Gentlemen Never Sail to Weather

The Story of an Accidental Odyssey

Gentlemen Never Sail To Weather

The Story of an
Accidental Odyssey

Denton R. Moore

Prospector Press
Bellingham, Washington
1993

Disclaimer:

The author reminds readers that while this book is a factual account, he is not a licensed master mariner, nor is he licensed to practice medicine or law. Thus where legal issues are raised, or when specific mention is made of mental or physical conditions (and/or the treatment thereof) the author is merely expressing a layman's opinion.

Similarly, equipment functioned exactly as reported, but the reader is reminded again that the author is merely describing his experiences. Others might well have different experiences with the same equipment. Readers are invited to draw their own conclusions, but **are expressly warned that the author assumes no responsibility if any reader should follow the experience, formulas of theories expressed herein. Readers do so entirely at their own risk.**

Publishing History

First Edition published June, 1992
Second Edition published July, 1993;
Reprinted, November, 1994;
Reprinted, May, 1995;
Reprinted, November, 1995;
Reprinted, June, 1996
Reprinted, February, 1998

Published by:

Prospector Press
PO Box 29175
Bellingham, WA 98228-1175

Library of Congress Catalog Card Number: 93-083834
ISBN: 0-9628828-3-6

Drawing of <u>Prospector</u> by Madelline Ann Bodenham
Frontispiece courtesy of the Northern Advocate, Whangarei, NZ

MANUFACTURED IN THE UNITED STATES OF AMERICA

Table of Contents

Illustrations

Photos

Drawings

Maps

To Velda, my beloved wife:
Without whom
this trip would not have been possible.
A finer shipmate no man ever had.

Acknowledgements

Many readers, some from as far away as South Africa and New Zealand, responded to our request for comments and corrections to the first edition of this book. I found those corrections and comments extraordinarily helpful as I began preparing this second edition. To you, my many editors, I am particularly grateful.

In addition to the many people mentioned in the text and index, I should also like to express my gratitude to the people who designed and built *Prospector*. Our crew also deserves special mention. Each uniquely contributed to the success of our trip.

I should particularly like to acknowledge my indebtedness to Captain Jim Hogan, the cartographer who prepared the charts, and Betsy Lampé of *Rainbow Books* who drew the beautiful sketches.

I am also indebted to the *Whangarei Northern Advocate* of New Zealand for permission to reproduce two photos which appeared in that paper. One may be found in the frontispiece; the other appears on page 164. Similarly, I am indebted to *The Cape Times* of Cape Town, Republic of South Africa, for permission to reproduce a portion of the article and photograph appearing on page 404.

To all of you, and the many others who contributed to this work, and to my readers, I say gratefully, *thank you*.

Denton Rickey Moore
Moore Haven, Florida
March 31, 1993

Introduction

This book is unique. After following the adventures of Velda and Denny aboard *Prospector* as they made their uncertain way around the world, I'm delighted to share my thoughts about what they learned and accomplished.

These folks were not professional adventurers, or even at the outset of their epic voyage, especially competent sailors. On one level, this book is about a deep learning curve concerning basic seamanship which, somehow, they managed to scramble over.

In the process, they developed rare insights into small boat management. Denny shares his views and experiences on a wide range of topics, including automatic steering devices, refrigeration systems, and single-handed sailing. He is candid about his mistakes; any sailor, reading this book and sharing those experiences will benefit.

Denny and Velda are rare, because they survived a collision at sea. As a result of that experience, he circulated a questionnaire at a New Zealand Christmas party the following year concerning major risks facing small boat sailors. His respondents included such well known authorities as Dick McIlvride and the late Eric Hiscock.

This book will appeal to many people other than sailors, because unlike many other books about long cruises, Denny has brought his inquisitive nature to bear, and he tells about the people he met, their lives, ambitions, and the worlds in which they live. For example, through the experiences of a convalescing South African soldier from an antiterrorist unit, and the anguish of a Malay mother in Cape Town concerned for her teenage daughter's education in America, you get an inside look at the awful consequences of apartheid for all South Africans.

Beyond that, however, his insights and perceptive descriptions of other social systems enriched my understanding of our own system. For instance, he describes New Zealand's medical program, where all medical costs arising out of *accidents of any kind* are routinely paid by the State. I haven't yet heard that option mentioned in our national debate on health care, but perhaps it ought to be.

Similarly, in describing Australia's submarine Navy (why does Australia need *submarines?)* he makes the provocative suggestion that perhaps the Australian taxpayer, like his American cousin, is ". . .being taken on a military snipe hunt" to satisfy the emotional needs of the military elite. In our frustrating search for peace dividends, that's food for thought!

Denny found that West Indian youth uniquely in the English–speaking Caribbean were becoming increasingly alienated from the larger society. If his observations are accurate, why should this be so? Has he noticed something that might also explain the rise of youth gangs in our major cities?

The appendix will be of special interest to many sailors because it offers an easily applied method for accurately measuring the windage of any boat, and translating that measurement into pounds (or tons) of pull on the vessel's ground tackle. It also explains single–station weather forecasting, storm evasion tactics, and provides a reliable method for estimating your distance from an approaching ship, and the safest way to avoid collisions.

By the way, did you realize that at sea, radar reflectors (at least the small boat variety) are almost useless except in a fog bank? Denny explains why.

Not only is this book excellent reading in front of the fire on a crisp winter evening, it is a practical, insightful guide to a variety of interesting and exciting places in both hemispheres.

I highly recommend *Gentlemen Never Sail to Weather* whether you are ashore or afloat.

Captain Jim Hogan

Solomon Island, MD
January 25, 1992

Preface

When I try to explain why we've gone to the considerable trouble and expense of reprinting the second edition of *Gentlemen Never Sail to Weather*, I find I'm repeating the reasons I gave for writing the book in the first place.

I had three primary reasons for writing the book. Initially, the book was an extension of my response to the question posed on page 434, when someone asked, "Would you do it again?"

My answer was an unequivocal "Yes, but... " The only way I could describe what I would do differently was by explaining what had gone wrong.

My second reason was more personal. The world is a wonderfully diverse and interesting place. As small boat sailors wholly reliant on our own resources, we were privileged to see many of those places almost through the eyes of those who live there. I found that an extraordinarily interesting experience, and I wanted to share it.

Make no mistake. Travel by a small yacht cannot be compared with commercial travel. In my former life as a World War II Marine, and later, as a federal bureaucrat, I already had seen much of the world. Disappointingly, it all looked pretty much the same. No matter where I went, I found that international airports and Intercontinental Hotels, like troop ships and military camps, are so similar that the hotels find it desirable to create in their decor and on the menu a patina or artificial aura of local color. Otherwise, the traveler might be hard pressed to distinguish a hotel in Tokyo from one in Tahiti.

Perhaps the best way to explain the distinction is to tell you that I had seen the *Taj Mahal* in my earlier travels, but I **experienced** apartheid in South Africa when we hired Zulu laborers to work on our boat.

Finally, while there is satisfaction in knowing you have written a book, just as there is in knowing you've sailed around the world (even though you may have done it accidentally), for me, it wasn't enough just to write a book. I wanted to write the best book I was capable of producing. In this reprinted second edition, you will find maps, photos and drawings, and fewer typographical errors. I hope those that remain are regarded, in the words of *Woodenboat Magazine,* as merely tool marks on hand crafted furniture. Please enjoy the book.

DRM

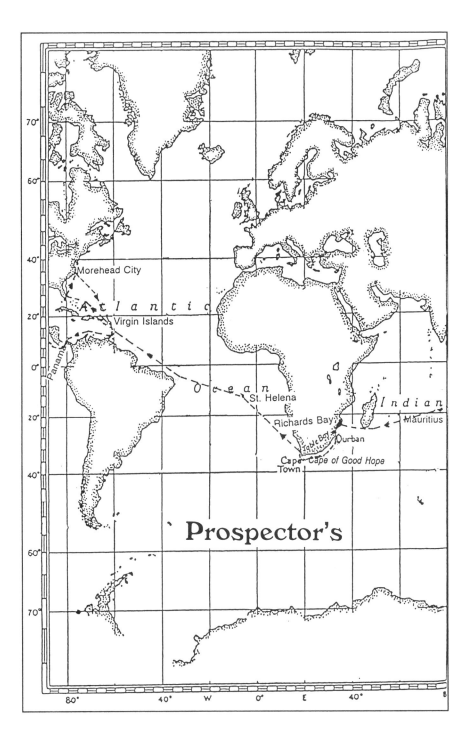

Morehead City
Virgin Islands
Panama
St. Helena
Richards Bay
Table Bay
Durban
Cape Town
Cape of Good Hope
Mauritius

Atlantic
Ocean
Indian

Prospector's

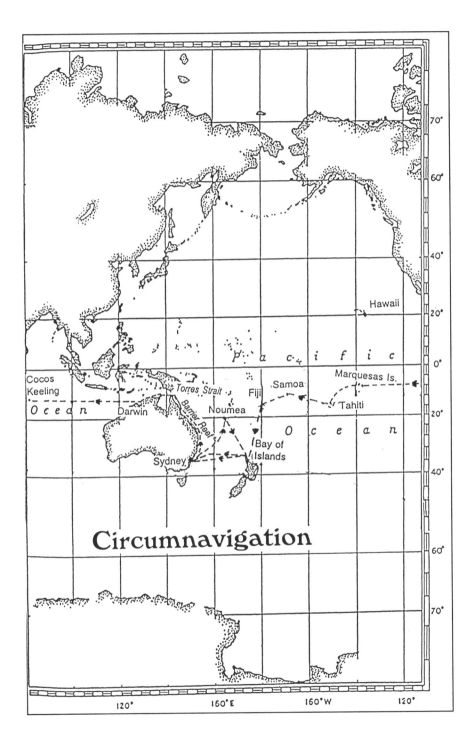

Cocos
Keeling

O c e a n

Darwin

Torres Strait

Barrier Reef

Noumea

Fiji

Samoa

Marquesas Is.

Tahiti

P   a   c   i   f   i   c

Hawaii

O   c   e   a   n

Bay of
Islands

Sydney

Circumnavigation

70°
60°
40°
20°
0°
20°
40°
60°
70°

120°   160° E   160° W   120°

Northern Advocate
Sport

WHANGAREI, NZ,   FRIDAY, JANUARY 11, 1985

A TALL SHIP
AND TRUE...

Prospector from Washington D.C. in the United States sailing on the wind in the spectacular annual Bay of Islands Tall Ships race last Sunday. The race was won by another American yacht, Cygnus. A fleet of 37 contested the event.

Prologue

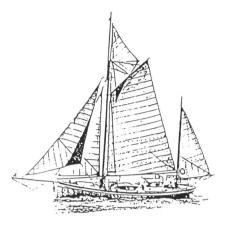

$\mathcal{A}$s I painfully climbed the companionway ladder returning to the cockpit, my horrified gaze was caught by an overtaking rogue wave dead astern, already looming above the taffrail, the lazarette, blocking the sky as it reared above us! I was as mesmerized as a rabbit staring at a snake. Water began sliding down that ugly, monstrous, moving face.

The spell was broken when, to my complete and utter terror, I saw the crest begin to topple forward, propelled by countless tons of water behind it. In that awful instant I knew *Prospector* was doomed!

"LOOK OUT!" I screamed at my wife.

Later, as we regained our senses and looked back on that awful moment, we realized we had survived another catastrophe that might have crushed a lesser boat.

Years earlier, when we had set out from Morehead City on that beautiful autumn day in 1981, we had no idea that we would wander around the world during the next five years, or that at times like now, our survival would hinge on the merest chance.

It had started with our first hesitant offshore cruise from North Carolina to the U.S. Virgin Islands.

Three of us; my wife Velda, a close friend John Kelly, and I, were aboard our 41-year old Concordia yawl (or ketch), *Prospector,* following the ketch *Starbound* down the channel that winds from Morehead City to the open waters of the mid-Atlantic.

It was a lovely, fall morning. The leaves we could see from the deck were almost garish in their autumn splendor — crimson and bronze, yellow and brown. North Carolina is spectacular in the fall, but my mind was not on the scenery. The famous 18th century English lexicographer, Dr. Samuel Johnson, said it best when he remarked, "When a man knows he is to be hanged in a fortnight, it concentrates his mind wonderfully."

Leaving port for the first time on a long ocean voyage had exactly the same effect on me. For the hundredth time, I mentally reviewed the list of stores, charts, tools, spare gear; the almost endless list of things that experts had recommended and that we thought we needed, and had crammed aboard.

Foolishly, we had even laid in a year's supply of food instead of merely provisioning for the passage to St. Thomas, because we were sure that food prices would increase the further out on the pipeline we went. We were right about the prices; you can't beat Food Giant's stateside prices anywhere in the Caribbean. But it was a false economy. We soon realized we had made a mistake.

I had no idea how efficiently salt air (and leaky decks) would destroy tin cans. Our savings were illusory because many cans quickly became dangerously rusted and had to be discarded.

Even more importantly, while a medium displacement boat like *Prospector* can handle an extra ton or two more easily than a light boat of the same size, we paid a serious penalty for overloading her.

Overloaded boats become stiff. Unnecessary strains are imposed on the rig. Also, overloading will slow a boat significantly, and speed is an important consideration.

The difference between average speeds of three versus five knots on the Morehead City–St. Thomas run is the difference between a 16 day passage and one requiring only ten days.

My reverie was interrupted as I watched Starbound, about 200 yards ahead of us, nudging her way through clustered fishing skiffs as an ice-breaker might clear a path through ice floes. Imperceptibly at first, her tall masts began to sway in time with the incoming Atlantic swells. I could feel a sympathetic tug in our steering wheel as our rudder also began to sense the surge of Atlantic currents.

The sun was almost overhead when we reached the last buoy marking the outer end of the infamous Lookout Shoals extending almost 20 miles offshore, like a slightly crooked finger, laying in wait to snare the careless skipper.

Starbound's squaresail had already been set. When her skipper,

Gordon Stuermer, set her raffee, a triangular sail that sets above the yard and draws like a miniature spinnaker, she quickly pulled away.

As I watched her disappear over the horizon, suddenly, I felt terribly lonesome and quite unprepared for my new responsibilities.

We had arrived in Morehead City a week earlier. The first thing that caught my eye as we motored around the bend coming into the city from the Intracoastal Waterway, was a big square-rigged ketch tied to Tony's Sanitary Market and Restaurant.

As we drew closer, I knew intuitively that I was looking at *Starbound*. Her people didn't know us, but they recognized kindred spirits when they saw our rig and realized that we too had an old wooden boat with a rudimentary square rig. They gave us a friendly wave as we motored past, and shouted an invitation to come for a visit as soon as we were anchored. We gladly accepted.

By then, Gordon and Nina Stuermer had written two books which we had eagerly read while preparing for our new life. The first book, *Starbound*, was an account of their 1973–76 circumnavigation, which we used as a cruising guide. His second book, *Deep Water Cruising*, contains a wealth of useful information and sound advice. Both deserve space on any ship's book shelf.

Although late October–early November is the best time to make the passage from North Carolina to St. Thomas, a late season hurricane was churning up the South Atlantic coast, and we waited for it to dissipate before we left Morehead City.

The Stuermers were as friendly as their books suggested they might be. We were fortunate because during our enforced delay, we gleaned a great deal of useful information from them.

Offshore cruising is a lot like sex. No matter how many books you read, or how much expert advice you receive, before your first time, there is really no way of knowing what it will be like, or even whether you'll like it.

Like an old-fashioned bride groom, I was long on theory, but painfully short on practice. I had taken several mail order courses in celestial navigation, offshore cruising, and marine meteorology, and I was sure I knew how, but in the back of my mind, I also knew I had yet to try it for the first time where it counted.

As it turned out, we were better prepared than we knew. Velda and I had spent our summers sailing a small sloop on the Potomac River. Our first shipmate, John Kelly, had gained most of his sailing

3

experience aboard *Prospector,* but he had served two hitches in the Marianas Islands as a Peace Corps Volunteer. What he didn't know about sailing, he more than made up in raw courage, enthusiasm, and a willingness to learn.

My background is unusual. I learned to sail forty years ago in the little two-man sailboats that were used in Alaska's Bristol Bay salmon fishery from the late 1800s until 1951. I had never heard of hypothermia, but the water in the Bering Sea is frightfully cold. A man overboard was almost invariably a goner. Sometimes boats capsized or swamped. Sometimes a luckless fishermen was snagged by his net and dragged over the side. Some fishermen simply fell overboard.

More than one fisherman has shaken hands with St. Peter with his pants down around his knees because he went overboard while perched on the gunwale answering a call of nature. It was a tough way to make a living; every year each cannery lost at least one boat, and sometimes several, depending on weather and fishermen's luck.

I survived five seasons in those little boats because I learned not to fall overboard. Don't smile. It's a learned skill, like the skills city children learn as they play in and around urban traffic. City children acquire such skills instinctively, shortly after they learn to walk. Not all of them survive, but most do.

There were other problems besides hypothermia. For instance, my partner (the captain) wouldn't allow me to share the tiny forepeak, where he enjoyed the luxury of smoldering mosquito coils. I spent many nights rolled up in a wet sail as my only defense against the most voracious mosquitoes in North America. It was good preparation for learning to live aboard.

John was a co-worker in the Washington, D.C. office of the National Marine Fisheries Service. He had given up his weekends to help us work on *Prospector*, and had sailed with us on our shake-down cruise around the Delmarva Peninsula.

Sailing around Maryland's Eastern Shore bears little comparison with crossing the Indian Ocean, but even so, it was an exciting experience. Looking back, I know I over-estimated my sailing skills, but I was still the most experienced sailor on board.

The first leg of the trip down the Potomac was easy. So was the second leg up Chesapeake Bay, past Baltimore. Even running through the Chesapeake and Delaware Canal wasn't difficult.

Our luck changed when we reached the Delaware River. I was

not prepared for the heavy river traffic we encountered, and dusk caught us three uncomfortable hours away from the nearest safe anchorage at Cape Henlopen.

At its mouth, the Delaware River is nearly 30 miles wide. According to the chart, the channel appears to be a meandering thread of deeper water known only to harbor pilots, tugboat captains, and God. Influenced, no doubt, by my memories of Bristol Bay's tidal estuary (where a 25 foot tidal range is not uncommon), I was convinced there was less than three feet of water immediately outside the channel, and I was terrified at the prospect of being forced out of the channel and running aground in the middle of the night.

John Kelly

Confused by the traffic, constrained by our draft, lacking local knowledge and uncertain of the rules of the road, we wandered around the lower end of Delaware Bay until midnight, when we crept into the shadow of the great Henlopen lighthouse. We dropped the anchor and went to sleep, blissfully unaware we were squarely in the middle of the Lewes–Cape May ferry lane.

We discovered our error at first light when an infuriated ferry captain attempted to levitate *Prospector* with his foghorn.

I was embarrassed, and we hurriedly started the engine, hauled the anchor, and made our way out of the harbor without further incident. The wind was calm, but we had ample fuel aboard, and ran three miles off the coast before turning south toward Cape Charles and the Chesapeake Bay entrance. We went past Ocean City and were abreast of Assateague Island when I happened to glance at the depth finder.

My God! Three miles off and we were in eight feet of water! I knew that much of the Atlantic seaboard was dangerously shoal with constantly shifting sands, but this was my first encounter with it.

5

Trying to appear calm, I grabbed the binoculars and began searching for a navigation aid. John and Velda were trying to decide whether, based on our speed and the elapsed time since passing Ocean City, the land we saw on our starboard beam was Assateague Island.

John took the wheel and began steering straight out to sea, while I continued to search the horizon, and Velda kept her eyes on the depthfinder. I heard the ominous message:

"We're down to seven feet," she said.

"Yell if it gets down to six feet," I said, trying to keep my voice steady. "Slow down, John, and steer 60 degrees," I said. I wanted to get more on a reciprocal course, backing out of our difficulty, and slowing the boat so if we hit a sandbar, we could get off as quickly as possible.

The weather was unpredictable. It was flat calm then, but the wind could rise at any moment. If *Prospector* being aground, was lifted and dropped hard on the sand by successive swells, she would be in serious trouble. No boat can take "pile-driving" long without breaking her back, or at least springing a garboard.

John slowed the engine as he took up the new heading. The boom swung slowly across the doghouse, dragging the sheet tackle along the traveler with the metallic grating sound of iron scraping on iron. It seemed uncommonly loud; then I realized how tense I was.

"How's the water, Honey?" I asked.

"We're hanging on to seven," she said. Then, "We have ten feet . . .11 feet . . . ten feet."

"John," I said, feeling better, "let's try to follow that 11 foot curve. Swing a little to the right, and see if you can get it back."

"We have 12 feet," Velda said triumphantly.

"We're not aground yet," I said. "Hey! I think I see something." John turned toward me.

"Where?" he asked, holding his hand out for the glasses.

I pointed to a speck on the horizon. Everything was quiet as he adjusted the focus. I was already beginning to develop the respect I would come to have for his remarkable eyesight.

"It's a buoy, all right," he announced quietly. "But I can't make out the markings."

"That's all right; that buoy is this one," I said, pointing to the chart. "It's the only buoy between Ocean City and Cape Charles."

"If that is Assateague Island... ." At that point I interrupted myself and performed a bearing "benediction" over the compass by raising my right hand vertically in the air, pointing at the smudge on the horizon, then slowing bringing my hand down over the compass, carefully reading the compass card.

"It bears 265 degrees," I said.

I put the parallel rule over the nearest compass rose on the chart, found 265°, walked the rule to the north end of the island and penciled a line from that point out to sea. I repeated the process with the dot on the horizon, drew the line, and found that the lines of position intersected about four miles off shore.

I pointed to the X on the chart. With an assurance I was far from feeling, I said, "That's about where we are."

Velda and John nodded respectfully, and watched as I plotted a course to the entrance buoys off Cape Charles. Straight face and all, I was already beginning to act like a navigator.

Once we reached the channel buoys, it was a simple matter of following them under the bridge and around the corner to the anchorage behind Cape Charles.

The next morning, sitting around the saloon table drinking our coffee, we discussed the trip. In many respects, it had been a disaster. That we came out of it without damage was dumb luck. Luck is a poor substitute for seamanship. It seemed appropriate to ask ourselves what had happened, and how could we do better in the future. I realized that abstractly "knowing" about something and having that information indelibly tattooed on my nervous system by experience was quite a different thing.

We had found ourselves wandering around Delaware Bay in the middle of the night because we had bucked the tide most of the way down the river. Had we looked more closely at the tide tables, we might have seen that we would have been better off anchoring near the entrance to the Canal and waiting for daylight and an ebbing tide before descending the river.

What about that episode off Assateague Island? We concluded that was plain carelessness. Misreading (or not reading) charts is a serious fault in a navigator. I promised myself that I would be more careful in the future.

However, being more careful in the future doesn't explain what I was doing with a big wooden boat in the first place. Many people have asked and I have given it serious thought.

The best explanation I can offer is that I bought *Prospector* at age 52 for precisely the same reason that I bought my first tattoo at age 14. My subconscious mind promised that exciting things would happen if I did.

I'm serious. Apparently, I'm one of those peculiar people with a powerful inclination toward inductive (as opposed to deductive) reasoning. People with my mental orientation appear to be in the minority. We're the folks who learn to rely on hunches, who do things intuitively.

No doubt the male menopause also had something to do with it. The decision to buy a large sailboat seemed a congenial and perfectly reasonable way of dealing with approaching old age.

The mind set of the potential owner of a large and impractical boat seems not unlike that of the romantic who is in love with the idea of being in love. No one suggests these ideas and attitudes are rational, but who among us has made the really significant decisions in life on a basis of pure rationality?

Thus, irrationally, we decided to buy a boat.

Having made that decision, we began visiting showrooms and discovered that what used-car salesmen do with a spray-can filled with vinyl scent, new boat dealers do better with visions of sun-baked, blue-green lagoons filled with happy brown people dressed mainly in hibiscus blossoms. Unfortunately, a new boat of the quality we wanted was beyond our means.

Therefore, we began corresponding with used boat people, among others, Bill Page in Camden, Maine, who responded almost immediately with a large envelope crammed with boat pictures and descriptions. One of them was a boat named *Prospector*. Again, I have to shift gears.

I grew up in Seattle during the 1930s. The world was a simpler, safer, saner place in those days and like most boys, I found the waterfront an unending source of adventure, and incredibly interesting things.

I vividly remember seeing the great gray halibut, white with flake ice, being winched, one at a time, from the fish hold of halibut schooners tied to the old San Juan dock at the foot of Yesler Way. I even remember the sharp, clean smell of those huge fish, the odor of the deep cold waters of the North Pacific.

For me, those doughty halibut schooners with their stubbornly plumb stems, low working waists, high bows, and nearly uniform doghouses aft, epitomized the essential nature of man's relationship to the sea. *Prospector* in profile is a miniature halibut schooner. When I saw her picture, I could almost smell that rich briny odor. Her resemblance to those fishing boats is startling. She has the same stubborn plumb stem, the same high bow, the same waist, and the same doghouse. The only difference is that *Prospector* is smaller and is rigged for sail.

Her specification sheet indicated that her knees, floors, and other structural members were fashioned from Madeira. I had never heard of Madeira, so I wrote to Mr. John Gardner, a world authority on small wooden boat construction.

He replied, "Madeira is a dark,

Fitting out in Chesapeake Bay

hard, heavy lasting wood that grows in the West Indies." In reply to another question, he said, "Natural crook means that the curved shapes are grown in, that the frames were sawn from crooked trees selected to yield the curved shapes required by the shape of the vessel. For heavy, or moderately heavy, construction, I can't think of anything better than 'natural crook Madeira', a perfect mate for long leaf hard pine planking." Because *Prospector* was a Concordia design, he suggested I get in touch with Capt. R. D. (Pete) Culler, former chief designer for the Concordia Co.

"Pete" Culler and I had a brief exchange of letters. I asked his advice on evaluating an old wooden boat. His reply was pure Culler.

"Like all of us," he wrote, "she is getting on in years. What you want to do is sight along the sheer strake and sniff in her bilges. If she has kept her shape, and still smells sweet, there is a lot left in her yet."

9

Those are words to live by.

Prospector had undergone a major refit when I first saw her in April, 1978, in English Harbor, Antigua.

Her owner, Tony Maidment, had installed a new engine, new standing and running rigging, had cleaned and recaulked her decks, had new sails cut, brightened the bright work, and so forth. She hasn't looked that good since.

We struck a bargain, and he agreed to deliver her. A month later, our first crew, composed of Velda and me, her son Tom Adams, a friend named Phil Olsen, and Dr. Mike Orbach, our volunteer sailing master and a work colleague, were in Ft. Lauderdale waiting for our ship to come in. Mike's knowledge of sailing and seamanship is encyclopedic. He also enjoys a well earned international reputation in his field of social anthropology.

We had been waiting in Fort Lauderdale for four days. I was beginning to fret. Velda suggested we have a picnic. Mike and Phil had other things to do, so Velda, Tom and I took our little rental car to the beach. We had just spread out the blanket, I hadn't even sat down, when I glanced out to sea. I saw a little halibut schooner look-alike coming in from sea under her jib and mainsail. Stupidly, I thought at first that it was amazing how much that boat looked like *Prospector.* Suddenly I realized she **was** *Prospector.*

"Hey, there she is," I shouted, pointing to the boat, now less than a quarter of a mile away. She was on a broad reach, and I fell instantly in love with the cut of her jib and the shape of her mainsail's leech. I've always thought gaff sails presented more interesting and dramatic shapes than Marconi sails, and *Prospector* was proof of that theory, at least in my eyes.

My first impulse was to run down the beach telling everyone whose wonderful boat that was. Instead, we scooped up the blanket, ran back to the car, and drove to the hotel.

Our room overlooked the canal and as we watched out the window, *Prospector* approached the bridge. Her jib was already rolled, and as we watched, the gaff dropped and the mainsail slowly wrinkled down. We saw the English flag on her stern, the courtesy flag on her starboard flag hoist, and below that, her Q flag. This was Velda's first look at her, and the first time I had seen her under sail.

With two well placed phone calls, Velda found Mike. While we waited for him, Phil came strolling in. *Prospector* was still waiting for the bridge to open. When Mike arrived, we left to drive over to the customs facility at Pier 66.

For some odd reason, ignoring the customs sign squarely in front of him when the bridge opened, *Prospector's* skipper turned hard left and entered a maze of canals in a housing development. The chase, straight out of a Peter Sellers movie, was on.

We were tightly jammed into a bright red little Japanese subcompact. Although our view of the canal was restricted by the houses lining the water, we could see the top of *Prospector's* mast above the roofs.

We sped ahead of her, popped out of the car and sprinted down to the edge of the canal, only to see her stopped and maneuvering to turn around in the narrow waterway a block away. Then it was back to the car, and off we went racing past her mast in the opposite direction. When I found an opening between the houses to the canal, I would slam on the brakes, the five of us spilling out of the car to run once again to the water.

This was a serious business. But to any passerby, watching five large people jump in and out of a Japanese subcompact, run down the street, run back, drive a few hundred frantic yards, and repeat the process, it must have been an amusing sight.

Eventually, we flagged the skipper down, and directed him to Pier 66. That's where we met the crew.

While we stood on the finger pier waiting for the customs officer, I studied the rigging, trying to make sense out of the confusing array of lines seemingly belayed at random to the many belaying pins attached to various parts of the rigging.

I was so busy looking at the rigging and wondering, frankly, if I could ever sort it out, that I failed to notice a beautiful young woman with a stunning figure in a crocheted bikini, sitting quietly on the cabin trunk. *God*, I breathed quietly to myself, *this gets better and better*. Her name was Norma.

While she explained to Velda the mysteries of the stove and the water pump that would deliver water only after it was primed by sucking on the spout, I followed Mike and the delivery captain, English Harbor's sailmaker, Graham Knight, around the boat listening in quiet and happy amazement as they knowledgeably and intelligently discussed the rig and sails. It was wonderful knowing that I was in the hands of experts.

11

The delivery crew didn't waste time. They spent the night aboard, and by noon the next day, were gone. We checked out of the hotel, moved aboard, and went shopping for our provisions, charts, and other necessities.

The next day, I returned the car to the rental agency, and after paying the marina operator, we moved to the fuel dock.

Mike and I were in the cockpit as we approached the dock. Velda, Tom and Phil were standing on the foredeck. Mike nudged her bow through the current up against the dock, and handed the attendant a stern line. I was opening a fuel tank, when I heard Mike shout, "Pass a line quick!"

It was too late. The current was behind the bow by this time, pushing it away from the dock.

The stern was still tied, and as the bow swung out into the current, the stern line acted like a fulcrum, putting the weight of the current on the port corner of the taffrail which was hard against a dock piling.

Something had to give. With a terrible splintering crash, the corner brace, the end of the bulwarks, all four taffrail stanchions and the beautifully curved taffrail broke away from the stern.

It was my fault. Except for Velda, our foredeck crew was innocent of experience, and Velda's seasoning did not include 20-ton boats. I should have been on the foredeck, too.

After lashing the broken taffrail to a grab rail on the cabin top, we headed up the Intracoastal Waterway in search of an easy pass to the ocean. We found it at Jupiter Inlet.

While my optimistic outlook concerning diesel engines seriously eroded in the years to follow, my faith in diesel combustion then, based on little more than a gullible belief in advertising, was absolute. I suppose I was also driven by a macho desire to show Mike that I knew *something* about boats. There was no other explanation for my behavior as I drove *Prospector* past the long breakwater to the open sea.

I can't imagine what must have passed through his mind. I boldly shoved the throttle wide open, and bracing myself against the sharp pitching as *Prospector* encountered incoming rollers, I ignored the bellowing exhaust, the dense black smoke, and the hungry, slimy rocks twenty feet from my port beam.

A blocked fuel line, and we would have been on the rocks. But

I was lucky. Then, I had no idea how fussy diesel engines are about their fuel.

Neither, apparently, had Tony Maidment. When he replaced the gasoline engine with the Perkins, he had saved a few dollars by retaining the original gasoline fuel settling bowl instead of installing a proper diesel filter.

I had noticed, while at Pier 66, that the glass settling bowl was full of dirty, rusty, water and muck. I didn't understand its significance, or that our violent pitching probably was stirring more of it into the fuel feeding our straining engine.

I'm sure Mike realized it, but he no doubt assumed I knew what I was doing, and since it was my boat... .

The engine faithfully pushed us clear of the breakwater, and immediately, Tom and Phil became seasick.

But Velda was a natural. She took to the ocean as if she had been sailing all her life. She stood her watches, some of my watches, handled the cooking and helped Mike organize the boat.

I'm afraid I didn't do at all well. I was suffering a monumental case of buyer's remorse, thinking that this complicated, heavy, costly toy had little to do with the fantasies I had built up of tropical lagoons, exotic ports, and admiring and envious onlookers. I was facing reality, and I wasn't at all sure I liked it.

It is times like that when people with deductive minds have the best of it. When logical people buy boats, they usually know why. Unfortunately, the mental processes of inductive reasoners like me more closely resemble the popular image of Peter Pan. Deductive folks operate on facts, we rely on hunches.

Mike brought us safely to Charleston. After docking in the yacht basin, we went to Mike's hotel to watch him register, and to enjoy showers in his bathroom.

The next morning, we took stock. Although we were 1,000 miles from Washington, I felt confident that I could deliver the boat to Chesapeake Bay by sticking to the Intracoastal Waterway. I was still unnaturally attached to our engine.

The trip was a nightmare. To the best of my recollection, I ran the boat aground three times. The last time, in Swansboro, N.C., Phil gave up, and quit. That was immediately after I had broken the topmast and crosstrees trying to roll the boat down on her side to refloat her. I can recall the grim satisfaction I felt watching him stand barefooted on the fantail of the Coast Guard launch as he was leaving, not realizing he had left his shoes behind. That was the only time I smiled all month.

Another friend, Jack Wise, joined us for the final leg into Chesapeake Bay. I vividly remember he and his son coming aboard in Great Bridge, Va., looking wryly at the broken pieces lashed to the cabin top, and saying to me, "You're turning *Prospector* into a boat kit."

In addition to the physical problems we were having, I had looming before me, a serious reckoning with the Treasury Department. I had to pay *Prospector's* import duties.

Before leaving Ft. Lauderdale, I had been given a green keypunch card and a stern warning from a customs officer that we had 30 days to clear *Prospector* in Baltimore on pain of a certain fine and possible forfeiture if I didn't comply.

Immediately after we arrived in the Chesapeake, I arranged to meet a customs inspector on a street corner in Baltimore. We drove 70 miles to the marina where the boat was.

He knew his stuff. I watched him examine the engine. Ours is the green English version. He looked at the new Marlow braided running rigging (also English) and the new English–made standing rigging. He read the English sailmaker's labels. Finally, after well over an hour, he asked, "Do you think those sails are worth $2,000?"

I nodded.

"This is what I propose," he said. "Your boat was built in the United States; consequently, she is classified as American goods returning and there is no duty on her. However, you have a lot of English gear on board; none of it new, but none of it very old, either. Suppose we agree that the dollar value of this English gear is $2,000. Does that sound OK?"

"Well, sure," I said. "I guess so."

"The duty is six percent," he said. "You owe $120."

That is how *Prospector* regained her American citizenship.

The moral of this story is that although the rules sometimes seem incredibly silly and the penalties unbelievably harsh, it *always* pays to do it *exactly* the way the book says. You'll save much trouble that way. On the other hand, as this incident illustrates, within that rigid framework, as if to compensate for it, the processes can be astonishingly informal as applied by most Governmental officials here and abroad.

The next two years passed quickly. Most of my spare time was taken up with a renovation of *Prospector's* accommodations.

We owned a large house in Arlington, Va. The basement was filled with work benches, saws, jointers, lathes, and sawhorses.

We found an ancient cat boat boom that I converted to a yard (the original sailplan specified a squaresail) and Glen Housley, a first rate sailmaker in Annapolis, made our first squaresail.

I didn't know how to rig it, so a young Coast Guard officer, Bill Chappell, contributed his copy of *Eagle Seamanship,* the Coast Guard cadet's handbook to the training ship *USS Eagle*.

Meantime, I installed a new water tank and two new fuel tanks, redesigned the galley, altered the rest of the accommodations, moved the head out of the main saloon, installed a Racor fuel filter, a Grunert freezer, an Autohelm, a VHF radio, wind instruments, a depthfinder, a paddlewheel speedometer, a pres-sure water system and even a hot water heater. I had it bad. (You'll hear much about that freezer and Autohelm.)

An amiable young man named Mike Peacock designed the galley, and did much of the basic carpentry.

All the while, I was waiting for my subconscious to tell me why I was doing this. Then, one day Jack Wise, the co-worker who had made the boat kit quip, came into my office and casually observed that some people enjoy sailing boats while others prefer rebuilding them.

Jack's comment started me thinking. Had I bought *Prospector* as a glamorous fix-it project? That night, as I was driving home from the office, I experienced an inspirational flash of insight; the sort we inductive folks occasionally enjoy.

Quite unaware, we were operating a private museum. We had somehow become indentured to our possessions. When I wasn't earning the money to make the house payments and the monthly fuel bill, I was caring for things. Our house had many rooms filled with memorabilia, mostly mine. It occurred to me that I was behaving exactly like a medieval monk guarding a Holy Relic.

But where the monk would have been sustained by a devout belief in the hereafter, all I could look forward to were inexorably rising fuel and electrical bills. I was devoting my life and most of my income to the comfort and well being of things.

15

There was something else to consider. It's curious how our perception of time changes. Young people know they are not immortal, but few of them believe it.

"Goodby"

It isn't until you reach middle age that the passage of time becomes significant. I suddenly realized that intuitively I was reshaping what was left of my future by rebuilding *Prospector*.

I have an insatiable curiosity about myself and things around me. Luckily, Velda shares that point of view, and it was her prodding as much as anything that encouraged our purchase of *Prospector* in the first place.

We decided it was now or never. For me, it was already almost too late. I was in that awkward age — only 55 — too old to join the Army, but much too young for Social Security, but I was already feeling the pangs of serious arthritis. If I had known, however, that before long I would discover how painful a chest full of broken ribs at sea can be, I might have sold the boat and headed, instead, for a sheep ranch in Montana.

It was time to burn our bridges, and start over. We took the things we needed, and sold the rest in a series of garage sales.

16

Then we sold the house, bought food and basic spares for the rigging, for the engine, and spare sails, grossly overdoing it.

We enjoyed several farewell parties, and we were on our way.

"Up on the hard"
at Calvert Marina

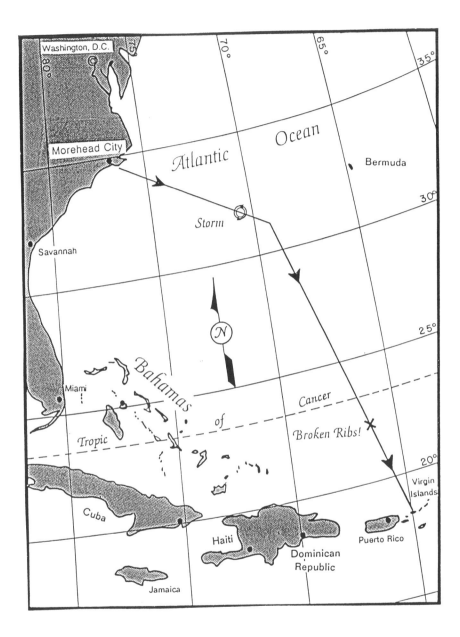

Morehead City, N.C. to St. Thomas, V.I.
(Chart 1)

Chapter 1

The Bermuda Triangle

*I*t felt as if we were making our way to sea almost surreptitiously. Instead of confetti and cheering crowds crying *bon voyage*, the dozens of fishermen sitting impassively in their skiffs, intent on their baits, neither knew nor cared that the two elderly wooden yachts passing by were headed for the Caribbean, and even less that the smaller of the two was skippered by me.

I was irrationally disappointed. It seemed such an ordinary way to begin an epic voyage. I wondered how many of our silent audience had ever dared to dream of such a trip? Or having dreamed of it, had the courage to try?

The temporary excitement that had buoyed my spirits as we were making our majestic way to sea faded as soon as land fell astern and *Starbound* disappeared over the horizon ahead.

It was lonely at the top, especially when I contemplated how really superficial my preparation was for the awesome responsibilities I had assumed. It was one thing to risk my own life, but quite a different thing to risk two other lives. Believe me, I was in a solemn and somber mood as I watched the sun drop below the horizon at sea for the first time. I'm only glad that I had no way of knowing what lay ahead.

During the first few days of our passage, after I recovered somewhat from my feelings of total humility, I found the sailing exciting. The winds remained westerly for the first 400 miles, and our squaresail pulled us along like a great silent steam engine.

John Kelly had joined us in Morehead City, and the daily rituals; the watch schedule, regular mealtimes and our individual sleeping cycles quickly became established. We made the transition from land to sea with a bare minimum of effort.

In his excellent cruising guide, Donald Street warns of local gales that can spring up between Cape Hatteras and Bermuda without warning, blow like hell for two or three days, raising huge seas, and then disappear without being noticed, except by an alert weather satellite and people like us who get caught. Those storms may have something to do with the frightful reputation of the Bermuda Triangle.

We reached 32°30′N at the end of the first week. This is about the same latitude as Bermuda. The barometer remained at the same comfortable 1012 millibars we had carried from North Carolina. The brief storm summary provided by the Bureau of Standard's radio station WWV beginning at eight minutes past each hour (broadcast simultaneously on 2.5, 5, 10, 15, 20, and 25 MHz) failed to mention bad weather in our part of the Atlantic.

The first inkling I had that something was wrong was when the westerly breeze abruptly died in midmorning, leaving us temporarily becalmed. During the few minutes we rolled aim-lessly on that glassy sea, I should have furled the squaresail.

When I saw a heavy catspaw coming from the wrong direction, I reached quickly for the engine starter switch, but it was too late. The sudden wind reversal slammed the yard against the mast, and the squaresail blanketed the foreshrouds. We had been "taken aback", an accidental maneuver dreaded by windjammer captains. A sailing ship being unexpectedly pushed backwards could experience serious damage to the rigging and rudder.

However, before the wind could begin pushing us back, I had the engine running, clutch engaged and we were beginning to make way in a circle to the left. When the wind, by now a steady fresh breeze, was full on our beam and the squaresail began to flog, John and I were waiting by the mast.

With the wind pressure off the sail, we quickly cast off the clew and tack, and hauled the big sail up into her gear. Then we set the mainsail and the staysail, and I spent the next two hours futilely trying to steer the boat to weather.

We would move slowly ahead, only to be slammed in the bow by a wave that stopped our forward momentum. Then, I would spin the wheel, letting her fall off. The sails would fill and we would begin gaining way and returning to our course, when another young

20

wave would smash into us.

I had no idea we were on the threshold of a major storm. But I finally realized that heaving–to and waiting for the weather to improve might be our best move. This was a bit scary because, while I had read about heaving–to, I had never done it. But this seemed like a good time to learn.

John and I began experimenting with the rig after lunch. The wind was still rising out of the southeast and the weather was beginning to look serious, but we took our time and tried various combinations involving the staysail, the mizzen and the rudder.

We found that by flattening both the staysail and the mizzen, and giving her about ten degrees right rudder, the boat would lie fairly and easily about 65 degrees off the weather on the port tack. More than that, she would move slowly forward, thus protecting her rudder.

By dusk, the wind, still out of the southeast, was blowing 25–30 knots and the waves were up to eight–ten feet. The barometer had started down, and by 8 p.m. stood at 1008 millibars. As it grew dark, John and I, in our oilskins, sat in the cockpit speculating about the weather. We could see the lacy white foam starting to mottle the downwind side of the waves rushing toward us. The wind was beginning to moan in the rigging, and we could feel the boat tremble as sudden gusts struck the masts.

I felt a strong sense of affinity with *Prospector*. I had thought from the beginning that her best quality would be her sea-keeping ability, and I was right. She rode those swells gracefully with the assurance of a true aristocrat.

Following her jaunty bowsprit, she would rise to the top of the swells. Her bow, catching the wind, would fall off, causing the staysail to fill, which drove the boat slowly ahead as she coasted down the windward slope of the wave.

Her wheel, lashed a bit to weather, would force her head up in time to meet the wind as she rose to the top of the next swell, repeating the same confident little journey over and over again.

Prospector's motion is so gentle and easy that we never found it impossible to sleep in the forward cabin. Most of our friends used their forward cabin at sea only for storage; the motion there even in good weather rendered that cabin almost uninhabitable.

However, as the seas continued to rise, and the boat's motion became increasingly violent, I found I was sleeping with my toes and fingers dug into the sheets to avoid being pitched out of my bunk onto the cabin sole.

Later, Velda and I fell into the habit, in bad weather, of hot-bunking it. Since one of us was always on watch when we were without crew, the "safe" bunk on the leeward side was always available. We also found that stuffing cushions under the inboard edge of the mattress was more satisfactory than using lee cloths.

Velda called me at four o'clock the next morning for my watch with a warning to wear my heavy oilskins. As I dressed, I knew from the boat's motion and the sound that the weather had deteriorated during the night but I had no idea how bad it was.

As I made my way up the companionway ladder into the cockpit, I was astonished by the ferocity of the wind and the wild plunging and rearing of the boat which made it necessary to hang on whenever you were standing. I could hear the roar of rushing water under the unremitting shriek of the wind, and feel the sting of flying salt spume on my face, particularly in my eyes.

Velda handed me a cup of steaming coffee, and began to perform the usual end of the watch chores. After she read the barometer, I heard the tension in her voice as she called out, "The glass is down seven millibars since midnight!"

A drop of one and a half millibars in an hour is serious. Seven millibars in four hours is very serious.

"How much has it fallen in the past 12 hours?" I asked.

There was a pause. "It looks like 15 millibars," she called back.

It looked now like we were really in for it.

"I love the way she handles in this weather," Velda said quietly behind me. I hadn't heard her approaching in the dark and she startled me. I looked at my watch. Almost time for the weather summary on radio station WWV. I went down into the snug security of the cabin and turned on the radio.

The measured tock, tock of seconds ticking away, WWV's radio signature, filled the cabin. At eight minutes past the hour, we listened to the weather bulletin.

I felt an odd glow of proprietary pride when I realized that our storm was the most significant feature on the weather chart covering the Western Atlantic.

The coordinates given, 31°40′N, 71°30′W, matched our position almost exactly. I found it strangely reassuring that others knew about our storm. The storm was more severe than I had realized. According to the radio, we were experiencing winds of 50 knots or more, higher in gusts, and wave heights to 35 feet.

That was only two notches below hurricane strength, and the same magnitude as the storm in England in 1978 that had shattered the Fastnet Race with serious loss of life.

Daylight came very slowly through the heavy overcast that morning. For a long time, I couldn't distinguish between the wave tops and the scudding clouds. I sat in the cockpit watching those monstrous waves rolling down on us, marvelling at the easy and almost casual way *Prospector* rode up and over them. Then I noticed our cat and dog.

Lara and Cap, the ship's cat and dog, seemed oblivious to the weather. About the same size, they were sitting side by side in the cockpit, ignoring the roar of the waves and the wind, unconsciously swaying in perfect unison as the boat rolled, looking exactly like an animal ballet.

When the cat's box was retrieved from the fantail and placed in the cockpit, Lara performed solo, gamely squatting in the litter while the box slid back and forth in the cockpit. She provided wonderful relief from the stress of the storm. Nobody could watch that poor cat and keep a straight face.

The wind increased all morning. Before the anemometer cups blew away into the scudding overcast, we were registering gusts to 85 knots. By then, the seas were huge tumbling masses of green–gray mottled foam and spray, capped by breaking rivers of white water rushing down the slopes toward us.

Later that morning, as I pulled on my oilskins to give John a break on his watch, the companionway door slammed open and he poked his head inside to announce that we had company!

No matter how empty the horizon may seem, I know now that the oceans of the world literally teem with humanity. There are people like ourselves in small sailboats, others running a spectrum of container ships, tankers, aircraft carriers, Oriental longliners and God alone knows what else.

I finished zipping my jacket, pulled the hood over my head and climbed the ladder. The wind struck like a physical blow.

"Hey, look there," John shouted over the thunderous roar of wind and waves. "Wait until the next swell passes." Shielding my eyes from the flying spume with one hand, as I held on with the other, I peered in the direction John had indicated. As the swell rolled past, I felt my skin tighten, as if the hair was rising.

A ketch about the size of *Prospector,* not more than 300 hundred yards away on our port beam, was slowly making way against the storm under a triple-reefed mainsail and a storm jib.

I rushed down below. Velda was in the galley preparing lunch. "There's a boat out there," I said, switching on the radio.

"This is the yacht Che"

My call was answered immediately; they had been waiting to be noticed. "This is the yacht *Che*," came the response to my hail.

During the brief conversation that followed, we learned that the *Che* with a crew of three, a man and two women, plus two very large dogs were also on their way to St. Thomas.

Although they were still making way against the storm, the captain said that he and his crew were worn out, and that if we didn't mind, they would heave-to within hailing distance.

I replied that we were delighted to have company. Seeing another boat had a positive effect on us, a sentiment I'm sure they shared, although if either of us had gotten into trouble, there really wasn't much the other boat could have done to help in those frightful weather and sea conditions.

Our new neighbors stayed nearby the next day, but by noon of the second day, after the wind subsided, they left. We followed as soon as possible. First, however, we had repairs to make.

Predictably, we had lost our masthead anemometer cups and

radar reflector. Inexplicably we had also lost the downhaul block for the jib topsail and our bobstay which was then fashioned from chain. The bobstay is essential, because by securing the end of the bowsprit to the stem near the waterline (see the diagram in the appendix), it supports the entire rig.

Also, the gammon "iron" — the bronze collar securing the bowsprit to the stem head — had broken. Apparently, the bowsprit had taken a serious shock during the height of the storm, but, because of the noise and commotion of the storm, nobody noticed it when it happened. We repaired the broken gammon iron by wrapping a wire strap around the stem head and the bowsprit, tightening it with a turnbuckle. We couldn't do much about the bobstay, except refrain from using the jib and the jib topsail.

Prospector never abuses her people. No matter how wild her environment may be, her motion invariably is gentle and restrained. I have already mentioned another lovely characteristic. While you cannot completely escape the wind's shriek or the feel of hundreds of tons of water smashing into the topsides, those effects are muted by the stoutness of her planking, and the skill of her builders. Regardless of the weather, when you go below, you'll find yourself in an oasis of relative tranquillity.

Her rig was well thought out, and her sail wardrobe is suited to any condition she is likely to encounter. When her rig is intact, *Prospector* can stand up to as much sail as you want to set. If you push her too hard, she will heel more deeply, and let you know in a ladylike way she's uncomfortable. But she won't capsize or break. That's because she carries much of her ballast deep. She has a 7,000 pound cast iron ballast keel, and carries 10,000 pounds of boiler punchings under her floors. The result is that her center of gravity is unusually low. This increases her stability, makes her a hell of a seaboat, but it also gives her a quick roll.

After we had made such repairs as we could, we raised the sails and got underway. The wind had returned to the westerly quadrant and was fresh enough so we scarcely missed our topsails. We overtook *Che* in midafternoon.

Ordinarily, I'm not a reckless person, but I had met my first real test, a serious storm at sea, and had found that we were equal to it. I felt like a kid out of school. I was sailing with such exuberance that *Che's* skipper called on the radio to warn me about the possibility of broaching as he watched us skid down the face of a wave.

My elation in the fair fresh breeze, bright sunshine and a lovely blue sky was further enhanced later that same afternoon when we saw a third yacht on the horizon. The newcomer had a satellite navigation receiver (satnav) antenna.

Those units are common today, but in 1981, they were found only on commercial ships and the more expensive yachts, sometimes called gold platers. We relied on clear skies, the sextant, our H.O. 249 tables, and opportunistic requests on the radio for position checks from passing freighters, cruise ships, and as here, upper-class yachts to find our way. We had been three days without celestial observations, and suddenly we had a satnav in our midst. Responding to my hail on the radio, the yacht's skipper identified herself as *Innocent Bystander* from Guernsey, and gave her position as 31°16′N, 71°23′W. After plotting those coordinates, I found that during the storm we had drifted about 30 miles southwest.

Then I reflected on the boat's name. *Innocent Bystander*, an unusual name; surely one that might tempt the gods. She soon disappeared over the horizon, but in the mysterious order of things, we would meet again in a different part of the world, and eventually the gods *would* have the last laugh.

By daylight the next morning, *Che* had disappeared. Again, we were alone in the middle of an immense arc of sky and water. The second day after *Che* disappeared, an English container ship appeared over the horizon. I gave her a call.

"Hullo, *Prospector*," came the reply. "This is the *Cape Fairliner*. Where have you come from? Over."

I replied that we were 11 days out of Morehead City, bound for St. Thomas, and that we had spent three days hove-to.

The captain of the *Cape Fairliner* replied that they were four days out of Baltimore, and that he had thought during the storm that they might lose their top layer of containers.

I explained what had happened to us. Finally, he said, "Several of the chaps on board are keen yachtsmen. We'd like to pass close astern so they can take photos. Would you mind?"

I assured him that we had no objection, and soon the ship crossed our wake. A small crowd of photographers appeared on her starboard bridge wing. An hour later she was gone.

The horse latitudes, a dreary 300 mile band of bad weather,

between 25 and 30 degrees north, gave us a bad time of it. I left the Autohelm in charge one evening, while I enjoyed a roasted pork tenderloin and mashed potatoes dinner. Suddenly, the boat lurched and heeled sharply to starboard.

I sprang for the companionway and peering at the compass, found that we were 80 degrees off course. A powerful squall had overpowered the Autohelm, and the boat was sailing herself.

Prospector's theoretical hull speed based on her wetted length, is only 7.76 knots. Displacement boats sometimes go faster when they are planing down long waves, but this is a stunt best left to the big racers. Apart from that rare exception, according to the experts, it is virtually impossible for a medium displacement boat like *Prospector* to exceed her theoretical limit.

I know this sounds like heresy, but I think the experts may be wrong. I watched the paddlewheel log needle flicker above eight, climb to eight and a half, and before I could cast off the mainsheet, pass a scary nine and a half knots and briefly touch ten!

Whether we could have exceeded our hull speed by almost 30 percent is a difficult question. Still, there's no doubt we were going like hell, and with *Prospector*, anything is possible. I should add that this was not an isolated incident. Years later, over a measured course, we were to have a similar experience.

Anyone planning to sail a small boat long distances must have confidence in the strength, and pride in the integrity of their boat. If they don't have both, they have the wrong boat. We have that sort of feeling about *Prospector*. She is one of a kind. She was designed in 1935 by Bill Harris of the then fledgling Concordia Co. for a mining engineer Jack Harper who needed a strong, self-reliant, solidly built, and easily cared for boat to serve as a base camp for his prospecting ventures in Central and Latin America.

The boat was built twice, first in 1936 in a contract yard that burned hours before she was to have been launched; the second time by Harper in his backyard on New River near Ft. Lauderdale.

After the fire, Harper had gone to Cuba on a prospecting venture, and while there, had bought likely looking pieces of wood that he shipped back to Florida. When the lumber pile was high enough, he recruited a building crew from among unemployed ship-wrights and furniture builders, and rebuilt her himself. She was launched on September 25, 1940.

Her keel and deadwood were cut from a Cuban Acana tree that

has properties similar to ironbark. Her stem, clamps, shelves, carlins, floors, natural crook knees, bulwark stanchions, beams and mast steps were cut from a Madeira log that came from a tree blown down in the 1926 hurricane. Her framing is double-sawn white oak, three by three inches on ten inch centers. Her planking, one and a half inches thick, is from now extinct Dade County pine, and according to a shipwright who cut a hole for a transducer, is tough enough to turn torpedoes. It is so resinous that shipworms won't touch it.

In his book, *A Life in Boats*, Waldo Howland, former owner of Concordia Co., quoted from a letter from Harper, dated May 8, 1940, written while *Prospector* was on her building ways, saying that a visitor to the project had remarked, "...you only see a boat built like this, and out of such material, once in a lifetime... ."

That was in 1940, remember, when seasoned boat lumber was cheap and abundant, and instead of today's high-tech production runs, boats were designed and built one at a time.

Shortly after I bought *Prospector*, an excited co-worker burst into an office meeting waving a new copy of Roger Taylor's *Good Boats*. Mr. Taylor had selected *Prospector* as one of his favorite older designs and had devoted five full pages to her description.

No matter how severe the weather, we can move freely about below decks, hanging on, of course, but never having to tie ourselves down, except that Velda wears a strap around her waist in the galley so both hands are free. Mobility is important when looking out for your boat and yourself, but even on *Prospector*, you can get into trouble if you fail to hang on when you should.

We were about 200 miles north of St. Thomas when my accident occurred. It was nearly four in the morning, and I was fixing a cup of coffee, getting ready for my watch.

No doubt I was careless. I should have been hanging on, but it is hard to stir coffee when one hand is needed to hold the cup in place while the other is gripping a hand rail. I thought I had wedged myself tightly enough into the galley, but I was wrong.

The boat unexpectedly fell into a trough, and coffee forgotten, I went flying full length across the cabin. My left side collided violently with the unyielding wooden trim on the edge of the settee where Velda was sleeping. I knew instantly that I was badly hurt. Even while I was lying on the cabin sole, gasping for air, I realized I would need a numbing shot of Demerol before trying to move.

When my breathing returned to normal, John administered the shot. After it took effect, we pooled our efforts and lifted me up on the settee. He and Velda then strapped my torso with an old sheet, reinforced with duct tape. We didn't know what the problem was, although I should have guessed when, with every breath, I felt and almost heard a series of clicks in my chest.

I thought I had suffered a shoulder separation. I knew how painful they were, having experienced one under almost identical circumstances in an Alaskan fish boat some 20 years earlier.

It was clear that my navigating and watchstanding days were over. Velda and John listened closely as I explained how to take noon sights. Fortunately, those lessons weren't necessary.

The following afternoon, Velda saw a ship on the horizon. She rushed into the cabin, and called the ship on the radio. After explaining our problem, the ship's radio operator notified the Coast Guard in Puerto Rico that we had an injured man on board.

During the next two days, I was in serious pain. I wedged myself against the backrest of the settee and futilely tried to prevent my torso from rolling with the motion of the boat. The persistent click-click-click in my chest continued, although over time, I grew accustomed to it. It was lucky that we had ample codeine on board.

We made landfall the third morning after my accident. It was a first landfall for any of us. John was the first to realize that the clouds on the horizon had substance. But instead of rejoicing as one might have expected, I was too sick to care, and Velda and John became nervously excited. Neither had any idea whether the land mass they saw was St. Thomas, or how far off we were. Velda persuaded me to climb the companionway to the cockpit. I was barely able to do it. The after cabin in *Prospector* is separated from the main saloon where I was, by a bridgedeck with a four and a half foot overhead clearance.

We normally duck under the bridge, and climb straight up the three-step companionway ladder to the cockpit. I couldn't do that. Instead, I slid off the settee to the cabin sole, and shuffled forward on my knees, holding my back as straight as possible.

When I reached the after cabin, Velda and John helped me to my feet. Carefully, I climbed the ladder. Even with codeine, I was nauseous with pain and slick with sweat when I finally reached the cockpit seat. Thus began one of the worst days of my life.

The main port on St. Thomas, Charlotte Amalie, lies on the southern side of the island. We had to choose between going around the island on the eastern side, through Pillsbury Sound and Current Cut; or sailing into the Virgin Passage, separating the Virgin Islands from Puerto Rico, and zip right up to Charlotte Amalie. That seemed the quickest, most direct route, but we were dead wrong.

Yacht people must read the Pilot carefully to extract significant information buried between the lines. That's no job for someone who should be in sick bay. Since Coast Pilots are not written for yachts, navigational factors like foul currents that trouble yacht skippers may be described, but are not emphasized.

The sun was setting as we entered the Virgin Passage. Sail Rock, so named because the 200 foot stone pinnacle rising from deep water bears a remarkable resemblance to a full-rigged ship, was reflecting the last rays of sunlight to our right.

The wind fell off, and for the first time I realized we were bucking a substantial westerly current. We started the engine, and began to motor toward Charlotte Amalie. The engine ran well until the light was nearly gone, and Sail Rock was dead astern. Then the engine abruptly revved up momentarily and stopped.

John inspected the Racor filter. "It's full of water," he announced. "Now what do we do?"

"John," I said, "you are going to learn how to change the fuel filters. First... ." Step by step, I led him through the process for changing filters, then bleeding air from the system, and finally restarting the engine.

Velda and John, armed with flashlights and wrenches, crawled around the engine while I answered questions and shouted instructions from my vantage point in the cockpit. Their concentration was undisturbed because, since they were wedged tightly next to the engine, neither of them could see Sail Rock bearing down on us at what seemed to me a breakneck speed.

I was becoming as terrified as a deer watching on-coming headlights, as that ghostly mass rushed toward us at about three knots. I was afraid if we hit it straight on, we might hole and sink the boat. But there was nothing I could do, except hope we would miss it. I forced myself to keep quiet while Velda and John, entirely oblivious, kept bleeding the system.

We were less than 100 feet away — I could hear the ominous

murmur of fast moving water striking and flowing around that massive obstruction — and I was about to call them out of the engine room, when the starter whirred and the engine fired!

Our joy as *Prospector* gathered way, was short-lived. As we drew away from Sail Rock, we could see what appeared to be airport lights on St. Thomas, and we decided to anchor as close to the beach as possible for the night. By that time, it was pitch dark. Knowing we were bucking a strong current, and aware that my strength was rapidly fading, I had the engine wide open. Unfortunately, I was confused by the lights, and mistook an airport beacon for a light shown on the chart.

I was standing in the cockpit steering the boat with one hand and bracing myself with the other, when simultaneously, I heard an awful splintering crash, and felt the deck heave abruptly beneath my feet while the boat shuddered to an instant stop.

I almost fell down. The boat was partly out of the water, heeled about five degrees on her port side. John rushed below to shut the engine off. In the shocked silence that followed, we could hear water running past the hull. John and Velda, armed with flashlights, began ripping open the hatches in the cabin sole, looking for leaks.

I sat heavily on the helmsman's seat, nauseated with fatigue and pain, sick with worry and remorse. I had driven *Prospector* on the reef at over five knots, and I was sure she was lost. I was almost at the point of giving up. There is no more terrible feeling than that.

Satisfied that she didn't appear to be taking any water, Velda and John came back to the cockpit, and we sat there in the dark, each absorbed in our own thoughts. I don't know what the others were thinking, but my mind was filled with images of kedges and tackles.

"I wonder if she could back off?" John asked quietly.

"I don't know," I said. "Start the engine, and let's see."

I was sure we were much too hard aground for our puny little Perkins to be much help. John reached down and turned the key. The engine fired, and I put the clutch into reverse and opened the throttle. The engine roared, and we could feel the vibration as the propeller shaft spun in the stern bearing. But nothing happened. I yelled to John to pull the kill wire.

Nobody said anything in the sudden quiet. I could still hear the current running past the boat. In despair, I began wondering whether, in the morning when the sea breeze began raising a little

31

sea, she would bounce off the reef, or would merely pound on the rocks when the waves lifted and dropped her. Suddenly, I realized she was moving! Still lying partly on her side, the current was washing her back into the sea. Or was she, recognizing my weak despair, and sensing her mortal danger, saving herself?

John quickly restarted the engine, but before I could engage the clutch, with a final groan, *Prospector* refloated herself.

We worked our way into Perseverance Bay, and dropped the anchor. My shipmates helped me renegotiate the companionway ladder, and I collapsed on the settee.

In the morning, the Coast Guard escorted us into Charlotte Amalie harbor and directed me to tie up at the Coast Guard dock. An ambulance was waiting and I was whisked to the hospital.

After a series of extraordinarily painful X-rays, I got the bad news. It's no wonder I didn't feel well. That click–click–click business had nothing to do with my shoulder. My problem was five, possibly six, broken ribs. The only cure for broken ribs is aspirin and time. My shipmates found a taxi which delivered us back to the waterfront. We had one last chore to perform.

Donald Street advises first–time passage makers to retire to Sparky's Waterfront Saloon as soon as possible after their arrival in Charlotte Amalie to reflect on what they have accomplished. We had relied on Street's advice to this point, and this last admonition seemed eminently sensible. Velda, John, and I quickly rediscovered what sailors have known since the days of Ulysses. Nothing tastes better than the first sip of that first beer when you are sitting in a real chair at a real table, and you know that when you set your beer glass down, it will stay there until you pick it up. That wonderful feeling is enhanced as you look out the window at the boats in the harbor, knowing one of them is yours.

Chapter 2

The Caribbean Sea

Charlotte Amalie, with a harlot's instinct, has always catered to the sailor trade. In the 18th century, her clients were freebooters, provisioned by pious and avaricious Dutch and Danish merchants who prospered by fencing pirate plunder. Her legacy of greed is intact. Now, late in the 20th century, she still has a transient trade. School children are taught cynical little jingles about welcoming tourists who bring "green" (money).

Where Blackbeard once swaggered, a bewildered gaggle of tourists; sweaty, red–faced, probably thinking longingly of a tall cool drink, are herded back and forth by grasping cab drivers. I'm certain the clearest memory many of them carry away from this island paradise is the relentless chant issuing from the driver's seat of a safari bus: "Back to the ship? Back to the ship, now?"

People who arrived in their own boats occupied a much different world. Few of us had much money, and what little we had, we spent carefully. Our social lives revolved around rum (then priced at $1.19 a fifth in the local supermarket) and continuous visiting back and forth with other yachties.

A Baltic trader named *Johanne Marie* was anchored next to us. We quickly became acquainted with her remarkably friendly crew. During my convalescence, I found I could crawl over her bulwarks without too much pain, and we spent many happy hours in the shade of her awning, sipping rum and orange juice.

Three months elapsed before my ribs healed sufficiently so we could haul *Prospector* to see what damage had been inflicted on her during that terrible grounding the night of our arrival.

In the meanwhile, my son, Harry, had joined us for an indefinite visit. One morning, a young man in an inflatable dinghy came alongside. He introduced himself as Mark Cernac, and asked, "Is this the real *Prospector*?"

We assured him she was, whereupon he explained his interest in classic wooden boats, saying he and his wife Debby had sailed a wooden Jim Richardson ketch down from the Chesapeake Bay.

Mark was also a first-rate shipwright and marine engineer. Like Mike Orbach, Mark's knowledge was encyclopedic. He and his wife, Debbie, quickly became warm and giving friends. They volunteered to help haul *Prospector* and repair any damage caused by the grounding. They even sailed their boat in company with us to Isleta Marina in Puerto Rico.

The brief journey to Puerto Rico was not without incident. Isleta Marina is, as the name suggests, a marina on a small island, and lies a quarter of a mile off the east coast of Puerto Rico in Sonda de Vieques, or Vieques Sound.

Because Vieques Sound provides a natural barrier to the criminals on the main island, the island has become a popular and expensive residential neighborhood. Three large condominiums share the tiny island with the marina. Immediately after we anchored, a man came out in his dinghy to call attention to a small sign that warned of a utility line crossing. It was too late.

Our anchor, a 60 pound Danforth, had snagged something. We knew it as soon as we took a strain on the chain. Thinking you might be hooked to a high tension wire inclines you to be gentle, and very careful. I did the only sensible thing. I buoyed and slipped the anchor chain and hired a diver. When you hire a diver who thinks you might have hooked a 10,000 volt cable, your potential for bargaining is not great.

Luckily, we had only snagged the water line. The power line was untouched. Still, it cost $100 to get our anchor back.

We found, when the boat was out of the water, that a large splinter of Acana had been torn from the port edge of the keel. Evidently, the fourteen foot cast iron ballast keel had taken most of the blow. The planking wasn't damaged.

Ten days later, after repairing the keel and painting the boat, we left Isleta, hoping to reach Culebra before dark. Unfortunately, the Christmas trade winds, at 20 to 25 knots, were squarely on our nose.

Vieques Sound is a dangerous body of water, foul with uncharted coral heads, shoal bottom, reefs, small unlit islands, and so forth. A poor place to be caught after dark, except that the water was shallow so it would have been possible to anchor almost anywhere and wait for daylight. But frankly, that alternative never occurred to me.

By mid–afternoon we knew we were not going to arrive in Culebra before

Launching day at Isleta Marina

dark unless I could coax more effort out of our engine. I shoved the throttle wide open. Because the bottom was freshly painted and slick, instead of our usual 1800 RPM maximum, I was able to coax 2200 RPMs out of the engine, driving us at nearly six knots, even into the wind. I was happily steering the boat, enjoying the unaccustomed speed and power, when Velda, standing next to me in the cockpit, wrinkled her nose, and looked around. "Do you smell something funny?" she asked.

I sniffed. She shook her head. "See what's happening below," she said. As soon as I approached the companionway, I smelled the acrid odor of painted wood smoke! I rushed below to see if the galley was on fire. At the bottom of the ladder, I could see smoke rolling out of the engine room under the cockpit sole. I quickly lifted the engine cover, grabbed the kill wire, and gave it a good yank. The engine stopped.

"Denny! Come quick!" Velda yelled. "The cockpit's on fire!"

I ran back up the companionway ladder, and saw smoke coming from the port cockpit locker. The locker door is hinged on top, and is protected from the weather by a heavy canvas flap.

I whipped the canvas back and raised the door. I saw embers smoldering in the bottom inboard corner of the locker nearest the exhaust pipe.

A quick bucketful of sea water quenched the fire, and the smoke turned to steam with a satisfying hiss. I was sure the fire was out, but I crawled back under the cockpit sole next to the hot engine just to make sure. The fire was out, but our troubles were not over.

When I tried to restart the engine, I discovered that the Morse control cables had melted in the heat, and were forever frozen in the position they were in when the engine had stopped. Thus, when the engine fired, the propeller instantly began churning the water, and the tachometer quickly climbed to 2200 RPMs.

We propped the locker door open, and we watched as a hair-line crack in the exhaust pipe began to glow a dull red. At the same time we could smell escaping exhaust gases. Harry kept busy throwing a fresh bucket of sea water in the locker every 15 minutes to prevent the fire from reigniting.

I wonder what Mark thought as he watched us roar into the Culebra anchorage at full speed, coast to a stop, drop the anchor, raise it again (we were too close to another boat), get underway at full throttle, whirl around the anchorage again, coast to a stop, and again drop the hook. He was too polite to say.

Harry had spent the first two weeks of his vacation with a paint brush in hand. Now on his third week, pliers replaced the brush as he and Mark squirmed around the engine.

Mark disconnected the control cables, and showed Harry how to adjust the clutch setting and engine speed by hand. They wrapped a piece of copper and asbestos tightly around the cracked exhaust pipe, and wired it in place.

That jury-rigging got us safely back to Charlotte Amalie. Mark convinced me that it would be foolish to continue using an old fashioned dry exhaust system. Mark and Harry went ashore to look for parts while Velda and I cleaned up the mess. A diesel engine is superior to a gas engine on nearly every count, and not just for propulsion. Diesels are more powerful, have far greater fuel efficiency and the fuel won't blow up. But diesel soot is the greasiest, grungiest, dirtiest, most awful stuff in the world.

Mark and Harry rebuilt the exhaust system, replacing the dry stack with a modern water-lift exhaust of Mark's design.

Nearly three months had passed since that awful night in November when I broke my ribs, and I was ready to do something rather than just lay around the boat. Everything, including my health, the necessary boat repairs, and my son's presence came together so we could participate in the now defunct Ridiculous Regatta Lulu

Magras sponsored in mid–February each year at St. Barths.

St. Barths (more properly, St. Barthélemy) lies about 110 miles upwind from St. Thomas. The normal route from St. Thomas is to sail up the Sir Francis Drake Channel, through the British Virgin Islands where Captain Kidd once lay in wait for the Spanish treasure ships, to the Anagada Passage, then southeast to St. Barths. We followed that route and the trip was uneventful.

St. Barths is small and steep–sided. About 5,000 people, mostly of French descent, call it home. Anyone calling in St. Barths can be assured of a warm welcome at the *Le Select* bar.

The port of entry is Gustavia, a small town at the head of a bay inside Fort Oscar. Those place names are not French.

According to Don Street, Sweden arranged with France in the 18th century to manage St. Barths as a free port, in a complicated deal involving trading privileges in Stockholm. The trade proved not to be profitable, and the Swedes handed the place back to the French in 1877. It is not surprising the Swedes found the arrangement unprofitable. They were dealing with a people who viewed the evasion of customs duties as a sacred obligation.

However, despite its reputation as a smuggler's roost, which has carried down to the present day, the police do not carry arms. There is not much crime in the French West Indies.

Five days after we arrived, Harry and I went snorkeling over a deep bed of seagrass. When I surfaced, I removed my mouthpiece to say something. I felt a sudden unaccustomed cold draft over my lower jaw. A quick confirming check with my tongue, and I knew the worst. I had accidently removed my plate with the mouthpiece, and the plate was gone.

The return passage from St. Barths to St. Thomas is an overnight, downwind sail. The trip normally requires 18–20 hours in the winter trade winds. Thus, the prudent sailor will leave St. Barths after noon, planning to arrive in the early morning.

I knew that, but I hadn't yet learned the most valuable skill a rag sailor can acquire — patience. We left St. Barths at 10 a.m. A series of squalls overtook us in mid–afternoon, and we ran under bare poles, straight downwind, in continuous squalls. At times, the rain was blinding.

Shortly after 3 a.m., we thought we saw lights off our port bow. We didn't have a lot of time to think about it, because at that moment, an intense electrical squall rolled over us, with dazzling jagged blasts of blue-white lightning on all sides, so close we could smell the ozone. The noise, almost incessant explosions of thunder, seemed to make the deck vibrate, and reminded me painfully of what it feels like to live through a mortar barrage. I found myself trembling as I held the wheel.

Caribbean electrical storms can be intense, but they seldom last long. This storm tormented us only a few minutes, then rolled on. By that time, it was nearly 4 a.m. None of us had any rest, and we were tired and jumpy. The seas were only moderate, but the wind was up to 30 knots and more. It didn't occur to me to heave-to, but that's what I would do today.

Instead, I turned on the radio direction finder. I don't know what I expected to hear at four in the morning, but it was something to do. Our RDF was my kind of machine. It required almost no intelligence to operate, had the stamina of a Cape buffalo, and was impervious to mistakes. Unfortunately, I understand that Heathkit no longer makes them.

I set it on the wheelbox and turned it on. As I rotated the antenna, a station came in strongly, then faded as the antenna reached the blind spot (null), only to strengthen as I continued to turn the antenna. I returned the antenna to the null position, noted the compass bearing, and turned the antenna 90 degrees to learn what station we had.

"This is the Voice of Prophecy, the Island of Anguilla, B.W.I."

Anguilla. A flat little island four miles west of St. Martin. Its elevation is so low that the lights of St. Martin are visible across it to boats approaching from the northwest. More than a few vessels seeing those lights, have run aground on Anguilla or on a nearby islands like Prickly Cay, or been stranded on the reefs surrounding them.

According to our RDF, Anguilla was behind us, bearing 085 degrees. I penciled that bearing on the chart, and realized that no matter where we were on that line, we were not in danger.

We were in the middle of the 40-mile wide channel that separates St. Thomas from St. Croix. The lights we had seen were probably fishing boats on Lang Bank northeast of St. Croix. By daylight, we were in the entrance to Charlotte Amalie where I would begin my search for a new lower plate.

Our culture makes a joke of dentures. It's probably in our early conditioning when grandfathers (but not grandmothers) amuse their grandchildren by doing tricks with their teeth.

Well, face it: False teeth *are* funny. Consequently, if you are foolish enough to admit that your teeth were lost snorkeling, expect no mercy. At least that was my conclusion after phoning practically every dentist in the Virgin Islands. They all had the same story: It will involve a six week wait, and cost $500.

Some day, if there is any justice at all in this world, I hope to see that grasp of dentists explain to a federal judge why their fee schedules only *appear* to be fixing prices and restraining trade.

Like most successful members of a minority, I had learned to survive by playing on the ignorance of the majority. Toothed people arrogantly assume the rest of us live on mush if anything happens to our dentures. Now all I had to do was find a young, impressionable, and sympathetic dental assistant. I knew the typical assistant would be hardened against economic complaints, so my strategy was to focus their attention on my "suffering." In response to the projected delay of six weeks, I protested: "But surely you can't expect me to live on mashed potatoes that long?"

Eventually, that plea got me the telephone number of a dental clinic in Puerto Rico. In less than 24 hours, I had a brand new plate costing $79 plus airfare. It pays to shop around.

But the story does not end there. The dentist running the clinic, Dr. Wayne Reid, was a young New Jerseyite who, besides being a fine dentist and oral surgeon, was a private pilot. He and I struck up an instantaneous friendship over the impression tray. Two weeks later he, his girl friend JoAnne, and two of her friends, unmarried young ladies, came to spend the weekend.

I suppose I will always remember the expression on Harry's face while we were loading their luggage after he had ferried the girls out to the boat.

"Thank you, father," he said in a tone that fathers seldom hear. The weekend turned out well, despite or perhaps because we were so overcrowded.

Somehow, that weekend was a turning point for me. I needed more room and something to do. When we had left Morehead City the previous November, we had no goal more ambitious than reaching St. Thomas.

After convalescing in St. Thomas for three months, I was becoming restless. A life spent in energetic pursuit of one goal after another (which I seldom attained, of course) had not prepared me for a life of ease. Idleness doesn't suit me well.

Some years earlier, I had become interested in Costa Rica as a potential retirement haven because of its reputation as a highly congenial but very inexpensive place to live.

We invited my brother, Buzzy, to join us in Martinique for the passage across the Caribbean to Panama, and through the Canal to Costa Rica. He accepted our invitation as far as the Panama Canal, and asked if he could bring a friend. That seemed fine; the more the merrier. He agreed to meet us at Fort de France on the island of Martinique on June first.

Buzzy and I seem to complement each other like the Grass-hopper and the Ant in Aesop's fable. I tend to be flighty and impecunious, while Buzzy is diligent and steady.

Velda and I had become a part of the social fabric among the boat folk in Charlotte Amalie harbor, and although everyone was a transient, we found it sad to leave our friends, who sent us off in a cacophony of horns, whistles, and loud–hailers. Velda stood beside me in the cockpit, tears in her eyes. We knew it was unlikely that we would see those friends again.

Our first stop was at a night club on a cay in Trellis Bay on Beef Island in the British Virgin Islands. The club is called The Last Resort and is owned and operated by an Englishman named Tony Snell. It offers, in addition to Tony's act, a delicious buffet supper. The club is served by a launch named, appropriately, The *Last Retort*.

Tony's whimsical humor extends to the livestock that share his island. There is a beer–loving donkey named Chocolate, and a dog named Chicken. Chocolate begs beer by thrusting his head through a hole in the door, cut for that purpose by canny Tony, and braying. I'm sure it amuses Tony to watch the luckless tourist seated nearest the door pouring his not inexpensive beer into the gaping maw of a jackass.

Tony's act, while it changes little from year to year, is funny. He plays the piano, sings, and tells jokes. It is a delightful way to spend the evening.

We didn't have reservations, so Tony fit us in with a large party of Englishmen, all in one stage or another of inebriation. Velda became the belle of the ball, except for one cranky fellow who kept insulting everyone his bleary eyes found. His pals kept apologizing for his bad manners, and eventually the sot rested his head in the mashed potatoes and went to sleep.

We left Trellis Bay the following afternoon. The wind was holding fair out of the nor'east, and we laid a course for Great Dog Island, and finally swung south into Necker Passage. It was marvelous sailing. As soon as we reached Necker Island, I struck the fore and aft rig and set the squaresail. The breeze was fair on our port quarter, and we bowled along, the bow rising and falling in the quartering sea.

At first light we saw smudges on the horizon. I hoped they were St. Barths and St. Martin, which are only ten miles apart. The wind freshened with the strengthening light. By full daylight, we were on a broad reach under the four lowers watching those smudges become islands.

St. Martin (or St. Maarten) is divided almost equally between the Dutch and the French. The southern portion (St. Maarten) is part of the Netherlands Antilles. The northern half is administered by the Department of Guadeloupe, French West Indies.

We planned to spend several days on St. Martin and decided to anchor first in Great Bay on the Dutch side.

Great Bay is approximately half a mile wide, and the same distance deep. As we entered the bay, we saw five Oriental longliners tied to a pier near the eastern entrance to the bay.

Following Street's advice, we took the necessary bearings, and worked our way through the outer bay, across the bar that runs laterally inside the bay, coming to anchor in 20 feet of water about 200 yards southwest of the town dock.

In a place like Philipsburg you are expected to put your dinghy in the water and row ashore with the ship's papers, crew list, and crew's passports. You should go directly to the police station or Customs office and you should go alone.

After anchoring, I looked around the harbor. As I faced the beach, I saw a fleet of a dozen small beige and maroon charter boats anchored less than a quarter mile away in the southeastern corner of the bay near Bobby's Marina. The business district lay directly in front of us. Off to the left were several resort hotels.

Completing the picture, and somehow emphasizing the historic significance of the place, a lovely three-masted schooner with sparkling brightwork and newly painted green topsides rode to anchor just outside the bar to the northwest. Our nearest neighbor was a native sloop, anchored between us and the dock. A small trimaran was anchored 50 yards south of us.

I'd say, being mindful of the size of the place, there may have been 100 sailing vessels of one kind or another anchored in the inner bay, most of them south and east of us. A few larger boats, like the three-masted schooner, were anchored outside the bar.

Philipsburg is the sort of place where anything you might want could be found in a single afternoon. It is a small commercial town with many duty free shops. I believe prices for the usual tourist plunder such as perfume, watches, cameras, electronics, linens and china, may be the most reasonable in the Caribbean.

The day after we arrived, three West Indians rowed out to the native sloop behind us. They climbed aboard and broke out a second anchor, which they set at an angle to the original one.

When local folks begin setting extra anchors, it's wise to pay attention. With hindsight, we should have followed Street's advice, and moved around to the French side of the island.

But it was getting dark, and with me it is always a case of better a devil you know than one you don't. I had no idea what we might find in Marigot, and I had confidence in our ground tackle. It never occurred to me to wonder what sort of ground tackle those charter boats had.

We carried three anchors. The 60 pound Danforth, on a three-eights inch chain rode, was our working anchor. When we needed a second anchor, we generally used the 75 pound fisherman with a three-quarter inch nylon rode. I carried that anchor out in the dinghy. After dropping it, I started the engine and backed down to set it.

Then we sat back to see what would happen next. We didn't have long to wait. At sundown, the sky turned a sulphurous yellow as wicked looking clouds, roiling and tumbling, began scudding across the sky. Blasts of cold wind coming out of those clouds swirled across the bay toward us, scooping water off the surface and sending a fine spray of mist into the air.

The wind, out of the southeast, began pushing rollers into the bay. Gusts were no longer discernible because the surface wind was blowing so strongly. Looking to my right, toward the western side of the bay, I could distinctly see, even in the gathering dusk, a long line of curling breakers following the line of the bar.

I was surprised that the seas could rise so fast. *Prospector* was beginning to pitch and roll against her ground tackle, and I began to wonder nervously how the fisherman anchor was faring in the sandy bottom. We soon found out.

We began hearing distress calls over the radio from boats anchored further out, even before it was fully dark.

"Look out! One of those damned charter boats has gone adrift, and has snagged my anchor. My God, here comes another one!"

Dimly, through the flying spray and the wildly rolling fleet, we could make out the shapes of boats lying broadside to the weather upwind from us. They were obviously adrift.

God, I thought. *If those boats get this far, they'll pull our anchors out, and we'll go straight on the beach!* It looked as if half the fleet was bearing down on us. I had been running the engine off and on, keeping it warm. Now, I turned the key.

The engine fired. "Velda," I yelled, "Get those anchors up. We've got to get out of here before those boats reach us."

I put the clutch in gear and slowly began inching her ahead. Velda was on the foredeck and faintly, over the sound of wind and sea, I could hear the whine of the windlass's motor and the rumble of chain falling into the chain locker.

By this time, the wind was approaching 50 knots. Channel 16, the VHF radio's calling frequency, was plugged with cries for help, each call blocking the previous one. There was no help in Philipsburg that night.

I sensed our bow begin to fall off, and I turned the wheel to weather, hoping to meet it. I was afraid to open the throttle for fear of picking up the nylon rode in our propeller.

Velda was standing on the side deck next to the cockpit. "The anchors are tangled," she yelled. "I can't get them up!"

"Are they off the bottom?" I asked, wondering if we would have to drag our anchors across the bay.

Velda nodded. "They're under the bobstay," she said. "But the nylon rode is still in the water."

"Haul it as quickly as you can," I said. "If it washes into the propeller, sure as hell, we'll go on the beach!"

43

I saw a boat running northwest, parallel to the beach and away from that catastrophic pile-up in front of the town dock. I pointed to it. "I'm going to try to follow him," I yelled.

Velda ran forward again. I waited a few moments while the bow continued swinging toward the beach. Hoping I had given her enough time to get the bight of the line from under the boat and away from the propeller, I increased power to swing the bow back into the wind.

Velda leaned over the corner of the doghouse. "I think I have all the anchor rode on board," she said. "Come and see."

I motioned her to take the wheel, and grabbing a flashlight, ran forward. A quick glance told me what I needed to know. The light showed an insane jumble of twisted chain and fouled anchors woven together by a complicated web of glistening wet nylon. The whole mess was drawn snug under the bobstay.

The beach was now only 100 yards away. I ran back to the cockpit and relieved Velda at the wheel. As I increased power, *Prospector* began to answer her helm. I held the wheel hard over until the bow pointed out to sea. Holding her like that, we crabbed along the beach trying to think of what to do next.

We had three choices. We had a third anchor and a new 300 foot five/eighths inch nylon rode. Since we were safely away from the other boats, we could now try to re-anchor using that line and our 75 pound C.Q.R. (plow) anchor.

It would be a grotesque mismatch, an anchor rated at 5,000 pounds shackled to a line officially rated at only 900 pounds. I wouldn't have considered it except I knew that new nylon is incredibly strong, and the rating was very conservative, being based on only ten percent of its 9,000 pound tensile strength.

The second option was for Velda to keep the boat jogging into the weather while I tried to bring that pile of junk over the rail. But I wasn't sure I could do it alone in the dark on that wildly pitching deck without getting hurt or breaking something.

Our last option was a desperate one. We could go to sea and hope none of the sharp points of the anchors slung under the bobstay were driven through the planking as the waves smashed them against the hull.

Clearly, reanchoring was our best bet. I shouted over the roar of the storm what I was going to do. and Velda took the wheel as I knelt on the side deck cutting the lashings holding the spare anchor. Luckily, I had already spliced an eye with a strong thimble on one end of the new line. A bowline, even behind a fishermen's bend, would have weakened, perhaps crippled, an already inadequate anchor line.

I shackled the eye securely to the anchor, not forgetting to mouse the pin. Then I passed the bitter end of the rode outside the shrouds, careful to make sure it was clear of the rigging. I was grimly aware that we wouldn't have a second chance.

The toughest part was crawling out on the wildly pitching bowsprit to lead the rode under the whisker stay and over the roller on the bowsprit. I hauled back as much slack as I could get, and took three quick turns around the Sampson post.

By that time, Velda had slowed the boat so she barely had steerageway. I hurried back to the side deck where I had left the anchor, picked it up, and praying I hadn't forgotten or overlooked anything, threw it as far from the boat as I could, and ran forward to seize the other end of the line.

I had underestimated the speed at which we were being blown toward the beach. Even though I tried to check the momentum of the boat gradually, the strain on the anchor line came sooner and was much greater than I had expected.

I threw two more turns around the Sampson post. When the boat's weight and momentum came full upon the line, it creaked like a rusty gate and stretched like a rubber band. But it held.

That was the first time I had imposed anything near a maximum strain on a nylon line, and watching it take the load, I felt the same superstitious awe — and fear — toward it that I usually feel toward high voltage power lines.

That line looked and felt like a bar of reinforcing iron. It seemed to have shrunk to not more than half an inch in diameter. I can't begin to think how much potential energy must have been stored in it, but had it parted while I was standing there, it might have inflicted serious injury.

When I was sure the anchor was holding, knowing how susceptible nylon is to abrasion, I thought I had better make certain the anchor rode was leading fair and there was no chafe.

Not more than ten minutes had passed since my previous foray on the bowsprit. Then, we had been jogging into the weather, losing ground, but holding the bow into the wind. Now, we were stationary, taking whatever the wind and waves chose to throw at us, and the difference was startling. Worse than that, we had inadvertently anchored right on top of the bar.

By this time the seas were regularly breaking on the bar, one every 15 or 20 seconds. Three or four times each minute, a great curling arc of water would roll toward us, the foam reflecting back the lights from the beach.

As our bow fell into the trough immediately in front of the advancing breaker, a wall of solid water would crash down on the bowsprit and foredeck, rolling over the deck and trunk cabin, breaking against the doghouse, and pouring off the stern.

At the same time, as the bulk of the wave passed under her forward sections, *Prospector's* bow was thrown high into the air. I'm sure her bow was rising and falling at least 15 feet, which meant the tip of the slender bowsprit was rising and dropping through a 25 foot arc. Possibly more.

I clenched a piece of rag between my teeth and crammed a fathom of marline in my shirt pocket. Then I straddled the bowsprit, and when I thought the bow was beginning its upward thrust, I gave myself a mighty shove with my feet against the stem. By the time the bow began its sickening downward plunge into the trough, I was exploring the line where it turned around the bowsprit roller with my right hand, searching for tell-tale wisps and strands of nylon.

Suddenly, the slippery wood I was desperately clinging to seemed to fall away as we plunged into the water. Curiously, in that maelstrom, I was aware of a peculiar sucking sound as the wave rolled over me, pulling at my clothes.

I clung desperately, eyes and mouth tightly closed, feet braced against the whisker stays. I couldn't have been under the water for more than four or five seconds, but my lungs felt as if they would burst from the stress.

When I emerged from the water, while gasping for air, I took the rag from my mouth, and as the bowsprit fell again toward the water and the anchor rode went momentarily slack, I quickly wound the rag around the line twice where it passed over the bow roller. This time, I wasn't as frightened when the water closed over my head, and as we shot back into the air, I was tying marline around the rag to hold it in place.

I very likely set a world's record for sliding back the length of that bowsprit to the safety of the foredeck. The feeling of disorientation as I had gone under water was scary. No wonder they called those long bowsprits "widow–makers."

The next thing was to get that jumble of line, chain and anchors on deck and sorted out while our makeshift ground tackle was still holding. Crawling out on the bowsprit had just about used up my strength and luck.

I passed a light line outside the lifelines, and under the whisker stay to the anchor chain just forward of the chain stopper, and made it fast with a bowline through a link.

Velda, meantime, unshackled the staysail from its halyard, and handed the halyard's moving block to me.

I tied the other end of the light line to the block Velda was holding, and after passing several fathoms of chain through the stopper so the weight of that tangled mess was taken by the line, we began hauling on the halyard.

It was dangerous and very difficult, working in the dark, constantly off balance because of the boat's erratic pitching and rolling, and with solid water breaking over the bow, sweeping past our knees, continually drenching us. The job was even more difficult because the jumbled gear constantly fouled on the guard rail, and Velda pushed that frightful tangle away from our topsides a dozen times while I held the load on the halyard. After changing our purchase twice, we finally tumbled the lot over the lifeline onto the deck.

With Velda's help, I removed the shackle pins from the anchors. It went faster than I had expected. In minutes, we had the mess sorted out and put properly back together. I felt a huge sense of relief, knowing our anchors were operational again. We were giddy with fatigue, and sopping wet when we returned to the cockpit. It wasn't until then that a nagging question surfaced in my mind.

I had noted the sound of breaking wood immediately after throwing the heavy anchor out into the darkness and filed it in the back of my mind. I was much too busy to worry about it at the time. Now I knew what had caused it.

The after starboard pinrail, fashioned from two sturdy pieces of teak bolted together and clamped to the mizzen shrouds, had broken, and the dinghy was gone.

This wasn't hard to figure out. We had been towing the dinghy with its painter (or tow rope) tied to a belaying pin in the missing pinrail. While Velda was steering the boat, the whirling propeller had snagged the dinghy painter. In a fraction of a second, the painter would have wound itself around the propeller shaft until the slack was gone; then, with a healthy yank, the pinrail broke, and the propeller blade cut the painter. We were left with no dinghy and a broken pinrail.

I persuaded Velda to lie down and rest. I sat in the cockpit, listening to the distress calls on the radio. Other people were having much more serious problems than we.

The unfortunate man on the trimaran, for example, apparently had broken his leg while fending off a drifting boat. He was obviously in terrible pain as he pleaded for a doctor.

The wind began subsiding around two in the morning, and by daylight had died away almost completely. As the morning light strengthened, I took the binoculars and examined the beach for a sign of our dinghy. I couldn't find our boat, but the beach was littered with layers of flotsam. I was shocked to see that the big green three-masted schooner I had admired had been driven ashore, and now seemed to be resting in a sea of sand about five feet above the water.

I never found out the extent of her damage, but when sailing vessels sit vertically on the beach that way, probably not much of the keel remains. Modern sailboats are not flat-bottomed.

I was so busy looking at the wreck on the beach that I failed until then to notice that we had company. A big 63' charter boat, *Sandcastle*, was anchored 200 yards off our port beam. I have no idea when she arrived, but her people later told me they had watched me crawl out on the bowsprit the night before.

Seeing activity on deck, I waved my arms to gain their attention and yelled "Channel 68!"

The person on deck waved an acknowledgement and ducked out of sight. The radio contact was quickly made, and when I explained that I needed to go ashore to look for our dinghy, the skipper offered to give me a ride.

Within minutes, *Sandcastle's* Boston Whaler was alongside. The skipper introduced himself and said that a six-gallon gas can had washed out of the Whaler during the storm. I got into the boat, and

48

after a brief run, we tied up to the city dock.

The beach was a shambles; much worse than I had realized, peering through the binoculars. The native sloop was aground, and as I looked down the beach toward Bobby's Marina, the sand was strewn with beige and maroon charter boats laying on their sides. Sea grass and Sargassum, tangled with odd bits of yacht flotsam, an occasional oar, boat cushions, a torn life vest, bailers, and chunks of broken dinghies, littered the beach.

In places, the debris was almost knee deep. The trimaran also had come ashore. While I was gawking at the sights, Bob said, "Well, well. Look here."

I stopped and turned around. Bob was pointing to a six-gallon fuel tank stowed away on top of the seawall, just below eye level, hose neatly coiled. "Is that yours, Bob?"

"Sure is," he said. "Looks like we're getting warm." We walked on. Then he asked, "Would you know your dinghy?"

"Of course," I said.

"Well," he said, "is that it?" He pointed to the bow of a rubber dinghy poking over the edge of the seawall. It was ours. I would know those patches anywhere.

We scrambled up to the top of the seawall, and found ourselves on a patio covered with neatly stacked chairs and tables. Just then a small boy wandered into the yard rubbing his eyes. He saw us and ran back into the house crying, "Papa, Papa!"

A senior version of the boy came out of the house. "Is dot boat yours?" he asked in a strong Dutch accent.

I nodded. He went on, "Ve poot de oars and motor in de toilet to protect dem from de vedder. It vos de best ve could do," he added apologetically. Suddenly I realized we were on the patio of a small restaurant.

I expressed my appreciation, and offered to pay him for his efforts. He would have none of it. Feeling embarrassed, I tried to make some meaningful comment about the terrible storm, unfortunately illustrating my point by gesturing toward the green schooner on the beach only a few hundred yards away.

"Ja, I know," he said quietly. "Dot boat vos mine."

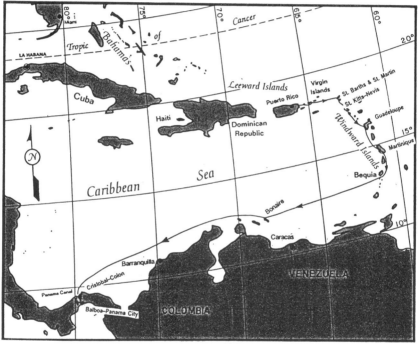

Prospector's Caribbean cruise
(Chart 2)

The Lesser Antilles

St. Martin is not a large island; it covers only about 37 square miles. Still, because it is irregularly shaped with lagoons, bays, peninsulas and off-lying reefs, it seems larger. It also seems larger because it has two capitals, Marigot for the French, and Philipsburg for the Dutch. Marigot lies on a wide indentation on the island's western coast, facing the British island of Anguilla.

If you were to call in Marigot today, you would find a courteous English speaking gendarme on the dock who would provide the necessary directions. Outside business hours and on holidays, you would be expected to row ashore, find the police station and announce your arrival.

If you arrived outside business hours in earlier years, you were expected to display your national flag at the stern and both a courtesy flag and a quarantine flag from the starboard flag hoist. There was a tacit understanding that you could remain at anchor for 24 hours before declaring yourself. But even in 1982, since we arrived on Saturday, I should have gone ashore to advise the police of our arrival.

We climbed into the dinghy on Monday morning and rowed ashore, carrying passports, crew list and our Philipsburg clearance. Dinghies and brightly painted fishing boats were clustered near the end of the town ferry dock. We squeezed our way into that raft of boats and found a place to tie up. After asking directions, we hiked up the hill past the fire station, the Catholic Church and cemetery, and a small hospital, coming to a building on the crest of the hill under a large French Tricolor rippling lazily in the breeze. We paused, recovering our breath and admiring the view.

The scenery was magnificent. Anguilla lay directly before us. could imagine how the French might have intimidated the British. It was not by coincidence that a battery of rusting cannon was pointed toward Anguilla. The Napoleonic Wars left an indelible imprint on the development of modern Caribbean politics and culture. Rival European powers, primarily but not exclusively, British and French, fought over the more easily defended and strategically placed islands. That is why the former British and present French islands present such a mixture of political affiliations.

We were ushered into the Inspector's office. A solemn Frenchman sat behind his desk staring at us with a somber gaze. Rows of ribbons decorated his uniform. Over his shoulder, through the opened window, I could see *Prospector* resting at anchor, her Stars and Stripes boldly waving in the sunshine.

If you have retained any high school French, now was the time to use it. French and Spanish–speaking officials genuinely appreciate the courtesy of a greeting in their language, even if *bon jour* is the extent of your vocabulary.

"When did you arrive?" This question is invariably asked, although the examiner may have watched you sail into the harbor. I'm sure the police knew exactly when we had arrived, but I told him, and he began leafing through our passports.

Frontier police invariably do that. For a long time, I foolishly thought they were vicariously enjoying our travels. Then I realized that by matching entry and exit stamps, they quickly learned whether we were sufficiently law abiding to comply with required clearance procedures. Yachties are sometimes rather lax about this requirement. This is especially important because clearance certificates are no longer issued to yachts in many places, and the exit stamp in your passport may be the only evidence you have that you left your last port lawfully.

I mention it because sometimes the exit stamp is overlooked by the clearing official, and you may have to request it. If necessary, do so; it is an important record.

You may expect questions about animals, firearms, and narcotics. The rituals must be observed. Answer all questions carefully, truthfully, and fully. ***But do not volunteer information.*** Babbling can cause embarrassment on both sides of the table. Frankly, there are some things your examiner may not want to know.

Satisfied, but not before the standard admonition against allowing the animals ashore, and a special one against both of us coming ashore to clear in, the examiner selected a stamp, and with a forceful thump we were formally admitted to the French end of the island.

I was amused to discover, several days later when I was driving back to the Dutch side, that in sharp contrast to the starchy treatment given yachts, the only way a motorist can tell when he has crossed the frontier is when the texture of the road surface changes. I don't even recall seeing a sign.

Marigot was not a complicated place. It wasn't as large as Philipsburg, but it seemed more foreign. That's because the French almost always do things differently.

English is commonly spoken in Philipsburg. Merchandise often is priced both in guilders and dollars. If you offer dollars in payment for merchandise, likely your change also will be in American currency.

The French also will accept U.S. currency — after all, the American dollar is the nearest thing there is to a universal currency. But your change always will be in francs and centimes.

Goods in French shops were always priced in francs and centimes. Usually a small card near the cash register would announce the current exchange rate being offered by the store. Bars were a different story. The exchange rate you got in a bar depended largely on the bartender's memory and his expectations concerning a tip.

Unfortunately, unlike their European counterparts, educated Americans are notoriously poor linguists. We were no exception. It certainly does we Americans no credit to complain when foreign nationals prefer to speak their language in their country. But that meant there was more of a language barrier in Caribbean French-speaking territories than we encountered elsewhere.

Like Philipsburg, there wasn't much to see in Marigot after the first few hours. We enjoyed cups of *café au lait* and rich, buttery *croissänts* in a tiny coffee shop on the waterfront before returning to the boat. Then we decided to go to Grande Case, which we thought was a fisherman's village, four miles north along the coast.

The entrance to Grande Case's shallow bay was easy. We anchored 100 yards from the town dock and rowed our dinghy ashore. Our only concern was an abnormal tide, because dinghy theft was almost unknown in the French islands.

We climbed up to the road and walked from one end of the village to the other. Buildings were tightly packed on the land side of the road, but only a handful stood on the beach side. One of these was a small hotel near the dock, where we paused for a refreshing beer.

Several small boys rode past on their bicycles in the heat of the afternoon sun. Otherwise, the village seemed deserted.

After we resumed our walk, we made an astonishing discovery. What at first we assumed were private homes, on closer examination, turned out to be small restaurants. At least a third of the buildings — 15 to 20 of them — had small discreet signs, often hand lettered, near the gate. Most also displayed menus. We had stumbled into a gourmet's paradise!

At the northern end of the village, where the road passed over a small bridge at the outer end of a salt pond, four restaurants — two Vietnamese, one Chinese and one Filipino — were clustered together. At the opposite end of the community, on the beach side, we found the Rainbow Restaurant.

Although we couldn't read the handwritten menus, we assumed the restaurant's offerings would be similar, so we selected the Rainbow restaurant strictly by price and appearance. It had a clean, freshly painted look, and it was neither the cheapest nor the most expensive establishment on the road.

Surprisingly, the owners turned out to be Americans, but the cuisine was French, and dinner was excellent. Velda had lobster. I'm sure it was delicious, but lobster is never my first choice. I like it well enough; but other things suit me just as well.

My entree was a chicken dish in a white wine sauce I thought exquisite. Even the check was a delight. Imagine two gourmet dinners, wine, pre-dinner drinks, post dinner coffee; the whole works, including tip coming to only $75!

If you ever find yourself on St. Martin, make it a point to visit Grande Case. If you are lucky, and the Rainbow is still in business, give them my best regards and order chicken. You won't be sorry.

The next morning, we got underway for Orient Bay on the Atlantic side of the island.

Orient Bay was a pretty place. A coral reef guarded the lagoon north and south of the entrance. We entered the lagoon by taking Caye Verde on our port bow, turning slowly to the left behind the cay as our depth allowed, until we had come a full 180 degrees. We were in a pool 12 feet deep and completely protected, with the cay on our left and on our right, a sandy beach about 200 yards away. The water was so clear that when our anchor hit the bottom, I could see the resulting puff of fine particles rise like smoke from a miniature explosion.

With the anchor down, I shut the engine down and we looked around. We shaded our eyes against the sparkle of the brilliant sun reflecting off the water. The dark blue sky fringed at the far Atlantic horizon with low white, uniformly flat clouds that looked as if they had been sheared off by the prevailing tradewinds, set the stage for the muted rumble of surf on the reef, the excited cries of seabirds wheeling over the water on the reef, the muttering of land birds in the island jungle behind us, and the faint laughter of people we could see tossing Frisbees on the beach. This was our introduction to a French *au naturel* beach.

A dozen huts, seemingly placed at random, and a large semi-enclosed pavilion close to the beach, appeared to constitute the hotel. We put the dinghy in the water and I rowed it to the beach, where we dragged it up on the sand.

We were surrounded by people of all ages in various stages of dress or undress. The Frisbee tossers were young people, displaying youthful enthusiasm and sleek, tanned bodies. Older folks sedately sat in beach chairs, or lounged on beach towels, carefully rubbing sun lotion on the pink parts.

A smattering of dedicated sun worshipers, burned an even dark mahogany shade by countless hours in the tropical sun, sat on beach towels chatting, playing cards, or in one or two extreme cases, jogging briskly along the beach.

We wandered into the pavilion. As we had guessed, it was the hotel lobby, restaurant, souvenir shop, and bar. The only part of the room with a wall was behind the bar. The roof was supported by wooden posts resting on the cement floor. Ice cream parlor tables and chairs were scattered around the lobby.

Velda and I went to the bar and ordered two beers from a matronly lady who welcomed us with a broad smile.

"Welcome to Fantasy Island," she said in a strong New York

accent. "That will be five francs, please."

Five francs, I expected. But not a New York accent. She was a combination room clerk, bartender and short order cook. She was also a widow from Yonkers and a very nice person.

"It doesn't pay much, this job," she said in answer to my question. "But Herman and I wanted so badly to come down here, and it would have been good for him. . .." She excused herself, slid down from her stool, and walked to the counter to wait on a cute little blonde wearing only a waist chain, a broad smile, and a startling bikini shadow, white against her otherwise tanned body.

We looked around the room. There were a half dozen groups, lounging in the shade of the open-air pavilion. Like the girl standing at the counter, they appeared to be wearing white swim suits, but they were "cottontails," or novice nudists. Velda and I had visited nudist resorts many times before, and minutes later I was comfortably padding across the hot sand to the dinghy with our clothes in my hands.

I was intrigued by our hostess's calm acceptance of a life style many Yonkers widows might have regarded as outrageous.

"I don't mind them kids," she said with smile and a wave of her hand, "you get used to it. Besides, I've seen it all before." She paused, then added, "Takes a lot to shock me."

She wasn't the only American on the staff. Joe and Cathy, a young American couple, also worked at the hotel. They were the proud parents of a brand new baby daughter.

Cathy was the program director. Joe operated the hotel charter boat service. I don't believe I ever met a man who enjoyed his work as thoroughly as Joe did. And why not? Even from a pure business point of view, he was an object of envy.

His charter vessel was a 16 foot Hobie catamaran. He charged $20 a head for a two hour cruise in the lagoon. He usually had six passengers for the morning cruise, and six more every afternoon.

Thus, he was paid $240 a day in a business with practically no overhead, for sailing a Hobie cat in a tropical lagoon and looking at naked girls all day. Not bad. His uniform consisted of a baseball cap, a pair of dark glasses, and zinc oxide liberally daubed on his nose, his lips and his foreskin. His only cash outlay was for zinc oxide and cleaning fluid to get the suntan oil stains out of his ship's trampoline.

The hotel owned the boat.

Orient Bay was special, flavored as it was with a hint of bagels and cream cheese and the robust American couple, Joe with his zinc oxide, and Cathy with her cries of "Volley Ball!"

It was hard to imagine a greater contrast than that between the sophisticated island we were leaving, and our next port, the former British colony of St. Christopher, known throughout the Caribbean as St. Kitts. British colonial policy was a variation of the English caste system, where there were two kinds of people, us and them. At home, the "thems" included everyone outside the British peerage. In Her Majesties' tropical colonies, "thems" were mostly useful for cutting sugar cane, fighting wars, and caring for the horses.

As Toffler points out in his insightful book *The Third Wave*, universal education was invented by the English at the outset of the industrial revolution to supply the new factories and mines with child laborers who could tell time, accept discipline, and do jobs by rote. Colonials were treated much the same way, except that cane cutting required no formal education, and consequently, none was provided. It was a remarkably efficient system for converting black sweat and white youth into great fortunes. The colonials bought the cloth and machetes produced by English child labor, paying for them by cutting sugar cane.

Other than the English language, the only legacy the British left when they pulled out of the Caribbean in the late 1960s was a semi-literate society rooted firmly in the 19th century.

One result, almost exclusively peculiar to the English-speaking Caribbean, has been the radicalization and alienation of young West Indians, and the rise of pan-African cults and religions.

We anchored in the tiny harbor at Basseterre, St. Kitts' capital, and rowed ashore. A ten-year old businessman was waiting for us, a wide confident grin on his face, as he took our dinghy painter and expertly made it fast to a dock cleat.

A missing front tooth took nothing away from his raffish appeal. "Yo' need laundry? Ice? Find de Custom House? Watch yo' dinghy?"

This kid had met yachts before.

"Jes' one dolla, I watch yo' dinghy. Or I get othah fella watch yo' dinghy," he said, pointing to an obviously shy youngster leaning against a piling. "Yo' give me dolla, I take yo' 'Gration, show yo' aroun'," he added. We opted for the package deal, leaving the other lad in charge of the dinghy. Our young guide led us to a building on the commercial dock, and indicated the staircase. "Top ob de stairs," he said, and finding a shady place, he sat down to wait. The customs officers didn't allow those kids in the building.

Our guide was waiting when we emerged. After a quick tour of the town, he led us back to the dock, reciting the other services he could perform. He was waiting for us the next morning with a new catalog of services. However, we told him we were going to try it this time on our own.

St. Kitts was a quiet place. There were no glittery duty free shops. The stores near the waterfront were in dark cool buildings, air-conditioned by opening more shutters. Velda and I wandered around the town, peeking into shops, visiting the graveyard, chatting with people on the street, and enjoying the 19th century ambiance of the place. The police still wore the cork helmets and white uniforms of colonial times. There was a large open air market near the waterfront which, like nearly all similar markets the world over, opened before daylight and closed shortly after most people have had breakfast. This market had an unusual cleanup gang.

Five or six prosperous hogs were turned loose in the recently abandoned aisles to clean the place up. Very efficient, except we wondered who cleans up after the hogs.

Possibly to prevent the spread of unwelcome and divisive ideas like labor unions and social justice, the population was sequestered until 1978. Visitors were discouraged, and visiting yachts were barely tolerated under rigidly controlled conditions. Even as late as 1982, we found it necessary to obtain a boat pass to visit Nevis, a politically linked neighboring island. We knew the customs office would be closed over the weekend, so I obtained our pass late Friday afternoon. We spent Saturday morning in the market, and early Sunday morning, we motored out of the harbor. We ran under power slightly over three hours to reach the anchorage in Charlestown, Nevis' capital.

A scowling and suspicious customs officer was waiting for us on the dock. "What took you so long?" he demanded. Had he been waiting three days, I wondered. He was certainly acting that way.

We explained we had wanted to see market day in Basseterre. He nodded and said curtly, "Follow me."

He led us to the police station. The officer on duty was a friendly chap who examined our passports and our boat pass. He then asked the liturgical questions: Did we have animals, firearms or narcotics?

My "yes" to all three questions bothered him. I explained the narcotics were in the ship's medicine chest, the animals were on board and would not be brought ashore, and that we carried a rifle and shotgun.

He warned against bringing the animals ashore, told us to keep the medicine chest out of sight, and ignored my statement regarding firearms. Then he turned to the customs officer, and asked if he wanted to add anything. The officer was still sulking, and shook his head. The policeman handed back our passports.

"Enjoy your stay with us," he said, smiling. We shook hands. I took our passports and we left. It was Sunday morning. No shops were open. We saw only churchgoers.

Velda and I went back to the boat and spent the day lazing around. We didn't care for the police state atmosphere, and since we didn't see anything particularly interesting about the place, we decided to move on to Guadeloupe.

The next morning, I went to the customs office and obtained our clearance certificate; an archaic document that informed the world that *Prospector* was of "12 tonnes burden, 0 guns, laden in ballast, bound for Guadeloupe."

The distance from Nevis to Guadeloupe is only about 70 miles, but the trip took well over 24 hours. We left Nevis shortly after breakfast. It was late in the afternoon when we finally saw Guadeloupe through the haze. The wind was dying. By dark we were still some ten miles away, and barely had steerageway.

As we ghosted along, we became aware of puzzling lights on the water directly before us, seemingly less than a mile away, appearing and disappearing at random.

I had no idea what they were. The sensible thing was to stop and wait for daylight. We dropped the mainsail and rolled the jib. The wind died, and the mysterious lights began to fade.

By daybreak, Guadeloupe had disappeared in the haze. We were completely becalmed. The pilot chart indicated we were in the grip of the northwesterly flowing Guyana Current, which filters through the leeward islands into the Caribbean, and forms the nucleus of the mighty Gulf Stream.

According to the chart, in May the Guyana Current had a velocity of between two and three knots. Thus, we probably drifted some 15 to 20 miles during the night.

We had plenty of diesel, so I started the engine. We motored for hours over an oily, heaving sea, steering what I hoped was a reciprocal course. In early afternoon, the faint, shadowy bulk of Guadeloupe began to appear through the haze. By late afternoon we could distinguish landmarks on the island, and shortly before dark we entered Baie Deshayes.

Baie Deshayes is a jewel. Located in the northwestern corner of Guadeloupe, the bay opens like a fjord into the island, tall hills on all sides. The deeper you go into the bay, the more sheltered the anchorage becomes.

We motored past a cluster of open fishing boats, and I saw what had caused those mysterious lights. Each boat sported a gasoline lantern hung from a sturdy bracket bolted to its gunwales. The lights were intermittent because in the open sea they were hidden as a boat dropped into the trough between the swells. It was well we had stopped when we did. Who knows what might have happened had we blundered into that fleet in the dark.

We anchored in 12 feet about 100 yards from the town dock. Everywhere we looked we saw lovely shades of green punctuated by black rock on the steep hillsides and the glistening narrow white strip of sandy beach in the soft glow of the setting sun.

The only sounds, other than children laughing and screaming as they leaped off the dock and splashed in the water, was the occasional bleat of a goat on the hillside.

Our first impression was misleading. Behind that tranquil screen of fringing palms was a small village. Not a center of commerce certainly, but a place large enough for our needs.

The next morning, after launching the dinghy, we ran ashore to the tiny dock, which was little more than a dinghy landing, about 100 feet long. There was three feet of water at the outer end. A small restaurant/grocery store was located on the shore.

Across the street from the grocery, a signpost in French (with English subtitles) directed the visitor to the *Bureau de Poste*, the *Gendarmerie*, and the *Douanier* (customs officer). We followed the sign to the customs officer up the hill, and eventually were rewarded with a small sign announcing the *Douanier's* residence.

The officer invited us into his home, and in moments, we were formally admitted into Guadeloupe by a gracious gentleman who enhanced our welcome by expressing pleasure for the opportunity to refresh his English.

The town occupied six blocks between four parallel streets. The business district was centered on the street nearest the water. The next street over was the highway which descended the hill where we had found the customs office, passed through town, and ascended another hill. The road eventually led some 20 miles to the main city of Pointe-a-Pitre.

Anse Deshayes has an odd distinction. Where Grande Case, for no apparent reason, was a gourmet's delight, Anse Deshayes appears to be a center of driver education, with five *École de Auto*. How is it possible that a village of possibly 300 souls, with a social orientation so rural that the town laundromat was a stream at the edge of town, support five driving schools?

I'm sure there's a logical explanation — if anything, the French are excessively logical — but we shall never know because English is not commonly spoken on Guadeloupe and the question was far too subtle for pantomime.

A small bus passed through Anse Deshayes on its way to Pointe-a-Pitre about every two hours. The fare for the 20 mile journey was 12 francs. The ride took you through the agricultural backbone of the island, winding through little country towns, past cane and tobacco fields, and banana plantations.

Seen from the air, Guadeloupe resembles a lopsided butterfly heading north. Pointe-a-Pitre is the butterfly's head. The city was built at the edge of a marsh which arguably splits the island in two. The butterfly's two wings are called Basse-Terre and Grande-Terre respectively. Pointe-a-Pitre is a small city of about 30,000 people. We wandered through the streets, and found a peculiar order in the way the stores were arranged. For instance, we found a street devoted solely to fabric stores. On the next street was a collection of hardware stores. We also saw many pushcart peddlers selling food, beverages and vegetables.

We decided one evening to try the local restaurant in Anse Deshayes. I wish I could tell you we discovered a genius in the kitchen and enjoyed impeccable service, but that would not be true. We had very ordinary dinners.

In common with most small French restaurants, the menu and the price were fixed. Our only option was between two entrees. Velda ordered lobster, and I had overdone fish of some sort. The service was provided by a sullen 12-year old daughter. The ambience was provided by a young cat that was sick under a neighboring table. All I can say is that Anse Deshayes had better forget haute cuisine and stick with driving schools.

I wish we could have lingered, but we had to keep an eye on the calendar. My brother, Buzzy, would be waiting for us in Martinique on June first, and he hated to be kept waiting, so reluctantly, three days later, we raised our anchor and motored back into the Caribbean, again turning south.

Another former British island, Dominica, lies between Guadeloupe and Martinique. The anchorage at the Port of Entry, Roseau, is an open roadstead where the boat would roll incessantly, making launching the dinghy very difficult. It just didn't seem worth the effort to stop.

Shortly before we came within sight of Roseau, a large, low flying helicopter bearing the legend *U.S. Navy* painted on her hull flew toward us. The chopper hovered for a moment, raising hell with the draft in our sails, then flew on.

Immediately afterward, a ship which I thought at first was a cruise ship going into Roseau, turned suddenly toward us. Minutes later, *USN-69*, the biggest aircraft carrier I had ever seen, was steaming across our bow. She wasn't more than 500 yards away. Hundreds of sailors stood in the elevator wells and lined the flight deck, cheering and waving as she swept past.

Martinique has an interesting World War II story to tell. The island joined the Vichy Government after France surrendered to Germany. According to the story, the Vichy regime asked President Roosevelt's permission to store their treasury bullion on Martinique. The President acquiesced only on condition that the French deny Nazi submarines access to Fort de France's harbor.

Martinique has a much different flavor than Guadeloupe. Guadeloupe is more West Indian than French, while Martinique, birthplace of Josephine Bonaparte, is infinitely more European. Brisk and businesslike, the city radiates the cosmopolitan character of France.

When you arrive in Martinique, after anchoring in the yacht

anchorage, you row ashore. Customs is located in a house trailer at the end of the dock, where a sign in French and English warns you not to go further until you have completed the necessary formalities. There was none of the provincial starch we encountered in Marigot, and none of the charm we enjoyed in Anse Deshayes. Instead, the officials were courteous, efficient, and professional. A question or two, stamp, stamp — the appropriate marks were recorded in our passports — and we were admitted.

Buz and his friend, John Black, were waiting for us when we arrived. I liked John Black from the beginning. I knew he didn't have much offshore experience, but I felt that a person who had paddled a kayak 800 or 900 miles from Seattle to Alaska would be a great help on a cruise across the Caribbean. I was glad to have him aboard. They had brought with them, all the way from Seattle, four gallons of expensive bottom paint and two five gallon pails stuffed with hardware for the boat.

They wanted to see the ruins at St. Pierre, several miles north of Fort de France. Since they had already rented a car, we took the day off and went with them to visit the site of the most disastrous volcanic eruption in modern times. Unbelievably, 32,000 people died when Mt. Pelee erupted in 1902. Ships in the harbor were set afire by the unimaginable heat of the lava flowing over the city and into the sea.

Parts of the city have been excavated, and some houses restored, but the lava flow is still the dominant feature of the landscape, and most of the city will remain forever buried.

On the return trip, we stopped in a suburban supermarket. The market had color, style and flair. The vegetables and meats, especially the pâtés, were beautifully displayed. It was arranged exactly as you might expect a French supermarket to be, especially since the supermarket concept is a French invention. John and Buz had both spent time in Europe and had fun filling a shopping cart with wines, pâtés, and cheeses.

But it was expensive; and man cannot live on pâté alone, so the next day we began provisioning in the small, dingy markets near the waterfront. We bought perishables we thought would keep, filled the freezer with meat, and refilled the propane tanks.

We cleared out, stowing the dinghy in its accustomed place on the cabin top, and motored to the fuel dock where we topped up our diesel and water tanks.

On the third of June, we left Martinique for Bequia, about 95 miles south. The wind, after we cleared the harbor, was broad on our beam, and we set the four lowers.

St. Lucia, immediately south of Martinique, is another high island. To avoid being trapped in a wind shadow on its leeward side, and remembering our experience in the Guyana Current, I decided to go out the St. Lucia Channel into the Atlantic.

Shortly before noon, as we began to feel the Atlantic swell, I watched *Rocher du Diamant* (see the cover) slide past our port side, and remembered the Stuermers had mentioned Diamond Rock as the point where their outbound and inbound tracks had crossed, thus signaling the completion of their circumnavigation. As it turned out, that rock would also come to have special meaning for us, as well.

The passage to Bequia was uneventful. We ducked back into the Caribbean north of St. Vincent, and by noon the next day came to anchor off Port Elizabeth in Bequia. Almost immediately, a bumboat with two boys was alongside. You don't see bum boats many places in the Caribbean, but in Bequia they swarm around the yachts like seagulls around a fishing trawler.

Our lads, one about 12, the other possibly 15, offered an amazing range of goods and services; from ice and laundry, to souvenirs, and an evening's musical entertainment. They even offered to run interference with the customs officials: "Ol' Bob's on the table, today, mon. I kin take keer 'a ol' Bob fer ya . . .."

That was in addition, of course, to the usual offerings of bananas, mangos, papayas and limes. Had they not seen Velda, I think it very likely that other, more exotic attractions might have been offered. Their sales patter was very practiced, one lad asking rhetorical questions and the other answering, all by rote.

While West Indians enjoy a well deserved reputation for open-handed friendliness and generosity, those who put on the uniform of a customs officer in the English–speaking Caribbean unfortunately tend to be arrogant, boorish, ill-tempered and very bad mannered. Regretfully, I include the American officials in the Virgin Islands in this indictment.

I don't know if it was Ol' Bob I ran up against, but whoever he was, he stands head and shoulders above his sorry peers for rudeness and bad manners. He was sullen, unresponsive, and uncooperative. He was also a shakedown artist.

I knew I was in trouble when I first stood in front of his desk. He was a middle-aged man, slender, with short-cropped hair, whose gaze was fixed on anything except me. His short fingers played with our passports.

He wanted a crew list. Fair enough. At that time, I was sufficiently green not to have come prepared. But I did have the four passports, so it was a simple matter to prepare one if he would just loan me his pencil.

"De sto' nex' do'," he said in the broadest West Indian accent I ever heard. So I went to the store next door and bought a pencil and a single sheet of paper. You can't always find a store willing to sell you a single sheet of paper — but not every store had an Ol' Bob next door. Then I paid the harbor dues of EC $67.50 (US $22.50), and, at Bob's urging, ten dollars EC each for four tickets to the Ladies Social. It wasn't until I was back on the boat and read the fine print that I realized these were tickets left over from a social that had been held a year earlier.

Bequia is quaint. They still hunt an occasional whale from open boats, but they do better building elegant and expensive whale boat models to sell to tourists.

Walking along the sandy road that followed the curve of the bay, you would see goats and chickens, hibiscus and palm trees. Here and there, back from the road, were small buildings. Some were homes, some were shops and many were both.

While we were there, an inter-island freighter had been hauled partly out of the water on the beach for work on her rudder. The gear used was primitive, but the procedure must have been spectacular.

A huge tree growing on the beach served as the deadman. The second part was a massive tackle made up of a heavy bright yellow polypropylene hawser rove through two six-part blocks. The third was an antique ship's capstan — the kind that required eight men and a hearty sea chantey.

Unlike their brethren in the Leeward Islands, which stretch from St. Lucia through St. Kitts to the Virgins, the Bequia West Indians are avid boat people. Bob Dylon's beautiful schooner *Water Pearl* was built here by local craftsmen.

Port Elizabeth was once a major whaling port, so it is not surprising that Bequia should be so salty. The small boats, although heavily and sometimes crudely built, are classic New England peapods. They appear to be over-canvassed, with their huge spritsail rigs, but their young captains handle them skillfully, and those little boats go like the devil during their semi-weekly races through the anchored yachts in the harbor. Even young children get in on the fun. A coconut husk shaped like a boat, with a stick for a mast, and a piece of paper for a sail was a very common toy. The little tykes race them with great enthusiasm.

On the third day, we visited two shops where elegant, but very expensive ship models were on display. Then, while we were walking back to the landing where we had left the dinghy, we passed a small native bar. The door opened and a young black couple walked out on the porch.

"Hey, white man," the man called, "you like my sister?"

I knew he couldn't be talking to me; Velda and I were together. Buzzy and John were trailing along behind us.

My dumb brother, wanting to be polite, muttered, "Yes, she is very pretty."

John, considerably more worldly, hissed under his breath, "Shut up, you idiot, and keep walking!"

We quickly returned to the beach and cleared out that afternoon. Luckily, Ol' Bob was off duty when I presented myself for our exit stamps. Our next port was Bonaire in the Netherlands Antilles, straight downwind for 420 miles. We left at 11 the next morning. This was not a tranquil passage. For instance, on June ninth, the strap securing the yard to the mast broke. After bagging the squaresail, we lowered the yard, and cradling the spar in our arms with great difficulty and greater awkwardness, staggering back and forth on the rolling deck, we stowed it and its gear on the deck, where we tripped over it all the way to Costa Rica.

On June tenth, we raised Los Roques, an isolated reef belonging to Venezuela, well marked with stranded and wrecked ships. In a fit of absent-mindedness, possibly influenced by the sad appearance of those wrecked ships, I made a classic navigator's error. Plotting our course from Los Roques to Bonaire, I subtracted the variation instead of adding it, resulting in a 14 degree error. Although Bonaire was only 30 miles away, we missed it by a country mile.

But there's one thing about the Dutch. Their navigational aids are always in good working order. When daylight was nearly gone, we distinctly saw the measured flash of a navigation light over the horizon behind us to the southeast. The wind had died completely by then, so we started the engine. The current had a strong westerly set, but at daybreak the next morning, we were preparing to anchor off the beach at Kralendijk, Bonaire's city.

I nosed the boat in as close as I dared and we let the anchor go in 20 feet of water. I backed slowly as the chain dribbled off the bow, and by the time we had 150 feet of chain in the water, our depth finder was indicating a depth of 200 feet.

Meanwhile, a man in a gray uniform came to the water's edge and beckoned to me. We put the dinghy over the side, and I rowed ashore. "Go there," he said, pointing north along the beach. "Better place."

Anything would be better than trying to anchor against the Empire State Building. We hauled the anchor back aboard, and putting the helm over, started moving north along the beach.

After running a short way, we came to a breakwater guarding the entrance to a tiny bay that seemed from our vantage point to be crowded, except an open space in front of a bulkhead.

I realized that was where we were expected to dock. It was either go in there or forget Bonaire. I decided to do it, although by then a brisk breeze was blowing across the entrance.

Prospector is typical of her full-keeled breed. She hates to make tight turns. Also, she is so heavy she is hard to stop when she is under way. Consequently, I avoid getting into tight spots when possible, but here, I had no choice.

I slowed the engine so I barely had steerageway, and crabbing against the wind, aimed for the tiny channel. Once we squeezed through, it was a simple matter to bear off to the left and slide up against the bulkhead. Mr. Gray Uniform was waiting for us.

He wanted to search the boat. God only knows what he was looking for, but *Prospector* was something of a novelty; for obvious reasons, Bonaire didn't get much transient traffic.

The inspector gave us a cursory once over: "What's in that locker?" He would point. He opened things at random. It was mildly annoying, but eventually he stamped our passports, gathered up our arsenal, and bid us a good morning.

John went to inquire about plane schedules. He had decided to visit Venezuela and rejoin us in Panama. Buzzy left to seek a rental car. That was something we couldn't do.

When we severed our ties with civilization, we made two serious mistakes. First, we should have left Virginia with fresh driver's licenses, because a valid driver's license was necessary if we wanted to see the countries we visited. Failing to appreciate that without a fixed address, it's impossible to get one, when we left Virginia, our licenses would expire within the year.

The other mistake I made was cutting my American Express Gold Card in two when the annual renewal fee went from $35 to $50. That was important because plastic is ubiquitous, accepted everywhere. But, like the issuers of driver's licenses, those who hand out credit cards do not knowingly do so to nomads.

If you have access to a car, you can see everything there is to see on Bonaire in two short days. We started at the salt pans at the southern end of the island. Those pans — gigantic earthen cookie sheets, each covering acres of ground — as neatly diked as though they were still being used, dotted the landscape.

They were being used, but not by people. We saw scores of spectacular pink flamingos walking stork-like in the shallow water, searching for brine shrimp. The birds were not tame but they are used to people, and we were able to approach within fifty yards of a small flock feeding near the road.

Two huge antenna farms, each covering several acres with a complicated and seemingly random scatter of poles and wires, lie in the center of the island. One is the main transmitter for Dutch World Radio. The other belongs to a religious group and broadcasts world-wide evangelical messages.

Continuing north, we soon came to the hills. They were covered with brush and small trees, and reached an elevation of possibly 100 feet. They offered a pleasant change from the flat, arid, sunbaked southern part of the island.

Other than flamingos, the evening news, and government subsidies, the only thing that keeps Bonaire economically alive is the world-class scuba diving offered by its spectacular reefs.

It's a pleasant place, but unless you're a scuba diver or a pink flamingo, I didn't imagine it would be very exciting to live there. We topped up our water and fuel tanks. On June 13th, after retrieving our arsenal and the necessary exit stamps, we waved farewell to John, and made our way out of the marina.

It may have been the 13th, but you can bet it wasn't a Friday. It's a odd thing about superstitions. Black cats, walking under ladders, spilling salt, none of those things bother most yachties, me included. But please don't ask us to leave port on a Friday. It just isn't done. This silly quirk seems practically universal in the yachting community. I don't know anyone who, all things being equal, will voluntarily leave port on a Friday.

The passage from Bonaire to Cristobal at the Atlantic end of the Panama Canal is about 700 miles, straight down the Spanish Main. We were following the path of the conquistadors, and later the plate ships and the pirates who preyed on them.

We stayed well away from the Colombian coast and gave Cartagena a wide birth. Cocaine smuggling gets the headlines, but piracy is practically a cottage industry on that coast.

The constant tradewind remained on our port quarter during that six–day passage from Bonaire to Cristobal, and we rolled the miles off at a steady five knots.

The closer we came to the Canal, the thicker the traffic became. Of the five major straits and constricted waterways in the world, I believe the Panama Canal handles as much traffic as any two of the others. Cruising in a small sailboat, you get to where you notice things like that.

On our last evening, just a day from Cristobal, I was sitting on the doghouse at twilight, shooting a round of stars. I took my eye from the sextant, and saw a huge shape directly astern of us. "Turn on the running lights!" I yelled.

I jumped off the doghouse just as the lights flashed on, and ran below to switch on the radio. "Hello, ship," I said, feeling small and vulnerable, "this is the yacht *Prospector*."

"Hello, *Prospector*," came the instant reply. He had been waiting for my panicky call. "This is *Exxon Lexington*. I notice you just turned on your navigation lights," the Mate said dryly.

I explained I had been taking a series of star sights, and then asked if he could give us a position.

"I'll do better than that, *Prospector*," came the response. "I'll give you your position when we pass in a few minutes. By the way, you needn't have turned on your lights for us; we've had you on radar for the past 12 miles."

Shortly after noon, on June 19, we saw the two huge cement structures, one painted red, the other green, marking the Atlantic entrance to Colon harbor, door to the Panama Canal, gateway to the Pacific Ocean. Luckily, as we passed between those massive quoins, we hadn't the slightest notion of the terrible few minutes, and almost certain catastrophe, waiting for us in the upper Miraflores lock chamber.

Cap and Lara
ship's mascots

Chapter 4

Spanish America

$\mathcal{E}$ntering the breakwater off Cristóbal, a yacht was a gnat among giants. From a yacht's deck, everything seemed huge. Ships of all nationalities crowded into the bay behind the breakwater, patiently waiting their turn to be lifted over the spine of the Americas from the Atlantic to the Pacific.

An alert Panamanian customs launch came alongside as we inched our way into the crowded anchorage, and I was handed a sheaf of papers and directed to the small boat anchorage near the fuel dock. We anchored in 15 feet of water and sat back to wait for developments.

Less than an hour later, the boarding officer returned. He made a cursory examination, and helped me prepare the necessary documents. He hinted that life might be a good deal more pleasant if we hired an agent. He was undoubtedly right, but agents are a luxury most of us can't afford. Consequently, I had to go ashore and complete the entry formalities personally. It was a chore, but not as bad as I feared.

When the U.S. Army Corps of Engineers was in charge, Cristóbal was an Army base, with armed guards and a high chain-link fence. The fence was still there in 1982, but the guards were gone, and the gates were permanently open.

Most of the government offices that concerned transient yachtsman were located in yellow frame buildings, left over from World War II. If there is anything the Army is obsessive about, it's signs, tags and labels; in the old days, I'm sure those buildings and the offices inside were identified by neat signs in English.

However, like the guards at the gate, those signs probably

symbolized, for Panamanians, the more undesirable aspects of what they viewed as an American occupation. The signs have disappeared. Port agents, of course, don't need them; they know where the officials are. For that reason and my lack of Spanish, it was difficult in 1982, three years after the U.S.–Panama Canal Treaty had gone into effect, to work my way though the system because while Americans still operated the machinery and paperwork pertaining to it, Panamanians ran everything else.

The crews of vessels passing through the Canal do not need Panamanian visas if they do not leave Cristóbal. The same is true, of course, for the crews of yachts. However, cruising people will want to see more of Panama than the stained cement walls of the lock chambers, and in any case, most yachts will want to replenish perishable stores. Since we fell into that category, I had to go into downtown Colón to find the Panamanian immigration office on the second floor over a drug store on Frente Street to obtain our tourist visas.

The city of Colón lies just outside the gate, across the train tracks from Cristóbal. Following directions, I followed the street and found the drug store, and the staircase leading to the second floor. A poorly lit hallway opened off the landing. Through the gloom, I could make out a sign bearing the word INMIGRACIÓN, about halfway down the hall to my left.

Three ladies were seated at desks inside the room. I produced our passports. The lady nearest the door removed a box from a desk drawer. "Ten dollars, Americano," she said, adding, "for one visa," when she realized I was holding three passports.

I paid her. The second lady stamped our passports, and the third one licked and pasted the stamps in their proper place. The first lady then signed the visas and handed the passports back to me. The only thing left then was to go back to the *Inmigración Inspección* booth on the docks, so our lawful entry into Panama could be recorded in our passports.

The Panamanian formalities taken care of, I had to arrange our transit through the Canal. This procedure also seemed elliptical, but at least signs were posted in the Canal Administration Building and everyone there spoke English.

The Canal Authority building, like the Canal itself, was built for the ages. It was constructed early in the century of stone, a natural insulation against the tropical sun, and featured outside galleries and open stair cases to facilitate the circulation of air. It stood slightly apart and seemed aloof from the yellow wooden barracks surrounding it. The first step to be taken in arranging our transit through the Canal involved measurements. Canal fees are based on the vessel's dimensions.

The dimensions in our ship's document didn't count. Therefore, I made an appointment at the admeasurer's office. The next day, a Canal launch with two young Americans carrying a long tape measure came alongside. To my surprise, the distance from the tip of the mizzen boom to the end of the bowsprit is almost exactly 60 feet. That's a lot of overhang for a 43 foot boat.

After *Prospector* was measured, I returned to the Administration Building where I paid the necessary fees and made an appointment for our transit interview with the Port Captain.

The fees came to $96. Of that sum, $34 was charged for the measurement, and $31 was refunded. The actual transit fee was $31; undoubtedly one of the world's greatest bargains.

The Port Captain's interview was formal. I was required to sign a waiver because, like all but the biggest yachts, we lacked Panama chocks and bitts.

The Captain explained that we needed four line–handlers (in addition to the captain) and four pieces of line, each at least 100 feet long. We also discussed the relative merits of center tying as opposed to side tying. I agreed to side tie if necessary. The Captain gave us a transit date of June 25, only three days away.

In the meanwhile, we had settled in at the Panama Yacht Club in Cristóbal, which is a remarkably hospitable place. The club had several highly desirable attributes. The most desirable of these was that we were granted access to the facilities gratis.

For a small deposit, we were given a key to the showers and laundromat. In the bar, we found a tasty local brew, PANAMA BEER, that cost only 50¢ a bottle. The dining room featured a very reasonable menu featuring Chinese as well as Panamanian and American dishes.

Regular club members were as friendly as the club itself, and it wasn't long before we began receiving warnings about gangs of muggers that roamed Colón's streets in search of victims.

Frankly, I wasn't impressed. Over the years, I had scoffed at similar warnings about Jamaica, Manila, Singapore, Jakarta, Tehran, and even Washington, D.C., and I had yet to be attacked on the street. Perhaps I was just lucky.

Discounting the warnings, since we had already gone as far as the train station to catch the train across the Isthmus to Panama City, and hadn't seen anything that seemed threatening or hostile, we decided that a simple stroll downtown in mid-afternoon, couldn't be that dangerous in a civilized country.

Velda and I wandered first into the back streets, taking pictures of children playing in the street, little boys throwing balls against the peeling stucco walls, little girls holding dolls with one hand, their mother's skirts with the other.

We tried to talk with people, but not many spoke English, and because the sun was very hot, we retired temporarily to the shade of a native store/bar, where we ordered a couple of beers. The two young women behind the counter seemed nervous and asked us to leave as soon as I paid for the beer. I thought they were just shy, so we sat at the counter until we finished the beer. They wouldn't sell us a second round, so we walked back to Cristóbal, still oblivious to danger.

The next day we took another walk along the main street to see what the duty-free shops were offering. We hadn't gone more than five or six blocks from the gate, when a heavy older woman rushed up from behind, and after passing us, wheeled around and spread her arms as if to restrain us.

"No, No, No!" She cried in a quick breathless voice. Her eyes were wide, and her face was taut with emotion. Something was wrong; she was very upset. A torrent of rapid Spanish poured over us. Seeing no comprehension on our faces, she rolled her eyes up, and graphically drew her right forefinger across her throat. Then she rushed into the nearest store.

In a few moments, she returned with a clerk who said apologetically, "This lady say bad mans follow you. She say go back to Cristóbal before bad thing happen."

Then I remembered the peculiar conversation I had with a barber right after I had obtained our visas. I had badly needed a haircut, and seeing a familiar barber pole after I completed the Panamanian formalities, I had crossed the street and entered the shadowy shop. The barber expressed his surprise and delight at seeing me, and congratulated me on my — *courage*(?). I had discounted the implication underlying his remarks, thinking I hadn't properly understood his broken English.

Now, I understood it too well. However foolish we may be, we are not suicidal. We thanked the old lady and turned around. Briefly scanning the faces of people who had been walking behind us to see if we could identify the "bad mans," we walked quickly back to the yacht club.

The same thing happened to another yachting family, also Americans, a few hours later. They had also gone window shopping along *Frente* street. Suddenly, a knot of five young men appeared in front of them, on the sidewalk 50 yards away.

A passerby, undoubtedly taking a serious risk, spoke to them, warning that the gang they could see was preparing to rob them. The young mother was fluent in Spanish, and she asked their benefactor a few questions.

According to him, this gang and their accomplices closing in from the rear, regularly stopped and robbed foreign pedestrians on the sidewalk in front of the most expensive duty-free shops in Colón. Apparently, they were immune from police intervention as long as the victim was a *Norte-Americano*. Like us, our friends heeded that advice and quickly crossed the street. They hurried back to Cristóbal and the safety of the chain-link fence.

The next day, Velda went to a local supermarket to buy our provisions. The store provided a heavily armed guard to escort her and her groceries to a waiting taxi.

I can't say whether the danger was exaggerated, but that was 1982. In the ten years since, the hoodlums have turned Colón into a ghost town populated by poverty-stricken natives.

During the 1989 American invasion, the Panamanian Government foolishly distributed small arms to any civilian who wanted them, exhorting them to help repel the invading army. Thus armed, the criminals quickly went on an orgy of robbery and theft, forcing the tourist-oriented shops along *Frente* street to move to a fortified area called *Zona Libre* where retail shops, banks and small businesses now exist behind barbed wire, protected by heavily armed guards. For tourists, Colón has become one of the most dangerous cities in the world. A European or North American walking the ten blocks from the yacht club to the *Zona Libre* would almost certainly be mugged at least once, and possibly several times en route.

It's a pity, but because of the crime problem, the picturesque narrow-gauge railway running through the jungle across the Isthmus connecting Colón with Panama City no longer offers passenger service. Ten years ago, the one-way fare of $1.25 was a terrific bargain, and the trip through the jungle to Panama City was one of the highlights of our visit to Panama. Panama City was like every major city in Central and Latin America. Beautiful buildings in the expensive part of town, terrible slums elsewhere. Parts of the city even then were dangerous. Today, most of Panama City is off limits for a gringo wearing a watch or carrying a camera.

John Black had rejoined us by this time. He and Buzzy were busy. They went sightseeing, traveled through the Canal as line handlers on other yachts, and even did some horse trading. Three days was not much time to see a place as complex and interesting as Panama, but Buzzy's impending grandfatherhood was setting our pace. For reasons I never quite understood, he seemed to believe he was an indispensable party.

The horse trade was really a dinghy trade, but the moves were identical. Unlike most horse trades, however, the great dinghy swap had its genesis in fear instead of greed. Buz and John were certain our rubber dinghy, the one the Dutch restaurateur had rescued the night of the southerly gale in St. Maarten, was tottering along on its last legs. With a horse trader's instinct, they decided to trade up while the beast could still stand. I had been away on an errand, and when I returned, I found them lolling on the yacht club veranda, smugly congratulating themselves for having traded our old Achilles and $100 for a smaller and much newer Avon.

When the time came to leave, I decided to clear from Panama in Cristóbal rather than Balboa, but even in familiar surroundings, clearing out was much more difficult than I anticipated.

In addition to being shunted from office to office, I was required to produce a photostat of the ship's document, which in those days, was a sheet of stiff salmon-colored paper about four times the size of an ordinary sheet of paper. The requirement has not changed, but the new ship's document is now much smaller. Even so, anyone planning a trip to Panama would be smart to carry certified copies of their document with them.

I succeeded in finding an agent with a big copier however, and completed our clearance on schedule. The morning of our transit, I began transporting our line handlers from their boats around five thirty. Two young women, Jean and Elizabeth, in charge of a Seattle yacht, had asked to come along so they could see what they were facing. We were glad to have them. A young German couple had volunteered to join us at the last minute so they, too, would know what they faced.

When I had collected the last of our crew, we hauled the dinghy aboard. A scruffy Canal launch pulled alongside, and a stocky little man with a brown weathered face, wearing a railroad engineer's hat and carrying a battered briefcase, swung easily over the lifelines.

"I am Ricardo, your advisor," he said in a quiet, confident voice. "Which of you is the captain?"

I introduced myself, and we shook hands. Then he repeated the process, introducing himself and shaking hands with everyone. On a ship, Ricardo would have been the pilot, but on *Prospector*, his official standing was that of "advisor."

I'm guessing, but I think the distinction said a great deal about the hazards small boats faced in the Canal. The difference between serving as pilot and someone merely offering friendly advice might be the difference between the Canal Authority assuming liability and not assuming it. I'm not sure this distinction would make much difference in court, and it certainly did not accurately reflect Ricardo's true role on board, but it probably helped the Army lawyers sleep better.

Ricardo was a Colombian, about 50 years old. He had worked as a pilot and advisor for more than 20 years, and had "advised" thousands of small boats during his career. While he was fully qualified to pilot ships, he preferred the informality of yachts.

His pay was the same as other pilots with his seniority and qualifications. He told me later that he earned about $70,000 a year, an enormous salary for that time and place.

We gathered around him — it was fully light by that time — and he explained what we would find when we entered the first chamber. Then, looking at his watch, and after conferring with someone over a portable radio he took from his briefcase, he nodded to me.

"Time to get anchor up," he said.

77

"Go slow," he said, after the anchor was secured. "Follow that fellow." He pointed to a Canal launch 100 yards in front of us. I looked behind. Another sailboat was getting underway, and I imagined his advisor pointing to us and saying, "follow that sailboat."

The waterway narrowed, and soon we were in a tight gut, with high hills on both sides. I could see cement works in front of us, and as we drew closer, the superstructure of a large ship.

"Go very slow," Ricardo said. I lifted the throttle arm, and the engine slowed to 700 RPMs.

"Stop," he said.

I pulled out the clutch pin, and we coasted slowly to a stop. He turned away from me and began talking over his radio. A few minutes later, he turned back. "Is OK now. Go slow and inside, go next to salvage launch."

We moved slowly past the massive lock gate recessed into the stained cement wall, and entered the chamber.

I knew a big ship would be ahead of us in the chamber. I had even had a glimpse of her superstructure as we approached the first chamber. But I still recall the shock and surprise I felt when I realized that curving gray wall in front of me was her bulging stern. I looked up and saw her flag almost directly overhead.

I could see her massive propeller just below the surface, and I shuddered to think what her prop wash would be like. Her name, *Act V*, was carved in raised steel letters on her stern, as was her hailing port: *London*.

Worried as I was about the ship, I was more seriously concerned about the chamber's width. We had been allotted space next to the salvage launch, which was tied to a Canal tug, which was tied to another Canal tug, which was tied to the south wall. Between us and the north wall was about seven feet of air.

The sailboat following us turned around. There was no room for her in the chamber. The scheduling office had made a mistake, or those Canal tugs had usurped her space. Ricardo was disgusted and very apologetic. "We're too damn crowded," he said. He began talking on his radio again while we made ourselves fast to the launch.

Ricardo insisted we set up spring lines, and haul them taut with the anchor windlass. "Is very important," he said. He was thinking about that big propeller, too. He continued to talk over the radio, while I looked around the chamber.

We were at the bottom of a deep well with stained cement walls. The surface of the cement was pitted and scarred, and decorated with bathtub rings of green algae alternating with black rings of tar. From the stains, it was obvious that we would be lifted about 30 feet when the lockmaster opened the flood valves.

The lock gates began their ponderous closing movements. Watching them, I was seized with a claustrophobic feeling of doom. There was no backing out now.

As if sensing my mood, Ricardo said reassuringly, "We're OK. The lockmaster'll take it easy; he knows there are too many boats here. Also, I talk to my frien's on the ship. They take it easy, too. We'll be OK."

He was right. Instead of flooding the chamber in the normal eight minutes, the lockmaster only let the water trickle in; it took 15 minutes for us to reach the next level. Watching the water level climb that pitted and stained wall was like being in a huge freight elevator. All at once, we were at eye level with the top of the chamber.

Ships are towed from one chamber to the next by electric mules, small locomotives that look like yard switching engines. The mules, however, were designed in an era of smaller ships, and lack the necessary traction to overcome the inertia of the 50,000 deadweight tons typical of modern ships. Consequently, the initial thrust is always provided by the ship's engines, but in such a confined space, the prop wash can be devastating to small boats sharing the same space.

Act V's captain was as considerate as the lockmaster. We scarcely noticed any commotion when I suddenly realized *Act V* was gliding smoothly away from us.

Ricardo waited until *Act V* was nearly out of the chamber, then had us cast off, and warned me, "Wait, let tugs go first." I started the engine while our crew picked up the lines.

One after the other, the tugs first, then the salvage launch, followed by *Prospector*, we paraded into the next chamber and eventually into the one after that, without difficulty. Finally, we entered Lake Gatun, 85 feet above sea level.

Folks on yachts have a better chance to see wildlife on the numerous jungle-covered islands in the lake, where wild monkeys and parrots screech and whoop at passing traffic, than people on ships because yachts take short cuts. People on yachts do other things, too.

"Pull behind that buoy, and stop," Ricardo said, pointing to a large round white buoy anchored near a small island. I was puzzled, but I complied.

"Rig your swim ladder," he said. Then, louder, he said, "It's time to go swimming. Everyone in the water!"

Jean and Elizabeth looked at each other. "We didn't bring our suits," they said.

"That's OK," Ricardo said cheerfully, "no one will look."

Armed with that assurance, the girls forgot about swimming suits, and within minutes, seven naked bodies were splashing in the warm, fresh water. It was novel and very refreshing.

Note that I said seven naked bodies. Buzzy had modestly kept his underwear on, but when we made a second unscheduled stop to repeat the performance, he got more into the spirit of things. The trip was turning into a party. Velda had prepared a lovely buffet lunch and we had plenty of cold beer.

We were the only boat scheduled in the first lock on the Pacific side, so we enjoyed the luxury of center tying. Ricardo had me bring *Prospector* to a complete stop in the middle of the lock chamber. The lock attendants standing on both sides took careful aim with their heaving lines, and abruptly four monkey fists were in the air. Two of them missed the boat. One went into the awning, and the other wrapped itself around the bowsprit.

There was some fancy scrambling by the line handlers and explosive Spanish from Ricardo, but soon we sent four docklines up to the attendants who dropped the line's eyes over convenient bollards. Ricardo instructed the line handlers how to ease away as we dropped in the chamber. As soon as we reached the next level and the gate opened, the attendants dropped our lines into the water. Our line handlers hauled the wet lines aboard.

Minutes later, we entered the upper Miraflores chamber. A Canal tug was tied to the wall near the lower end of the chamber.

"We tie up to that tug," Ricardo said.

Pause and picture the lock chambers. Each was a rectangular cement box 1,000 feet long, 110 feet wide, and about 70 feet deep. Unlike the Gatun locks where we began our vertical journey at the bottom of the well, the chambers handling down traffic were full as we entered them, filled to within five feet of the top.

Facing us at the far end of the chamber was a steel gate shaped like the bow of a ship, the two gate halves joining at an acute angle to resist the weight of some 200,000 tons of water.

The tug we were headed toward was tied about 200 feet from the gate. Shortly before reaching her, I happened to glance over my shoulder and noticed a large ship entering the chamber behind us, but I concentrated my attention on the tug. As we came abreast of the tug, and before Ricardo could stop me, I brought the engine control lever up into the neutral position, then over into reverse, as I normally do when making a landing.

Without warning, **Prospector** *suddenly went out of control!*

As if by some malevolent magic, we found ourselves in a strong current being swept broadside to our doom against that sharply pointed gate, *now less than 30 seconds away!*

There was no time to maneuver or shift gears. We were in reverse gear, and I frantically shoved the throttle wide open. Thick, black smoke billowed from the exhaust. Gradually, the propeller began to bite into the water and slowly, ever so slowly, we backed out of the invisible current across the chamber to the opposite wall.

Even while we were backing out of that mysterious current, it occurred to me that the ship behind us was a huge self-propelled hydraulic ram, pushing the water in the chamber ahead of it to the gate where the water escaped by flowing down to the bottom of the chamber, and back under the ship as a submerged counter–current. We had been caught in the surface current.

I shuddered at the hideous vision of *Prospector* crashing broadside into the gate, breaking her back on its sharp edge, and, in pieces, being sucked beneath the approaching ship.

Ricardo suggested we stay on the wall until I regained my nerve (that's the way he put it), but I wanted to get it over with, so we ran across the chamber to the tug.

He *then* told me how to make my landing. "Put your best man on the starboard quarter. Have him pass the line to a man who will be standing near a bitt on the tug. Maintain your forward speed until you see the line pass. Then, but not before, put the clutch into reverse, and back like hell!"

I put my best man on the key corner, and throttled down as slow as I could while maintaining steerage. We passed within two feet of the tug. My best man tried to hand the line over, and missed. Ricardo grabbed it out of his hand, and flung it to another deckhand standing closer to the bow.

He didn't miss. In a swift practiced motion, the deckhand dropped the eye of the line over a bitt welded to the tug's bulwarks. Ricardo yelled "**REVERSE! REVERSE!**" while he threw three quick turns around the sheet winch and began winching us back to the tug.

That was a close escape. Luck, and a reliable engine that was well bolted down is all that saved us. Otherwise, we might have been seriously holed, and at worst, we could have lost *Prospector* and perhaps even our lives.

When the gates swung open at Balboa, I saw for the first time the magnificent mile–long Bridge of the Americas connecting North and South America silhouetted against the setting sun like a picture post card. Ricardo must have sensed that my mind was elsewhere, because he urged me to make my best speed. This was partly to get out of the way of the freighter behind us, but most likely he wanted to arrive at the Balboa Yacht Club while it was still light. I'm afraid his confidence in me as a skipper, while probably never high, may have been seriously eroded by the awful events in the second chamber. However, nothing could dampen my elation at having reached the Pacific Ocean.

We stopped briefly at the Balboa Yacht Club to discharge our passengers and line handlers. In the excitement, I forgot I had promised Buzzy money for cab fare to the airport. He and John had tickets and credit cards, but no cash and no reservations.

Unfortunately, they also forgot about money as they boarded the yacht club launch with the girls and the German couple. Consequently, they hitchhiked 20 miles through the Panamanian jungle that night to reach the airport.

Meanwhile, Ricardo called the Canal launch, which met us in the yacht transient anchorage adjacent to Flamenco Island. Velda and I said farewell to him, and alone for the first time in weeks, gratefully rolled in for the night. It had been a full day.

Early the next morning, we raised the anchor and began motor-sailing through the Gulf of Panama. Our daylight watches were pleasant. But after dark, things went to hell. Ships were constantly in view, seemingly all headed toward us. Early in the evening, we tracked ships easily. But after the squalls began rolling in, it was a different story. We would be watching a ship, trying to estimate her bearing and speed relative to our own, when, without warning, she would disappear behind a heavy curtain of wind-driven rain.

Of course, that ship was still there, still bearing down on us, but we couldn't see her, and I doubt whether her radar could see us through the deluge. Then, with a terrifying *craaaacCKK-BOOM*, a spurt of lightning would show us the silhouetted ship for an instant, much closer, now, but our eyes would be so dazzled by the flash that precious minutes would go by before normal night vision returned. Meanwhile, where in hell was that ship?

Weather and ships continued to plague us like that all night. However, by late afternoon the next day, as we rounded Cape Mala at the western entrance to the Gulf and began following the coast, the shipping thinned out. Of course, we still had to keep a close watch, but now we had to deal with only one ship at a time, and their courses were almost parallel to ours. Moreover, steaming that close to the coast, I was sure they would be monitoring their radar. The weather was a continuing problem. The log put it this way:

June 27: Motorsailed all day. Coast obscured in low clouds. At 5:30 p.m. ran into intense squall that lasted about an hour. Lots of rain, wind, lightning. Actually saw bolts striking the water!

I don't think the most hardened or saltiest sea dog among us is entirely oblivious to lightning. It is more than scary; it is dangerous. A close miss could blast the watchstander right off the boat. When lightning is that close, I think it is more prudent to heave-to and bring everyone below, than it is to ignore the lightning. Even a direct strike won't necessarily sink the boat, but it probably would kill anyone on deck. Even with all hands below, we still would maintain a watch for other traffic.

We saw several small fishing boats during the night of July second and we entered Golfo de Nicoya at daylight on the third. Late that same evening, we came to anchor in the roadstead outside Puntarenas. Velda and I were very tired, and we went to bed as soon as we were satisfied that our anchor was properly set.

The next morning, after drinking my coffee, I flew the Stars and Stripes from our stern in honor of the Fourth of July, and hauled the Costa Rican courtesy flag and the Q flag up the starboard signal halyard. The skipper of a nearby American boat, seeing me begin to pump up the Avon dinghy, cautioned us to sit tight; this was not one of those places where you put the dinghy in the water and went looking for the nearest police station.

Shortly after lunch, we heard the roar of large diesel engines. I looked out, and saw a big patrol boat, cannon and all, bearing down on us. At the last possible moment, the captain reversed his engines, and the boat shuddered to a stop inches from our port bow.

A small crowd led by a big man in a naval captain's uniform stood on the foredeck looking down at us. He was the port captain who had come along for the ride (and the overtime) since it was a Saturday. He and the boat's skipper were the only people who stayed behind. The rest of the crew, all wearing leather soled shoes, scrambled over the lifelines. One of them even used the lifeline as a step. What a lubberly crew!

After they crowded below, we found we had representatives aboard from customs, agriculture and immigration. I never knew what the fourth man's role was. They sat on the settee. One of them examined our passports while another peered into our freezer.

Since we were in a roadstead, we were rolling a good bit, although neither Velda nor I noticed it. But they did. Sweat was beginning to appear on their faces, when their spokesman somewhat foolishly asked for beer.

I don't much care for officials who come aboard and ask for refreshments. As usual after a long passage, *Prospector* was almost as dry as a Baptist revival. Almost, but not quite. We had the dregs of a bottle of the sweetest, most sickening home-made liqueur I have ever tasted, and I had no compunction about giving the last of it to our visitors. After the first sip or two, those beads of sweat turned into rivulets and abruptly, they craved fresh air and sunshine much more than free drinks.

Again using our lifelines as a ladder (one klutz even tried to step on our Bimini top), the inspectors tumbled over our rail to the patrol boat like so many bear cubs returning to mother.

The port captain collected our passports and asked us to come to his office that afternoon to retrieve them. He also suggested we change our money at Frank's barbershop, and went to great pains telling us how to find the place.

I didn't realize until later how cute he was. He didn't want his pals to witness the squeeze he was about to perform — they probably would have demanded a cut.

The patrol boat backed away from us and was gone. We finished inflating the Avon on the foredeck. We could see a surf running on the beach and decided to row ashore, rather than take the outboard.

Although it was windy, the beach was crowded. We carried the boat up above the reach of the tide, and for good measure, tied the painter to a tree. Two young men approached us and struck up a conversation. Their English was good. They offered to show us the town when they learned that we had just arrived, but after our experience in Panama, we tended to be shy around strangers, and we declined with appropriate thanks.

I wish I had looked more closely for identifying marks; it would have been helpful later when I was making my police report.

We walked several blocks east to the center of town, and after paying the $40 fee — I'm sure it was simple larceny — for our passports, we found Frank's barbershop.

Frank obligingly put his clippers down when he discovered we had business to conduct, and reaching in his pocket, withdrew a huge roll of *colones*, Costa Rica's currency. He told us his rate of exchange was 60 to one, and how many colones did we want?

I changed $100 into ¢6,000. Enjoying that wonderfully rich feeling that comes from having a pocket stuffed with currency, we went looking for a liquor store. In Puntarenas, like money changers, bars and liquor stores were easily found.

The afternoon was wearing on. I slung a crate of beer on my shoulder, and Velda cradled a sack of cigarettes and rum in her arms. We had the essential stuff. Then we retraced our steps to the beach where we had left the dinghy. It started to rain.

We reached the place where I thought we had left the dinghy, but I was apparently mistaken; the dinghy wasn't there. The rain was coming down much harder. I left Velda sitting on the beer crate in the shelter of a low palm tree, while I went back and forth on the beach in what I soon realized was a hopeless search. The weather was getting worse. The rain had changed from a downpour to a deluge with an almost constant crackle of nearby lightning accompanied by ear-splitting explosions of thunder. The dinghy was gone.

At moments like that any action is better than none. Velda and I held a brief conference. Looking around for a possible shelter, I saw a sign gleaming through the early rainy dark announcing the "**Aloha Restaurant**." I sloshed across the street and asked the lady in the cashier's cage if she would call a cab, preferably one with a driver who could speak a little English. She politely heard me out, staring at this wet gringo who had come in out of the night, white hair plastered against his head, beard dripping, and water squirting from his shoes. When I stopped and searched her face for signs of comprehension, she fled into the kitchen for reinforcements.

"May I help you?"

I wheeled around. An attractive young woman stood behind me, a concerned expression on her face. I explained that our dinghy was missing, and that we needed to find shelter for the night. If she could help me get a cab.... .

"Is your wife with you?"

I nodded.

"Where? I don't see her," she said.

I was almost afraid to tell her that I had left Velda under a tree across the street. After I explained, she said more sharply than she probably intended, "Bring her here this minute!"

Obediently, I went back out into the storm, found Velda's tree, and brought her to the restaurant.

Maria Quackenbush — we learned her name later — invited us to sit at a table while she ordered hot coffee. She listened to our story with keen interest, her intense eyes never leaving my face.

"You must go back to your boat," she said. "The thieves will know the boat is unprotected and they will steal everything."

I hadn't thought of that unpleasant possibility. But I had to agree with her logic. By this time, Tom, Maria's American husband, had joined us. He is a big man, impressive, with a no nonsense style who appeared to know what he was talking about.

He nodded. "Maria's right," he said. "You must go back to your boat."

Maria then called a cab. When it arrived, she gave the driver explicit and detailed instructions. I suspect she didn't think it necessary that I know what she had in mind; she probably guessed that I would have objected.

I got into the cab, leaving Velda with our new friends. Our first stop was the police station. Third-world police stations, Costa Rica's among them, are occasionally attacked by terrorists. Therefore, they find grills and barred gates necessary. If you have business at the police station, you must first stand on the sidewalk and, talking through a barred window, negotiate your way inside. Only when the duty officer is satisfied that you are a peaceful citizen are you admitted inside.

My cab driver talked our way in, but unfortunately, the officer who interviewed me had as much English as I Spanish. Maria had foreseen that possibility, and driver made the police report.

I was told to come back the next day; that an English speaking detective would be on duty and I could make a full report. I nodded, and we were escorted to the door. I heard the bolts rattling behind us as we walked down the steps.

Instead of returning as I expected, to the Aloha Restaurant, we went in the opposite direction, leaving the main road, and driving along the river.

Puntarenas was built on a narrow sandspit between the sea and a river. The town is about 20 blocks long but only seven blocks wide. It was laid out in neat square blocks, except near the river; there the roads begin and end seemingly at random.

Twice the driver stopped to ask for directions, but eventually he pulled up in front of a small house. He left the cab and went to the door, where he talked briefly with a woman standing in the doorway. Then he returned to the cab and we drove back to the restaurant in silence. Maria met us. She and the driver had a long conversation. Then she turned to me.

"It is all arranged," she said. "The fishermen will take you to your boat tonight. Tomorrow you must go to the police again. The fishermen will come for you."

She embraced Velda briefly, then put us and our purchases into the car. Things were happening almost too fast for me. On the way back to the fishermen's house, Velda explained why she was wearing what looked like an evening gown.

After I had left, Maria had taken Velda next door to her home, and put her into a hot shower. Then she found dry clothes for her. When we had returned, Velda was clean, dry, fed and looking, if a little peculiar, much better than the drowned cat I had left.

The cab delivered us back to the fishermen, and I paid the ¢300 fare ($5.00). Victoria and Pedro, our fishermen-hosts, were waiting for us. Pedro was a successful fishermen. His wife, Victoria, taught art and crafts at the girl's high school. Their comfortable little home backed against the estuary. They owned the small dock and fish-house directly behind their home.

Victoria greeted us formally. *"Mi casa es suya,"* she said.

Her English was limited, but with patience and pantomime, she helped us understand that Pedro and his helper were waiting to take us out to our boat, and that Pedro would come for us tomorrow morning so we could complete our report to the police, and arrange for another dinghy.

Watching her strong face as she struggled with an alien tongue, not for the first time I regretted my linguistic short-comings. She smiled when we nodded our comprehension. Apart from the communication problems, she was so matter-of-fact about our plight and her involuntary role, that you might have thought this an everyday occurrence.

Victoria was a big woman, with a strong presence, who appeared to be in her mid-30s. Her husband, Pedro, was shorter than she, stocky, and quite dark, with an aura of quiet competence. Pedro came into the room and spoke to Victoria. She turned to us. "Is time," she said, motioning us to follow Pedro.

We followed him out the back door, and down a planked walk to a rickety old pier. Peering through the dark over the edge, I barely made out a launch about 20 feet below us. It was afloat, but it seemed to be in the mud. Evidently, the tide, was out.

We climbed down a shaky ladder. First Pedro's helper, who had materialized while we were standing on the dock, then me, then Velda, who had an awful time with that long skirt, and finally Pedro.

After pumping her bilges, the helper opened the compression releases on the engine — it looked like an old air-cooled three cylinder Lister — and spun the flywheel. Expertly flipping a release lever, he smiled when the engine fired in that cylinder, and he quickly closed the remaining release valves. When the engine was warm, Pedro and his helper untied the docklines, and pushed the boat through the gooey mud into deeper water.

Pedro motioned for us to sit where our weight most effectively trimmed the boat. She was top-heavy because of her large house, so when we met the Pacific swells at the end of the spit, she rolled slowly and heavily before settling down to a permanent starboard list. Within minutes, the ghostly shape of *Prospector*, her white topsides faintly reflecting the town lights, appeared out of the darkness. We came alongside, and quickly climbed aboard.

It was choppy, and Pedro's boat was making heavy weather of it against our topsides. Consequently, he pushed off immediately on his return trip, while Cap was barking and dancing in excitement, welcoming us home. It was wonderful to be back aboard. Taking advantage of our replenished liquor stores, I poured us each a good stiff drink. Then, with Maria's warning ringing in my ears, I loaded the shotgun and laid it on the cabin sole where it was within reach.

Fortunately, it wasn't needed, but the next morning, we still had to deal with the dinghy problem. Without a dinghy, we were in trouble. We had heard in St. Thomas that there was a marina in Puntarenas. Marinas the world over have in common the probability they will maintain a watch on channel 16 (or its local equivalent) during business hours. I wasn't very hopeful, but Velda switched the radio on and keyed the mike.

"Pacific Marina, this is *Prospector* calling; do you read?"

I was surprised and delighted to hear a man's voice, decidedly American, answer.

After Velda explained our problem, the man said, "If you can get up here, I'm sure we can take care of you."

Things were looking up. At that moment, Pedro and Victoria came alongside in their skiff. They declined our invitation to come aboard, so we climbed down into their boat, and Pedro steered the boat around the end of the spit.

This was the first time we had seen the place in daylight. I watched closely as we went past 30 fishing boats, identical to Pedro's, anchored in the river. They were about 25 feet long, top-heavy with oversized pilot houses ornately decorated with carved gingerbread moldings and bright yellow, blue and red paint.

A heavily constructed ferry dock was the first major structure on the shore to our right, as we passed the boats. Rising from the ferry slip, the shoreline became a steep cutbank, about 25 feet high. Small buildings crowded precariously close to the edge.

I wondered how deeply the river was eroding that bank each year, and how many buildings slid over the edge. Judging by the clumps of grass and mud breaking the surface of the water at the foot of the bank, this was a serious problem. Dozens of ladders dangled from structures at the top of the bank, ending about three feet above the water. Pedro landed the skiff at the base of a ladder, and Victoria, sitting in the bow, expertly passed the painter around its lowest rung. In the daylight, the ladder looked even shakier than it had felt the night before. However, I thought that if it held us then, it would hold us now.

We called a cab, which quickly arrived. While I was in the police station trying to formalize our theft report, the cab driver took Velda out to Pacific Marina, where she talked to the people, and got piloting information.

I was standing on the street corner when Velda returned in the cab, and we rode back to our friend's house where Victoria was preparing a huge Sunday dinner. We sat in the living room, practicing our slender Spanish vocabulary on Victoria's eldest daughter, a charming and vivacious youngster named Maria, then 11 or 12 years old, who was simultaneously practicing her English on us. Another visitor arrived.

We were introduced to Ralph who had arrived on his bicycle. I'm sure his appearance was not accidental. Ralph had an excellent command of English, having fished on American tuna clippers out of San Diego for several years.

We explained again what had happened to us. I was worried about navigating the estuary. I knew this estuary, like most at low water, was a maze of channels, mud flats, and sand bars. Unlike many, however, this estuary was not navigable at low water, and only marginally so on top of a ten foot tide. I asked Ralph to inquire whether Pedro would be willing to grant an additional favor, and pilot us up the river to Pacific Marina.

When he understood the question, Pedro grinned, and enthusiastically said, *"Sí!"*

Then I raised a more delicate question about something that was troubling me. "Ralph," I said, "we have been imposing on these nice people so much that I feel very indebted to them. I wonder if you could ask Pedro what he thinks would be fair payment for all he has done for us?"

Ralph didn't bother to confer with Pedro this time. I suspect that issue had already been discussed and settled. Looking me in the eye, he said, "We are sorry about your trouble, and we want you to regard our help as a gift from the Costa Rican people."

Victoria came into the living room to announce that dinner was ready. Already moved and nonplused by Ralph's statement, we were seriously embarrassed when we discovered the dinner was intended only for Velda and me.

Everyone stayed out of the kitchen until we could eat no more of what amounted to a feast. I was really bothered because there was no practical way we could reciprocate, and our heartfelt thanks seemed shallow and inadequate.

After dinner, Maria produced a Spanish–English dictionary and with much lighthearted laughter, we found the words we needed to communicate. We didn't really need to rely on the dictionary, because the warmth of the friendship we were receiving was so intense and genuine that verbal communication was almost superfluous. Besides, bright little Maria already had a basic command of English. But the dictionary was fun, nevertheless.

When the tide was right, Velda and I, Pedro, Maria, and two cousins Maria's age, climbed down the ladder and into the skiff. We ran around the spit out to *Prospector*. Because of the expert way she fended the skiff away when we came alongside *Prospector*, it was likely that Maria frequently accompanied her father.

While Pedro trailed his skiff astern, I started *Prospector's* engine, and raised the anchor. I gestured to Pedro to take the wheel, which he did with obvious pleasure, and we made our way around the end of the spit and into the estuary.

Puntarenas is much more interesting from the river than from the ocean. On the ocean side, all you see is another tropical beach. The other side of the Puntarenas spit tells a different story.

After we passed Pedro's dock and fishhouse (where Maria took great delight in saluting her mother, who was waving to us from their dock, with our freon fog horn), we came next to a commercial dock with large boats tied alongside. This was the Ice House.

A few moments later we passed the *Centro Mercado*. The Coast Guard dock was next. The patrol boat with the cannon was tied there. Next we passed several marine railways, two tuna canneries, three large cement tanks, and wide mud flats. The houses had thinned out, and beyond the cement tanks, we saw only occasional houses on the bank.

A series of mangrove islands populated by troops of noisy monkeys and parrots defined the opposite shore. The river turned slightly to the right, and narrowed. Most of the flats were behind us as Pacific Marina came into view. At first, I saw a cluster of yachts anchored and moored in the river. Then I noticed a small dock and several buildings roofed and clad in rusty corrugated iron.

Velda had been talking on the radio, and Pacific Marina was expecting us. Before we could anchor, a dinghy came roaring out from the marina dock. A slender, older Costa Rican waved us ahead, and ran the dinghy in a tight circle, pointing down at the water.

Our anchor was ready. In a matter of minutes, the hook was down and set, and I killed the engine. Pedro and I shook hands. Velda gave Maria a hug and a kiss, and our benefactors disappeared down river in their skiff.

The fellow in the dinghy clung to the caprail and introduced himself as Carlos, the Pacific Marina foreman. "Anyt'ing you need," he said, "I get for you." He took us ashore, and introduced us to the owners and the marina manager, all Americans. Bill, the manager, explained how the place worked.

"We charge you three dollars a day for the use of the facilities," he said. "That includes the head and the shower, work benches, and access to the beer cooler." Everything operated on the honor system. Help yourself; just remember to mark it down in your charge book.

Some amenities were skimpy by Chesapeake standards; the laundry facilities, for example, were two stainless steel tubs on the dinghy float. You filled a tub with fresh water, adding soap and bleach, and put your clothes in to soak. Then you went to sit in the shade of the cabana with a cold beer. You always had company. Usually, someone would already be sitting in the shade thinking of things remaining to be done. If not, when you sat, you'd quickly attract company. Indolence was infectious.

When you thought your clothes had soaked long enough, you could either plunge them up and down with an old fashioned plumber's friend, or trample them with your bare feet as if you were pressing grapes in a European vineyard. We met Hans and Elly Lutt at the laundry.

They were a young couple from the Netherlands, living aboard a steel sloop named *Solitair*. When we met, Hans was paddling a replica of a dugout canoe he had fashioned from a sheet of Formica, and Elly was energetically sloshing around in the tub with her bare feet. There is nothing a Dutch lady hates worse than dirt.

Despite Hans' arguments to the contrary, I didn't think we could solve our dinghy problem with a sheet of Formica. The problem had been somewhat alleviated by our move to Pacific Marina because the marina staff provided ferry service, but I hated to be a nuisance.

Velda and I quickly fell into the habit of going to the Aloha nearly every day. Sometimes we took a cab, which cost ¢40 (or 65¢ U.S.). Other times we'd catch the little bus (¢5 fare) and on those days when the big bus arrived first or we were feeling particularly egalitarian, we'd take the big bus which cost only two and a half colones, or slightly over four American cents.

We became close friends with Tom and Maria. To help us find a new dinghy, Tom introduced me to Herman who was a young Costa Rican living with his beautiful bride, Evelyn, in a basement apartment in his father's house near the Aloha. Herman was one of those rare and gifted people who are truly bilingual. I think he was born in Costa Rica, but because his father was a fishing captain sailing out of San Diego during Herman's childhood, he grew up and had gone to school in California.

He was a great help. We looked at many dinghies, but none of them would do. Finally, he led me to a small government ship yard where dinghies were occasionally built on a custom basis.

The mold bore a slight resemblance to a small Boston Whaler, and came in two sizes. The smaller eight foot version cost about $200. The larger ten foot boat was $50 more.

I can't tell you how often I regretted not having ordered the larger boat. The first rule about the selection of dinghies must be this: Buy the biggest boat you can safely handle.

In many ways, selecting a dinghy is not unlike choosing a mate. Think about it. There are plenty of pretty dinghies around. Some are more sea kindly, more tractable, more completely equipped than others, but you want three things from a dinghy. You want safety, reliability and capacity, probably in that order. We have sailed many thousands of miles. Yet, in a single calendar year, we have never spent more than 120 days at sea. Thus, at least two-thirds of each year was spent at anchor, when our dinghy became the family station wagon, endlessly hauling loads from the beach to the boat, and people from the boat to the beach. Our new boat had one serious flaw. Until we had flotation installed, she was not safe.

Our new boat was built like a Sherman tank. She would carry three adults on calm water. Views differ regarding a dinghy's style. Some experienced sailors want a long, lean pulling boat. Such a boat would be drier than ours, probably would carry as much, and couldn't be any heavier. By definition, it would be nimble under oars, should sail well, and would tow adequately at sailboat speeds. In short, it would be the better dinghy, except that long, lean pulling boats tend to be delicate, temperamental, and cranky.

Our boat is impossible to row in a breeze, is cranky, and far heavier than she ought to be, but she is the biggest eight foot dinghy I have ever seen. She bounces off the rocks, stands dragging across the beach, and hasn't yet let us down.

Costa Rican farmers had a different solution to their small boat problems. Dugout canoes carrying bananas and other farm produce destined for the *Centro Mercado* floated past our anchorage almost every morning.

People associate dugout canoes and rafts with illiterate savages. That stereotype did not fit these facts. Costa Ricans enjoy both a much higher degree of literacy and far better public health standards than Americans do, and are infinitely more sophisticated than people in neighboring countries.

They know it is easier to ride to market with produce than it is to carry it. A dugout canoe, like our dinghy, may be short on style and flair, but it's efficient and cheap.

Cap had much to say to those canoes. Eventually, the paddlers learned Cap's name and when he didn't convey his usual morning greeting, we would hear, *"Hey, Capitán, Capitán!"*

Cap always responded to that.

With our preoccupation about dinghies, we nearly lost sight of the calendar. We had been given 30-day tourist visas when we entered Costa Rica. When these expired, we visited the local immigration office, seeking a three month extension, because we had yet to haul *Prospector*, and we were planning extensive work while she was out of the water. Unfortunately, the local office could only issue extensions one month at a time. We knew the work would take longer than that.

While we might have gotten monthly extensions in the local office almost indefinitely – that's the way most yachties handled the problem – I preferred more structure in my life.

To obtain a three month extension, we had to go to the main immigration office in San Jóse. As the clerk in the local immigration office was explaining this, she handed us a mimeographed instruction sheet that listed what we needed to do before going to San Jóse.

Naturally, the sheet was printed in Spanish. Velda and I stood on the sidewalk trying to make sense of it when, providentially, Ralph and Diane happened to stroll by. Since our introduction to Ralph in Victoria and Pedro's home, we had met Ralph several times by chance on the street.

He and his wife, Diane, lived in a ground floor apartment near the Aloha. We had often walked past their doorway. When the door was open, as it usually was, he or Diane would call out a greeting, and on occasion, invite us in and offer us a glass of orange squash.

These were the very people we needed to see. I explained the problem, and Ralph read the instructions aloud. We were required to furnish passport photos, several sheets of official paper (available in any stationary store for two colones per sheet), and a sworn statement from an *abogado*, or lawyer, attesting to our character. We also had to provide proof of our solvency.

Diane swung into action. She was a large woman, not fat, just big. Her hair was dark with a reddish tint. Her strong facial characteristics were a legacy from her father, a Slavonian–American tuna fisherman. She had high, flat cheekbones and brilliant blue eyes with a slight oriental tilt. She was an attractive woman with a powerful presence. Nobody fooled with Diane.

We had no time to waste. Technically, we were illegal aliens because our visas had expired that morning.

"First we get pictures," she said. Immigration offices are always flanked by shops offering passport photos. Puntarenas was no exception. There was one directly behind us.

Fifteen minutes later, pictures taken and promised for delivery in two hours, Polaroid technology not yet having reached Puntarenas, we walked down the street to the lawyer's office.

Diane found it necessary to telephone the Immigration office for clarification. Satisfied, she dictated a statement to the lawyer's secretary — I haven't the least idea what it said — which was duly typed on two colone paper. I signed it and the lawyer, who I never saw, signed, notarized and sealed the document.

The photos were ready when we returned. The only thing left was proof of solvency. That requirement is a common one in many parts of the world. Normally, the officials expect to see stacks of travelers checks or cash, but sometimes a statement from a bank or brokerage house will do.

Diane and Ralph had a private conversation, then turned to us: "We go with you to San Jóse," Diane said.

I started to object, "We can't... ."

She interrupted me, saying firmly, "This is very difficult. You need help. We give help."

We agreed to meet on the eight o'clock bus the next morning, but we were alone. Ralph and Diane didn't show up.

Nevertheless, we enjoyed the novelty of our first trip to San Jóse. The buses were different. They were built in Mexico for short-legged Mexicans, and I found the knee room a bit snug for comfort. On the other hand, there was none of the drab uniformity you get from Greyhound. Each bus was unique and reflected a Latin flare for individualized, dramatic decoration.

The drivers were conscientious and careful, and they obviously took their responsibilities seriously. Understandably, they tended to swagger a bit as the caballeros they are.

The highway was well engineered and the road surface was in excellent condition, but it was a mountain road and rose steeply with many sharp turns as it climbed from Puntarenas at sea level to San Jóse, Costa Rica's capital, at 3,000 feet, in less than two hours. Much of the trip was made in the lower gears.

We were spellbound by the scenery as the road led from the jungles surrounding Puntarenas, through coastal barrios and small towns, past open farm land, to metropolitan San Jóse.

The mountain meadows were steep, but well stocked with brown and gray colored, big-eared, hump shouldered cattle that looked to my inexpert eye like Charolais or Indian brahmas.

The farms grew smaller, and factories bearing names like *Firestone, John Deere* and *Toyota* appeared as we approached the city. We passed the local brewery on the right. The two Costa Rican brands of beer, *Imperial* and *Pilsner*, were brewed and bottled there. The driver was willing to stop at the airport if any of the passengers wanted to catch a plane. A mile or so further on, the bus always pulled up to the big, modern Mexico Hospital. That facility, I understand, was part of a Mexican foreign aid package to Costa Rica several years ago.

San Jóse seemed much larger than the quarter million population it had. That was because the older downtown section was so crowded. Most of the buildings were only two or three stories high. But the newer buildings and hotels were larger.

The city was dirty. Trash littered the streets, and the general impression of urban neglect was reinforced by the broken curbs, the irregular pavement, and the universal coating of grime on the downtown buildings.

The bus station, like other bus stations around the world, was strictly utilitarian. Nobody goes to a bus station for fun. The restrooms were cesspools, and the restaurant wasn't much better.

A cab took us to the immigration office. Without Ralph and Diane's help, like children in a Grimm's fairy tale, we wandered into the swamp of Costa Rican bureaucracy, protected only by our wide-eyed innocence.

Centro Inmigración, in San Jóse, was a scene from a Hollywood extravaganza, *circa* 1940. Imagine a large cobbled courtyard surrounded on three sides by a grimy, decrepit two-story stone building with outside staircases and overhanging galleries protected by rusting iron railings. The only access to the courtyard was through a narrow cobbled passageway guarded by a high iron gate. I had the same feeling passing through that gate as I had when the Canal locks closed. There was no turning back.

A small cement building of more recent architecture stood on the fourth side of the square. I would know that building well before the day was over, because that was where the copying was done and the excise stamps bought.

Add to this medieval setting several hundred bewildered, frightened, and confused petitioners milling about, trying to solve problems that, in extreme cases, might have meant the difference between life or death. I'm sure this could have been true for some Nicaraguan refugees.

Ellis Island must have been like this. Signs were posted for various purposes. One we won't soon forget said in English and Spanish, PLEASE DO NOT WASH UTENSILS IN THE DRINKING FOUNTAIN.

Where do you begin? We saw older people, possibly American *pensionados*, relying on their high school Spanish. Unfortunately, lacking Spanish, we were hopelessly in over our heads. Therefore, we decided to hire a guide.

We selected a young man named Carlos (or perhaps he selected us; one can never be certain about these things). He had sufficient English so we could communicate. He was a dapper little man, with slick black hair, a razor sharp moustache, and a facile smile that didn't quite mask the hard, predatory glint in his black eyes. Incongruously, he wore a three-piece suit, patent leather shoes, and carried a small briefcase. He closely resembled an ambitious junior law partner in a large firm. He was highly effective with the officials, particularly the female clerks.

The business of the place — at least the overt part — was conducted through ground floor windows opening on the courtyard. Lines had formed in front of the key windows long before the shutters were opened.

Carlos was not the sort of person who stands in line. In his line of work, time was money and standing in line was not his style. After darting in a side door, thus avoiding both the tedious waiting and any unpleasantness crashing the line might have caused, he would dance over to us for a brief conference, another signature, or help in phrasing a self-serving statement concerning the unquestioned benefits that would accrue to Costa Rica when our visas were extended. He ran, non-stop, from office to office, writing the required documents as he went. God only knows what perjuries they may have contained.

I began to feel like the Sorcerer's Apprentice as I ran back and forth to the small cement building on the fourth side of the courtyard, and responded to his commands: "Have four copies of this made," he would say, or "we need three more sheets of two colone paper," or "he wants 74 colones in stamps."

I was busy in our joint enterprise but one small worry was

beginning to niggle in the back of my mind. I had seen Carlos' aggressive (and successful) approach to the bureaucracy, and I had noticed how well he manipulated the officials. There was no doubt in my mind that he was on equally good terms with the police, and I was painfully reminded of another situation, years earlier, when an apparently rosy future had dissolved instantly into a nightmare.

It was during my younger, more innocent days when, after whiling away an evening in a Tokyo bar, I was presented with a bill that included a charge of ¥10,000 for companionship. When I objected, the pretty little bar girl with whom I had been falling in love turned into a prosecutorial virago:

"You wan' I call poreece?"

Then as now, I had foolishly violated the first rule of a happy coexistence. I had failed to first negotiate the price. Here, in my anxiety, I had allowed myself to be lulled by Carlos' assurance that "it won't cost very much."

Now, however, we were approaching the moment of truth. Carlos had persuaded the officials to accept our most recent broker's statement as proof of our solvency; a document he no doubt studied with great interest as he ran back and forth. He also managed, on our behalf, to sidestep the fingerprint requirement that would have obliged us to return to San Jóse the following day.

This last accomplishment was the ultimate demonstration of his virtuosity. I had just taken a deep breath and asked, "How much do we owe you, Carlos?" when I happened to glance toward the gate.

Like the Seventh Cavalry, bugles blaring, and flags flying, I saw Ralph and Diane pushing through the crowd toward us. I knew it was a crime for a nonresident to be unpleasant to a Costa Rican, and up to now, Carlos had been holding all the cards. He knew it, we knew it, and worst of all, he knew we knew it.

But he hadn't noticed we had company. He was too busy looking at me with the appraising stare of a butcher examining a lamb. He started to say something, but I deliberately interrupted him by turning to greet Ralph and Diane. In that instant, when he got a good look at Diane, the odds shifted.

Carlos looked at me and then back to Diane. I almost felt sorry for him. He was mesmerized by her stony expression and glittering blue eyes. She said something to him in Spanish that sounded like air coming out of a tire. He cleared his throat. Dapper Dan was gone.

99

In his place stood a worried young man who was having trouble getting his thoughts together.

"Two hundred colones," he whispered, then seeing no reaction on Diane's face, he bravely added, "each."

That seemed fair. I paid him, and we treated Ralph and Diane to the best lunch we could find in San Jóse.

Ironically, that expensive and traumatic ordeal was nearly nullified a week later when an anonymous junior bureaucrat classified *Prospector* as a motor vehicle.

The government was concerned about the number of foreign (i.e. Nicaraguan) vehicles in Costa Rica, and had imposed a 90-day limit on the length of time they could remain in the country. As often happens in any bureaucracy, an overzealous clerk decided to go his boss one better, and mindlessly interpreted the order to include foreign yachts.

I talked to Herman, who discussed the problem with his father. The father, whose name was Hermoso, had served as head of the local fishermen's cooperative, and enjoyed considerable political influence in Puntarenas.

Hermoso arranged an appointment with Señor Ronaldo Vargas, then Member of Parliament for Puntarenas, and *Vice Ministrio de Hacienda*. Hermoso went to San Jóse with me, and acted as interpreter. Señor Vargas listened carefully as Hermoso explained the problem. Then he turned to me and said, "I t'ink we help."

He sat at his secretary's desk and with two fingers typed a letter, which he signed and sealed, then handed to me with instructions where to deliver it.

In Spanish, which Hermoso translated, he said: "I would enjoy your company next Sunday at my *finca*."

"*Gracias, Señor,*" I said to Señor Vargas. Then to Hermoso, I asked, "Please ask him what time and where."

The following Sunday, Velda and I presented ourselves at the Vargas apartment in Puntarenas. Young Herman was with us; we needed his help as an interpreter, while he was not insensitive to the potential benefits that might accrue by associating socially with the area's leading politician.

We crammed ourselves into Sr. Vargas' little car, and he drove with great enthusiasm through several small barrios on the way to his *finca*. Judging by the reception he received whenever we stopped, he was very popular in his district. When we arrived at the *finca*, a five acre farm, several members of his permanent entourage, including a body guard, were already present. We found during subsequent visits that one or more members of that group were in almost constant attendance. Señora Vargas looked as if she might have had a Chinese ancestor, and she cooked Costa Rican food in a Chinese mode. It was delicious.

During the next few weeks, we enjoyed several visits with the Vargas family. Shortly before we left Costa Rica, we decided to reciprocate their hospitality by inviting them and their friends to join us aboard *Prospector* for a daysail in the Golfo de Nicoya.

We assumed we would be hosting the same small group we had met at the *finca*, and made preparations accordingly. But we were wrong. By the time Sr. Vargas arrived with his family, we were already crowded, with twenty guests on board.

It was a lovely day, with just enough breeze so when we cleared the estuary, we shut the engine down and sailed on a broad reach to a group of islands six miles away. Our guests were enchanted. None had sailed before, and they were visibly impressed by the silent power of the sails. One by one, I gave the more adventurous guests a turn at the wheel.

While I was sailing the boat, Velda was in the galley, held at bay by three determined Costa Rican women who made sure their men didn't starve by insisting she cook a large pot of rice to supplement the spaghetti she had already prepared.

After lunch, I rigged the swim ladder. Most of the men and a few of the younger women went swimming. None were very skillful, but they had a good time jumping in the water. On the way home, the wind was fair, so I set the squaresail and raffee for an exhilarating sail up the Gulf. It was a tired, happy bunch of excursionists we brought back to the marina.

One thing about places like the Pacific Marina — places somewhat isolated from the larger society — is that because we were more or less thrown together, we learned to rely on ourselves and on each other to get the things done that needed doing. People who sail small boats long distances tend to be egalitarian. Some have more money than others, but others are better equipped with relevant skills and tools. Take the two Bobbies as an example.

"Big" Bobby Seigleman and his wife, Sandy, were an attractive young couple. Bobby had worked for Hughes Aircraft as a computer programmer before going sailing. He was a highly skilled electronic engineer and could fix any electrical gear. He was also a terrific guy. Sandy was just as clever. She was from Mexico, which explained Bobby's fluency in Spanish. He and Sandy had sailed south along the Baja coast with another boat, also operated by a Bobby, that one accompanied by a pretty Filipino girl named Carmine.

To avoid confusion, it was necessary to distinguish between them. Since Bobby Seigleman was physically smaller than his pal, in the perverse way such things are done, he became Big Bobby, while the other one became Little Bobby.

Little Bobby was a good carpenter, and in his way just as friendly as Big Bobby. We all became close friends.

One evening, just for the hell of it, Velda, Sandy, Carmine, and Sylvia Fox, a young Englishwoman who, in Velda's words, was 33 going on 19, decided to go out on the town.

The two Bobbies and I watched the women go ashore, and we looked at each other — what should we do? There was only one answer. Like boys let out of school, we were off.

Puntarenas is a seaport town. While not exactly a sewer of iniquity, neither was it run by the Moral Majority. In Puntarenas, the prevailing public attitude toward weaknesses of the flesh was a tolerant live and let live.

By 11 p.m., we were seated around a table in Madam Lily's bar. The three young whores sitting with us had a limited command of English that they probably had picked up from the crews of American tuna boats, but they were pleasant and congenial company. I was having a good time, oblivious to things going on around me, totally engrossed in the conversation, when I felt a tap on my shoulder. Annoyed, I glanced up and saw two men staring down at me.

"*Por favor, Señor,*" the youngest of them said, "may we see your passport?"

Of course, none of us had passports, so we were ordered outside, and told to get into the paddy wagon, which was a pick-up truck fitted with a wooden bench.

That's when Big Bobby's fluency paid off — for him. Neither Little Bobby nor I understood a word, but as he stood by the tailgate, Big Bobby held the officers' undivided attention. Beautiful cadences of Spanish floated from his lips. I could see he was making a sale when the officers began nodding in agreement with his argument.

Then the officers withdrew and while they conferred, Big Bobby said, "I just told them they would look like fools for arresting you guys on suspicion of being Nicaraguans." He paused to let the "you guys" sink in.

Not even bothering to conceal his grin, he said, "So I offered to go to the boat, find our passports, and bring them to the jail."

The huddle broke up, and much to my disgust, one of the officers shook Big Bobby's hand. *Muchas gracias, Señor, muchas gracias!* Big Bobby turned to us. "See you around, guys," and with a wink, he turned and headed downtown in search of our women.

Little Bobby and I spent four uncomfortable hours in jail. Yet, if the doorman hadn't been carrying a submachine gun, I might not have guessed that we were in detention. A steady flow of humanity came and went, seemingly at random.

The novelty of the thing lost its appeal as the wooden bench we were seated on grew harder. I knew if we were seriously relying on Big Bobby to spring us, we would have a long wait, perhaps several days. Besides, I was goaded by a bitter fantasy of Big Bobby finding the ladies, and I could picture him explaining between gasps and paroxysms of laughter, where we were. I also could envision their incredulous reaction when they comprehended what Big Bobby was trying to tell them. That's about the way it happened, only Big Bobby was so overcome with emotion as he delivered the news, that he was blinded by tears streaming down his face.

Nearly all the visitors approached the uniformed officer with sergeant's stripes seated at a small desk in the middle of the room. Obviously, he was the person in charge, and had the keys to the gate. I decided to have a little chat with him. Luckily, I had Vargas' card in my pocket and I showed it to the sergeant.

"Do you know this man?" he asked. I assured him I did. I also told him that if they intended to keep us much longer, I would have to be given a bed; it was long past my bedtime, and I was becoming very tired.

I must confess that by that time, had it been necessary, I would have left Little Bobby as a hostage, just as Big Bobby had left us.

Clearly, there is no honor among jailbirds.

The sergeant extracted a promise from me that we would bring our passports first thing in the morning, and released us. *"Buenas noches, Señores,"* said the man with the machine gun politely, as he opened the door for us.

More than any place we had been, Puntarenas was a crossroads. Yachts arrived from California, from the Caribbean, from Hawaii, and even from Alaska. They stayed for days, weeks and even months, but when they left, they went to such places as Panama, Cocos Island, Hawaii, the Galapagos, the Caribbean, and the Marquesas. Some even sail around the world.

Sylvia and friend

As we became more a part of that tight little community, and heard more about other people's experiences, we began to think that turning back into the Caribbean, as we had originally planned to do, might be a mistake.

I'll be honest about it. After our experience in the Miraflora lock, I was scared to death of a return passage through the Panama Canal. I have no doubt that fear had much to do with my part of the decision we were beginning to make.

It is about 4,280 nautical miles from Puntarenas to the Marquesas Islands in the mid-Pacific. If you ignore the Galapagos Archipelago, that passage is one of the longest uninterrupted voyages in the world. What must it be like, we wondered, to spend not days, but *weeks* at sea?

I don't recall prolonged or sensible discussion about it, and neither does Velda. I can't even tell you when we decided to sail west rather than return to the Caribbean. The genesis of that determination was as obscure as our original decision to buy the boat. The idea was planted; it took root and flourished.

It never occurred to us that our timing was off; that we were proposing to leave for the South Pacific at the *beginning* of the

South Pacific hurricane season. But even if we had, it probably wouldn't have made any difference, because then we would have been sophisticated enough to know that hurricanes never occur in French Polynesia.

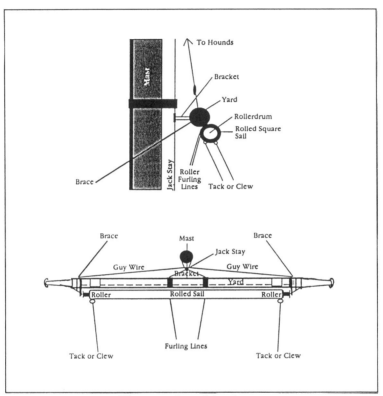

The yard and jackstay

Things began to snowball. Sylvia Fox wanted to join us. We were more than glad to welcome her aboard. She was a robust young woman with an easy laugh and a splendid sense of humor. There never was a moment on that long passage when she failed to pull her full share of the load, and then some.

It required several trips to the French Consulate in San Jóse to obtain six-month visas for French Polynesia — strangely, it was necessary for the Consul to obtain approval in Paris — but eventually our visas were granted. Then we began assembling the necessary

105

stores and provisions.

We had difficulty finding navigation gear. Filling our propane tanks was awkward and inefficient, but ordinary hardware was cheap and abundant. Hans had called my attention to an illustration in Conor O'Brien's book *Across Three Oceans* which showed how he had rigged a chain jackstay aboard *Saoirse* parallel to, and about eight inches forward of his mast to give his yard lateral support so it could be raised and lowered but was prevented from chafing against the mast. I found the necessary chain and other hardware in a Chinese hardware store.

"Wooding" the hull

Our hull was in good shape. Laborers in Costa Rica worked for $5/day, and we had wooded the hull and applied the paint Buzzy had brought from Seattle.

Also, remembering Gordon Stuermer's insistence that it would be possible to design a raffee around our complicated standing rigging, I had drawn one to our dimensions. which was was cut by Cheong Lee in Hong Kong and delivered in Costa Rica. To my surprise, it fit and functioned very well.

It was time for our final provisioning. The abundance of food in Costa Rican markets was overwhelming. The displays of tomatoes, cabbages, and other fruits and vegetables were works of art. The market was truly a cornucopia. Since eggs were sold by the pound. We found it necessary to buy six plastic egg cartons in the Chinese variety store.

Velda and Sylvia were very busy. They canned over 50 pint jars of meat. We stowed 20 pounds of tenderloin, 45 pounds of pork, 40 pounds of hamburger, three turkeys, and ten pounds of sausage in the freezer.

We bought 12 dozen eggs, 200 pounds of potatoes, 50 pounds of onions, five cabbages, 20 pounds of carrots, a stalk of green bananas, and large quantities of limes, oranges, and celery. The vegetables and eggs had never been refrigerated. That's essential if you plan to hold them at ambient temperature.

Then came the hardest part. Saying goodbye to wonderful friends like Ralph and Diane, Tom and Maria, Pedro and Victoria – and little Maria, of course – the Bobbies and their ladies, Señor and Señora Vargas, Herman and Hermosa, to say nothing of the gang at Pacific Marina. The list was a long and emotional one.

We left Puntarenas, after obtaining our *Zarpe,* on December fourth, outbound for Nuka Hiva in the Marquesas Islands, French Polynesia. But no matter how well prepared we were, we couldn't have guessed that 1983 would be the year of El Niño; or that *six* hurricanes were gestating just west of our far destination.

REPUBLICA DE COSTA RICA

MINISTERIO DE SEGURIDAD PUBLICA   CAPITANIA DE PUERTO

ZARPE

Se hace constar:

Que el Capitán ____RICKEY MOORE DENTON____

al mando del ____YATE DE BANDERA AMERICANA   "PROSPECTOR"____

de ____12____ toneladas neto, de registro, y ____3____ tripulantes

sale hoy de este puerto con destino a ____ISLAS POLINESIAS, FRANCIA____ vía

____PUERTOS INTERMEDIOS____ de acuerdo con los requisitos de la ley.

Está solvente,

Administrador de Aduana

Dado en la Capitanía de Puerto de ____PUNTARENAS____

a los ____3____ días

del mes de ____DICIEMBRE____

de mil novecientos xxxxxxxx ____OCHENTA Y DOS____

Válido hasta las ____11:15____ horas

del __4__ de ____DICIEMBRE____ de 19&82

Capitán de Puerto
PEDRO VARGAS HIO

4249 - Imp. Nacional - 1968

107

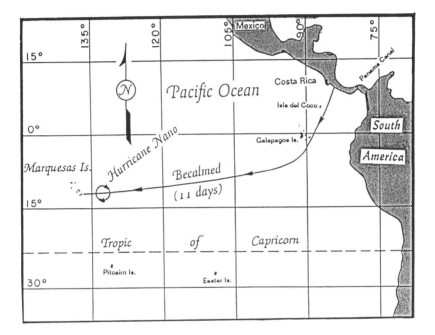

Puntarenas, C.R. to Hiva Oa
(Chart 3)

Chapter 5

The Wide Pacific

Something magic happens when you unshackle your anchor, lash it to the bulwarks, and tie the hawse-pipe plug to the end of the chain. This is the moment when you have severed your last connection with land, which will not to be renewed until you have successfully completed your passage.

That feeling has as much to do with the uncertainties that lie ahead, and a humbling appreciation of your limitations, as it has to do with the voyage itself. By now, we were no strangers to passage-making, and we were almost painfully aware that the difference between a seven day passage and one lasting seven weeks was considerably more than the time involved. Things age at sea. Unexpectedly, they break, wear out, and run dry.

Knowing that your landfall is 4,295 miles away, and that your best daily runs will only average 100 miles or so, will put you in a thoughtful mood. Have you stowed enough water? Is there enough fuel? What about food? Shouldn't you have an additional type of antibiotic? Even such prosaic items as toilet paper, radio batteries and pencils must be counted. You also must think of the repairs that might be needed to keep your boat moving.

Our first day at sea set the pattern for most of the passage. The wind was almost flat. We had started with 180 gallons of fuel. We used 12 precious gallons of it the first day to travel 66 miles. Using nearly seven percent of our fuel in the first 24 hours was not a good beginning.

The next morning, rolling on the slow Pacific swell, out of sight of land and almost completely becalmed, we found ourselves in the midst of a porpoise convention. Hundreds of the animals surrounded us. Cap was in a frenzy. I have no idea what porpoise's breath may smell like, but the slightest whiff would make him crazy. The calm of the moment, whatever time it might be, was shattered by his shrilly outraged barking. He would race madly from one end of the boat to the other, jumping up with his front feet braced against the cap rail, his black fox–like ears cocked forward, body quivering with excitement, and bark his defiance at the invaders.

Fortunately, they ignored his bad manners, and continued to play around the boat, in stunning display, diving in front of the bow, and leaping into the air. Sometimes two or three would jump in beautifully choreographed unison, again, again, and again, seemingly on a collision course with the boat, diving at the last moment to swim gracefully under our keel.

After only our first week at sea, while we still had some 3,800 miles to go, already we were running out of things. Our beer was nearly gone. More importantly, fully *half* the diesel was gone. I calculated that if we used fuel only for refrigeration and keeping the batteries charged, the remaining 80 gallons would last 60 days. Thus, already we had reached the point where we either sailed or waited for wind.

The log described our situation this way:

December 13: *Enjoyed 6–7 hours NE wind last night. First breeze of any consequence since leaving Costa Rica. Also saw water spout about half a mile away off stbd bow. Awesome and frightening. Measured and computed remaining fuel.*

December 14: *Autohelm died at 9:45 this morning. First, spreader lights died, then steaming light, now autopilot. Worked out new watch bill. Good to have third person on board. Light SE breeze. I hope we are out of doldrums. Noon position, 03°13'N, 87°47'W.*

Boat chores are never ending. I cleaned the Autohelm's electrical connections and temporarily revived the little beast. When it comes to desirable boating accessories, I think automatic steering — a functional "Iron Mike" — rates just below a dry bunk.

As we approached the Galapagos, the weather gradually turned humid and cloudy. We were in an almost constant drizzle. We could have stopped in the Galapagos Islands; indeed, we should have. But we sailed through the Archipelago without stopping because lacking visas and knowing what the Ecuadorian Navy had done to the American tuna fleet, frankly, I was afraid to test the local commanding officer's good nature. Also, our little ship's company had settled into a comfortable routine, and I was reluctant to disturb it.

I can rationalize all I like. The decision not to stop was a bad one, and I wish I had it to do over. We could have replenished our fuel and water, and seen the unique life forms that have evolved on these isolated islands. It is also possible that we might have learned the significance of the peculiar weather we were experiencing.

The Galapagos' climate is usually dry and arid; not rainy and foggy. Therefore, I should have guessed something was wrong when, for the five days we were near the islands, it drizzled and rained constantly. With the benefit of 20/20 hindsight, I now know that the unusual weather was part of the environmental anomaly that made possible the unprecedented series of hurricanes in French Polynesia during 1983. Had I known then what the weather gods had in store, even I might have had sense enough to turn around and return to Puntarenas.

I later learned that the heavy, cold waters of the Humboldt Current sweep up the west coast of South America from the Southern Ocean. When that current approaches the equator, it turns west and becomes a part of the westerly Equatorial Current. The Equatorial Current is wind driven. For atmospheric reasons not completely understood, the southeast trade winds had temporarily stopped. Like us, the current was becalmed. Without the trade winds to urge it along, the Humboldt water, being colder and denser than the surrounding water, sank.

It was replaced by *El Niño,* a temporary warm water current generated by the California current, augmented by warmer water flowing out of the Gulf of Panama. El Niño's long tongue of warm water floated thousands of miles west, significantly increasing surface temperatures, and resulted in the unprecedented flurry of hurricanes in the central South Pacific.

The continual gray overcast was reflected in the water, but while we were near the Galapagos, we saw a rich assortment of whales, porpoises, turtles, and an incredible mix of sea birds.

On December 16, we picked up a pair of hitch-hikers. *Large, white stork–like birds* is the way I described those Galapagos albatrosses in the log. They had no fear of us or the animals. They made themselves at home on deck, and perching uneasily in the rigging. Lara, the ship's cat, put on quite a show.

Guided by instinct rather than common sense, she began to stalk them. Belly flat, ears back, tail twitching in nervous excitement, she crawled across the deck toward them. They watched her closely, but without alarm. When she had crawled to within reasonable striking distance, and was gathering herself for her final lethal rush, one bird took a step toward her, probably to get a better view.

Galapagos albatrosses seldom if ever see cats, just as Lara had never seen birds like this. Possibly they thought she was good to eat. Fortunately, common sense prevailed, and Lara broke off the engagement before she got hurt. Cap solved the problem by pretending they weren't there.

I hoped to pick up the southeast trades while remaining in the equatorial counter-current. I didn't realize that by staying so close to the equator, we unnecessarily were prolonging our exposure to the unpredictable weather and calms associated with the Intertropical Convergence Zone (ICZ). This area is similar to the horse latitudes we had encountered on our first passage.

The log gives a good picture of the weather:

December 20: Ran into another heavy squall. Lots of rain. Wind gusty, veering all around.

December 21: More squalls today. Winds light and variable. Course changes from 210° to 180°, back to 225° because of wind shifts. Dull, unpleasant day.
December 24: Wind continued all night. Obviously we are in trades. Best run yet: 146 miles, crossed Equator at 11 a.m. Only 2,592 miles to go.

Christmas Eve, we tuned in the BBC Christmas Program, which featured portions of the 1939 Lionel Barrymore radio version of "Christmas Carol."

The wind died at daylight. *Prospector* celebrated Christmas Day by rolling heavily in the swell. Rather than endure the slash and bang of the booms and sails crashing back and forth with every roll, we struck the mainsail and staysail, and set the squaresail. It didn't help our motion, but it was much quieter.Sylvia's bouncy exuberance had led her to decorate the cabin with colored paper chains and other home-made ornaments. Velda had decorated a little plastic tree.

We exchanged gifts right after breakfast. One of Sylvia's favorite expressions then was "On yer bike". Velda had embroidered the expression and a picture of a Gay '90s high wheel bike on a blouse for her. Sylvia had brought Costa Rican wooden ware; a 1930s roadster for me, and a bowl and tray for Velda.

The high point, as far as I was concerned, was a gift Velda had commissioned Sandy (Big Bobby's talented wife) to make. It was a stuffed pantyhose doll, a remarkable caricature complete in every anatomical and clothing detail – makeup, rhinestones and gown – of Madam Lily, in commemoration of that dreary night I spent in jail in Costa Rica. I gave Velda a hammock, and had made an elaborate Turks-head bracelet for Sylvia. It was a lovely Christmas.

Velda prepared a tremendous Christmas dinner of roast turkey, stuffing, cranberry sauce, mashed potatoes and gravy, yams, and even a pumpkin pie. The meal was a monument to Velda's skill, patience and perseverance. The way we were rolling, I still wonder how she kept the pie filling in the crust. Our stove is on the centerline facing forward, and is not gimballed. When the boat rolls, despite the fiddles, pots and pans sometimes come adrift.

After dinner, we exchanged Shellback Certificates, officially stamped with the ship's seal, and decorated with left-over Costa Rican postage stamps.

We were becalmed for the next week. The log shows that on December 28th, we made good 18 miles. We were in a heavy cross-swell, and poor *Prospector* (and her unfortunate crew) rolled and rolled and rolled. We drifted back across the equator into the Northern Hemisphere. I was very discouraged.

December 29: *Boat rolling heavily. LAN puts us at 00°31-'N, 100°59'W. The boat rolled so heavily last night that we lost the radar reflector. Lots of rain; very unpleasant weather. Lost Walker rotator. No star sights, Noon to noon: 34 miles.*

For me, that was the low point of the trip. I remember sitting in the cockpit, reflecting that we were about midway between Costa Rica and the Marquesas, aimlessly drifting around while our precious fluids: water, diesel and propane, dribbled away. By that time, we had long been out of beer. I didn't know it then, but Velda foresight-edly had cached a bottle of rum, knowing that its medicinal qualities might be sorely needed at some future time.

My imagination was beginning to run wild. I was beginning to wonder if we, like ants on a chip of wood, unknowingly were drifting toward the edge. I can better understand now why single-handing sailors sometimes seem a little peculiar. Neither Velda or Sylvia seemed to waste much time worrying about such extravagant nonsense.

Sylvia's strength derived from her sunny disposition and incurable optimism. She had a wonderful outgoing personality, and nothing seemed to trouble her. Even a losing streak at a game of solitaire didn't bother her. She would simply shuffle the stock and play on. She is clearly one of life's winners.

On New Year's Eve, things changed dramatically. I had just completed my star sights, and was sitting at the navigation desk plotting our position when I felt the boat stiffen and heard water begin gurgling along the waterline inches from my left ear.

"We're moving!" I heard Sylvia's excited cry. I ran up the companionway ladder.

The moon was up, and I could see catspaws riffling the surface of the swells, coming toward us from the southeast. The squaresail was full and drawing and we were sliding through the otherwise calm water. The gurgling I had heard down below was even more pronounced on deck.

I took the wheel, relieving Sylvia, who had been standing in for me while I was reducing my star sights, and gently, ever so gently, so as not to offend whichever god had sent the breeze, I brought *Prospector* back to her course.

By coincidence, as if sharing our joy at being released from our windless prison, a large pod of porpoises began frolicking around the boat, stirring the phosphorescent water into a froth of glistening bubbles and aquatic fireworks. We were enchanted by the magnificent display.

Later that evening, after the moon had set, a large flying fish, it was over a foot long, flew on deck. It was large enough to fillet, and provided breakfast for the three of us.

New Year's Day was bright and clear, and the southeast wind continued all day. We crossed the equator for the third time. Velda fixed cherry-chicken crepes for dinner, and we saw our first strangers in almost a month.

First it was a helicopter. You don't ordinarily see helicopters 2,000 miles from land. However, you may see a tuna boat anywhere in the tropical Pacific, and they use helicopters to search for porpoise since, in the eastern tropical Pacific, big yellow fin tuna are often found with porpoise.

At noon, we saw the helicopter's mothership, a California tuna seiner, on our port bow. I switched on the radio, and soon I was chatting with the *Sea Queen's* skipper.

He asked if we had seen porpoises. To spare the magnificent animals we had seen from possible capture and death, I lied and said no. He told us our weather worries were probably over. We were still experiencing squalls, but our glass was steady at 1009 millibars. He also confirmed our position which put us 1,825 miles west of Puntarenas.

We were then beginning the fifth week at sea. So far, we had averaged only 65 miles a day. If we continued at that snail's pace, we could look forward to another 36 days at sea before reaching the Marquesas.

The log continues:

January 3: Brisk force 3–4 east–southeast breeze contin-ues. Set raffee. Still rolling badly.

January 4: Terrible night. Struck squaresail and raffee and set four lowers. Wind southeast force 4. The ride is much more comfortable under the fore–and–aft rig. Foot contin-ues to drain. Now using our old antibiotics since those we got in Puntarenas are gone. Red alternator warning light came on while charging refrigeration. We continue drain-ing water and sludge from the Racor filter. Refrigerator not working properly. Noon to noon, 135 miles.

This entry requires explanation.

A scar on my right ankle, resulting from a World War II wound, had opened while we were in Costa Rica. I had seen several doctors, each of whom had prescribed different medicines, but nothing seemed to work. It wasn't disabling, but it looked terrible, and the fluid draining from the scar stained my socks. It never occurred to me that the infection might caused blood poisoning or have spread into the bone.

I didn't know then that antibiotics have a relatively short shelf life, or that some of them can even become dangerous if stored too long. It would be helpful to know what the consequences might be from taking outdated antibiotics. Most of my fellow yachties are as ignorant as I about such matters.

I believe that every ship's medicine chest should have an assortment of antibiotics, so in case one doesn't do the job, the patient can be switched to another. But when buying antibiotics, try to make sure the labels on these medicines indicated their expiration dates. You don't want to accidently poison the patient.

The log continues:

January 6: Patched a large crack on bottom of sink holding tank with Marine–Tex. Also changed salt water intake for refrigeration unit, which now seems to work better. Crossed into Time Zone 8. Noon to noon, 126 miles. Position: 03°59'S, 112°47'W.

January 7: BAD NEWS! Main water tank empty. Our situation is now this: An unknown quantity of water, possibly 25 to 35 gallons in the reserve tank. Ten gallons in jerry jugs on deck. About two gallons of fruit juices and other potable liquids. We are still over 1,500 miles from the Marquesas. If our present speed holds, about two weeks. Wind southeast force 4–5, logging seven knots at times. Refrigerator seems OK at the moment. This is our 32nd day from Costa Rica. We have logged 2,480 miles.

January 8: Winds continue. Squaresail lashings parted, had to bring yard down to repair. Velda patched main sail again. Noon to noon 143 miles.

January 9: Barometer down to 1004 mb. High thin overcast, may have bad weather ahead. Surprise, surprise. Velda has been holding out on us. She had hidden a case of beer, and today was Beer Day.

January 10: Winds becoming light and variable, I knew it wouldn't last. Rubber tank still providing water.

January 13: Heavy squalls all evening. Collected about three gallons of rainwater. Saw porpoises today; at first thought they were pilot whales. Crossed into Time Zone 9. Noon position: 7°26'S, 127°38'W. 700 miles to go. Glass back up to 1010 mb.

January 14. Out of propane. Velda rigged the kerosene cooker, but it takes two people to use it. Collected about eight gallons of water in a squall this morning. Boat was making close to 10 knots at times.

The barometer began to drift lower on the 17th of January. At the same time, the wind backed into the north and strengthened briefly, then died away. The glass continued its slow descent, and by 8 p.m. was registering 1005 mb. The winds remained fitful in the northerly quadrant all day.

On the 18th, as if a cold front were approaching, the skies became overcast with increasingly dark clouds. We began experiencing thunder squalls and heavy rains. The wind strangely remained in the northerly quadrant.

January 19: Hazy, overcast day, wind still northerly, watch stopped; now must rely on chronometer for observations. Glass down to 1002 mb. LAN position: 08°15'S, 139°08'W. We'll be there tomorrow. Only 70 miles to go.

I was wrong. It would be nearly a week before we saw the Marquesas. The next day we got into trouble. Perhaps foolishly but understandably, considering how long we had been at sea and how badly we needed to see land and to replenish our stores, I was carrying the full twelve hundred feet of sail in our fore–and–aft rig, trying to keep moving against a northwest breeze and a stiff little chop that was developing.

The boat hit a wave, bigger than the others, which stopped her cold. At the same moment, we fell into a deep trough, and rolled violently to port. It was like a slow–motion demolition derby. I was listening to things tumbling about in the galley, when suddenly I heard a splintering **SNAAAP–CRACKKK** overhead and looked up in time to see the topmast fall forward, pulled down by the jib topsail, now partly in the water.

Velda came running up the ladder and took the wheel in hurried response to my startled cry, trying to hold the bow into the weather, while Sylvia and I went forward to drag the sail out of the water. Almost immediately, we stopped and were rolling in the trough.

Some 12 feet of the topmast was dangling upside down, suspended from its splintered stub by electrical wires and bits of rigging. The boat was rolling heavily, and with each roll, the broken mast swung out and back like a huge wooden flail, hammering the

117

complex rigging at the crosstrees 35 feet above our heads. Bits of wood, broken blocks and other debris fell with each blow. I knew I had to go aloft and secure that broken mast quickly, or risk serious, possibly irreparable and disabling, damage to our top hamper. The boat was now lying ahull in the trough, rolling 20 degrees or more from the perpendicular.

First we tried the bos'n chair. Well, actually, we tried it twice. The first time, as soon as my feet left the deck, I became a wildly gyrating pendulum bouncing off the mast, and smashing into the shrouds. Although I was in good physical condition, I was not strong enough to hold myself in place. So we tried another stunt.

This time, I put on the life harness, and passed its lanyard around a shroud. I thought if I could prevent myself from swinging across the foredeck, at least I would no longer be catapulted into the mast as I was flung back and forth. It was a good idea, but again, I wasn't strong enough to prevent myself from getting hurt as I spun around and became entangled in the shrouds. *Prospector* has a quick roll, now made even more lively by her shortened rig. The chair idea was sound in principle, but in execution it was murderous.

I hated to think about it, but I finally realized there was only one way to do the job. I had to climb the ratlines. Wearing a life harness, and with a short piece of line in my pocket, I climbed up on the starboard pin rail. I needed the harness to lash myself to the mast so I'd have both hands free to secure the broken mast. Looking longingly at the deck, I took a deep breath and began to climb.

On a port roll, while the boat was falling away from me, gravity was on my side. But when the boat was on a starboard roll, flinging me backwards, I was obliged to cling to the shrouds with locked fingers and toes; desperately willing myself not to slip or fall. Then, as the mast again began its upward swing, I prepared myself so as it reached the vertical, I could scamper up, trying for three rungs while the mast was falling away from me, before I had to lock my hands and feet again for the backward ride over the water.

The higher I went, of course, the wider the swings became and the more vicious the snap. It was almost like a vertical game of crack-the-whip. When I reached the crosstree, where I had to dodge the wildly gyrating broken mast as it swung out and viciously crashed back, I lashed myself to the mast.

Once, I leaned too far and my foot slipped. I barely caught

myself. I wouldn't have gone overboard, but I would have dangled, and I can tell you, *that* prospect scared the hell out of me.

After regaining my footing, I caught the broken spar and tied it as snugly as possible against its splintered stub; then I took an extra few minutes to look for other damage which might make sail handling dangerous or difficult. Finding none, I carefully untied my lashings and started climbing down.

The return trip was as hairy as the climb had been except I was becoming very tired. When I finally reached the pinrail, my legs were trembling so badly I could scarcely stand. Suddenly, my lashings came adrift, and the broken spar renewed its vicious attack on the rigging.

There was no help for it. I *had* to climb those ratlines again! Ignoring the fatigue in my burning legs and cramped fingers, I forced myself, step by agonizing step, up those ratlines to the crosstree. Again, I lashed myself to the top hamper, and again I captured that wildly swinging mast. This time, after restoring the lashings, I tied a lanyard to an eye in the upside down masthead band and secured it to the mast stub. Now if the lashings carried away a second time, the lanyard would prevent the broken piece from resuming its destructive punishment of our top gear. I knew with absolute certainty that I could not climb that mast a third time.

Again, I disentangled myself and cautiously began my painful descent. When I finally reached the pinrail a second time, my shipmates helped me to the deck. My legs would no longer support my weight, and I sat abruptly on the deck, oblivious to the wash of boarding seas surging over the cap rail. Velda had broken out the hidden bottle and pressed a cup of restorative rum and water into my trembling hands. We rested a few minutes, then tackled the yard. Since the break occurred above the yard's rigging, we could have left it in place, but because the weather was obviously deteriorating, I thought it would be best if we brought it down.

Handling a 26 foot spar on a slanting, rolling, wet deck is neither safe, nor easy. I remembered the four of us staggering around the deck burdened with the spar under far more benign circumstances in the Caribbean. That we three were able to do it at all was a tribute to Velda and Sylvia.

January 21: Weather turning ugly. Glass at 987 mb. North-west wind increasing with frequent heavy squalls. Force

*6—7 sea, higher than winds warrant. Was called out at 3
a.m. in a blinding, suffocating rainstorm to strike mainsail
and jib. Running off under staysail, keeping weather on
starboard quarter.*

Again, the log tells only part of the story. When the barometer
falls 17 millibars in 12 hours, something serious is developing.

When Velda had relieved Sylvia at midnight the barometer stood
at 1004 mb. and the wind was rising, still from the northwest, a
most unusual direction.

By some miracle, despite the rising gale and the wild, hard
slamming of the boat on her weather course, I had fallen asleep.
Suddenly, Sylvia was shaking me, and I heard the urgency in her
voice as she yelled, " *...right now!"*

Even though the boat was rolling and pitching like a thing
demented, I was shocked and surprised when I emerged from the
relative comfort of the cabin into the fury of the storm rising around
us. The wind almost knocked me down as I grabbed the mizzen
shroud and stepped past Velda out of the cockpit.

Water driven horizontally by the wind, like a fire hose, lashed
and stung my bare skin. It was impossible to see without shielding
my eyes. The incessant roar of the wind, waves, and spattering
spume made verbal communication all but impossible.

Sylvia was already on deck, struggling with the halyards. She had
hardened the topping lift, and was casting off the peak and throat
halyards when I arrived. In an effort to slow the boat, Velda had let
the mainsheet run, and the wind was holding the boom hard against
the port shroud. The sail had wrapped itself around the shroud and
was firmly held in place, like a sheet of iron, under the unrelenting
pressure of the wind.

It was impossible to round up in that wind and sea, and it would
have been disastrous to have attempted to wear around. Even with
a double reef in the mainsail, a jibe in that wind might have
dismasted us. The only sensible thing was to haul the boom
sufficiently to ease the sail away from the shrouds.

The mainsheet is a five/eighths inch dacron line rove through a
five-part tackle. Putting my mouth to Sylvia's ear, I shouted that I
would tie a handy billy to the mainsheet. I told her that after I got
the rigging set up, I wanted her to tail the winch while I heaved on
it. She nodded her comprehension, and waited while I tied the

120

necessary hitches. The handy billy doubled the power of the five-part sheet tackle, and the whole setup multiplied the power of the winch by a factor of ten.

Yet even with her keeping the line snug on the winch, it was all I could do to pull the boom sufficiently far from the shroud so the sail was only touching it. We then made our way forward again, and gripping the sail lacings, managed to bring the sail down and furl it. Just to make sure, we passed a line around the gaff, sail and boom, and lashed it securely to the gallows. While we were struggling to claw that sail down, something I read once that was attributed to the late Spike Africa kept running through my mind: *"Any fool can raise a sail, but it takes a sailor to bring one down!"*

Heavy weather

Sylvia and I went back to the cockpit to rest. Although we were both naked, that heavy exercise had warmed us so we were more comfortable than Velda, huddled in her oilskins, was in the helmsman's seat. The glass was still falling. Velda had tried to roll the jib, but the dangling outer headstay – wreckage from the broken topmast – had jammed it. I certainly wasn't going to risk my life trying to save the jib in the dark, but I thought at daylight, we might be able to cast off its halyard and lower it and its swivel to the deck when we could see what we were doing.

Velda's watch

Daylight was slow in coming. The seas were wild; hissing and roaring around us. It was impossible to tell, except by taste, whether the water flying through the air was salt or fresh. It was flatly contrary to the published information we had on board about central South Pacific weather patterns, but I was serious when I said to Velda, as we were eating breakfast after securing the jib, that if I didn't know better, I would think we were in a hurricane!

It doesn't much matter whether you call it a gale, storm, cyclone hurricane, or typhoon. Basically, these are the same to a small boat skipper, differing only in degree. They are revolving storms with high sustained surface winds. Much about them is predictable, even from the heaving deck of a small yacht. They are not usually as bad as they seem, and even when they are, there are measures you can take to improve your situation.

Nowhere does that old adage about an ounce of prevention have greater meaning than for the small boat skipper facing a serious weather problem. While it is always best to read the signals accurately and take appropriate evasive action *before* a storm strikes, it isn't always possible.

The next best thing is to learn what you can about the storm when, as in our case, you might find yourself in the middle of one. You need to know where the storm's center is, relative to your position, where it's headed, and how fast. Theoretically, those things can be deduced by taking appropriate observations, which I was now attempting to do.

It might be interesting, but it isn't necessary, to know the wind's velocity because you will always react to your physical environment, not to the numbers on a dial. Besides, if it's something you want to know so you can tell your grandchildren about it, you can always calculate what it was after the storm is over. (See Appendix.)

I studied the clouds scudding past, trying to pinpoint the exact direction from which the wind was coming. I stood up, clinging to the Bimini frame, squinting into the weather. Just as I was satisfied the wind was coming from the northwest, a heavy gust would slam into the boat, 20 or 30 degrees away from what I believed the prevailing direction to be.

The author

You could see those gusts coming. They looked like a speeding white wall because they came with such force that they scooped the water off the surface and hurled it straight ahead. I would guess their velocity might have been well over 100 knots.

After taking several observations on the surface wind direction during my watch, I concluded the storm's center was sou'southwest, and it appeared to be heading in a southeasterly direction. (See the Appendix for detail regarding Buys Ballot Law.)

As soon as I plotted the storm's probable track, I realized that we and the storm appeared to be on parallel headings. Like being caged with a tiger, our present situation had little to recommend it. Our present course was only prolonging our exposure to the storm, and increasing the risk of additional damage if it intensified or turned toward us. We had to change course before the storm did.

Fearful of broaching or taking a knockdown, I called Velda and Sylvia to the cockpit, "We have to come about," I yelled.

They came up to the cockpit and stood to one side as I watched over my shoulder, waiting for the right swell.

This one was it; as soon as I felt the cockpit sole begin lifting under my feet, I swung the bow gently, delicately, to port. Not enough to cause her to trip over her keel and broach or, God help us, pitchpole – the seas by that time were big enough to fling *Prospector* end over end – but enough so that at the bottom of the trough, the staysail jibed across, and as we rose on the next swell, the little sail filled with a healthy snap!

Suddenly, we were on our new course of 030 degrees, running away from the storm. We heaved a collective sigh of relief. After changing course, even though I knew things would get better as we moved further away from the storm, looking at the seas from a new angle, I realized for the first time how truly monstrous they were. I felt a twinge of awe and fear. The forces raging around us were almost beyond comprehension. The storm was beginning to wear me down. I know now that I can take about three days of really bad weather before I begin to feel the numb despair that is born in fatigue. Now, the incessant motion of the boat, the crashing of errant seas and the shrieking of wind in the rigging was rasping on my nerves and getting though my psychological defenses.

The physical effort required just to keep from being thrown into things as the boat pitched and rolled was exhausting. The question, increasingly, was not "how much longer can this last?" but "how much longer can *I* last?"

My log entries were becoming shorter and more succinct:

January 23: 989 mb. at 4 p.m. Wind veering; now steering 045°. No observations for fifth day.

As abruptly as they had begun, the winds began to diminish that evening, and by morning had veered into the southeast. The storm was over. I expressed it this way in the log:

January 24: Storm over, but squalls persist. Wind southeasterly at 10–15 knots. Still collecting rain water, course 270°, glass rising. At noon, 1002 mb. Seas still very high.

I knew we must be close to land. While it was still dark, I had heard the muted thumping of things in the water striking the bow, and in the first light of morning, I could see that the water was thick with debris. Mostly coconuts, but here and there bits and pieces of wood, and finally logs and whole coconut trees. The logs and trees were a serious hazard, and by early afternoon, I felt it necessary to post a lookout in the bow.

The sky was still heavily overcast, and I was unable to take any observations until after sunset when, as if the curtain on a stage was rising, the clouds disappeared and while the horizon was still visible, stars began twinkling overhead. I observed five stars, our first celestial observation in as many days. It's necessary, in reducing celestial observations, to use a reasonably accurate dead reckoning position as a reference point.

I had plotted course changes when they occurred, but as I attempted to reconstruct our courses during the previous five days, I could only guess at our speeds and the distances we might have traveled. Moreover, I had no idea how the wind might have distorted the surface currents. In addition, when the storm was at its height and the boat's motion was most violent, I even had to approximate our compass headings.

Imagine my astonishment, therefore, when I found, after reducing the five lines of position, that the intersection of the five lines of position covered an area less than two miles in diameter, and put us almost exactly 25 miles east of Hiva Oa. With a five-star fix, there was no practical possibility of error. It was almost a miracle. We had been through a major storm, and had run blindly trying to get away from the storm. Now, five days later, we were only 50 miles from our last known position, and 50 miles closer to our landfall. Pure blind luck. Fearful of going past the islands, running aground or hitting a log during the night, we struck all the sails except the staysail, and ghosted during the night toward our landfall.

It was a silent and solemn crowd in the cockpit at first light the next morning, as we strained for our first glimpse of land in seven weeks. It was a shared, yet intensely personal moment. Velda thought she had seen lights on her watch, but we discounted that; even though our evening fix had put us only 25 miles from Hiva Oa, we had stopped out of range of all but the most powerful lighthouses. According to Earl Hinz's excellent cruising guide, *Landfalls in Paradise*, the most powerful lighthouse in the Marquesas Archipelago was a kerosene lantern. We failed to consider that she might have seen another boat.

The light strengthened, and we began to see silhouettes; dark mounds on the horizon that could only be land masses against a brightening sky. We set the mainsail and jib, and began sliding through an almost glassy sea. In minutes, the hulking beehive shape of uninhabited Motane Island passed to port. To the left behind Motane, we could see another island. The jagged mountains of Hiva Oa loomed dead ahead.

We still had two gallons of diesel, but I was waiting for a land breeze, and before noon we were sailing past the eastern headland into Baie Vipihai, otherwise known as Traitor's Bay. Velda started the engine while Sylvia and I furled the sails.

We made a terrible picture, with the broken mast lashed to the topmast stub pointing defiantly at the sky, and the slack and dangling topmast rigging hanging from the top hamper.

Through the coconut palms lining the beach, we saw the village of Atuana, Gauguin's burial place. Off to the right was a stone breakwater, behind which were several sailboat masts.

Like calls to like, and we motored around the breakwater, carefully dodging uprooted coconut trees floating in the little harbor, and came to anchor near another wooden boat, *Windjob* from Portland, Ore. *Windjob* had arrived a few hours earlier. (Remember the lights Velda thought she saw?) Her skipper, Dirk Winters, then in his 76th year, was singlehandedly retracing an earlier circumnavigation. Like us, he had experienced the full weight of the storm. We later concluded we must have been within a few miles of each other during much of the storm.

Also sharing the anchorage were three modern ketches. Two, *Carioca* and *Kulkuri* were from California. The third, *Summer Seas*, hailed from Hawaii. *Carioca* was a real gold plater. Don, her owner and skipper had supervised her building in Taiwan, and saw to it that all her specifications were met or exceeded. Don's crew was a happy, bubbly little woman named Mary who had answered his ad in a cruising magazine. They seemed well suited to each other.

Kulkuri was family owned and operated. Her crew included her skipper, Jack Curley, a retired commercial diver, who strongly favored his Irish ancestors and was an extremely likable guy; his wife, a pretty and friendly blonde from Finland named Ritva, and their precocious 12–year old son, Benjamin.

Even before we had the anchor down, Jack was alongside in his dinghy, inviting us to *Kulkuri* for a drink, offering to help us through customs, and asking about our experiences in the storm.

He could see the broken topmast, of course, but apparently we had come off much better than the island did. He gave us the bad news. The storm had destroyed the water system and the roads, so we could get neither water nor diesel. Also, the only source of propane in the islands was in Nuka Hiva, 90 miles away.

We spent a lovely quiet hour in *Kulkuri's* cockpit munching sugar cookies and sipping the first social drinks we had since Christmas dinner on the equator a month earlier.

Then Jack rowed us around the headland to the beach at Atuona village. A heavy surf was running, and he put us ashore on some rocks on the right hand side of the entrance. It took skill to land the dinghy on the sandy beach in the surf without swamping, but Jack managed it. We dragged the dinghy up the beach where he tied it to a tree. Then we walked through the village to the police station.

As Jack had said, the police had their hands full trying to locate missing villagers and help restore services. Nevertheless, one of the gendarmes, fluent in English, took the time necessary to help us prepare our entry documents. The visas we had obtained in Costa Rica greatly simplified the entry procedures.

We were issued a green passport for the boat, but we still had to post the required cash bond. I had known about the bond, and had arranged with Buzzy before we left Costa Rica, to have $4,500 waiting for us in Nuka Hiva when we arrived. I explained that to the gendarme. No problem.

Then Jack took us to the local store, and introduced us to Hinano beer, brewed in Papeete. He also told us we had run into a hurricane named *Nano*, which would prove to be the second of six hurricanes that would batter French Polynesia in 1983.

In the Southern Hemisphere, the hurricane season begins in mid–November, and ends around the first of April. Our arrival in late January was right in the middle of the season.

Jack also took us to the post office. The postmaster obligingly called the post office in Nuka Hiva to learn whether mail was being held for us (it was), and to the bank where we exchanged our last $100 bill for 14,200 CP francs. Now, at least, we could buy our own beer and fresh bread.

Unfortunately, we needed more than bread and beer. Being unable to replenish our water, diesel and propane was serious. Consequently, three short days after our arrival, we reluctantly raised the anchor and wearily got under way again.

Nuka Hiva and Hiva Oa are at opposite ends of the Marquesan Archipelago, but are only 90 miles apart. Nevertheless, the trip took two days because there was no wind. Most of the time, since we had almost no diesel, we drifted, surrounded by small, oddly silhouetted islands that looked like the beginning of time. The islands are volcanic, and are crowned with black igneous rock that froze the instant the molten magma hit the atmosphere. The resulting bizarre spires, and jagged surrealistic silhouettes give these islands a forbidding, other-worldly appearance.

When you combined their primitive appearance, their mysterious isolation, and their folklore which abounds with stories of magic, cannibalism and human sacrifice, and the almost incessant rain, it is easy to understand why these are called the Misty Isles.

Geologically speaking, these islands are very new, which accounts for their appearance. Their harsh profiles will eventually weather into soft contours. Gradually, in the cosmic order of things, the uplands will wear away while corals build fringing reefs. And ultimately, the upland will vanish altogether, leaving behind another colorful and picturesque lagoon in mid-ocean.

Taiohae Bay was an excellent harbor. As we entered, we noticed that the hillside to the left looked cultivated. Next to that area, and tucked behind the headland, was a collection of round huts that resembled the beehive huts found in Africa, clustered near a larger building. This, we later learned, was the Keikahanui Inn, owned in part and managed by an American couple, Frank and Rose Corser.

The village occupied nearly all the crescent of the beach, but was concentrated near the big cement pier across the bay to the east. The post office, the police station, hospital and Governor's residence were located on or near the small hill that rose immediately behind the pier.

Yachts were clustered directly below the Inn on the western side of the bay. Frank and Rose may have quit cruising for a time, but they had not forgotten what it was like to live on a boat in places like the Marquesas. Every morning at eight, after turning on the VHF radio, we would hear Frank's cheery "Hello out there. Is anyone up this lovely (rainy) morning?"

We would also hear a dispirited series of acknowledgments from our fellows. When it was raining — most of the time — Frank invariably invited everyone to the lodge for chess.

Frank and Rose never tired of answering questions, helping people find things, and generally being helpful. Giving aid and support to transient yachts was not their only civic activity. The plowed area we had noticed when we arrived was a reforestation project on Corser property. The plot was planted in teak, mahogany and sandalwood seedlings provided by the government. They had also published an excellent guide to Tahiti, then in a revised edition.

The population of Nuka Hiva was about the same as Hiva Oa, approximately 1,500 people. Nuka Hiva was the administrative and commercial center for the archipelago, and Taiohae Bay was much larger and better organized than Atuona. Taiohae Bay had six stores, compared to one in Atuona. Taiohae Bay also had two banks, two hotels (besides the Corser resort) and a hospital.

When we arrived, the island was recovering from the hurricane. But Nuka Hiva had not taken a direct hit as Hiva Oa did. Most of the storm damage on Nuka Hiva appeared confined to washed-out roads and ruined bridges. We saw no wind damage. Government workers had constructed foot bridges out of coconut logs over the two streams flowing through town. Cars were obliged to ford the stream between Corser's place and town, and to detour down on the beach if they wished to cross the stream next to the Town Hall.

The water system was intact, and we quickly ferried our water jugs to the pier's free water tap. The propane and diesel problems were not so easily solved. Both fuels were unavailable until some indefinite future date when the next copra schooner would arrive with supplies. This posed an immediate problem for us. Since we were out of diesel, and couldn't buy any, I had to find a way of preserving our frozen meat that did not involve running the engine.

Most stores were owned and operated by Chinese. Dealing with them was strictly a matter of cash and carry. However, one store was operated by an amiable Marquesan with the improbable name of Maurice McKittrick, who not only understood the problems we faced, but was genuinely sympathetic.

Of course, I didn't know Maurice then, and it was with considerable trepidation that I approached him with my problem. I told him I needed to find a place where I could store our meat, and I hoped he could point me in the right direction.

"How much meat you got?" He asked.

"Not much," I said. "Maybe a cardboard box full."

"No worries," he said. "I put it in my reefer. Plenty of room."

I brought the cardboard box of Costa Rican meat ashore, and he tucked it away in his cold storage locker.

That was one problem solved.

I was worried about our bond. I had yet to post it, and I knew the local gendarme's patience wouldn't last forever. The days when you could set up in business as a beachcomber in the South Pacific are long past. The French Government was making every effort to prevent people seeking that supposedly romantic life style from getting off the airplane (or boat).

People arriving by air were not allowed out of the airport without a return ticket. People arriving by yacht were required to hand over an amount of money equal to the price of an airplane ticket back to the country that issued their passport. This rule also applied to the boat's skipper.

There was much bellyaching and bitching about this by other yachties, but I thought it was a sensible arrangement. I couldn't think of any reason why the French Government should support foreign bums, or provide free transportation for them.

Our bonds (Velda's and mine) were $850 each. Sylvia's was $1,500, London being further away from the South Pacific than Los Angeles. Following my request in early December, Buz had instructed his bank to send $4,500 to us. A receipt from the Bank of America was waiting at the post office when we arrived. I took the receipt to the local branch of the Indo–Suez bank that conducted most of the Government business. The teller examined the receipt and called the bank's central office in Papeete. A short conversation in French ensued, and though I heard only one side of the conversation in a language I did not understand, the expression on the official's face told me what I needed to know.

The young man replaced the receiver and turned to me.

"I am veree sorry, Monsieur, ze monee 'ave not arrive." He shrugged his shoulders to demonstrate his sorrow.

I protested. The receipt was dated December 15, 1982, and now it was the second of February, 1983, nearly seven weeks later. Something had gone astray. The receipt indicated that the money was to have been transmitted through two corresponding banks after leaving the Bank of America.

I'm convinced that when money passes through that many hands, something is almost certain to fail. I called Buzzy, who was glad to learn that we had arrived. He promised to put a tracer on the money. I then went back to my young friend in the bank to report the results of my call.

He suggested I speak directly to his managing director in Papeete, something he couldn't do. Following his advice, I called the Director, who spoke excellent English and who listened carefully and sympathetically to my story. He asked me to call back in an hour. I did; he had checked all the Indo-Suez branches in French Polynesia, and nobody had seen the draft.

However, less than 18 hours later, as I was walking down the road in front of the Indo-Suez bank, my young banker friend came running out waving his arms and shouting, "Monsieur! Monsieur! Ze funds 'ave arrive!"

Somewhat cynically, I imagine the funds had arrived about *six weeks* earlier, and had been misplaced. No sensible clerk would admit receiving such a document until they could put their hands on it. Transferring money by mail is now obsolete. Funds are now shifted throughout the world instantly by the ubiquitous Telex or telegraphic transfer, or by the even more prosaic expedient of cash advances on a credit card.

We had temporarily solved the refrigeration problem, and had posted our bond, but there were still a few loose ends that needed attention. The scar on my ankle was still weeping, although by this time I had almost forgotten about it.

But one lazy afternoon, even that was taken care of. Velda and I were in the cockpit catching up on our reading, when a young couple in a modernized version of a native canoe came alongside. They introduced themselves and inquired about our damaged rig.

That's how we met Claudine and Lucius. Claudine was an attractive Frenchwoman in her early to middle 30s. Her friend, Lucius, was a very handsome young Polynesian, about ten years her junior, who strongly resembled Johnny Weismuller or any of a succession of young movie Tarzans. As we chatted — they declined our invitation to come aboard — I noticed that her gaze kept returning to my ankle, which was about on a level with her eyes.

Finally, curiosity got the best of her, and she asked about it, explaining that she was a nurse attached to the local French Army

131

medical unit. After I explained my problem, she urged me to come to the outpatient clinic for treatment. The French Army had acquired much experience treating tropical infections, and she thought they might heal it.

Army medicine is Army medicine. The treatment of choice is always the one that will get the patient back to duty in the shortest possible time. When you combine that result–oriented attitude with the difference that I think exists between American and European medical philosophies — the American doctors relying more heavily on technology, while their European colleagues rely on technique — you might guess that my visits to the Army clinic were uncomfortable, but the treatment *was* successful.

Unfortunately, the French system didn't always work. Bill Cribbs was an unhappy example. Bill had retired as a welder from Boeing Aircraft in Seattle. He and his wife, Janet, on a circumnavigation, were stuck in Taiohae Bay on board their Westsail 32, *Kalakala*, waiting for Bill's appendectomy incision to heal. Apparently, he had an attack of appendicitis shortly after arriving in the Marquesas, and an Army surgeon had operated several weeks earlier. But the incision would not close. It was still open when we left Taiohae Bay six weeks later.

By this time, the people we had met in Atuona had shifted to the more cosmopolitan Taiohae Bay. But the weather was still acting as if forces beyond human ken were at work. The prevailing easterly winds had become westerlies. The rain was incessant. Tensions were rising. People felt trapped, and for some, paranoia may have been just around the corner.

Frank Corser arranged for an island tour in a Land Rover. Six of us took the tour, jammed into the sturdy little truck. The driver took us up the road that runs along the spine of the island. Luckily, the day chosen for the tour was clear and sunny. When we stopped for pictures at the highest point on the road, we could see the whole archipelago to the south and east.

In the last century, Herman Melville wrote a damn good novel called *Typee* about the early Marquesans. The story is about war, intrigue, magic, and human sacrifice and was set in the Taipi Vai valley, lying green and mysterious before us. Taipi Vai extended well into the interior of the island. The lower valley was an alluvial plain that faced the ocean, and supported an old coconut plantation.

We drove through that grove of trees, past small houses, the copra shed and the drying racks, up a bumpy road, scarcely more than a trail, and came to a stop in a small farm yard. An old woman sat on the porch of the one-room house, fanning herself and watching us. Half-wild chickens were scratching in the dirt, and we saw goats in a nearby pen. The driver shouted something in the local dialect to the woman. She grinned and responded in kind. The driver turned to us:

"Guide coming," he said.

We assumed that meant we were to dismount from the truck. I don't think at that moment any of us knew where we were, or what we were to see that required the services of a guide.

A teen-age girl came strolling along, swinging a long switch. She neither smiled nor acknowledged our presence, other than by gesturing imperiously with an abrupt motion of her head, and by swinging the switch in the direction she wished us to take.

We stumbled along in her wake as best we could as she skipped over roots, scrambled up moss-covered rocks, and took short-cuts, from one level of our fiendishly steep switch-back trail to the next. There was no pity in her for any of us as we struggled behind her. I was completely out of breath when, after a climb of a mile or more, we stepped into a level clearing.

It took a moment, but then I realized that the stone structure before us was the famous marae described by Melville and other writers during the last century. The marae was a huge stone platform possibly 150 feet square. Slightly uphill from the platform was a small amphitheater, not much larger than the platform, where the spectators probably lounged while the business of the place was conducted, and sacrifices were made.

The platform was constructed of massive basaltic blocks, each weighing several tons. It's beyond my comprehension how a people who did not have the wheel or advanced mathematics could have built such a structure. I can't even imagine how they cut the stone. Yet the platform was guarded at each corner by bellicose Tikis beautifully carved from the same incredibly hard rock.

This marae was the most sacred temple in their religion, and was populated by vengeful spirits who apparently have neither forgotten nor forgiven the awful things done to them there. Even today, many Marquesans refuse to go anywhere near the place. The Tikis guarding the place were thought by the local people to be "alive."

We didn't know that at the time, and even if we had I doubt whether it would have deterred our irrepressible Sylvia who, with the Englishwoman's inborn contempt for heathen idols, sat on one. I'm sure it was only coincidence that a week later, Sylvia was a patient in the Army hospital, writhing and sobbing in agony over a badly infected finger.

There is a brooding quality about these islands – something alien and disturbing – which I have never felt elsewhere. Even the weather had a supernatural feel to it. Three hurricanes passed south of the Marquesas in quick succession during the six weeks we waited in Taiohae Bay. From January 19th, when hurricane *Nano* rolled over us, to April 18th when hurricane *William* died in infancy, French Polynesia was battered by five hurricanes, and threatened by the last one. Six hurricanes in a place where the last one occurred 100 years ago is astonishing.

It may have been a sense of confinement that led the people from two boats to leave prematurely for Tahiti. The skippers of those boats even planned a stop in Ahe in the Tuamotus before sailing on to Papeete on Tahiti.

I thought at the time the side trip to the Tuamotus was unwise, but the skippers of *Secret Sharer* from Boulder, Colorado and *Summer Seas* from Hawaii, were determined to make the trip. The Tuamotu Archipelago, also known as the Dangerous Archipelago, is a 400-mile chain of low lying atolls and coral reefs. Ahe is an isolated Polynesian village in that archipelago.

Both boats were equipped with ham radios, but only *Secret Sharer* had a satnav, and neither boat had radar. *Summer Seas* was crewed by Ike and Debby with whom we had dinner in Traitor's Bay. The other boat also carried a young crew. Larry was a tall young man, and Molly, a lovely young woman.

Before leaving, they had arranged with *Carioca's* crew to maintain regular radio schedules on a ham frequency. As the two boats approached the Tuamotus, a fast moving hurricane, *Sara*, overtook them. The boats were separated in the storm. *Secret Sharer* survived. Larry's functioning satnav enabled him to furnish *Carioca* with a constant up-date of his position. With that information and the meteorological detail coming from Papeete, Don suggested courses most likely to carry *Secret Sharer* away from the storm and helped them avoid the more prominent reefs.

Ike and Debby were lost. No trace of *Summer Seas* was found. We don't know what happened, but it is likely that at some point, as the weather deteriorated, Ike and Debby would have made a conscious and tragic decision to proceed. If they did, I am certain that unfortunate decision must have quickly become irreversible.

It's a sad story and I have no wish to dwell on it, except to point out that, based on the scraps of information we gleaned from Don's radio conversations with Ike, apparently they were caught in a trap based on their physical and emotional exhaustion. It's not hard to imagine how the incessant trauma of their tiny environment might have imposed terrible stresses leading to a numbing fatigue and a foggy lassitude, where judgment was eroded and even the simplest problems became insoluble. Rest, in such circumstances, would have been all but impossible. When they slept, it was probably only a brief twilight loss of consciousness, rather than meaningful rest.

In addition to their other problems, Ike had reported that water was inexplicably rising in their bilges. In his last message, Ike reported that the leak they had been searching for during the previous 18 hours had been found in the stern bearing, and that he had repaired it by putting a hose clamp on the bearing's rubber sleeve. He concluded that broadcast by saying they were exhausted and were going to rest. *Summer Seas* was never heard from again.

If Ike and Debby taught us anything it must be this: no matter how inconvenient it is, or what sacrifices may be required, and even if it means violating the first rule of seamanship concerning the watch, you and your crew *must* get adequate rest. If necessary, use Valium or some similar medicine. A rested crew is your most precious asset.

That sad episode cast a pall over the yachting community, but there was a lighter side to Taiohae Bay. Every time I hear "Old McDonald," I'm reminded of a group of young boys, 10 or 11 years old, I saw regularly in the village, diving off a foot bridge into a shallow pond, and playing running–chasing games.

Those kids were a friendly bunch, and they apparently recognized in me a kindred spirit. They spoke no English, but when I sat to rest, they invariably sat with me. The only French I knew, other than a greeting, was some lyrics to *Frere Jacques*. I thought they might know the song, so while we were sitting on a coconut log one day, I began to hum a few bars.

They recognized the melody immediately. The bolder boys began singing with me, and the next thing I knew, we were all lustily singing "Morning bells are ringing!" That's when I decided to teach them an American song.

What could be more American than *Old McDonald*? Throughout the remainder of our stay in Taiohae Bay, whenever those boys saw me, it was always "*EEEi, EEEi oooH.*" And I'll bet if we were to land in Taiohae Bay tomorrow morning, some kids would be singing "Old McDonald had a farm... ."

I mentioned Maurice McKittrick, but I haven't said much about him. He deserves the credit, with Frank and Rose Corser, for our pleasant and successful visit to Taiohae Bay. He was in his '70s when we knew him and he wore his years well. A big man, usually clad only in shorts and sandals, he would close the store during the noon hour and stretch out on his counter for a siesta.

Any customers arriving while Maurice was taking his nap were welcome to wait on the wide veranda until he chose to open his door. The islanders didn't mind. Time is relative, and the concept certainly was not invented in Polynesia.

Maurice had helped us buy a drum of incredibly filthy diesel fuel from a copra schooner, had loaned me his adapter so I could decant propane from an 11 kg. French tank into my smaller American container. He had also provided free cold storage, and had arranged for repairs to our alternator. He had a quick temper, and it was during one of his explosions that I came to know him better. I was climbing the steps to his store one afternoon when I heard him roaring in obviously profane French at a small man standing silently and unhappily before him. Maurice was in full cry, and I was beginning to pity his victim, when Maurice leveled his finger at the door, obviously ordering him to leave.

The man brushed past me on his way out, and Maurice was still muttering and sputtering when I made my presence known.

"What was that all about?" I asked.

"Doze French bastards!" He said, "gimme dis, gimme dat, take, take, take." He paused for breath. "I fought their damn War for them. Dat's enough!"

I knew Maurice the South Pacific storekeeper, and Maurice the patron saint of South Pacific yachties, but I hadn't yet met Maurice the war veteran.

"Were you in the Pacific War?" I asked.

"Non," he said, "I vos in England. I flew over Europe in a B-25 as a navigator in the Free French Airforce."

You can never tell about people. He went on to tell me about his sea-going career after the war, before he decided to come back to the Marquesas and settle down. We traded war stories and discovered we were both disabled veterans.

In the meanwhile, we had an engine problem. The manifold fitting Mark and Harry had devised to repair the exhaust system in St. Thomas had cracked and began to leak.

Maurice and Frank Corser jointly owned a small electrical welder. Bill Cribbs' unhealed appendectomy scar did not interfere with his welding skill. I took the broken piece to him, and together, we found a piece of pipe we could cut to fit; then with both Frank and Maurice looking on, Bill welded it together.

At the end of March, after we had been in the Marquesas about two months, the prevailing winds had returned to their normal trade wind orientation, it looked as if the hurricane season was over. Besides, we were depressed by the loss of our friends, by the endless rain, the ubiquitous mud, the infections and insects, freezer-burned chicken, our teeth turning black from the bulk rum Maurice sold, and finally, on the 24th of March, we left Nuka Hiva for Tahiti. We were wrong about the hurricane season. It wasn't over yet.

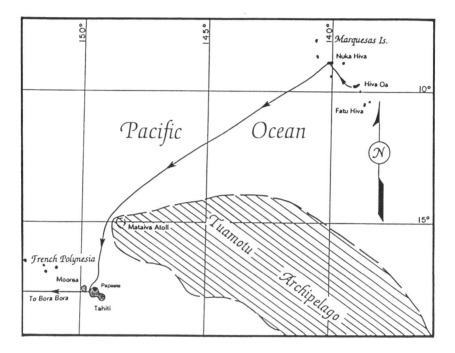

French Polynesia
(Chart 4)

Chapter 6

Tahiti

$\mathcal{F}$or a change of scenery during our last night in the Marquesas, we anchored in Daniel's Bay next door to Taiohae Bay. It was different, but not better. The sheer cliffs on both sides and behind us were primarily black rock interspersed with occasional dark green patches of vegetation where a plant or shrub had gained a foothold. It was a dreary and depressing landscape.

We motored out of the bay at first light. The wind, which had gone back into the proper quadrant, was light and fitful and rain was falling with a steady, persistent monotony. At dusk, Nuka Hiva was still high on the horizon behind us, but at least it appeared that we had left the rain.

The next morning, Nuka Hiva was gone but not forgotten. During the night, Velda had come down with a bug, no doubt the final salute from an offended Tiki. It was one of those "God, I feel awful" type of things that goes around from time to time. She was under the weather for two days; then it was my turn. Sylvia escaped. Apparently, she had been punished enough.

The weather continued calm. On our first full day, we logged only 17.7 miles. The following day, when I got sick, we made only eight miles. Then, appropriately on April Fool's day, we ran out of eggs, and I found I was a day behind in my navigation.

Even under the best of circumstances, the moon was not my favorite navigational subject. It moves so fast that timing is especially critical. Also, you often had to use its upper limb (which I was not accustomed to doing) because the lower limb was in shadow much of the time. Finally, two pages of the Almanac were devoted to parallax corrections, and corrections to the corrections.

While the procedure seemed complicated, it was only tedious, and when things were slow, I enjoyed plodding through those complicated reduction procedures. It gave me something to do.

My April Fool's joke had to do with the Almanac's moon data, and I suppose it also tells you something about me. Although it seems unbelievable as I write about it, I actually thought the data were off by about 45 minutes. If nothing else, I suppose that shows you how much faith I had in my government.

That peculiar fit of temporary stupidity persisted until the next day, when I checked my time against radio station WWVH (the Pacific Ocean's equivalent to WWV), and realized my watch was displaying *yesterday's* date.

The moral of this story is obvious but I seem to need constant reminding. As in most things, when the engine stops, always check the fuel level before starting to take the engine apart.

I also mention this incident so if you find a gross error in your navigational calculations, don't forget to check the calendar as well as the sweep hand on your watch.

The search for *Summer Seas* had developed into a major coordinated US–French effort. The *USS Glacier Bay*, a U.S. Coast Guard ice breaker en route to San Diego from the Antarctic, was diverted to Papeete so her helicopters could join in the search.

An American research ship from San Diego (cynically thought by many to be under charter to the CIA for monitoring the atomic bomb tests the French were conducting in the Gambier islands) entered the search with the French Navy.

Although *Summer Seas* had vanished a month earlier, naturally we hoped to spot a life raft with survivors. Once, on my evening watch, I saw a shooting star which so resembled a white flare that we stopped and spent two hours listening and looking. Before the search was abandoned, almost every atoll in the Tuamotu Archipelago had been examined, most of them on foot.

At daylight, on April third, we sailed into a strangely configured wall cloud. It was a uniform light gray color and extended across the horizon in a line so straight it might have been laid out with a stupendous chalk line. It rose straight up from the water's surface to an altitude of possibly 15,000 feet. It was a scary thing to see.

I would have avoided it if I could, but it was upon us before I could take evasive action. Sailing into it was like sailing into the wall of a huge windowless building. At the very least, I expected a severe wind sheer, and had Sylvia standing by the pin rail, ready to scandalize the mainsail by dropping the gaff if necessary. Instead of the expected turbulence, the light nor'easterly breeze we had been enjoying died away, and again we were becalmed.

The cloud moved overhead, and in less than an hour, we had a breeze out of the southeast. We later learned that another major weather system was forming northwest of us, and I suspect that peculiar cloud and the erratic winds were somehow related to it.

Two days from Papeete, still on a heading of 250 degrees, I was turning the watch over to Sylvia, who was standing on the side deck having a look around, when she leaned over the doghouse. "Let me have the binos, please," she said. I handed her the glasses, which she focused on an area directly off our port beam. "Come have a look," she said. The Autohelm was steering, so I stepped up beside her. She handed the glasses to me.

"Look just there," she said, indicating an area directly abeam. "You'll see it between the swells."

I took the glasses, and looking down the trough of a wave, almost immediately saw what looked like rows of densely packed telephone poles about five miles away.

It was Mataiva atoll, the westernmost of the Tuamotus. The telephone poles were coconut palms that had been defoliated by the hurricanes. I spun the wheel, and hauled the sheets. Having the Tuamotus behind us gave me a splendid lift.

The easterly wind freshened, and for the last two days, we sailed on a broad reach with a reef in the mainsail. At daylight on April sixth, Tahiti loomed high above the horizon, not more than ten miles away. By 8 a.m., we were sailing through the pass, and an hour later, we were anchored off the small boat customs dock in company with a dozen other recent arrivals.

Every landfall is an occasion for rejoicing, but making a landfall in Tahiti, land of *HMS Bounty*, Count von Luckner and his *Seeadler*, and countless legends, was a special occasion, because Tahiti is a very special place.

I think Velda captured the sentiment for all when, as we were sailing through the pass, she murmured, "I never thought I would be sailing into Tahiti in my own boat!"

We were assigned a berth off the boulevard south of town, near the canoe sheds. We were required to moor Tahiti style, perpendicular to the beach with our bow out. Instead of being tied next to a cement quay, our stern was about 50 feet from a steep gravel beach that separated us from the road. Our stern lines ran to cast iron bollards less than a 100 yards away, sunk in the ground at 100 foot intervals along the road. We relied on our anchors to hold us perpendicular to the shoreline.

Fresh water was available from water taps attached to pipe showers that dotted the beach at the same intervals as the bollards. These conveniences were wonderful, but they weren't free. We paid 4,200 C.P. francs per month (U.S. $30.00) for them.

A Polynesian family lived under a half dozen sheets of rusty corrugated iron and carefully arranged cardboard boxes on the beach directly behind us. We enjoyed their company. So did Cap. He was always ready to say hello, particularly when the children were in the water, which was most of the time. We never got beyond the smiling and waving stage because other, more momentous events were on our immediate horizon.

A Canadian boat named *Daydream* was in the slot next to us. We had met her owners, Charlie and Pauline, earlier in Taiohae Bay, and now they helped us organize ourselves. Even before we settled in, Charlie broke the unpleasant news that French meteorologists were tracking a cyclone, already at hurricane strength, which appeared to be bearing down on Tahiti. They called it *Veena*.

Hurricane or no, on arriving in Tahiti, our first quest was for a grocery store. I don't mean to disparage Maurice McKittrick, or the Marquesan people who treated us to local fruits and vegetables, including avocados the size of footballs, but there are only so many things you can do with canned mussels, and I thought it very unlikely that the chicken here would be freezer burned.

Using Corser's guide book, we found a neat little supermarket only two blocks from our mooring. The store was well stocked. It's well that we replenished our stores while we had the opportunity, because by April tenth, there was no doubt whether Tahiti would be hit by the approaching hurricane.

The French were magnificent in their response. Shortly after lunch, a young English–speaking French naval officer and an enlisted man carrying a clip board came walking down the beach, hailing each yacht in turn. They came to *Prospector*.

"Are you the *capitaine*?" The young officer asked.

"*Yes*," I said.

"Are you aware of the impending cyclone?"

"*Yes*," I said again.

"Do you have sufficient anchors and ropes to make yourself secure?"

I was surprised. Unexpectedly, the French Navy was actually offering to lend ground tackle to foreigners, if necessary. I couldn't help but wonder whether, if our situation were reversed, American officials would have been that generous. "I think so," I said.

The enlisted man was writing my responses. The young officer smiled and waved his hand. "I wish you good fortune," he said, and they walked on to the next boat.

Possibly because of the large number of foreign boats in port, the French extended another courtesy. They began translating the radio and television weather updates into English. For the benefit of those who could not receive commercial broadcasts, a French-Canadian yachtsman began reading the weather bulletins in English over channel 16 on the VHF radio.

We now had to make serious, and possibly irrevocable, decisions. I couldn't make those decisions alone. Velda and Sylvia were involved, since their lives, too, were at risk. We urged Sylvia, somewhat halfheartedly, I confess, to stay ashore and seek shelter where she would be safe. I was privately relieved when she refused to consider it. Then we had to make a conscious decision whether to go to sea, although in Papeete, with its sturdy seawall, for me, that wasn't a serious question.

Of course, not all ports were as secure as ours. Jack and Ritva Curley, on board *Kulkuri*, were in Ahe, in the Tuamotus, when the alarm sounded. Jack successfully took *Kulkuri* to sea. Dirk Winters was in the same situation, and he took *Windjob* to sea.

The only other serious decision we had to make, since we had no intention of going to sea, was whether to leave the beach and take a chance on our ground tackle, hoping to snag the hurricane chain in the harbor. About half the fleet did just that.

I tried to estimate our vulnerability to the expected winds. If we went into the harbor, no matter what direction the hurricane took, there was no doubt we would catch hell. But on the beach, as I saw it, there were three possibilities.

We were lying facing the northwest. We were protected by the town to the northeast, a high hill behind us to the southeast, and a curving beach to the south and southwest. If *Veena* passed north of the island, we would be in the so-called **navigable** semicircle, and the winds would be north, northeast, east, southeast and southwest in that order, mostly coming over the hill behind us.

On the other hand, if the hurricane passed south of the island, the winds would back from the north, through the northwest, to the southwest as the storm went past. In that case, we would be in the *dangerous* semicircle (with winds from 20 to 40 knots higher depending on the hurricane's speed). Since we were exposed to the northwestern quadrant, with nearly a mile of fetch before us, we would be totally reliant on our anchors to hold us off the beach, with little margin for error. However, as I reminded Velda, we still had the 75 pound C.Q.R. that had saved us in the gale in Great Bay, and I didn't see how the weather could possibly be worse than that.

The third alternative would be that unhappy situation where the hurricane rolled right over us. If that were to happen, we would experience a rising northeast gale, followed by a calm, and an abrupt reversal of the winds to the southwest. In our present location, we were well sheltered from the northeast, and only marginally exposed to the southwest.

We couldn't completely avoid risk, no matter what we did, but it seemed clear to me that we would be better off to stay where we were because we were sheltered from the strongest winds, and had serious worries only if the storm passed to the south. Moreover, those cast iron bollards on the beach looked as sturdy as anything we were likely to find in the harbor. Velda and Sylvia endorsed my proposal that we stay where we were.

I carried the 75 pound C.Q.R. anchor with the 300 foot, three-quarter inch nylon rode in the dinghy as far as possible to the northwest, about 30 degrees from the 60 pound Danforth, which was already well set, and dropped it overboard. Then, back on board, I hauled on the rode with the anchor windlass until it refused to come any further. Then we stripped off the sails and carried them below with the awning, jerry jugs, and anything else that we thought might blow overboard.

We tied the boom securely to the gallows frame, and brought the storm trysail up and lashed it to the mast. If my reasoning was flawed, or if the northerly weather overwhelmed our anchors, that little bullet-proof sail might be our only chance to save the boat. The engine might help the rudder, but 40 horsepower is no match for 100+ knots of wind. We were putting a great deal of reliance on our ground tackle. Not to the extent our friends out in the harbor did, but I couldn't see a better alternative.

We brought the dinghy aboard and secured it under double lashings where it would protect the galley hatch. The latest forecasts predicted that gale force winds would begin shortly after midnight. I decided to start the engine at regular intervals during the night to make sure it would start if we needed it.

Velda prepared her favorite crisis dinner: spaghetti. You can eat it hot or cold, and there are always leftovers. The radio was left on, and we listened with half an ear to the nervous chatter of our fellows. Some of those who had abandoned the beach were having second thoughts. Rumors about the weather, about other boats, and so forth, flew back and forth. The slightly accented voice of the Canadian from Quebec interrupted the noise.

"I have the latest weather bulletin," he said quietly. The silence was instantaneous. He then read the ominous weather report. *Veena* was on schedule. The French naval frigate *Commander Bory* had been sent out to monitor the approaching storm. Armed with her findings, the French weather bureau predicted the hurricane would pass slightly to the north of the island, and the authorities urged people living on the coasts to leave their homes, and seek shelter in designated safe buildings.

We silently stood in the cockpit, each wrapped in our own thoughts. For once the traffic on the boulevard was still. It seemed as if everyone was looking and listening, and except for the radio, being very quiet so as not to attract attention. I found that as it grew darker, we began conversing in whispers. Apparently, we're not so far from the Tikis after all!

This, I imagined, was the proverbial calm before the storm. It was *very* calm. The water was glassy, and city lights reflected from it in shimmering, glistening streaks of color. With the last hope of reprieve gone, the nervous chatter of our colleagues on the radio became even more brittle.

We re-established our watch schedule. I was concerned about people off watch getting adequate rest. Lying awake in the dark worrying about tomorrow was a poor way to prepare for it. I passed around two mg. Valium tablets, not neglecting to take one myself. I asked to be called as soon as the wind began to blow.

It was just before midnight when I felt a hand on my arm and saw the muted beam of a covered flashlight. "The wind is just beginning," I recognized Sylvia's English accent. "I think it's nor'east," she added.

I grunted an acknowledgement, and sat up, reaching for my pants. The night was over as far as I was concerned. Velda started to get up. "I want to watch this," I said. "Why don't you get some more rest? I'll call you if I need help."

Sylvia was right. The wind was northeast, unmistakable evidence that the center of the storm was almost due north. By this time, Velda had joined us in the cockpit.

By one o'clock, the wind had risen to 40 knots, still coming over our starboard quarter. Everything seemed under control, and I decided to try for more rest. Neither Velda nor Sylvia wanted to leave the cockpit.

Velda urgently roused me just before daylight. "The big schooner's coming down on us," she said.

Not bothering to dress, I rushed up to the cockpit. Even as I passed through the cabin, I could hear the shriek and moan of wind in the rigging, and the pounding of halyards against the mast. The storm was upon us.

A Danish schooner anchored immediately north of us, was in trouble. Like us, she had planned to ride the storm out stern to the shore, but being in a more exposed position, her anchors were apparently dragging.

She was less than 50 feet away and in imminent danger of swinging into us and ultimately fouling our anchors. The wind, by now, was up to 50 or 60 knots, still blowing across our starboard quarter.

Cupping my hands to my mouth, I tried yelling, but the words were lost in the shrieking wind. The captain had only one choice, and I prayed that he was seaman enough to recognize it. Almost too late, he ran to the stern, and I watched him cut through his stern lines. In the meanwhile, his all-girl crew was readying fenders in case he crashed into us. Even then, despite the excitement and poor light, I noticed that the three girls were stark naked. But so was I.

The last strand on his stern line parted, and instantly her stern began to swing out, barely grazing our topsides as she turned. Her anchors apparently were fouled, because the boat quickly drifted out to the harbor. I later learned that she had snagged the hurricane chain and rode out the rest of the storm safe as houses.

"Safe as houses," that morning, was an unfortunate metaphor. There was nothing safe about the houses on Tahiti. Standing in the cockpit with our backs to the wind, we had front row seats to the devastation occurring around us.

As the wind reached 100 knots with stronger gusts, we saw whole roofs rise in the air and go spinning out into the harbor. Glittering, whirling, corrugated sheets of aluminum and iron roofing flew in a deadly blizzard over the boats at anchor.

Prospector shuddered under the hammering those gusts inflicted on her masts and rigging. There wasn't a thing we could do now except hang on. It wouldn't even have been safe to leave the security of the cockpit without a life harness.

I watched the third floor of an apartment building across the street disintegrate. The rupture began in a cornice, where the wind had worried loose some tiles. Once a hole was open, it was only a few moments before the roof seemed to explode.

A stream of debris — tiles, insulation, personal effects, and anything that might have been stored there — sailed off into the harbor. When the roof was gone, the leeward side of the building began to bulge outward; the windows disappeared. It was only then I remembered that people lived in those rooms, and I was suddenly concerned for their safety.

We lost track of time. Daylight came almost unnoticed. The storm was at its savage height and we were shouting to each other to be heard over the roar of the wind and the incessant clamor of things ashore crashing into each other.

Sylvia pointed to the church across the road directly behind us. I followed her gaze, and as a fresh gust tore at the trees lining the boulevard behind us, I saw the bell-steeple of the Protestant Church tremble and begin teetering. If that thing landed in our cockpit, we wouldn't have had a prayer. What an ironic end. Imagine how the

147

Tikis would have laughed! There wasn't a thing we could do about that tower, except get out of its way if it became airborne. But that was only a sideshow. The real dramas were being enacted in the harbor. It must have been crazy out there. The yachts were listing about 40 degrees under the constant pressure of the wind.

Gusts of 150 knots were blowing across the harbor. One would skim water off the surface, temporarily obscuring everything downwind. Gradually, the boats would reappear through the mist, and slowly, like tired old pensioners, bringing themselves back to their original list. It's hard to imagine how the people on those boats survived the hammering the winds inflicted on them.

A small tugboat, smaller than many yachts around it, worked without pause, energetically pulling dragging yachts apart, helping other yachts re-anchor, and towing those that had lost their ground tackle to a dock where the crew could save themselves if not their boat. I'm not sure whether the tug belonged to the Navy or the harbor master. It doesn't matter. It was one thing to be out there hoping to save your boat because it was all you had in this world, and quite another to be out there risking your life to save other people's boats. The agency that owned that tug, and the heroic crew manning her, richly deserved the appreciation of the yachting community.

Yachts were not the only vessels in trouble. The wind had gotten behind the bow of a big container ship, *Nedlloyd Korea*, tied to the International Terminal across the bay. Her headlines, probably doubled and tripled, had carried away.

The determined effort of a big 12,000 horsepower tug pushing on her bow was the only thing that kept her from being blown away from the dock and swinging like a huge scythe, obliterating anything in her path, possibly even destroying the Navy Yard.

Dirk Winters was also in trouble. Early in the afternoon of *Veena*, as the storm was beginning to abate, someone heard a faint broadcast over the nervous chatter on the radio. It sounded serious so someone uttered the magic word *"Mayday!"*

Instantly, the chatter stilled. Faintly we heard, "Hello, hello, hello. This is Dirk Winters on *Windjob*. I'm about 30 miles northeast of Point Venus. I've just been through another hurricane, my sails are gone, my rigging is slack, and I'm tired. I'm all alone, and I'm 76 years old. Goodby."

The French also heard Dirk's message, and within 20 minutes, the *Commander Bory* was standing out of the pass. Shortly before dark, the *Bory* found *Windjob*. Despite what must have been mountainous seas, the *Bory* launched a Zodiac with three spirited volunteers. Somehow, those young Frenchmen got themselves on board *Windjob* — frankly, I don't see how — and found Dirk on deck. They urged him to go below. "We see what we can do," they said.

When Dirk came back on deck, it was still dark, but those young men had repaired the rigging and jury-rigged some sail, and the boat was slowly making way back to Papeete.

By daylight, that strange little convoy — the crippled old wooden ketch, and the *Commander Bory* guarding her like a jealous mother hen — was standing off the pass. *Windjob's* jury rig was not equal to bringing her through the breakwater.

"If ze *Bory* tow you," one young man said, "Ze Navy charge ten percent of ze boat for salvage. But if one of your frens come, it cost you nozzing."

Dirk made another call. A big American motor sailor named *Baranita* — she was another boat we had seen in Costa Rica — went out to give Dirk a hand. Later, the officers of the *Bory* gave Dirk a dinner party. That gallant old gentleman genuinely deserved it.

By late afternoon, *Veena* was history, and people began assessing the damage. Incredibly, only one life was lost. After the storm was over, a little girl tragically came into contact with a live wire and was electrocuted.

Three days later, Betty and Gary Parker, co-captains of the California ketch, *Calaveras*, whom we had met in Taiohae Bay, invited us to join them for a drive around the island. We gladly accepted. The French Army had done a monumental job clearing away the rubble, but the surviving palms were still wearing broken window frames and twisted sheets of galvanized roofing.

The most bizarre thing we saw was a housing project on the east coast. For blocks, all that remained of what apparently had been single family bungalows were scores of neatly spaced cement slabs, each with properly installed toilets and refrigerators. Everything else; walls, roofs, partitions, furniture, personal possessions, even the kitchen sinks, was gone.

The poultry industry was destroyed. It was reported that 20,000 chickens had been killed. While people amused themselves asking how long it would take the feathers to circle the earth, it was months before eggs were available anywhere but under the counter to friends and relatives.

Roughly 50 yachts suffered serious damage, despite that heroic little tugboat. Seven boats anchored inside the reef down by the airport were blown up on the reef, another one was photographed with its bow in a hotel cabana. Some yachts sank.

Boats that had been taken to the dock were in particularly bad shape. Fiberglass is no match for cement bulkheads or sharp metal. I saw two fiberglass boats that looked as if they had been flayed on one side. A dozen small wooden fishing boats were overwhelmed by the seas in the harbor, and had sunk at the customs dock. Masts rising from the water near the Navy Yard marked the resting place of a big ketch that had holed herself by rubbing against a sharp corner of a copra schooner's stern.

A row of sailboats up on the hard in the Government boatyard were knocked over domino-style when the roller jib on the windward boat accidently opened during the storm.

Four days later, we learned about Hurricane *William*, then forming in the same area where *Veena* had been born. *William* worried us, but fortunately, he died in infancy. He was the *sixth* hurricane in French Polynesia during 1983.

The French were as well organized cleaning up as they had been trying to minimize damage during the storm. The fishing boats were lifted by a portable crane, and repaired on the spot by their owners.

A floating crane was sent to the reef, and the yachts that could float were returned to the water; the others were loaded on a barge and taken to level ground near the ferry dock where they were blocked up so that repairs could be made. The authorities even ran electric power to the impromptu repair yard for the convenience of the vessel owners.

After the hurricane, our Polynesian neighbors accumulated additional building materials, which I think may been a serious error. It probably elevated their profile to an unacceptable level because their pile of roofing materials and cardboard now looked too prosperous and permanent. The gendarmes chased them away. We were sorry to see them go, even though we never got beyond the smiling and waving stage. I don't know if they spoke English, but I'm sure we could have communicated.

The people on every island in the South Pacific have a story to tell. If you want history, there are many places, like the Marquesas, where the present is more involved with the past, than it is in Tahiti. Papeete epitomizes the modern South Pacific. Most island-countries in the South Pacific reflect a blend of ancient and modern cultures enriched by successive waves of immigration, but I doubt if any have succeeded as well as Tahiti in accommodating and assimilating the diverse and frequently conflicting cultural mores of its settlers. I don't mean to suggest this has occurred without stress. We heard many complaints directed toward the Chinese community – Chinese storekeepers in particular – but the assimilation process appears to be well advanced.

Three widely diverse cultures, French, Polynesian, and Chinese, complement and enrich one another. In fact, if you confined yourself to Papeete, and didn't know better, you might think yourself in a bustling small city in the south of France where all the clerks and customers were Chinese and Polynesian.

Ubiquitous motor-scooters, often with two passengers, whizzed back and forth on the boulevard, the staccato roar of their exhausts almost lost in the cacophonous din of a modern city. Yet for all the noise and confusion, the people you meet on the street are gentle, friendly, and courteous. I was always warmed by the murmured "*Bon jour*" with which passersby almost invariably greeted me.

Nearly every evening and on weekends, cars and scooters were parked on the shoulder of the boulevard near our mooring, while their owners engaged in a sport rooted deep in Polynesian culture. Every evening at sundown, we watched canoes carrying 15 to 20 paddlers glide across the still water, their wakes a burnished and rippling mass of color, reflecting the reds, purples and yellows in the clouds and the setting sun. With the contrasting irregular silhouette of Moorea in the background, the scene was both a living postcard and a step back to prehistoric times.

As we listened to the ancient chants floating across the still water and watched the precision of deeply thrust paddles driving those fragile craft forward, we didn't need to understand the language to feel goose bumps rise. I had much the same reaction to those races as I had at a deeper level of my subconscious to the primitive and erotic rhythms of the Polynesian *tamure*.

But when we went downtown, we found little evidence of that

early culture. The city reflected a European heritage rather than a Polynesian ambience. Logic rather than emotion had dictated the way Papeete was laid out. When we climbed the five-foot bank beyond the gravel beach behind *Prospector* to the sidewalk paralleling Boulevard Pomare, named for a prominent Polynesian king, we left one society and entered another.

Upon reaching the sidewalk, when we were heading downtown from the boat, we would turn left and follow the boulevard along the waterfront for three blocks until we came to tiny de Gaulle park on the right. Across the street was a block of small restaurants, shops, travel agencies and other storefront businesses. Coco's Bar was on the second floor of a building on the corner directly across the boulevard. Bougainville Park occupied the next block, and in the block after that, we'd come to the post office. The modernistic Viama Center, in the heart of Papeete, was two blocks further north.

Most people going to town stopped first at the post office in case someone had sent money. English was not universally spoken, but the *Post Restante* line was easy to find. You looked for people wearing tattered sneakers, ragged cutoffs, torn shirts, and sunglasses.

The clerks sometimes had difficulty with our names. I found it useful to present a card with our names (and the boat's name) spelled out in block letters with our passports.

The French revere their history. When you walked past the park you had to walk around two naval cannon eternally pointing toward the harbor pass and mounted in such a way that they stuck out over the sidewalk at knee height. I can only guess that they were placed in that awkward way so you avoided noticing them only at serious peril to your knee caps.

The older of the two was an antique naval cannon with a bell muzzle, cast in 1879. It was recovered from a French gunboat that was scuttled in 1914 to block the pass into Papeete harbor, thus preventing two German cruisers from entering the harbor and sacking the town. The strategy was successful. In frustration, the Germans shelled Papeete before they left, destroying a few houses and killing two people.

Although the second gun was also a World War I relic, it was of a much more modern design. It came from the famous German "Q" ship *Seeadler*, commanded by Captain Count Felix von Luckner during the latter part of that war.

Seeadler was a sailing ship, disguised as a Norwegian lumber carrier, and was sent to the South Pacific to sink Allied merchant ships. She had a remarkable career. Although she sank 14 Allied ships, her activities cost only one life. One of her crewmen was killed when an intended victim unexpectedly opened fire. She hoodwinked British patrol officers more than once. She was lost when a hurricane caught her careened on Huahine. Her captain, Count von Luckner, was decorated after the War by the French for his humanitarianism. He lived out his days on Tahiti.

Daydream, our next–door neighbor, left to return to Canada. Her place was taken by a big German steel Colin Archer ketch named *Atair II*. My introduction to her people was prophetic.

I was sitting in our cockpit, admiring our new neighbor's classic lines, when I realized she was a lot closer to us than she should have been. A slender young woman was bustling about her deck, and suddenly I realized she was rigging fenders to cushion an apparently inevitable collision between our boats.

I quickly called to her, asking if she had another anchor. She did, but it was buried in the forepeak. She was alone, so I put our spare anchor in the dinghy and carried it out to windward from our new neighbor, and after dropping it, passed the bitter end of the rode up to the woman. Then,

Atair II

after climbing aboard, I helped haul her boat away from *Prospector*.

That's how we met Babs and Klaus Kurz. They are lovely people. She is slender and attractive and he is a big, handsome man with an engaging personality. They are a good deal younger than we, but he is even more of a romantic than I.

It will be a long time before I forget the reverent look on his face when, as I was showing him around and we were walking to the post office, I introduced him to the gun from *Seeadler*. I didn't know then that he had served aboard the German Navy's sail training ship. Now I can understand why that gun had almost religious significance for him.

At first, after I told him the gun's origin, he didn't believe me. Then, after reading the proof marks on the gun's breech, all he could say was, "Is it really from *Seeadler*, Denny? Really?" He read the proof marks again, and stroked the barrel. "*Seeadler*," he said quietly, almost reverently.

Klaus's arrival dovetailed perfectly with the end of the hurricane season, and if we thought the harbor was crowded when we had arrived, it was now jam-packed. By Bastille Day, July 14, there may have been over 200 yachts in the harbor. I can't tell you from personal experience because by that time I was in the hospital, and the view from my window was limited to the vacant lot next door.

Most of us have physical weaknesses with which we have learned to live. The problem may lie dormant, possibly even forgotten, until one day you wake up to an unpleasant surprise. That's what happened to me.

My weakness, as I have mentioned before, stems from an old war wound. I woke up one morning to discover a bright red rash on the inside of my right thigh extending from the shrapnel scar just below my groin down to a point about four inches above my knee. It was very painful, and it was obvious that I needed a doctor.

With Velda's help, I hobbled across the street and down the block to the *Clinique Piofai*. The doctor diagnosed my problem as phlebitis. He prescribed antibiotics and alcohol soaks. As he predicted, the symptoms disappeared in about five days.

But I'm a worrier. I remembered that President Nixon had a bout of phlebitis while in office, and I recalled much concern about the possibility of a blood clot coming adrift and lodging in his lung, heart, or brain. I didn't know of any reason why I wasn't equally at risk, so I took what I thought was a reasonable precaution.

Since there was no doubt in my mind whether this attack was related to the old war wound, I was certain the Veteran's Administration was responsible for necessary medical care. The nearest VA facility was in Honolulu. Consequently, I decided to go to Honolulu for help. We had enough cash on hand for a one-way ticket, so I called Buz and asked him to send $2,500 to me in Honolulu, bought an airplane ticket, and flew to Hawaii.

The Veteran's Clinic sent me out to the Tripler Army Medical Center. The doctor there assured me that no clots could come adrift in my case. However, he pointed to a lump next to my shin on the same leg that looked like an extra shin.

"What's that?" He asked.

I didn't know. It had been there a such long time, I'd grown accustomed to it. Out of curiosity, he had it X-rayed. He and the radiologist concluded it was merely a calcified muscle, nothing to worry about.

A week later, five days after I returned to Tahiti, I woke to a throbbing pain in my lower leg. I thought the phlebitis had returned. But wise to the ways of the VA, before I went back to the *Clinique Piofai*, I insisted that Velda call the VA doctor in Honolulu for prior authorization. I knew that without that authorization, no matter what the circumstances, I would likely have to pay the bill.

Velda obtained a verbal authorization. Armed with that, and with Velda and Klaus' help, I hobbled back across the street to the French clinic. The doctors quickly assured me that I was not experiencing another phlebitis attack. They were interested in that "calcified muscle," and took a much closer look than the American Army doctors had.

Then I was tucked into bed in a private room. Almost everyone spoke a little English, the Polynesians more than the Europeans. I mention this so you will understand that what follows may have lost something in translation. I had barely settled in my new quarters when I received the first of many injections.

Shots and hospitals, like a horse and carriage, go together. But shots in the abdomen? Every six hours, right around the clock? Starting at four in the afternoon, then at ten at night, and four the next morning, I could expect a shy nurse's aid, a local girl, to come tiptoeing into my room, turn back the covers exposing a bit of abdomen, and zap!

You can bet I raised the question with the doctor the next day, and I think he said something to the effect that this medicine was a sure way of defeating thick blood. Well, the needle was a short one that barely penetrated the skin, and philosophically, I suppose it's better to get stomach shots than watch them attach leeches.

Three days later, the doctor decided to do a biopsy on that calcified muscle. The next day, I was wheeled into the operating room and a needle was shoved in my arm. The next thing I knew, somebody was shaking me, trying to wake me up, and I was doing my groggy best to oblige them. When I became aware of my surroundings, I realized I was in the "recovery room," which, in the pragmatic French way, was the hall outside the nurse's station.

During the next few days, while waiting for a pathology report, my doctor explained that what the doctors in Hawaii had mistakenly thought was a calcified muscle was really a tumor about the size of a Polish sausage that had to be removed. Every day when the nurse changed the dressing over the biopsy wound, it appeared be oozing pink tooth paste. Ug! No wonder I wasn't feeling well. There was no question about it. Whatever it was, it had to be fixed.

Four days later, the chief surgeon, Dr. Blanquart, came into my room, bringing with him a young woman from the business office who was reasonably fluent in English. First, he described the pathologist's report.

As I understood it, that tumor had acted like a oil filter, straining and accumulating all the vile things to which my body had been exposed during the previous 40 years. For instance, although I lived for several years in an Eskimo village where TB was rampant, I never had the disease. But they found TB bacillus in the tumor.

He had scheduled my surgery for the day after tomorrow. At about that same time, I discovered through the hospital grapevine that the chief surgeon's wife was going to have her new baby in Honolulu. As a prospective surgery patient, I found that troubling. It didn't seem to reflect much confidence in the clinic. I consoled myself that I was not having brain surgery, and I was sure that removing a tumor from a lower leg couldn't be that complicated.

It was interesting to compare this hospital with similar American institutions. While hospitals everywhere have basic similarities, there are also differences. For instance, I was disappointed in the food. I had expected much better, considering that this was a French hospital. But it was as dreary as any I had in American hospitals, civilian or military. But some of the differences were startling.

In an American hospital, during the evening before your surgery, your loved ones would be asked to step out in the hall while the lab technician withdrew a blood sample. Also, in an American hospital, about halfway through that fateful evening, a young doctor dressed in casual clothes will stroll into your room and look at your chart. The more suspicious ones will verify what they have just read.

"Are you Mr. Moore?"

This was your anesthetist. You would hope he was better at his job than he was at making small talk. Now that he was sure who you were, after introducing himself, and perching casually on the edge of your bed, he would begin by saying with false cheerfulness, "This is what we'll be doing tomorrow morning,"

There was none of that medical glad-handing in a French hospital. There were no frills at all. They didn't even take my blood pressure. As for allergies, well, we can hope for the best.

However, the functional differences between American and French hospital procedures are most apparent on the morning of the surgery. In both cases, you would be cautioned against eating or drinking anything. But your craving for coffee in an American hospital would be blunted by a nice little shot that immeasurably improved your attitude. Evidently, the way the French look at it, a shot before breakfast is for sissies. They want you to have the full experience, I suppose, so you'll feel you got your money's worth.

Two big guys in green suits wheeled a hospital cart into my room about ten o'clock. I flopped over on it, and they covered me with the sheet. Off we went. Did you ever notice how strange a hospital looks when it is seen upside down? I had never noticed it in an American hospital, but neither had I ever made that journey awake or entirely sober.

Judging by the way my heart was beating, my senses were functioning at about 150 percent efficiency. I was fascinated by the collection of pipes and wires in the ceiling. We took an elevator ride. I don't know whether we went up or down, but soon we were rumbled along a passageway where no attempt had been made to conceal the plumbing. Eventually, we arrived in a small room next to padded double doors. We were early, and had to wait some 15 minutes. I'll leave it to your imagination what was passing through my mind at that point.

I had heard, of course, of hospitals becoming so contaminated with strange and virulent forms of streptococcus, that the only way they could clean them up was by burning them down. Why *had* Dr. Blanquart send his wife to Honolulu to have her baby?

157

Things happened fast, once the padded doors opened and I was wheeled into the operating room. The table was extremely narrow. I was prevented from falling when my arms were lashed to outriggers that projected at right angles from the table.

Like matadors entering the bullring, the doctors came in, en masse. Dr. Blanquart was gowned but not yet masked. He came over, looked down at me for a moment, smiled and said "*Bon jour.*" The anesthetist stuck a needle in my arm while someone else fitted a tourniquet around my thigh. There was something terribly important I needed to tell them; the tourniquet had reminded me, but the anesthetist, seeing my agitation and thinking I was merely frightened, patted my arm reassuringly.

I was trying to think of a way I could tell the anesthetist this vital information in words he would understand, but he was looking at Dr. Blanquart. There was none of this "I want you to count backwards from ten to zero" business. The man standing at my shoulder received a signal from the surgeon, nodded and pulled the trigger. My last waking thought was that I was the only person in that room who knew my blood type.

I have always thought of myself as a robust specimen, but I went into serious shock as I was coming out of the anesthetic. Velda was there to take care of me, so they had put me back in my bed rather than leave me in their impromptu "recovery" room. Velda knows when I'm in trouble, and she kept piling the blankets on, and finally crawled into bed with me, to warm me with her body.

After that rocky beginning, I healed rapidly, and the stitches were removed ten days later.

The difference between French and American practices lie in those little things like crutches that we take for granted. I didn't realize until the day I was discharged, that the French didn't loan them out like some American hospitals did. If you wanted crutches, you bought them. Otherwise, if you have a leg injury and needed to go to the toilet, you could hop, hobble, crawl, or do what I did; use a chair as a knee crutch and scoot the chair across the floor when the need arose. That practice inflicted a certain wear and tear on the chair and the floor tiles, but the staff didn't seem to care, and as far as I was concerned, *c'est la vie.*

Primarily because of the many nurse's aides, the nursing care was outstanding. Most of the girls were boarding students from outlying islands, living in the nearby Piofai Girl's Boarding School. They were mostly teenagers, and shy at first, but after they realized that I was not much different from other older males they knew, they treated me with friendly familiarity.

As I said, the food was barely adequate. One girl took a keen interest in making sure I cleaned my plate Her mock scolding seemed at times a bit over done. But how could I complain in the face of her obvious concern? That was another thing. Most of these girls had a better command of English than the professional staff. Yet even the professional staff seemed to enjoy small conversations with me in English. Of course, I was expected to reciprocate by trying my few words of French on them.

Dr. Blanquart was a fine doctor and a good surgeon; and the medical standards at *Clinique Piofai* were as good as any I have seen anywhere. The few problems I had were mostly a result of the language barrier and cross cultural expectations.

I was treated much better, I'm sorry to say, than the clinic was treated by the Veteran's Administration. I don't know about others, but I find it deeply offensive that a branch of my government would behave in a way that compelled me to feel ashamed of it. I only wish there were some way to punish those responsible. Unbelievably, in spite of the prior authorization, and even despite direct intervention by Congressman (now Speaker) Tom Foley, it took the VA over *three years* to pay that bill. Their delinquency had a direct adverse impact on us later because, knowing the bill had not been paid, we shied away from French ports fearing that *Prospector* might be seized.

Years ago, long before sexual harassment became popular, I worked with a young woman who remarked one day, apropos of nothing at all, "It ain't no good if it don't hurt a little." Maggie might have been talking about physiotherapy because physiotherapy hurts. If it doesn't, you're not trying hard enough. After the stitches came out, I began physiotherapy and continued it for almost a month. Its purpose is to stretch, tighten, strengthen and retrain muscles, nerves, joints and related parts.

The therapist, a young Frenchman named Emil, was glad to welcome an American into his domain because he had found an advertisement in an American sailing magazine offering to trade a health spa in Wyoming for a yacht suitable for world cruising. He owned a 41 foot ketch in wonderful condition, worth $100,000 to

$125,000, which was eminently suitable for world cruising, and he wanted to make an offer. I told him what little I knew about Wyoming, and helped prepare his proposal. We left before a deal was consummated. However, I remember the unlikely name of his yacht, and I'd like to hear about it if anyone out there sees a Wyoming sheepherder sailing a 41 foot Benateau named *Chocolate*.

Two young amputees came into physical therapy for treatment when I was there, and I asked Emil what had happened to them. He shook his head and said, "motorbikes and infections." He went on to explain that the kids in Tahiti were at greatest risk from traffic accidents. Motorbikes were very hard on legs.

The infection cases came from the Marquesas, the Tuamotus, the Gambiers and the outlying Societies. As Emil put it, "Ze kids get ze scratch from ze coral. Mama treats it with a banana skin and poof! Big infection. By ze time they come here, eet is too late. Leg goes, or kid dies."

Each patient was interested in the progress the other patients were making. And it wasn't just a case of misery loving company. The group interest and concern was genuine and supportive. That's how I met Jacque Longines. His business card indicated that he was an expediter of some sort, but he was injured when he slid off a tile roof he was repairing. I imagine expediting has its slow days.

He had a back injury. His doctor couldn't find the cause of his constant pain, and Jacque was very discouraged. I've been around orthopedic wards enough to know how tricky it can be to diagnose some back injuries, and I wanted to help him, if I could.

Jacque was a good cook. Velda and I enjoyed several delicious dinners in his home. He came by that skill honestly, since he was a living embodiment of Tahiti, being approximately one third Chinese, one third French and one third Polynesian. He showed us a side of Polynesia that few tourists see.

One evening as we stopped at a traffic light, while Jacque was driving us back to the boat, two young men, heavily made up and in drag, walked across the street in front of us, holding hands.

"Am I seeing what I think I'm seeing?" I asked.

Jacque smiled. "Oh, yes," he said. "That sort of thing is common here."

Now that it was pointed out to me, there did seem to be an

extraordinary number of effeminate Polynesians clerking in the stores, waiting on tables, and hanging out in the bars. I asked Jacque if he could explain why. I had assumed earlier that what I saw was merely the overflow from San Francisco. When I told him that, he laughed and shook his head.

"Most of these young men are local," he said. "They were raised that way." He went on to explain that when a family had too many boys, and they desired a girl, the next born, regardless of sex, would be raised as a female. This practice, I later learned, was common in the central South Pacific.

I persuaded Buzzy and my sister–in–law (who was then a Public Health nurse in King County) to invite Jacque for a visit to Seattle, and help him get a proper examination and possible treatment at the University of Washington School of Medicine. They graciously extended an invitation, which he accepted. He spent three weeks with them. Jo, Buzzy's wife, arranged the appropriate examinations, and I'm glad to say the specialists found the problem.

Papeete was a great place to meet people. While I was in the hospital, Velda brought two visitors, red–headed Tom Lemm, and his partner, D.L. Benton. They were co–owners of the steel pinky schooner *Le Papillion*, which they had built in Baltimore. D.L., as she is known, did the rigging, while Tom did the welding.

Velda brought them to the hospital because she knew I would enjoy meeting them. After I was back on my feet, I met Roger and Molly Firey. *Sundowner*, their Westsail 32, had replaced *Atair II* in the berth next to us while I was in the hospital. Roger was a retired Naval officer, and a first rate sailor.

Hans and Elly Lutt, the Dutch couple on the lovely steel sloop *Solitair*, were also there. We had met them originally in Puntarenas. Another Puntarenas couple and fellow Alaskans, Roger and Cleon O'Brian on board *Robrian*, were tied near us. The influx of yachts was so great that the spillover extended well past the canoe sheds.

Dirk Winters was determined to complete his second circumnavigation, and was having extensive work done on *Windjob*. He hired Sylvia and another girl, Diane from New Zealand, to paint the interior of his boat.

Diane had an interesting story to tell. We had met her in Taiohae Bay shortly after we arrived. She was part of a crew that had quit their boat *en masse* in Taiohae Bay, leaving the skipper stranded.

Since the hurricanes were still threatening, she failed to find another yacht headed for Tahiti, so she booked passage on a copra schooner. That proved to be an awful mistake. The first night out, the cook strangled a dog and cooked it for dinner.

Diane was not the sort of person who held things in. She promptly called upon the captain, demanding a refund of that portion of her fare that paid for her board.

The captain insisted that the dog was intended only for the crew, that the passengers had a different menu, but Diane stood her ground and eventually got a refund and spent the next three days fasting. As it turned out, so did everyone else, because they ran into hurricane Sara.

I find it unbelievable that the captain would have taken his tired little motorship into the very teeth of a hurricane. One unfortunate passenger was washed overboard and lost. It was miraculous that the vessel wasn't lost.

Sylvia could never stand still. If she didn't have two or three things going on, she wasn't happy. While the girls were still painting Dirk's boat, Sylvia was cutting a deal with Coco and Victoria.

Coco was a Polynesian, and Victoria was his American wife. They owned Coco's Bar upstairs in the building on Boulevard Pomare, directly across the street from de Gaulle park.

Sylvia began promoting the bar along the waterfront by distributing crudely mimeographed handbills advertising free drinks and extended happy hours. As enthusiastic as Sylvia could be, she cajoled and harangued the boat people personally and individually, all but dragging them off the sidewalk. The bar was convenient for yachties, and although it had long been patronized by them, after Sylvia moved in, it became the only yachtie bar in town.

She was the perfect bar hostess. She greeted you by name at the door, made sure you met everyone in the room, kept the drinks moving and the people happy. When things grew quiet, as they will in any bar, she would get the party moving again by singing in a slightly off-key voice an incredibly filthy parody of a well known sea chanty. She knew many of them.

Eventually, she and Diane signed on as part of a delivery crew for a big steel ketch, *Aldebaran*, built in Germany for the infamous Nazi Air Marshal, Hermann Goering. I never went on board, but the captain (who I met in Coco's — where else?) told me that her sailing abilities had been sacrificed for strength, and that the plating on her bottom was 14 millimeters thick! It's a wonder she floated.

Originally, *Aldebaran* was to have been delivered to her owner in Darwin, Australia. However, plans change, and the boat was diverted to the Philippines. She eventually wound up in Hong Kong, with Sylvia still on board.

Meanwhile, time was moving on. I was discharged from the hospital on August fifth, and after a brief convalescence, I began to stir around, getting things fixed that needed fixing, buying supplies and generally making ready to continue our voyage toward the setting sun. I was still open-minded on the subject of circumnavigation. Still, I agreed that New Zealand would be the absolute, no waffling, no turning back, point of decision.

Just before we left Tahiti, Dr. Blanquart and his lovely wife, Elizabeth, came aboard *Prospector* for a visit. We almost talked them into sailing with us as far as Bora Bora. They had their new baby with them, and Madam Blanquart was all smiles as she held up her little **American** baby for our inspection.

At nine thirty, September fifth, Velda and I sadly sailed out of Papeete harbor bound for Bora Bora.

Prospector with a bone in her teeth

Chapter 7

From Cannibals to Caulkers

Bora Bora is 140 miles west from Tahiti. It is reputedly the most beautiful lagoon in the world. For that reason alone, it seemed foolish not to call there.

Two things about that lagoon stand out. First, the water was so clear it was almost transparent. Second, the lagoon is a terrible anchorage because the water is so deep. Hauling a chain and a 60 pound anchor through 90 feet of water is not fun.

We arrived off the pass on the western side of the lagoon at dusk. Rather than enter an unfamiliar lagoon in the gathering dark, we decided to heave-to and wait for morning.

The night was beautifully calm and lit with the rich shades of dark shadow and creamy light associated with a full moon. Until the moon set, the twin peaks of the main island, although slowly withdrawing to the east, were clearly visible.

We drifted about ten miles during the night, but the mountains were still in view at sunrise. We ran for three hours, bucking a light current, before we again stood off the pass.

The main island was directly in front of us as we went into the lagoon. We could see the sweeping curve of the palm fringed beach to the right, ending about two miles away in a small group of buildings, a cluster of boats, and a short dock.

Immediately to the right, as we cleared the pass, was a small motu (or islet). Three yachts were anchored in its lee. On our left was the main island, and as we motored along its beach, we slowly went past a Club Med, and abruptly came face to face with a large sign in English that said, FREE MOORINGS. Even though a sign like that might as well read "free ten dollar bills" to a suspicious yachtie, I decided to check into it.

The moorings — there were a half dozen, but only one with a boat on it — looked new. On the surface, they appeared to be substantial. A man stood on the dock watching us, and I slowed the engine, drifting near him.

"Does that sign mean what it says?" I yelled.

"Sure does," came the answer in unmistakable American accents. "Help yourself," he added generously.

I untied our boathook and fished a floating pennant out of the water. It took only a minute to bring the line on board and drop its eye over the Sampson posts. As soon as we had the dinghy in the water, I rowed over to thank our hosts and find out what free moorings cost.

The deal was on the level; we were the guests of a young American couple who had recently bought the OaOa Hotel, and who thought moored yachts would add to their South Seas ambiance. Also, not to be overlooked, yacht folk have been known to visit bars from time to time, and even to eat out occasionally. Greg and Elaine were wonderfully hospitable and friendly hosts. Lunches and dinners were delicious.

Unfortunately, because they were relative newcomers themselves, they were unable to help us locate a repairman who might have solved our continuing problem with the alternator.

Two days after we arrived, an Australian sloop named *Ardright* picked up the mooring directly behind us. After watching one of the two men aboard row back and forth to the hotel several times, I interrupted his homeward journey by hailing him and inviting him aboard for a drink.

Waving a bottle of Scotch whiskey is a great way to make friends. We were just getting acquainted with our new friend — his name was Mike Davidson — when he looked at his watch and abruptly excused himself. After hastily inviting us for a reciprocal visit, he dropped into his dinghy and rowed back to his boat.

I thought his behavior was peculiar and even a little rude, but I was oblivious that momentous events, particularly from an Australian yachtie's point of view, were occurring in the opposite hemisphere. I soon learned, however, that the America's Cup race, which the

Aussies eventually won, was underway. Mike was eager to hear the latest Australian sports news broadcast, which explained his hurry.

I'm one of those cranky people who find that the interests of the racing crowd in general, and the New York Yacht Club in particular, have little relevance for me. Instead of vicariously involving myself in a contest waged by millionaires dueling with 19th century toys fashioned from 21st century materials, I had serious and very real problems to solve.

The brush holder at the rear of our alternator housing had cracked, then broken, causing the brush holders to wobble. This was a fatal flaw in an alternator. Replacing the alternator in Bora Bora was out of the question, so Mike and I tried mechanical repairs, mostly involving large hose clamps, before we gave up.

I now think we may have given up too quickly. We should have tried modern chemistry. Marine-Tex is wonderful stuff – I've even repaired false teeth with it – and I think we might have been able to tie the housing together by molding the stuff around the end of the alternator. It would have been worth a try.

Inconvenient as a broken alternator housing may be, it can't begin to compare with the mental stresses imposed by running a diesel engine without *discernable* oil pressure. I knew the fault was in the gauge – it would have been insane to start the engine if I had seriously thought the engine was running without oil pressure. But even so, from a purely psychological point of view, it took a certain amount of courage and optimism to run a diesel with the oil pressure needle resting on zero.

How did I know the fault was in the gauge and not some vital part of the engine? A diesel engine will run a minute – possibly even two – without lubrication before it seizes up. Our Perkins had run for hours with the oil pressure needle resting on zero.

Still, it was foolish to run a diesel engine under those circumstances. *Relative* oil pressure provides a warning and can be symptomatic of various problems. You should always know what's going on under the hood, so to speak. Without that gauge, we were flying blind.

Actually, we were in a double bind. Starting the engine took a lot out of the batteries, and without the alternator, we had no way of replacing that electricity. I was sure we would want the engine when we arrived in Samoa. That meant we would have to save the batteries by doing without lights (except for the binnacle), without the Autohelm, and since we couldn't start the engine every day to drive the compressor, without refrigeration.

Ardright left the next day, but not before Mike and his deckhand kindly gave our bottom a scrub. After they left, we found that Mike had left behind in our cockpit a copy of an Australian yachting magazine, *Cruising Skipper*, which identified him as editor.

September was more than half gone. The door was closing on the 1983 cruising season. The next cyclone season was fast approaching. Much as we hated to do it, it was time to leave French Polynesia. We obtained our exit visas, presented them at the bank and retrieved our cash bonds. We said goodby to our hosts, and early on September 17, after ten days, we sailed off the mooring.

Regardless of the tide, the current in the pass at Bora Bora (and many similar lagoons) is always out-flowing. The wind was light but fair, and we ghosted through the pass, headed west for American Samoa, 1,200 miles away. Hand steering is not ordinarily hard work, but it is tedious, boring and always a waste of time. In selecting an automatic steering system, we had weighed and compared electrical and mechanical systems. I chose our Autohelm, an electrical system, for several reasons.

Being mindful of our outboard rudder, the shape of the transom, and the low overhanging mizzen boom, I didn't think we could accommodate a mechanical steering device. Even if we could, I knew a mechanical system would be more difficult to fit, cumbersome to operate, and would be twice as expensive as an electrical system. What I failed to take into account was that the mechanical system would be more reliable.

My inherent gullibility was as much to blame for that decision as my desire to find the most convenient solution. I *believed* those ads which boasted that single-handed racers successfully relied on Autohelms. I suppose those ads were accurate to a point, but half-truths can be more damaging than outright lies. I'm now told those single-handed racers carried several identical machines and changed them like you or I might change our socks.

If I had it to do over, I'd look long and hard at mechanical windvanes. The electrical Autohelm was husky enough for our old-fashioned wheel steering system, and it was convenient, but it was too delicate for our environment.

Speaking of lies, I suppose there are as many lies told about steering as there are concerning boat speeds and passage times. And why not? A *really* expert seaman (so I'm told) can trim the sails so the rudder is practically superfluous.

Of course he is long gone and can't defend himself, but who among us really believed Slocum's claim that he sailed the breadth of the Indian Ocean with scarcely a twitch of the tiller? Personally, I think that claim, like his assertion about boiling his alarm clock, was a sailor's yarn, intended to gull the gullible, and amuse the more knowledgeable.

Moreover, any self steering device is a mixed blessing because, like a case of rum, it is easily abused. The *first* rule of seamanship is to maintain the watch. That's why I think today's single-handed racing as a sport is like flagpole sitting; it's a good way to show off, and if you make a mistake, someone else will pay for the search and clean up the mess. Single-handed passage making, on the other hand, is more like riding a bicycle on a freeway. It begs the issue to argue that single handed cruising folk do not expect expensive rescue efforts if they get into trouble or that sailboats pose no threat to tankers. Real seamanship means accepting responsibility for your own survival; not pushing that responsibility off on the other guy.

Therefore, although the Central Pacific is a long way from more populated parts of the globe, and shipping is sufficiently sparse so I was comfortable running without lights, we *always* maintained regular watches whether the Autohelm was working or not.

It wasn't easy. Besides spending 12 hours every day on the wheel, Velda did the cooking, and maintained a regular meal schedule. I took the other 12 hours and did the navigation, sail changes and deck maintenance. I suppose that distribution of chores may seem chauvinistic, but it is not the time to experiment with roles when you are standing running watches — six on and six off — twice a day, seven days a week. That's when we must maximize our respective efficiencies. We were much more concerned with survival than with whose turn it was to wash the dishes. Velda is a better and more efficient cook than I. I was stronger, and at that time I was the better navigator. That's all that mattered.

People have varying sleep needs. I've read about Edison and other compulsive geniuses who regarded sleep as time lost, but most of them are dead, and I have never designed a watch bill with Edison in mind. Six hours of uninterrupted sleep is necessary for me, and my guess is it's probably essential for most of us, if we hope to keep firing on all cylinders.

The passage from Bora Bora to American Samoa is straight downwind. Like most gaff boats, *Prospector* took the long way around by tacking downwind under her fore and aft rig. I very much regretted not having the squaresail, but the yard was still on the deck. We had tried to replace the topmast in Tahiti, but we couldn't find a big enough piece of timber, even though Sylvia had arranged for the gift of a spare longboat sweep from the latest replica of the brig *H.M.S.Bounty*. The sweep was long enough, but lacked the necessary strength.

Even having to tack, we made excellent time, averaging 135 miles a day for seven consecutive days out of Bora. Then, with only 200 miles to go, the wind stopped.

We were totally becalmed. After a week of running watches, we were hovering on the edge of exhaustion, and the forced immobility gave us a chance to get more rest.

The log for the last days of that passage told the story:

September 26: Still no wind. Zero miles registered.

September 27: SE wind began last night. Made 73 miles.

September 28: Wind continues. Walker (log) turned 1,000 miles at noon. Star sights confirm that we drifted 37 miles while becalmed. Position: 14°44'S, 167°47'W.

September 30: Arrived Pago Pago and anchored by 7:30 p.m. We sailed a rhumb line to Samoa, but had to motor-sail last two hours to make the harbor before dark.

American Samoa, even by tropical standards, is a peculiar place. Not to be confused with Western Samoa, a former German colony 80 miles away, American Samoa is the only American possession in the Southern Hemisphere.

The harbor at Pago Pago is an ancient blown–out volcano, and because of the steep hills that surround it on all sides, is possibly the best hurricane hole in the South Pacific. The harbor isn't large. The town docks and warehouses are clustered on your left just past the last dogleg turn you make as you enter the harbor. Two tuna canneries lie deeper in the bay on the right.

Dotting the upper bay, by the canneries, where the yachts were required to anchor, were massive rusty mooring buoys. Dilapidated and seemingly abandoned Oriental longliners were tied to them.

The water was shallow in the upper bay. We anchored in about eight feet of water near a small crumbling multi-purpose cement pier that served as a customs dock, a breakwater for a small shallow-water marina, and a dinghy landing. Clearing in, we were required to go to the little cement pier and tie up alongside a disabled Canadian yacht for the convenience of the customs officers, who wore lava-lavas, a native wrap-around skirt, as part of their regulation uniform.

Even though we were an American yacht, the entry formalities were almost as complicated as those in Panama. After our customs clearance, I was obliged to call upon the Port Captain for anchoring instructions. Another example of make-work.

Pago Pago was the only American port we visited where transient yachts were required to pay anchoring fees. Like Panama, the services provided were inversely proportional to their cost. The more you pay, the less you get.

The Canadian yacht was disabled, with serious clutch problems, and was waiting for parts from Honolulu. Her captain, John, a tall rugged man with a stiff shock of wiry black hair and a chronically worried expression, was fortunate to have as crew a young Australian named Pete with good mechanical skills. We shared John's good fortune simply because we had tied alongside.

While I commiserated with John, I managed to direct his attention to our problems. Bingo! That afternoon, John, Pete and I were in Pete's rented car hunting for the nearest NAPA store.

Pete and the store clerk compared the bracket on my Lucas alternator with the brackets on a half-dozen rebuilt alternators, and concluded that a Ford was as close as we were going to get.

The alternator cost about $50, and it turned out that Pete worked largely for the experience. In less than a day, Pete had the new alternator installed and the oil pressure gauge fixed. I felt seriously indebted to the Canadians.

With repairs out of the way, we had time to look around.

Across the road from the customs dock was a small Burns and Phillips, Ltd. store. Burns and Phillips is to the South Pacific what Safeway is to California. Pago Pago, without question, is the best resupply port in the central South Pacific. Consider these prices: Budweiser at $11/case. Potatoes were 20¢/pound, and Campbell's soups sold for $18/case. I bought a fifth of Wild Turkey for seven dollars. Vodka sold for two dollars a quart. We bought a case of tuna at the cannery for $28.

We were on a roll, considering the success of the alternator repairs and reprovisioning, so I thought I would check out the famous Lyndon B. Johnson Center for Tropical Medicine. Here, I hoped, was the perfect opportunity for a definitive consultation that would finally end the recurring infections in my ankle.

What a disappointment. After waiting for several hours, I saw a Hindu doctor who gave me five minutes of his time and who prescribed about $50 worth of pills, which I had to pay for, even though they were prescribed in a U.S. Government hospital for a service-connected injury.

We also renewed our friendship with Len and Georganne Ackley, from Boise, Idaho, whom we had first met on McKittrick's store veranda in Taiohae Bay. They had followed us to Tahiti, taking a more adventurous route, and had left Papeete while I was in the hospital. They had preceded us, and were still aboard their little sloop, *Melusine III*, anchored nearby. They had decided to replenish their cruising kitty by spending a season in Samoa. Len was teaching in the local high school and Georganne had also gone to work.

Len, Georganne and I decided to take the aerial tramway ride that runs nearly half a mile across the harbor and up to the top of the mountain directly opposite the town. It was built by Navy Seabees during World War II to transport lookouts and radio operators up and back from the top of the mountain across the harbor. The mere existence of such a structure built for the convenience of enlisted personnel tells you how steep and high those hills are.

The ride cost five dollars, and it was certainly well worth it. The trip took about an hour; 15 minutes up, 15 minutes back, and half an hour on top of the hill. The view was spectacular. The deep inner valleys on the island were open to view, as was the harbor and the tiny boats tied to the cannery docks. There was something almost indecent about looking straight down on vessels, as if by peering into their funnels you could see secret things best hidden from ordinary view.

Huge plumes of bloody water poured from the cannery docks into the bay as frozen fish from those foreign longliners were thawed, gutted, and prepared for canning. Whether EPA (the Environmental Protection Agency) didn't know that Samoa was an American possession, hadn't found out what was going on, or simply didn't care, the two tuna canneries were apparently dumping offal into the harbor. If they were, I'm sure the local government was industriously looking the other way. I've seen the tuna companies throw their weight around local governments before, threatening to leave if community leaders objected too strenuously to various practices the canners wished to continue. Here, the sour smell of putrid water and rotting offal was the smell of tax revenues, payrolls, and general prosperity. Who could complain about that?

Our Canadian friends had obtained the necessary parts for their transmission and, with Pete's expert help, had their engine running again. John's boat was a 36 foot sloop, a handy size for a couple, but seriously overcrowded when you jam four adults and two children aboard as John had done. One of those adults was his youngest son by an earlier marriage, a lad named Jim, about 20 years old, just at that most abrasive age.

John had recently remarried. His new wife was an attractive young mother who had brought her two lively young sons to the marriage. Unfortunately, Jim and John's new bride were barely on speaking terms. I didn't envy him at all.

He and I were sitting in a small bar near the town square one afternoon, when he decided to unburden himself.

"Denny," he said, abruptly shifting gears in our conversation as we poured our second beers, "did you know you can fly from Suva to Vancouver, B.C. for only $293?"

The man must be desperate, I thought to myself, hiding my surprise at his candor. I made the appropriate noises and waited for him to continue.

"That's why I want to get Jim to Suva," John continued. He paused, then blurted, "But I dread that passage." He looked wistfully at me for a moment, then said, "I couldn't afford to pay you, but Jim's a good strong boy. Do you suppose you could find room for him on *Prospector*?"

"Well," I said, feeling suddenly very uneasy, "what does he think about it?"

173

"We've talked about it," John said. "He'd like it. We'll be there as soon as you are, and we'll take him right off your hands."

Still uneasy, but remembering those long hours on the wheel from Bora Bora, and mindful of John's generous help with my mechanical problems, I said, "I'll have to check with Velda."

I imagine Velda also remembered those long hours on the wheel. She agreed, and we had a full crew again.

While we were in Tahiti, I had discovered chart sets. They are common today, but that wasn't true in 1983. Chart prices had just begun their meteoric rise and since American charts are not copyrighted, enterprising firms had started photocopying sets of them for sale. Those early sets had only two things to recommend them. They were cheap, and being reduced in size and copied on thermal paper, they were much less bulky than the originals.

Buzzy sent two kits from Seattle. One, covering the Fijian Archipelago, contained 57 copied charts and came in a tight roll about five inches in diameter and two feet long. The originals would have filled a sailbag.

Unfortunately, those advantages were offset by their lack of durability and legibility. I wasn't concerned about durability at first, because unless you live there, people rarely call in a place like Pago Pago more than once a lifetime, and a magnifying glass would take care of the fine print. Unfortunately, there was another problem.

I didn't know until we were approaching the Fijian Archipelago and its 322 islands, islets, cays and motus, that cockroaches ate thermal paper. Then it was too late.

The passage from Samoa to Fiji is a short one, only about 750 miles. Most people stop a few days in Tonga, but we didn't because we had Jim on board, and I wanted to deliver him to Suva as promptly as possible. Also, it was getting late — it was already well into October. The hurricane season begins in November, and the area surrounding the Samoa-Fiji axis was a prolific hurricane generator. Most importantly, however, we did not have a chart for Astrolabe Reef, which lies fair on the route between Tonga and Fiji, and which has snagged many yachts. The cockroaches had eaten it.

The prevailing wind was dead astern, so again we were taking the long way around, tacking 50 miles to the right of the rhumb line, 50 miles to the left, sailing about 35 degrees on the wind.

As we approached the Fiji Archipelago, and begin examining the chart more closely, I realized there were two archipelagos running north and south. To reach Suva, it was necessary to pass through or go around the Lau Archipelago to the east. According to the *Sailing Directions,* the safest approach to Suva was from the northeast. You sailed through Nanuku Pass, then keeping Welangilala Island lighthouse on your port beam, you turned south into the Koro Sea.

On October 15th at sunset, we passed an off lying island that fit the description of Niua fo'ou. We had a so–so LAN on the 16th, and judging our speed to be five knots (the Walker log having gone to lunch soon after we left Samoa), we changed course at 6 p.m. to 220 degrees, estimating the pass to be 50 miles dead ahead. I thought we should arrive at daylight.

At midnight, just to play it safe, we doubled the watch. Two pairs of eyes were better than one when you're sailing into unknown but constricted waters in the dark and looking for a lighthouse. No light house was seen. My watch began, as usual, at four in the morning. By five-thirty, the horizon was bright enough for celestial observations. The sky was clear. I took sights on Venus, Rigel Kent and Vega, and was beginning to reduce them.

Velda, who had momentarily relieved me at the wheel, suddenly yelled "There's a rock dead ahead!"

I sprinted up the companionway. It was still twilight, although the stars were nearly gone. Sure enough, off to the right, less than a quarter of a mile away, was either a small island or a big rock looming out of the water!

Running forward to the pinrail, I quickly cast off the peak halyard, dropping the gaff and scandalizing the rig. In the meanwhile, Velda cast off the jib sheet, and together, we rolled the jib. That took most of the way off the boat. By this time the light was almost full, and with a big knot in my stomach, I anxiously climbed into the lower ratlines while Velda started the engine. At first glance, I felt sick and weak. White, foaming breakers lay directly ahead of us, only a few hundred yards away, anchored on the left by the island Velda had seen. The line of breakers extended across our bow and around us in a deep crescent, ending off our port quarter.

I could see the jagged teeth of rock and coral in the surf. I could even hear the sullen roar and sucking wash of the seas beating on and retreating from that terrible barrier.

175

I yelled to Velda to turn hard right! Then I heard the comforting bellow of the engine reaching its maximum power.

It was still too dark to see into the water. As soon as Velda had the boat on a reciprocal course, I called to her to slow the engine while I studied the surface, looking for eddies, rips and whirls that might indicate concealed hazards.

I stayed in the ratlines, my feet and legs almost numb with tension and fatigue, until I heard Velda's welcome shout that the depth finder was showing 100 feet.

Somehow, in the dark, we had blundered into the middle of a big reef. It was Velda's alertness that saved us. Luckily it wasn't windy or rough, and by now it was light enough so I could see the shallowest water clearly from my perch. In the meanwhile, Jim studied the chart. While Velda steered, the reef slide past on both sides. I was still trembling as I climbed down to the deck.

Jim examined the chart for several minutes, then stood up on the side deck looking around. Then he returned to the chart. Finally, he looked up. "I think we must be about here," he said, pointing with a pencil to a place immediately north of a large broken area faintly and almost illegibly identified as Heemskercq Reef.

I laid a course from that area south into the Koro Sea. He was right. We reset the sail and shut the engine down.

When we were in clear water, and could identify islands as we passed them, the near grounding at daybreak receded from the forefront of my memory — although in the months to come, as I stood my watches in the darkness of early morning, I found myself speculating: *Suppose daylight had been delayed 15 minutes, or the wind had been slightly stronger and we had arrived 15 minutes earlier*. It was a long time before that memory faded into a past remembrance.

We sailed south all day in the Koro Sea, passing easily identified islands. Despite our narrow escape that morning, we continued sailing after dark, when sensible people would have found a place to anchor.

Shortly after midnight, we saw the Nasilai Island lighthouse ahead, and when I came on watch at 4 a.m., it was only about ten miles away. There was no need to take morning star sights. The light was in plain view, and I could see dozens of fishermen working the dawn tide between us and the lighthouse.

But something was wrong with that picture.

Suddenly I realized those boats were strangely immobile. A closer look through the glasses, and with an sickening feeling of *déjà vu*, I realized those boats were really large rocks sticking out of the water, the nearest one only 200 yards away.

The wind was on our port beam. I yelled at Velda to start the engine while I spun the wheel to the left.

The engine fired, and abruptly, we were on a starboard tack standing away from the rocks. I have no idea what was lurking beneath our keel, but as we turned I thought I saw sinister shadows beneath the water's surface off our starboard bow.

The reef extended seaward from the lighthouse about half a mile. We studied the chart for clues. It was hard to be sure because of the condition of the chart, but it seemed to show deep water right up to the light. Unfortunately, the copy we had failed to indicate how old the original chart was, or where it had come from. Most likely, it was an old British Admiralty chart.

The remaining few miles into Suva harbor were easy. Three rusting hulks — they looked like fishing sampans — decorated the outer flats to the right of the harbor channel.

Unlike most of Fiji's 7,000 square miles, the harbor was well marked. We had no difficulty following the wide ditch between drying patches of mud on both sides into the harbor mouth.

There is always a moment of uncertainty when you enter a harbor for the first time. Later, we learned to announce our arrival while still at sea on the radio to the harbor master, but we weren't yet that sophisticated.

As we hesitantly motored into full view of the port, our quarantine and courtesy flags fluttering from the starboard flag hoist, a busy little launch with the word QUARANTINE painted on her sides came toward us.

A portly little Hindu carrying a briefcase stepped aboard.

"How do you do?" he asked, holding out a plump little hand and smiling, a gold tooth twinkling in the morning sun light. "I am Doctor Ram, the quarantine doctor. You are all in good health, I trust?" He looked anxiously at each of us. We nodded. He looked around. "Is there somewhere I can sit?"

We were dead in the water. The quarantine launch was standing

177

by, 50 feet off our port beam. There was nothing else within a quarter of a mile. I ushered the doctor below. He looked around the cabin, and his eye fell on a well thumbed copy of *Playboy* we had bought in Samoa.

"Ah," he said, smiling, "that's contraband. May I have it?"

I nodded, and the magazine slid smoothly into his briefcase. He sat at the table and spread out forms he had taken from his briefcase. "You sign here, and here, and here," he said, indicating the appropriate places. I did as I was told.

He recited a list of illnesses. "Any cases of that on board?" he asked. I shook my head. "Sign here, please," he said.

"Here is your pratique," he said, handing me an official looking document. "You may take your quarantine flag down."

We went back to the cockpit and shook hands again.

He pointed to a huge cement pier on the waterfront. "Customs will meet you there," he said. The launch captain, seeing the doctor on deck, maneuvered his boat alongside. The doctor gave us a wave and was gone.

The customs pier was suitable for commercial craft, but was much too big for us because the bottoms of the huge tires hung on the face of the dock as fenders, came even with the tops of our lifeline stanchions.

The customs examination was as cursory as the doctor's had been, and the neatly uniformed young Hindu who boarded us took our rifle and shotgun ashore with him.

Visiting yachts were required to anchor either off the Royal Suva Yacht Club or near a hotel. We chose the yacht club, which provided a long list of amenities.

We quickly learned that it was the sort of place where you got to know the secretary, the doorman and the bartenders by name, and where you were certain to find old friends and meet new ones. For most members, the bar was the main attraction of the club. For us live aboards, the club had additional attractions such as a laundromat, a fuel dock and inexpensive meals when we didn't feel like going to the boat for dinner. Also, it was possible to make long distance phone calls.

Sunday evenings when the dining room was closed, members of the Lady's Auxiliary prepared a delicious barbecue on the lawn that cost only pennies. This wonderful hospitality wasn't free. Our temporary membership cost $12 a week. Money well spent.

I was concerned about Jim. John's earnest plea in Suva, "We'll be there as soon as you are, and we'll take him right off your hands," was beginning to seem a bit hollow. We'd been in Suva for a week, and his family was nowhere in sight. I didn't know then they had taken a leisurely side trip to Tonga. Almost another week went by before they showed up.

I knew John's bride would be looking forward to a family reunion with the same enthusiasm as a visit to the dentist for root canal work, and I also realized that John had my measure; he knew I wouldn't toss his last born off the boat, no matter how provoked I was.

And I was very provoked. Left to their own devices, post adolescents can be selfish and egocentric. Sad to say, Jim was a better shipmate than roommate. Perhaps that was because at sea, he was an adult among adults. Ashore, however, because of his proximity to other young people, he reverted to his adolescence. For those who may have forgotten what life with Henry Aldrich was like, let me refresh your memory.

On our first trip to town, Jim sat in front with the driver while Velda and I shared the back seat. I don't know what started the discussion between Jim and the driver, but I tuned in just in time to hear the driver describe the punishments handed out by the Fijian courts. The driver, probably a devout and likely very conservative Moslem, described the canings, floggings, and hangings with great ardor and enthusiasm. He was really warming to his dialogue, and the obvious fascination of his audience, when Jim interrupted him.

"But do they do those things to white people, too?"

Later, even after I explained to Jim that his question revealed a certain lack of racial sensitivity, which probably explained why we had been charged a double fare, he just didn't get it. His perception of the world continued to follow an antiquated theory of white supremacy. Nothing I could say made a difference. Even so, he had good stuff in him, and I'm sure once the rough corners were knocked off, he will have grown up to be a fine man. I hope his experience with us helped.

Fiji, like Tahiti and Puntarenas, is a major crossroads; sooner or later, everyone cruising the South Pacific will call. *Kulkuri* was there when we arrived. So was *Solitair* and a big Westsail 43 from Oregon named *Rain Eagle*. We had met her people, Bill and Sharon Wridge, in Tahiti. The Parkers, Betty and Gary, from their yacht *Calaveras* were also in town.

The yacht club was an interesting microcosm of Fijian society. Melanesians served as bartenders and porters. The place was guarded by Hindu watchmen. The kitchen staff was Chinese, and the management was European. The membership was a cross section of society, without apparent discrimination.

It was unfortunately true that Melanesians were unwelcome in some Indian stores, but I think that may have reflected more of an economic bias than a racial one. But it also underscored the deep racial and social divisions that existed in the population.

Fiji is near the eastern edge of Melanesia. When the Europeans arrived, Melanesians were already firmly in residence. Such quaint niceties meant little to early European explorers and settlers who, after usurping the land, began cultivating sugar cane. The settlers quickly discovered that the Melanesians lacked an aptitude for the work or the ability to endure the harsh working conditions of the time. Consequently, the Europeans imported a few thousand Indian coolies to plant, cultivate and cut the sugar cane.

After the industrious Indians paid their debts, they sent home for brides. I don't know when the first bride ship arrived from India, but I'll bet every Indian–Fijian school kid does.

When we were in Fiji, relations between the two groups were not cordial. No doubt as a result of Indian influence, Fiji was a highly puritanical society. Dr. Ram wasn't kidding when he said our tattered copy of *Playboy* was contraband. I wonder what changes may have occurred. My guess is that very little has changed. A political structure that I felt was oppressive in 1983 is probably repressive today.

The Melanesians we met were not overtly political, but that may have changed. A good indicator would be the change, if any, in the crushing tax on alcohol. A tax on booze affected only tourists — and Melanesians. Hindus are not heavy drinkers and devout Moslems abstain from alcohol.

Fiji's capitol city, Suva, is about the same size as Papeete, but hugely different. Where Papeete is an amicable blend of French and Polynesian cultures, heavily seasoned with a Chinese flavor, Suva uncomfortably straddles diverse cultures with a sharply stratified society, that is deeply divided along economic, ethnic and cultural lines. As far as I could see, there has been virtually no assimilation.

For example, the Fijian Government makes determined efforts in Suva to preserve the Melanesian culture in areas set aside for that purpose. By contrast, Papeete reflects a dynamic culture that is growing by incorporating desirable French and Chinese attributes into its Polynesian base.

Suva was devoted to commerce in discounted Japanese cameras and Korean electronics. Therefore, the gastronomic arts were not highly developed. But we enjoyed two outstanding dinners there, each memorable in a special and unique way.

The first came as a result of our friendship with Betty and Gary Parker from *Calaveras*. We knew that Gary was an accomplished gourmet, having shared many dinners with them in a favorite Italian restaurant in Papeete. Consequently, when he and Betty invited us to join them for dinner here, promising us a special treat, we gladly accepted, although our budget didn't allow us to eat out often.

After a short drive in Gary's rented car in the early evening dark through the city to a nearby suburb, Gary pulled into an opulent porte-cochere where he surrendered the car keys to a parking valet.

We were ushered into a downstairs drawing room elegantly furnished with period furniture. The polished parquet flooring was covered with antique oriental rugs. The walls were wainscoted, punctuated with attractively spotlighted oil paintings. The furniture was clustered in intimate groupings. Another party of diners occupied an Empire sofa and two wing chairs. A second group sat in club chairs gathered around a small table. There may have been half a dozen such groups of diners in that rich setting, each discreetly separated from the others.

It was the sort of place where you want to whisper. The murmur of quiet conversation was interrupted when a young woman sat at a grand piano in the corner of the room. Tentatively, then with increasing assurance, she began to play. My knowledge of classical music is limited, but I recognized a Chopin etude. The music completed the aura of quiet elegance in the room. People stopped talking, and listened to the lovely melody. When the girl finished her impromptu recital, the dinner guests and the staff joined in a round of applause. It was a special moment.

Each dinner party had a private dining room. Those rooms were in the back on the first floor, separated from each other by folding solid partitions.

Gary's was the only menu with prices, and he selected the wines, and ordered the dinner. He chose well. After several preliminary courses; soup, salad, and so forth, we were each served a large broiled lobster.

The food was superb. I'm not a connoisseur of lobster, but this one was exceptional, partly because of the unusual flavors, but mainly because of its texture. Lobster, in my experience, is chewy. Not this one. This one was moist and succulent.

After dinner, we were invited to tour the building. Gary and I preferred to relax, but the ladies accepted the invitation, and were gone for nearly half an hour.

It seems that our host, Scott — I don't know whether this was his first or last name, or whether it was his real name at all — had come to Suva on a visit from San Francisco several years earlier, had been shown this 19th century mansion, then in terrible disrepair, and impulsively had bought it.

He and a friend, also from San Francisco, moved into the top floor, and installed a wood shop on the second floor. Then the work began. He and his partner had refinished, recovered, repaired, or replaced, as needed, every square inch of the place. Walls were moved to make useful space for the restaurant.

While we were there, they were starting on the furniture. When they are finished, if they ever are, I hope they will look at what they have accomplished with the pride and satisfaction it deserves. I have a feeling, though, that either the job will never be completed, or if it is, Scott will stumble across another treasure that just needs a little fixing-up. The work they have done reflects an emotional commitment as much as it does wonderful manual skills. Scott's Restaurant is not merely a place to have dinner. It is a multidimensional work of art to be experienced and savored. Truly a masterpiece.

I have no idea what the dinner cost. I paid Gary what he said our share was — but knowing how generous Gary was, I think he may have forgotten to add the cost of the wine. I'm glad we went. It was a wonderful experience.

Enjoying such refined elegance while living as we were, was unreal, almost a surrealistic experience. Certainly, it emphasized the shortcomings of our living arrangements. Except for a leaky hull, I can't think of a chronic boat problem more troubling than leaky decks. Leaking decks means wet bunks, soggy crackers, disintegrating electronics and spoiled books. It means mildew, gloom, and a very unhappy partner.

The leak over Velda's bunk was so bad that in heavy weather she actually wore oilskins to bed. I'll leave it to your imagination how our breakfast conversations went. The guts of our radios, electrical distribution boxes and light fixtures turned into green slime. Half the books in the ship's library hardened into planks. The other half were so badly stained with mildew that the print became illegible, and the bindings melted.

While we were trying to find a solution to that problem, Jack and Ritva Curley introduced us to a young couple, Ralph and Cheryl Baker, from Arkansas. Jack thought that because the Baker's boat, *Flying Lady*, was so similar to *Prospector*, that we would have a lot in common. So we did. We had considerably more in common than Jack and Ritva realized.

They didn't know that *Flying Lady*, like *Prospector*, was a Concordia design. Or that *Flying Lady* was designed by the same "Pete" Culler I had consulted before buying *Prospector*. Much of *Prospector* shows up in *Flying Lady's* detail. I'm sure the similarity was not accidental.

Ralph, a stocky man with graying hair in early middle-age, was an architect. His wife, Cheryl, a lovely young woman, was a registered nurse. Although they came originally from Fort Smith, Arkansas, they had built *Flying Lady* in a little town north of Seattle on Puget Sound. They had very nearly lost her on a reef north of Suva. After striking the reef, partly to lighten the ship, and partly in hope of soliciting the sympathetic help of local natives, they had emptied their lockers and gave away canned food, lines, spare gear, and almost anything else the natives asked for.

That generosity evidently paid off for them; their boat was refloated at minimal expense, although she spent a considerable amount of time hauled out in the government shipyard in Suva.

When Ralph learned that we needed professional caulking done, he and Cheryl recommended a Melanesian family, several of whom had worked in the gang that repaired *Flying Lady*. I asked Ralph to put us in touch with them.

The next day, a tall, slender Melanesian with a solemn, almost lugubrious expression approached me in the bar. After identifying himself as Philip, Ralph's friend, he asked me what sort of work I had in mind. I took him out to the boat, so he could see the job first hand. *Prospector's* decks were built of solid teak planks three inches wide, and one and a half inches thick.

These were beveled, fitted together parallel to the keel, and nailed to the deck beams. After the planks were nailed down, a thread of caulking cotton was driven into the beveled seams, and molten pitch (a high quality tar) was poured into the seams on top of the cotton. Many things have to be just right to get a good job. The caulkers, the fellows with the cotton, the irons, and the mallets, must know exactly how much cotton to drive, and how hard to drive it. It is even important to know how tight to twist it. The temperature of the pitch is also critical.

In other words, caulking is an art. Traditionally, when boat carpenters and shipwrights grew too old to swing adzes or top mauls, they became caulkers. That was the natural order of things. Today's modern boat building trades, however, have more to do with chemistry and fancy welding than with spiling planks. Fiberglass hulls have little need for caulking.

I had thought the older trades might yet survive in places like Fiji, where most boat building is still done by carpenters with planes, saws, and hammers. Philip struck me as a competent journeyman. After we paced off the job, he gave me an estimate of $600. Prospector has about 1,500 linear feet of deck seams, so $600 equated to about 40¢ a running foot. Not cheap, but like open heart surgery, this is a job where the results are much more important than the price.

We learned a great deal about that Melanesian family during the next ten days. The patriarch was a nearly toothless, skinny old man called Papa who was in that indeterminate age somewhere between 90 and 120. Papa told me that among his many occupations, he had been a shipwright, a caulker, and a fisherman. I believed him.

He offered to cut a new topmast for me while his sons (grandsons, more likely) worked on the decks. We agreed on $150 for the job, with his furnishing the materials. I climbed up to the crosstrees, worked the mast stub loose, and sent it down so Papa would have a pattern to follow.

By now, we were nearly a week into the deck project. Philip's crew, under Papa's good natured heckling, had settled down. One fellow, using a reefing iron made from a bent file tang, scraped the brittle old tar out of the seams.

Another young fellow reset the cotton the scraper had loosened. A pot of tar bubbled in the cockpit, heated by an old Primus (Swede) stove. Either Philip or his brother poured the tar. A fifth member of the

Philip recaulking cockpit. (Note brass binnacle in foreground).

gang came along after everyone else with a hammer and chisel and cut off the worst of the globs. There were plenty of those, and he missed many of them. We still have several globs of tar on the cockpit sole.

I wish I could tell you that when the crew finished, the decks had been restored, but that wouldn't be true. They were better, but unfortunately and disappointingly, the level of craftsmanship they brought to this job was only appropriate to the level of village fishing boats.

It is a standing joke among the yachties who were in Fiji at the time to inquire, when we meet as we occasionally do, whether the mast has started to sprout coconuts yet. I don't know what sort of wood he used, but it is light, tough, and has a grain similar to Sitka spruce. The decks were a disappointment, but the mast worked out very well.

We toyed briefly with the idea of hauling the boat in Suva. The government yard was available, and the price was right. Moreover, a local chemist mixed bottom paint according to International Paint Co. formulas, adding as much additional arsenic as the customer requested. The stuff was deadly. But time was getting away from us; the hurricane season was just around the corner, and I wanted to leave for New Zealand.

When the deck job was completed, Philip and I exchanged gifts and he invited us and the Bakers to his village for a feast. Philip and a gaggle of wide-eyed kids met us by the side of the road after an hour's taxi drive out of Suva. They led us along a path bordering a field, then through a clearing past some buildings, one of which was a school. Philip grinned when I asked him about it. "Peace Corps," he said.

The path led down to an obviously new and elaborate foot bridge across a small river. The bridge was built on cement piers, and was paved with macadam. Philip gave the hand rail a proprietary pat and smiled again. "Him belong Peace Corps, too," he said. Ralph and Cheryl explained that the river had divided the village socially and physically; before the bridge was built, the only way people could cross the river was by boat. This was dangerous because during the monsoons, the stream became a raging torrent carrying brush and fallen trees. Also, salt water crocodiles occasionally came into the river looking for careless goats or hapless swimmers.

Ralph had met the Peace Corps teacher who initiated the project. The teacher had persuaded the local U.S. Agency for International Development office to make a $15,000 grant. Volunteers did the engineering, while the village provided the labor and the grant paid for the required materials. When the project was completed, the Prime Minister and the American Ambassador shared the ribbon-cutting ceremony. We were told that the ensuing celebration cost more than the bridge. I believed it, when I saw the celebration Papa's family had planned for us.

Papa met us across the river. After we shook hands, I looked around the clearing, and saw four huts facing inwardly in a circle. Three cows grazed behind the buildings. Half-wild chickens darted here and there, and although I didn't see them, I heard the soft grunts of pigs. Each building was roofed with corrugated iron and stood on piling about five feet off the ground, probably against seasonal floods and to provide shelter for the pigs, chickens and goats belonging to the household.

Papa was proudly standing by the new top mast, freshly varnished and painted, resting on two old oil drums in front of one of the houses.

"Is OK?" he asked anxiously. The broken stub lay next to it for comparison. Papa had done a fine job. the spar was beautifully tapered and nicely finished. The grain of the wood ran true, and there wasn't a knot or blemish in the wood. The only problem was, and I didn't have the heart to tell him, he had cut the tenon in the heel of the mast backwards.

Urged on by Papa, we climbed the steep staircase of the nearest house and entered the small room. The plank floor, worn smooth over the years by generations of callused bare feet, was covered with intricately woven grass mats. A few pieces of furniture were scattered around the walls.

Although I sat on the floor with everyone else during dinner, afterward, claiming the privilege of age, I sat in an overstuffed chair because my joints were more accustomed to chairs than the floor while everyone else remained on the floor.

The food began to appear. Lord, lord, what piles of food!

It was Costa Rica all over again. Only instead of a private banquet for two, four of us sat on the floor stuffing ourselves. Platters of pork (the delicious kind that comes deep roasted from a fire pit in the ground), plantain, three different dishes of chicken, yams, rice, breads and several foods I didn't recognize, were heaped on platters in the middle of the dining mat. Solemn, big-eyed children lined the walls, watching us eat.

Papa sat next to me, pointing out particularly succulent morsels and urging me to eat, eat, eat. I looked around. Thomas, Philip's eldest brother was leaning over Velda's shoulder pointing to prize tidbits. It seemed the most natural thing in the world to be eating with our fingers out of a communal bowl and from communal platters. It wasn't until we were back on the boat that I made the inevitable comparison between that feast and the elegant dinner party we had enjoyed a week earlier at Scott's.

The comparison was stunning, because I suddenly realized that each dinner was, in its own way, a highly ritualized event. The rituals of "civilization" that we encountered at Scott's were more sophisticated and certainly more stylized, but the Melanesian feast we enjoyed probably was also pregnant with hidden meaning.

Even as we sat on that Fijian floor gorging ourselves, and as course followed course, it began to dawn on me that we might be involved in an ancient rituale, the meaning of which might had been lost.

I thought that a feast of this magnitude might be significant in a society that had practiced cannibalism as recently as the early years of the present century, certainly within Papa's lifetime.

Eventually, we could hold no more. The women and children cleared away the remaining food. Thomas stepped outside for

Let the party begin!

a moment. When he returned, he was carrying a large flat stone with a concave center that looked like a stone wash basin.

He carefully set it on the floor. Then he gestured to Papa who shook his head, grinning. Shrugging, Thomas knelt by the basin, and took from Philip a paper sack containing a tan powder. Another brother came from the cooking lean-to with a pitcher of water and a carved stick. These he handed to Thomas.

By this time, only the men and the two female guests remained in the room. With appropriate solemnity, Thomas began mixing powder and water to make a paste, then added more water until the stone basin was nearly full of a grayish liquid.

The men were making kava. This normally is the prerogative of the eldest male present, but Papa had relinquished the honor to his eldest son. A half coconut shell was used as a combined dipper and drinking vessel, and was passed from hand to hand around the circle. Somewhat to my surprise, Velda and Cheryl were included in the group. Normally, only males would have been offered kava. I tasted the stuff reluctantly, thinking it would be just my luck to contract tuberculosis drinking a beverage that tasted exactly like dirty Milk of Magnesia.

Kava is supposed to be mildly stimulating. Both Roger and Cheryl reported that their mouths were slightly numb, but to a person like myself, possibly more accustomed to beverages of a stronger nature, kava was as about as exciting and stimulating as a glass of muddy river water.

I suppose it's progress that instead of the womenfolk digging, drying and pounding kava roots into a powder for ceremonial purposes, this kava powder had been purchased from the same Indian storekeeper who had sold the rum and beer we were about to consume.

The kava ceremony over — nobody asked for seconds when a bottle of rum was in the room — the party got underway. Velda had brought her guitar, and handed it to Philip who began strumming chords. Other instruments appeared. A boy was sent for more rum and a case of Fiji Bitters.

The women came shyly into the room. Sitting on the floor, they and the children began singing and clapping their hands. Papa stood up, albeit a bit wobbly, and began to dance, first by himself, then with one of the women. Ralph and Cheryl also began to dance, and soon the little bungalow was shaking with stamping feet and the music that grew louder and louder.

Finally, around midnight, it was time to call it quits. Papa fell down the steps as we were leaving the house but didn't seem any the worse for the experience. The women carried him off to bed, and the younger men escorted us with kerosene lanterns down the path, across the bridge, through the clearing, and out to the road.

Then we discovered that no provision had been made for getting us back to the yacht club. A quick call to the taxi office from the Indian storekeeper's telephone solved that problem, and the four of us soon arrived back at the yacht club.

It wasn't until after we were back aboard *Prospector* that the significance of what I *hadn't* seen came to me. There were no fences. I didn't look for them, but on reflection, I didn't recall seeing any fences on the road, or in the village or even surrounding the pasture where the cows were.

As it happened, our visit to Philip's village coincided with an Indian religious holiday. Some celebrants had elaborately decorated their homes and yards in a style reminiscent of the way some Christians prepare Christmas decorations. I found it interesting that the places where those decorations were most elaborate were also the most heavily fenced. Another difference between two ethnic groups.

The mast was delivered to the yacht club the next morning, and I stepped it on the crosstrees under Philip's watchful eye.

Although the old man had cut the tenon on the wrong side of

mast, the remedy was simple. I merely stepped it backwards. It worked just as well and he never knew the difference.

Meeting the payroll had placed a serious strain on our limited financial resources, and we had to think seriously about obtaining New Zealand visas. I knew the New Zealand High Commissioner would want to see at least $1,500 in cash. It was always possible to arrange a 15-minute loan in the High Commissioner's ante room; we saw the same stack of greenbacks go through the door at least three times while we were waiting our turn. But that isn't my style. I prefer to play the game straight. Besides, we needed a fresh cash transfusion, anyway.

I called Buzzy from the yacht club. I explained we were running short, and asked him to see if there was a quicker way to transfer funds than the way we had been doing it. As always, I stressed with Buz both his duty and my undying sibling love and affection. The message got through. The next day, less than 24 hours after my telephone call, I received a cable reading: "Funds on deposit Westpac-Suva, whatever that is, love, Buz."

It's wonderful to walk into a strange bank, passport in hand, find the international transactions window, show your passport to the lovely person standing behind the counter, and be asked five little words, "How do you want it?" I don't know why it took over six months, and God knows how much anguish, to discover electronic transfers. It probably never occurred to Buzzy that there was a better way. I certainly didn't know better.

We were sorry to leave Suva, but the hurricane season was upon us and we had to move on. We left the customs dock at ten in the morning, November 12th, after retrieving our firearms and explaining to the workmen on the dock that Lara, our calico cat, was a real cat. They had never seen a calico, nor had they ever seen a cat as big as she.

We were outward bound for New Zealand, the Land of the Long White Cloud. That was the place of truth; where we had promised each other we would either turn back or get on with the program and continue sailing around the world.

Chapter 8

Land of Wool and Butter

Gordon Stuermer describes as giant scythes, the trailing cold fronts in the higher latitudes that follow the periodic low pressure systems originating in the Southern Ocean, cutting swathes across the southern South Pacific every week to ten days. To avoid them on the passage to New Zealand, some 1,100 miles south of Suva, his advice was to leave Suva immediately after a front had passed. With luck and a fast boat, you might get to New Zealand before the next one came along.

As usual, Gordon's advice was sound, but for *Prospector*, it wasn't so much a matter of making a trip between fronts, as it was minimizing the number we might encounter along the way. No matter how careful – or lucky – we were, we knew that we'd feel the lash of at least one. We also knew we would be especially vulnerable when we ventured as far as 35° south.

Our departure was without incident. The stranded fishing boats on the flats on the outer harbor were grim reminders to be careful, and I hadn't forgotten the lessons I learned on our arrival. I was concerned about Astrolabe Reef to the southeast, and Kandavu Island to the south, but the weather was good, and I was sure that by clearing Kandavu in daylight we'd be all right.

The Autohelm was back on the job. Thus, the drudgery of watchstanding was temporarily abated; the watchstander could move around the boat, keep up with chores that required attention, and get proper rest.

Three days out of Suva, the wind unexpectedly veered from easterly to southeasterly. Since we now had a topmast, we had been enjoying the unaccustomed luxury of topsails, but when we hardened the sheets to accommodate the wind shift, we began driving into a rising sea. Suddenly the jib topsail split.

After hauling the tattered fragments of the sail out of the water, I started the engine. While the starter motor was cranking the engine, I noticed gray wisps of smoke rising from it. Nothing serious, but certainly not the sign of a healthy motor.

The engine fired, ran for 15 minutes, abruptly revved up and stopped. Again, the filters had filled with dirty water. I spent most of the morning crawling around that damned engine, changing the filters, purging the air and restarting it.

The wind settled into the sou'southeast so it was impossible to maintain our rhumb line course of 190°; in fact, we were pinching badly on a heading of 210 degrees, 20 degrees west of our desired course. Sailing that close to the weather, we were taking a good bit of water aboard, much of it finding its way below through the newly recaulked decks.

I use a "systems" approach to boat management, which includes a regular pumping schedule for the bilges. Usually, I pumped the bilges once a day, immediately after my morning watch. However, if the volume of water in the bilge required it, we might pump the bilges twice daily, or after each watch, or even on an hourly basis if necessary.

The purpose of maintaining a regular schedule was to know as accurately as possible the quantity of water coming into the boat. For obvious reasons, this was critical information. That's why, although we carried a large electrical pump as a back-up, we did *not* have an automatic switch. Such a switch might have masked the amount of water entering the bilges, and its intermittent switching could inadvertently drain the batteries. Such a switch might be handy aboard an unattended boat tied to a dock somewhere, but I doubt they have a place on a cruising boat.

A mechanical Whale Gusher 25 was our primary pump. Each stroke of its handle delivered about a pint. I liked it because by using it regularly, I had a close idea about the quantity of water coming aboard every day. For instance, when it took 200 strokes to clear the bilge, I knew we were taking about 25 gallons of water aboard every day.

Compared to modern boats, *Prospector's* bilges are huge. If you had 25 gallons of water in the bilges of a modern boat like Ike and

Debby's *Summer Seas*, very likely you might think you were foundering. That illusion of imminent disaster may have been one of the factors that caused people to abandon their boats prematurely during the Fastnet Race tragedy in 1978, which undoubtedly contributed to the loss of life.

The wind backed into the nor'northeast during the night of November 19-20th, and we took advantage of it by steering 120 degrees until morning, when the glass began to fall. By noon, the clouds were growing black, ugly and threatening. By late afternoon, I decided to take appropriate action. Congratulating myself that I wouldn't have to shorten down after dark in a rising gale, I rolled the jib and struck the mainsail, continuing under the staysail and mizzen in an intermittent breeze on strangely calm seas. I remembered vividly how still the air had become that fateful night in Papeete hours before *Veena* struck.

The barometer was still dropping fast. Thirteen millibars in six hours was an alarming drop. It looked as if Gordon's scythe was about to descend on us and rip our masts out. The wind shift, the oily seas, the abrupt drop in the barometer and the sky spoke plainly to me concerning what was about to happen.

I put double lashings on the mainsail and dinghy. The sky grew darker and even more threatening. I thought all hell was about to break loose, and I was braced for it. I could feel the weight of the pending weather hanging over us like the sword of Damocles. Adrenaline was coursing through my bloodstream, and I felt ready for anything that might come — except what actually did.

We were becalmed.

I wouldn't have been more surprised if it had started to snow. The wind veered into the southwest, and faded to a whisper. By morning, we barely had steerageway.

Then the breeze died completely, and we started the engine. Even with the engine, however, the log entry for November 22nd shows a noon to noon run of only 32 miles.

Meanwhile, the barometer was climbing; at noon on the 22nd, it stood at 1008 mb, and we were enjoying a broad reach in a force four breeze.

That rollicking sail continued, and on the 25th, the barometer registered a phenomenal 1026 mb!

193

The next morning, at first light, we raised North Cape, the northern tip of New Zealand. The long white cloud clinging to higher elevations was very conspicuous.

At 10 a.m., a solitary sperm whale swam across our bow, and an hour later, as we drew near to the coast, we encountered a large pod of porpoises, apparently sent out as a welcoming committee. They followed us all day as we explored the coastline.

New Zealand had for me the special meaning that Tahiti had for Velda; an exhilarating sense of accomplishment. Moreover, New Zealand enjoys a well deserved international reputation as a yachting mecca, and I knew we would be able to get things done there that we couldn't elsewhere.

The coastline is rugged, with shallow bays, surrounded by steep sided, rocky uplands. We stayed well clear of the numerous small rocky islands that lie close to the shoreline. The welcoming committee porpoises were different from their cousins in the Eastern Pacific. Apart from their more sedate behavior, the most striking difference was their size. These animals were small, about the size of harbor seals.

It began to grow dark as we approached the entrance to the Bay of Islands. Remembering the narrow escape we had a month earlier when we blundered into the reef north of Fiji, we decided to heave-to and wait for daylight. Besides, we were using another sepia colored chart set, which was hard to read by flashlight.

The powerful Cape Brett light stood watch with us all night, its flash lighting the cockpit every few seconds. We drifted about ten miles during the night. At daylight, the wind was calm. Fortunately, we had plenty of fuel, and I started the engine. We began motoring toward the harbor.

The name "Bay of Islands" is colorful but misleading. True enough, there are scores of small islands scattered around the bay, some scarcely larger than a dinner table. But the most distinguishing characteristic of this bay is its convoluted shape.

This may seem gross, but as you travel through it, from the outer entrance to Opua, you pass through three inner-connected bodies of water somewhat reminiscent in shape and relative size to the chambers of a ruminant's stomach. "Sheepgut Bay" might be a more accurate if somewhat less elegant name for the place.

Much of New Zealand's earliest history centers in the Bay of

Islands. The first community you'll find as you enter the bay — it lies to the left on the lee side of a small peninsula — is the quiet little town of Russell.

One hundred fifty years ago, Russell was considered the hellhole of the South Pacific. It provided rest and recreation for the Antarctic whaling fleet, manned by the hardest miscreants and rogues ever assembled. It also furnished supplies and repairs to ships years away from their home ports.

In later years, when its ship chandlers, coopers, thieves, saloon-keepers, crimps, murderers, pimps, cardsharps, and whores gave way to politicians, Russell served briefly as New Zealand's capital. Today, Russell has a polite, almost pastoral quality. About 800 people live there in a family oriented community of small homes.

Muted reminders of its lurid past remain. The Duke of Marlborough, for instance, is the oldest licensed premises in New Zealand. Three blocks away in a modest frame building is the oldest Anglican Church. The church dates from 1849. I don't know when the licensed premises opened its doors.

Because they were probably considered bad for business and therefore weren't welcome in Russell, but also because of the proximity of the Maori settlement at Waitangi, the missionaries built their community at Paihia, about four miles across the bay from Russell.

Paihia is still a preacher's town, and it's much easier there to find an ice cream parlor than a licensed premises. The town may lack a shady past, but it's enjoying a prosperous present because unlike Russell, it's on the main road from Auckland, and it is served by the National Railway Bus Line. Therefore, it's much more convenient for tourists.

Russell, on the other hand, is a genteel, polite and dignified old lady sitting on her porch, elegantly entertaining her friends with tea, matter-of-factly reminiscing about former mutual business acquaintances — pimps, whores and cardsharps. Russell is a retired madam, and I like her.

Besides other attractions, sailing ships found good shelter and holding in 15 feet of water off the beach at Russell. Vessels needing more time could go around the town and tuck away in Matawhi Bay, still a favorite anchorage.

The Port of Entry is at Opua, five miles deeper into the bay than Russell. After passing Russell, heading almost due west, you will enter a narrow waterway. The channel is well defined by green and red piling. These lead you around a bend to the left and dead ahead, on the right side of the river, a half mile away, is a big cement pier.

The pier is about 600 feet long and seems incongruous in such a rural setting. It was built by the government in what proved a futile effort to establish a northern port for agricultural exports. The National Railway System ostensibly operates it, and occasionally excursion trains use it.

While the Opua pier does not appear to have been successful as a shipping point, it shelters an extensive mooring area, the ferry dock, the Harbor Master's office, fuel pumps, a general store and the Opua post office. A commercial fish buyer has a permanent installation — ice machines and delivery facilities — on the face of the dock. The inside of the dock features a large sign reserving the space for **HMS** CUSTOMS.

Entering and exiting yachts were supposed to tie up there so the officials could conveniently and safely conduct their business. But when we arrived, the dock was crowded with yachts rafted two and three deep.

Because of our poor close handling characteristics and over-hanging yard, I had serious doubts about landing there, so we decided to anchor off and think about it.

While we were still trying to collect our thoughts, I heard someone yell *"Prospector!"*

I looked more closely at the boats. There, snuggled up against a bigger yacht, was *Windjob*. Dirk Winters was standing on his deck waving a bottle of beer. I shouted back that we were going to anchor off, and almost immediately, a small boat was alongside, the people having overheard me, kindly warning that the mooring area was much too shallow for a vessel of our draft.

We went across the river and dropped the anchor near some sheds. It wasn't long before two men in white uniforms came rowing across the river in a borrowed dinghy. This was Her Majesty's Customs Service and the New Zealand Animal Quarantine Service.

The customs officer, a prematurely balding young man, was very annoyed. He demanded to know if we hadn't seen him wave at us.

We had seen him wave, but I told him that if they expected people like us to come alongside the pier, they would have to make room by chasing the freeloaders away. I was sure not all those boats tied to the pier had business with Her Majesty's Customs Service, but merely found it convenient to tie up while shopping at the general store, and I told him so.

Unwittingly, I had identified a characteristic that I later came to regard as basic to the New Zealand psyche. Notwithstanding conventional wisdom about generalizations, I believe that except in situations where equivocation would be clearly inappropriate, as a general rule, Kiwis dislike and therefore instinctively avoid confrontations.

Human conduct is nudged along desired channels by indirection; by consciously making the alternative as inconvenient as possible. Take, for example, the problem facing Cap and Lara as we signed in.

New Zealand shares the English phobia about rabies. It meant nothing to the quarantine officer that your animals had been as effectively sheltered from other animals for the last two years as if they had spent that time on the moon. To be welcomed into New Zealand, your little furry friend must be a graduate of a six-month quarantine in Australia or be an immigrant from Mother England. That was where the Kiwi genius for indirection manifested itself.

Instead of a flat prohibition against foreign pets, New Zealand simply made it terribly inconvenient to have them on board. Most yachts arrive in New Zealand as we did, at the beginning of the six-month southern hurricane season. Under New Zealand law, *Prospector* was eligible to remain in the Commonwealth for up to 12 months. Velda and I had visas good for six months. Presumably, if we behaved ourselves, those visas could be extended. However, our animals, Cap and Lara, were allowed to breathe New Zealand air for only 90 days.

There were no extensions or exceptions. Although I never heard of a case where that threat was carried out, we were told that they would be put to death if they overstayed, or somehow got ashore. Since the only route open to an animal-lover forced out of New Zealand in the middle of the hurricane season was sailing west to Australia, or an easterly passage in the roaring forties toward the Americas, the authorities believed that the 90-day restriction would

197

discourage people with animals on board from calling in New Zealand.

On the face of it, that 90-day arrangement was not a bad compromise. It allowed people with pets to visit, yet it was politically soothing to the general population with its fears concerning rabies. Although I knew they were merely following orders, I made it clear why I felt that policy was absurd. The officer's response neatly summed up the argument from the Kiwi point of view.

Naturally, he had heard my arguments before, and he smiled as he said, "Why should we be sensible about a possible hazard that is completely unnecessary?"

If I were a New Zealander, I would be infinitely more concerned about the people who arrive daily by air from places like Mexico, Latin America, and Africa; places where anthrax, hoof and mouth disease, and rinderpest exist.

The customs officer whose name, we later learned, was Lou Sabin, was a gentleman. His annoyance soon evaporated. While he was signing us in, the animal quarantine officer, a Scot named Gordon, was examining and photographing the animals.

I was required to sign a $1,000 (note) bond for each animal, guaranteeing that they would not escape or be taken ashore. The photography was for purposes of identification, to prevent us from avoiding the penalty by bringing a ringer off the beach if one of our animals got away. Local cats are much cheaper that a $1,000 bond. After signing the bond agreement, Gordon handed me a green plastic pennant bearing the stylized likeness of a kiwi bird. We were to fly this symbol while we remained in New Zealand waters to indicate we had pets on board. About once every week as long as we remained in New Zealand, the quarantine launch would come alongside and we would be required to display our animals. Ten years ago, we regarded those weekly quarantine inspections as a nuisance. Today, those inspections are an expensive nuisance.

They now cost NZ$25–$30 per visit. This illustrates an unfortunate but perhaps inevitable trend. Because of the novelty, cruising pioneers like Joshua Slocum and Conor O'Brien had things pretty much their own way. They were even received like heros most places they went. Today, however, since some 600 yachts, give or take a couple hundred, are always in the world-wide circum-navigation circuit, the bloom is well off the rose. Places like Tahiti, where yachts usually call, see an annual influx of yachts both as a source of revenue and pure trouble. For instance, in the wake of Hurricane *Veena*, French Polynesia no longer issues visas valid for the hurricane season. Everywhere, fees are increasing and restrictions becoming more onerous. Clearly, the ladder is being pulled up.

While I was talking with Lou, Gordon was impounding our egg shells (Velda was allowed to break the eggs into a jar and keep them; Gordon only wanted the shells).

We had known what to expect, but we had a brief argument about our canned meat; our home-canned meat bore only a grease pencil notation on the lid. Gordon didn't want the jars — just the contents. There went five pints of beef, an equal amount of chicken and four jars of pork. A jar of popcorn was another casualty. Even so, Gordon was not over burdened when the quarantine launch came alongside, taking the clearing officers back to Opua with the borrowed dinghy in tow. Considering how I had inconvenienced him, I never encountered another official anywhere so accommodating or willing to go that extra mile as Lou Sabin.

We were anchored near a building on the beach that bore a sign in faint, peeling letters: DEEMING'S BOAT SHED. I thought this might be the place Mike Davidson had recommended when we were in Bora Bora. The buildings had a worn look about them. They had been there a long time. Long enough, at any rate, so they seemed to belong, nestled against a rock outcrop behind them, partly on shore and partly standing on piling emerging from the water. Twin steel ribbons ran into the water from the side of the shed, and we could see the transom of a tarp–covered hull high out of the water.

Dirk Winters showed up after the quarantine launch left, and we made ourselves comfortable in the cockpit. Dirk told us that *Solitair* and *Kulkuri* were in Matawhi Bay. His boat also needed work, so we decided to go ashore in the morning to see what the prospects were of having the needed work done.

Our arrival in the shop the next morning coincided with the morning coffee, or mug–up (which the Kiwis call a smoker). Nine o'clock coffee is an international tradition in the maritime trades, but in New Zealand it is observed throughout industry.

Les Snowsill, the boss, was pointed out to us; we introduced ourselves and explained that we each had several projects in mind if he could take care of us. Les was a small man, slender and wiry, with a quickness that reminded you of a sparrow. His features were strong. His hair was a lank black, untinged by gray though he was then a grandfather twice over. In the shorts he habitually wore, he resembled a superannuated Boy Scout.

He had a strong New Zealand accent, which sounded cockney to my untutored ear, and when he was excited, as he was much of the time, I had difficulty understanding him. Like many Kiwis and Aussies, Les was addicted to rollies, hand-rolled cigarettes, and you seldom saw him without one stuck to his lower lip. He was gifted with a mind that moved even faster than his body. Blessed with a terrific sense of humor, chatting with him was not unlike playing straight man to Bob Hope. In sum, he was a nice guy, the sort of person you'd like as a life-long friend.

He came out to *Prospector* that afternoon in his yard boat. I introduced him to Velda. After a brief chat, we began the tour.

We started at the bow and worked our way aft. For a few giddy moments, I was the expansive ship owner, grandly pointing to this or that which needed to be fixed, made, or changed.

Les knows a good thing when he sees it; and for an hour we pretended I was a rich world traveler. Les trotted along in my wake, subtly egging me on by taking copious notes, asking respectful questions, and generally acting as if he thought I knew what I was talking about. We ended our little tour when, almost as an afterthought, I pointed to the starter and casually remarked that I had seen smoke rising from it, and suggested he ought to look at it.

It is remarkable how profoundly and inexorably the tide of human affairs sometimes can turn on the most casual event. Our starter offers an example. Most people would agree that smoke issuing from a starting motor is hardly cause for rejoicing, and that ordinary common sense says it ought to be attended to. But knowing what I know now, I would have done things much differently.

It's a little late, but I know now that you should never, ever, lose control of a job as important to your future as repairs to your engine's starting motor. Even then, had I realized that Les was going to subcontract the starter job out to an electrician in Russell, I might have gone with him to make sure the electrician knew what was going on. But I didn't. That was a costly error.

After our expensive tour, this is what my shopping list looked like, and the ultimate results we obtained:

Our shopping list

Project	Results
1. Build bow pulpit	Excellent
2. Grind valves	Excellent
3. Build new exhaust system	Excellent
4. Increase lifeline height by 10"	Excellent
5. Install roller furling on yard	Excellent
6. Haul and paint boat	Good
7. Repair head	Good
8. Rebuild galley	Good
9. Repair starter	Awful

Les was solidly booked until after the first of the year, so we picked up the hook, and joined our friends in Matawhi Bay, near Russell. *Kulkuri* was away on a cruise, but we spotted *Solitair* anchored near the Russell Boat Club, and worked our way toward her. Hans and Elly saw us coming, and I had scarcely set the anchor before they were alongside in their tiny dinghy.

"The dinghy landing is over there," Hans said, pointing toward the Boat Club landing. "Then just up the road you come to the Port and Starboard Deli... ."

Elly broke in, " ... where you can buy showers, and they have a washing machine!"

Hans looked at me and grinned. "Also," he added, "they have the best ice cream cones in town." He knew my weakness.

For any of a dozen reasons; deprived childhood, deprived adulthood, oral gratification, a craving for milk or a need for sugar, whatever, many yachties are inordinately fond of ice cream. I was no exception. The lady at the Deli knew her way into a yachtie's heart; she heaped almost a pint of ice cream on a 35¢ cone.

You could get a 15 minute shower for 20¢; most of the time there was hot water. They also had two coin operated washing machines. A veritable oasis of civilization.

However, there is more to life than the variety of flavors in the freezer chest, hot showers, or even a washing machine. The town of Russell was beckoning. Sidewalks began at the Deli. For three blocks, we walked along a row of cottages, each centered in neat little plots of lawn, flower beds, and tiny vegetable gardens, each set apart from its neighbor by a waist-high fence. Many of the homes had neatly lettered placards displayed on the fence or in a front window advertised space and lodgings. Tents stood in some yards; others had caravans or campers. These were retired folk living in a summer resort area, using their spare bedroom and front yard to supplement retirement income.

As we walked back and forth during the following weeks, we saw the same home owners and gardeners repeatedly. Nods of recognition grew into smiles, and smiles into greetings.

Kulkuri

The road gently ascended a modest rise, and after the third block, the street joined another. We turned to the left, and the road slowly dropped away from us in a wide circle to the right. All six or seven blocks of downtown Russell, former hellhole and one time capital of New Zealand, lay before us.

Beginning with the Captain Cook Museum on the left, and a small arcade on the right, you would quickly walk past a real estate agent, two boutiques, an ice cream parlor, and a doctor's office. Next to the arcade was another single-story building housing a book store, an electrical supply shop, a wine shop and a gourmet food store. Across the street was what the Kiwis primly call the public convenience or the loo.

A small supermarket shared the next building with the local branch of the Bank of New Zealand. The post office was on the corner. A hardware store stood across the street from the bank, next to a small Mobil Oil gas station on the corner. The cross street running past the Mobil station ended a block away at a large ferry dock. That block was occupied by a butcher shop, souvenir shop, travel agency and the local branch of Westpac Bank.

Diagonally across the intersection from the gas station was the Duke of Marlborough, one of the few licensed premises in New Zealand not owned by a brewery.

In a departure from English tradition, instead of a segregated men's bar, the Duke's public room where the pool players hung out and customers perched on high stools, leaning on narrow and equally high tables, catered to both sexes. The chatter here was louder and the beer was cheaper than in the Ladies, where the customers sat on overstuffed furniture and were waited on.

We spent many happy hours perched on those tall stools in the public bar, working our way through bottles of D.B. Brown, Lions, and other brews. As in Fiji, most beer was sold in 750 ml bottles, which wasn't surprising since the same company brewed both Fiji Bitters and D.B. Brown.

Most bars in New Zealand and Australia offered lunch in the bistro. The bistro usually was a steam table in a corner of the family bar offering salads and entrees. It was usually a good, filling lunch at a modest price. The Duke was unusual because the bistro was in a separate room.

When we wanted a bottle of rum, we went to the liquor store (another enterprise of the Duke's), where we found that spirits were taxed (and priced) according to their alcohol content. Some bottles were decorated with green stripes, indicating underproof (less than 40% alcohol) and others with red stripes to designate overproof (over 50% alcohol). The tax was brutal. A bottle of overproof liquor cost nearly twice that of a similar bottle of underproof.

Wine evidently was not taxed at all and probably for that reason, was fast gaining popularity. The wine store sold a variety of bottled wines, wines packaged in cardboard boxes (called casks) and bulk sherry, for which you brought your container.

Bulk sherry came in three flavors. Dry, medium and sweet. I thought it was a little like mixing paint, but it was cheap booze. For a dollar per liter, by judiciously opening first one tap, then another, you could blend exactly the flavor you preferred.

Wine casks ranged from the little two-liter box to the large six-liter carton. Boxed wines were popular, and there were many varieties from which to chose. I thought the wine cask was, in its modest way, potentially as significant a contribution to international yachting as the earlier invention of the Clorox bottle.

The wine boxes contained aluminum covered plastic bladders, which were easy to store. When you wanted to stow them, you simply removed the bladders from the boxes and stashed them in the bilge or anywhere. Because there was no air in them, they would limply conform to any shape. After the bladders were emptied, they made good radar reflectors. I have no doubt other beneficial uses will be found as they become more widely used.

Christmas was approaching, and after we had been in New Zealand about two weeks, we decided to join forces with Hans and Elly to do some Christmas shopping in Whangarei, the nearest large town. Because of the bus and ferry schedules, it was difficult to travel from Russell to Whangarei and return on the same day. The bus departed from and returned to Paihia. But we were anchored across the bay near Russell.

The morning trip to Whangarei was no problem; the 8:30 ferry from Russell would have delivered us in plenty of time for the 9:30 bus. It was the return trip that gave us problems. The only bus that left Whangarei after noon, didn't leave until 6:00 p.m. and it arrived in Paihia between 7:15 and 7:30. Unfortunately, the last ferry to Russell left Paihia at 7:00 p.m. This was clearly a case of not being able to get there from here — unless we used our dinghy, or made other arrangements.

We could have shifted one of our boats to Paihia, but it was a nuisance anchoring and reanchoring, and neither Hans nor I would have been comfortable leaving one of our boats newly reanchored in a strange place. Also, we knew a water taxi operated from Paihia, but we had become so conditioned to a penurious life–style and so self–reliant that it never occurred to me — and I doubt whether it occurred to the others — to wonder what it might have cost to hire the taxi for the return run.

Foolishly, we chose to use our dinghy. The water was like glass when we left Matawhi Bay that morning. We arrived in Paihia dry, in good spirits, and in plenty of time to find a place to tie the boat and stroll to the bus stop.

The ride to Whangarei was a rare treat. The road first passed through rocky, hilly terrain unsuited for agriculture. This area apparently had been reforested with trees that resembled loblolly pines of the southeastern United States. Perhaps they were.

A few giant tree ferns had been left near the highway. I think those trees, with their lovely shades of green, neatly capture the unique beauty of New Zealand. The first leg of the trip ended in Kawakawa, the town where the onion train had come to grief years earlier. Kawakawa is nearly a one street town. Not quite, but close. I particularly noted that the railroad tracks run down the middle of main street.

It was the location of those railroad tracks that defeated the purpose for which the Opua pier was originally conceived and built. It seems that shortly after the pier had been completed, the Ministry of Agriculture sent a train load of onions north to be shipped abroad from the new facility.

Railways in New Zealand, as elsewhere, were built before automobiles had replaced horses, and the tracks ran proudly down the middle of main street. The planners forgot that when the contest was between horse and train, there was no question about the outcome. Horses could move sideways, and had an innate desire to get out of the way. Automobiles have neither the agility of horses, nor their instinctive sense of self preservation.

The train was both unexpected and an unfamiliar sight in Kawakawa, and it caused a monumental traffic jam. When it was finally extricated, and completed its run to Opua, it was too late. In order to catch the tide, the ship had left. We were told that incident wrecked the government's hope of establishing a northern shipping terminus for agricultural commodities.

The government hospital was in Kawakawa, a few blocks up the hill. Both Velda and I had occasion to use those facilities, and I think I can speak for her that her encounter, like mine, with New Zealand's semi-socialized medical system was pleasant and very helpful. Plus we didn't have to mortgage the boat to pay for it. Experiences like that make you a believer.

The Whangarei bus usually discharged a few passengers here and received a few from the community and a connecting bus that came in from the country. The country bus was painted the same colors as the one we were riding, but unlike our modern German bus, was old enough to resemble a school bus.

As soon as the passengers were transferred, our bus retraced its way back to the highway. The countryside between Kawakawa and Whangarei is farm land, mostly pasture. We saw hundreds of prosperous looking cattle, sheep and horses grazing in the fields.

After several additional stops, mostly to deliver and pick up mail pouches in towns no larger than Russell, we rolled into the suburbs on the outskirts of Whangarei. After a quick unscheduled stop downtown to accommodate those who knew where they were going, we pulled into the railroad yards and stopped under an overhead shelter.

We hired a taxi and asked the driver to take us to the largest marine hardware store in town. He took us to Cater's Marine, where, over the next few months, we spent much time and a great deal of money. The store was across the street and about half a block from the marina on the Whangarei River that served as home base for the *HMS Bounty* replica whose captain had offered us a longboat oar in Tahiti as a temporary replacement for our broken topmast.

In the opposite direction, in the center of town, was a pedestrian mall. The largest building on the mall was the Whangarei Hotel. After lunch in the hotel bistro, we split up to do our Christmas shopping.

Although this was our third tropical Christmas, it was the first one where I was aware of crowded stores and sun burned Santas. My broken ribs had precluded much celebration in St. Thomas, and our second Christmas had been spent at sea.

Consequently, it seemed strange to see window decorations featuring cotton snow, snow flakes, and endless ersatz icicles dangling from make-believe cottage roofs on what may have been the hottest day of the year. Some northern traditions transplant better than others.

Whangarei, at 36° south, is as far south of the equator as San Francisco is north of it. But the southern Christmas sun is much more intense than the July sun in California because New Zealand has no smog. When I finished my shopping, I was glad to buy an ice cream cone from a street vendor and sit in the shade watching the other Christmas shoppers and Santa across the street ring the bell over his kettle.

Velda, Hans, and Elly arrived from different directions. All the stores close at 5:00 p.m., so we had more than ample time to stroll back to the bus depot with our packages. Because an hour's delay in Whangarei imposed such a burden on passengers bound for points beyond Paihia such as Russell, I decided to find out why the schedule was arranged that way.

206

I approached the lady behind the information wicket and asked why the north-bound bus didn't leave until six, when all the stores closed at five. She gave me a puzzled look, then recognizing my Yankee accent, she smiled as she might smile at a child.

"Because that's the schedule, sir," she said, reasonably. I could imagine her later telling friends, "Yanks do ask the most peculiar questions!"

The trip back to Paihia was a good deal faster than the ride down had been. There was less traffic and we had fewer stops, but the most important reason undoubtedly was that the driver wanted to get home to supper. Arriving at Paihia, we stowed our packages in the bow of the dinghy, hoping they would stay dry. A light breeze was blowing out of the northeast, kicking up a little chop squarely on our nose. Even then, none of us had sense enough to think of the water taxi. When people as experienced as we behave that way, you can understand how people in small boats get into trouble. They just don't think.

Running the outboard motor as slowly as possible, I steered a course quartering into the larger waves. Nevertheless, our blunt bow caused spray to come into the boat. Hans bailed constantly during the half hour it took us to get into the lee of Matawhi Bay.

The folks in Russell were of two minds about the annual influx of foreign yachts. Some business people, like the Deli, appreciated the extra business. But during the southern summer, with the seasonal arrival of tourists from Auckland and points south, most merchants had all the business they could comfortably handle.

As for the rest of the residents, the presence of 50 or 60 foreign yachts only meant longer lines at the post office and a more crowded public room at the Duke's.

However, the local folks did something special for us that Christmas. They graciously loaned the Russell Boat Club building to us for a Christmas party. I wish I knew who the organizers were; someone had to have taken the initiative to make it happen. My guess is that Doug and Mary Solomon, transplanted South Africans from Vancouver, B.C. whose boat, *Sundance Kid,* was well known in the South Pacific, were among those responsible. Doug is one of those people who seldom frowns. Mary is a bright, perky woman who put up with Doug, and was that rare person who could raise two teenagers on a 31 foot sloop, and stay sane doing it.

It was Mary, I think, who made sure the proper number of turkeys were purchased and saw to it that the appropriate number of gifts were accumulated around the tree. Bill Wridge, from *Rain Eagle*, was pressed into service as Santa Claus. He was provided with a costume, and made a splendid, if somewhat lascivious Santa. The supper was delicious, and the party an outstanding success. The tree, the Santa, the games and songs — it was a lovely time, made the more memorable because some Kiwi hosts joined us and shared our celebration.

New Years Eve was different. Hans and Elly asked us to join them on *Solitair* for a quiet dinner and a drink or two to welcome the New Year. Elly is a superb cook, specializing in Indonesian dishes, which the Dutch do well. Another couple, Martin and Gerda from the ketch *Kennemar* were also invited.

Martin and his wife undoubtedly have an interesting time when they pass through customs from place to place because they are a Dutch–American couple, but their boat is in British registry; her home port is Tortola, BVI.

This seemed an appropriate time to announce publicly our intent to continue sailing west. I think each of us had already made that decision privately, but it was time we acknowledged it to each other and to our friends.

Martin and Gerda have more blue water miles than most people, and after we made our announcement at dinner, they regaled us with stories of places they had seen and experiences we could anticipate as we continued our journey toward the setting sun. All the while, of course, our generous host continuously refreshed our drinks. After all, it was New Year's Eve.

The authorities had issued a temporary order permitting the yachties to fire flares, if they wished, to celebrate the New Year. Personally, I feel an adequate greeting can be conveyed with a dish pan and a large metal spoon. But this, admittedly, is prosaic, and was not at all up to Hans Lutt's standard.

Sitting in *Solitair's* cockpit, we heard people around us begin to count off the seconds. When the last second was sounded the anchorage erupted in a glow of pyrotechnics, and the hills echoed from a cacophony of whistles, bells, and cheers. Hans felt obliged to make his contribution, so he loaded his flare pistol and fired it into the air. Flare pistols have their purpose, but generating loud and satisfying *bangs* is not one of them. Even the flare, in a sky filled with similar signals, was quickly out of sight.

Hans ran below, and rummaged in his flare locker. He returned triumphantly to the cockpit with a huge handheld parachute flare of European manufacture, about a foot and a half long. I had never seen a flare that big.

I was quickly obvious that Hans had never fired one. Together, we read the directions. He translated the English instructions into Dutch as he went along while I was trying to make sense out of the pictures.

To be perfectly honest about it, neither of us was in any condition to be fooling around with something as potentially lethal as a 50,000 candle power parachute flare. Those big flares are not toys, and I said something to that effect, but seeing that he was determined, I got out of his way; particularly out of the line of fire.

A sight I'm sure I'll always remember – I was halfway out of the cockpit by that time – was Hans squinting owlishly along the tube fumbling with his right hand for the igniter. That was when I realized he was holding the flare upside down.

I should have tried to take it away from him, but the time for diplomatic intervention had passed. At that point, all I wanted was to put as much distance between me and that flare as possible. I almost got to the bow before Hans found the igniter.

An intense, unearthly, orange glow seemed to erupt from the cockpit, accompanied by a hissing sound like a blowtorch. I also heard human sounds. Yells, curses, moans.

Hans had fired the flare *upside down*.

Instead of gracefully and dramatically arcing into the sky, it had gone down the front of his trousers. It's lucky he wasn't wearing shorts. Actually, he was lucky to be alive.

The burning flare was quickly tossed overboard. Luckily it drifted clear of the plastic dinghy painters, and it also missed the two rubber dinghies hanging astern of *Solitair*.

Things happened fast after that. With great presence of mind, Velda grabbed a jerry can, and after tasting its contents to make sure it wasn't gasoline, she passed it to Hans who was battling a fire in his teak cockpit gratings.

Luckily, because *Solitair* was a steel boat, the damage was confined to blistered paint, charred cockpit gratings, and a nasty third degree burn on Hans' lower left leg. It was amazing how fast other yachties responded, even after hours of partying. Dinghies from neighboring yachts began arriving with fire extinguishers while the grating was still in flames.

The evening wasn't over yet. While we were alternatively scolding and commiserating with Hans and treating his burn, Elly was searching the boat for her cat. I was sure that had that flare gone off in our cockpit, Lara would have leaped into the nearest hole and stayed there until she thought the danger was past. It seemed logical to me that Elly's cat would behave the same way.

Elly didn't agree with me. She thought her cat had panicked and jumped overboard. Hans attempted to comfort her by pointing out that even if the cat had gone overboard and had drowned, it served it right for deserting them in their moment of trouble.

Then, possibly out of affection for the animal or possibly thinking about that $1,000 bond hanging over his head if he couldn't produce the cat when he was ready to leave New Zealand, he also began to wax emotional:

"I'm going to miss that old cat," he said.

I was still certain the animal would emerge when it thought the All Clear had sounded, but I tried to cheer Hans by promising that I would return at first light, and help him search the high water mark along the beach. If the cat had gone overboard and subsequently perished, we might find its little carcass along the water's edge. Hans seemed to brighten at that prospect, but poor Elly's sobs became more pronounced.

As we were leaving, I could hear Hans explaining to her, in English, how much the cat deserved to die for its disloyalty in leaving them to their fate. So far, I thought, 1984 had not been a very good year, and it was only about one and a half hours old.

After a short nap, I went back to *Solitair*. As I went alongside, I saw Elly, still wearing her long hostess gown, walking up and down the deck, crooning a Dutch lullaby to the cat that she cuddled in her arms. Hans, of course, was sound asleep.

Apparently, not all cats are alike. Their cat had abandoned ship. After we had left, Elly had begun rowing their dinghy around the fleet, calling her cat's name. Almost immediately she was hailed by a nearby Swedish boat with the improbable name of *Cool Runnings*.

Nearly an hour and a half after the excitement of the misfired flare had died down, *Cool Runnings'* people had heard a cat crying in the water, and had gone to investigate. Sure enough, there was a cat swimming around the boats. They had scooped it out of the water, and waited to see who would claim it.

Work on *Prospector* was scheduled to begin after the middle of January. We moved the boat back to Opua, and Les and his crew went to work. Some projects were more successful than others. The pulpit, which Les designed, was a great success. It reinforced the bowsprit and took the terror out of headsail handling. At sea, it also provided a safe and sanitary situs for a function traditionally associated with the ship's heads. This was one of those happy situations which are all benefit, especially from the captain's point of view. There is no possibility of a careless crew member plugging a bowsprit. I have been very pleased with it.

Dick and Pat McIlvride owned the Deeming property and lived on the hill above it. Dick was both a master mariner and a master carpenter. He graciously volunteered to repair our bowsprit which had developed a longitudinal crack, possibly from the impact that had broken the gammon iron in the storm near Bermuda in 1981.

We unshipped the bowsprit and Dick carried it up to his shop on a wagon towed behind a farm tractor. With consummate skill, he removed the damaged portion and replaced it with a sound piece of Douglas fir (Oregon pine to a New Zealander). It was a beautiful piece of work.

I wish everything had turned out that well. Most things did, but sadly, the human mind tends to dwell on misery and disaster, and now I must tell you about the starter. The appearance of smoke when the ignition key was turned was not a new phenomena. I had noticed it when we were in Costa Rica. Chico, Pacific Marina's mechanic, had taken the starter apart and cleaned it. No more gray smoke. I had thought that was what Les would do, but I was wrong.

I didn't realize that New Zealand's tradesmen respected each other's turf to an extent matched, in the United States, only by the medical profession. Les is a wonderful welder, a superb mechanic, and a highly skilled machinist.

He removed the starter and sent it to an electrician in Russell for repairs. Les phrased it differently. To use his expression, he "whipped it off" the engine.

More than anything, his choice of expressions reflected his unquenchable optimism. Nobody whips a starter off a Perkins 4-108 diesel engine. It is a long, dirty, complicated job requiring, among other things, the prior removal of the oil cooler lines.

Back from Russell came the bad news. The armature was shot. A new one wasn't available, but the electrician thought he could improvise by using one from an old Bedford truck if he could just make the bearings fit. **Oh, oh!**

That's a major danger signal. I knew, of course, that because of exorbitant import duties, improvision had been raised to an art form in New Zealand. But using old parts from an English truck seemed to be stretching it, even for New Zealand.

On the other hand, what was the alternative? You can't hand crank a Perkins. Reluctantly, I told Les to go ahead *because I failed to consider the most logical alternative*. There's a lesson here. But like everyone, I'm the product of my environment. I was brought up to admire and respect expertise and authority, and have developed what little skepticism I have, late in life and at great expense.

Therefore, it never occurred to me that the most logical response would have been to shrug and smile saying, "Well, if he can't fix it, have him put it back together." What's a little smoke?

The charge for this work came to $200 N.Z. Les added that amount to my growing bill and installed the starter.

So you can see why this starter problem was critical, let me first explain that unlike gas engines which rely on an electrical spark for ignition, diesel fuel is ignited by heat generated when the engine's pistons compress air in the cylinders. While that principle applies to all diesel engines, there are significant operating differences between heavy, bulky, slow–speed industrial engines and the light, high–speed engines found in small cruising yachts.

Because of their light construction, thin cylinder walls, and so forth, which permit the rapid dissipation of heat, this latter class of engines, of which our Perkins was a prime example, have special cranking requirements. All things being equal, a heavy industrial engine will fire no matter how slowly it is cranked. But light, high speed diesels must be cranked at a considerable rate of speed to generate the heat necessary to fire diesel fuel. Our Perkins will not fire unless the starter can spin the engine at least 280 revolutions per minute (RPMs).

While the starter I had sent to the shop had a bad smoking habit, it *would* start the engine. Sadly, the starter that came back from Russell $200 later, could only turn the engine about 90 RPMs, certainly much too slowly for it to fire.

Obviously more work was needed. The unseen electrician now reported, through Les, that the problem might be solved by installing new field coils (probably from the same truck) to match the armature. I was buying that truck by the pound. They cost an additional $180. As you might guess, by now I was devoutly wishing either I hadn't noticed smoke from the starter, or having seen it, I had forgivingly looked the other way.

Meanwhile, the other work was proceeding, and zero hour was rapidly approaching. We hauled the boat and Velda and I scrubbed and painted her. The mechanics fitted the new pulpit, reinstalled the stove and head, put the new exhaust system together; accomplished everything on Les's list *except fix the starter*. By this time, we had invested over NZ$400 in the starter, and it wouldn't start the engine. The electrician gave up. I guess he thought it was a terminal case. Then Les showed me how to start the engine on gasoline.

It was simple. You wet a rag in gasoline and wrapped it around the air intake filter. After closing your eyes and murmuring a brief prayer, hoping the electrical sparks created by closing the starter switch wouldn't cause the gas fumes to explode and blow you and the boat to Kingdom Come, you turned the ignition key.

Velda always stood by, fire extinguisher in hand. I don't think she really thought it through. I wondered what good a fire extinguisher be if the boat blew up? But I guess it made her feel better.

I have great power of concentration, but I become so focused on whatever is claiming my attention at the moment that I tend to become oblivious to most everything else. I almost overlooked the fact that since we had decided to go west when we left New Zealand, we needed Australian visas. Thus, during the last days of our New Zealand visit, Velda and I went to Auckland to obtain them.

The Auckland train depot/bus station, like similar places elsewhere, was located in a seedier part of town, where hotel rates are painted on the sides of old hotels, where not all the lights in the marquee work, and where, instead of air conditioning, you are likely to see a drape blowing out a half-open window — looking like a bag-lady with a drooping stocking.

Our standards may not be high, but we prefer a hotel that does not need to protect the room clerk with a barred grill. Consequently, after stretching our legs and collecting our gear, we slung our bags on our shoulders and started walking, following Customs Street along Auckland's waterfront.

The first modern hotel we found was the South Pacific. We shyly inquired at the desk for the rates. The clerk, knowing we didn't belong there, told us their rooms started at $120.

I doubt I could ever bring myself to pay more per hour for sleeping than I can earn standing up. Certainly not in those lean years. Which raises an interesting point; how do you reckon what a night's sleep in a bed is worth? We picked up our bundles and pushed our way through the doors back to the sidewalk.

Queen Street is the main downtown thoroughfare running perpendicular to the waterfront. We decided to follow it, thinking we might find a more reasonable hotel uptown.

The ground floors of the old buildings on both sides of Queen Street, for several blocks, had been gutted and turned into inside shopping malls. It was an excellent example of urban renewal. The new shops were bright and airy. The merchandise was attractive and well displayed. The malls were crowded, and business was good.

Like waifs, we wandered along the street, peering into store windows and down side streets. Tucked away on a small side street, we saw a marquee announcing the Hotel Debra Brett. Exactly the sort of place waifs should seek.

We know now there are at least a dozen middle class hotels in downtown Auckland named Debra Brett, Donna Baker, Darlene Brown, Diana Bellows, or Daphne Ball. Any name at all, if it was feminine with the initials D.B. We had also noticed a odd tendency by local hoteliers to name hotels after various Lions (The Green Lion, The Lazy Lion, and so forth) on earlier forays to Whangarei.

The only public bars we found in New Zealand were in hotels. Since the breweries own most of the bars, it follows that they owned the hotels that house the bars, including the Debra Brett.

The place we selected was sufficiently old–fashioned that the reception desk was on the first floor, at the head of the stairs. When I touched the bell on the counter, a pleasant middleaged woman bustled into the room. The rates were $35 a night for a double with bath. My kind of place.

I had noticed a high degree of uniformity earlier among the older folks at the Russell Boating Club, but I had attributed that to the insularity of the Bay of Islands, and the homogeneity of the people who chose to live there. Later, we came to realize that there was a great similarity everywhere we looked among the local population. New Zealanders tended to dress alike, talk alike, think alike, and to a surprising degree, look alike.

No doubt New Zealand's immigration policies were at least partly responsible. The country was settled by English and Irish farmers, who restricted subsequent immigration to people like themselves. New Zealand never imported cheap labor, and never encouraged immigration from Eastern Europe.

If the resulting culture seemed bland, perhaps that was only to be expected in an isolated nation of middle-class farmers and shopkeepers. On the plus side, because of her economic reliance on agriculture, New Zealand had escaped the environmental trauma associated with industrial development. The air was clean, the colors bright, and the people seemed extraordinarily healthy. But this utopian existence was not without cost. New Zealand was a debtor nation with very lopsided balance of trade. Sadly, the world is no longer fueled by wool and butter.

New Zealand's import tariffs offered another example of management by indirection. Japanese cameras, for instance, faced a tariff of approximately 100%. This steep tax wasn't calculated to protect a local camera industry; there isn't one. Its only purpose as far as I could tell was to discourage the purchase of foreign goods, and it applied not just to cameras, but across the spectrum of imports, and was wholly consistent with New Zealand's basic foreign policy, as I understood it, which was pure isolationism, politically, socially and economically.

Americans were liked and well treated, but the United States was perceived as a warmonger nation. The enviable nuclear-free policy which served to hold U.S. warships at bay was popular with the general public, but as a Marine veteran of WW II, I thought it was merely a recent opportunistic manifestation of the old, underlying antagonistic attitude that had caused the dockies in Wellington in 1942 to go on strike while my buddies in the 1st Marine Division were embarking for a landing on Guadalcanal for the purpose of preventing the Japanese from invading Australia and New Zealand.

Our Kiwi friends were curious about America and somewhat envious of our commercial arrangements, such as Sears Roebuck's unconditional tool guarantee, which was frequently mentioned, but no interest was expressed in emigrating to America.

Life in New Zealand, in many ways, is civilized almost to the point of being idyllic. Wages are low, but so is the cost of living. Life moves at a leisurely pace and except the continuing Maori-European controversy over the Treaty of Waitangi, there wasn't much social conflict. I've already mentioned that medical services were subsidized. But if your medical problem arose from an accident, all medical services and medicines were free. That generous policy extended to visitors as well.

An American friend of ours suffered a mild breakdown while we were in Opua. He was briefly committed to the mental hospital at Carrington, where he received splendid care, and was quickly restored to health.

But to an American, governmental intrusion into private lives seemed excessive. For instance, unlike the United States, a private yacht owner planning to go offshore must first obtain a license. Similarly, the boat must stand a stiff survey. Most Americans, I think, would be uncomfortable with that. On the other hand, a little intervention by the government before we left Opua might not have been such a bad thing.

The process of saying good-by to so many close and dear friends was drawn out and involved so many bottles of D.B. Brown and other, similar refreshments, that when the time came to leave, both of us were hung-over, sick, and exhausted.

Admiral Lord Nelson is credited with remarking that men and ships rot in port. As far as we were concerned, he was right. Since time immemorial, seafaring folk have turned to the health-restoring qualities of blue water for succor after the excesses of the port. That's what we did. Our problem, to be honest about it, was that we were too sick to leave.

However, we didn't have much choice. The final jobs in the boat yard had been completed. The boat (except the starter) was back in working order, and, most important of all, Cap and Lara's time had all but expired. We had entered New Zealand on November 27th, and on February 28th, according to everything we had been told, the animals were living on borrowed time.

It was late in the afternoon of the last day in February when we exchanged final embraces and shook hands with our friends for the last time. I had foolishly planned to do the final tying down as we motored through the outer chamber to sea. But we were too busy being sea-sick by turns, and the necessary work simply didn't get done.

When we emerged from the shelter of Cape Brett, we encountered a cross chop out of the southeast, curling around the Cape. Because we were still under power in the absence of any wind, we were tossed about with a jarring motion that utterly destroyed any interest I had in getting on with my responsibilities.

I didn't even have the dinghy secured, so blinking the tears from my watering eyes, and swallowing the bile that kept rising in my throat, I forced myself to move forward on hands and knees and begin the task of securing the boat.

Just as we came abreast of the Needles, a cluster of slender islands guarding the entrance to the Bay of Islands, a breeze out of the southeast began to blow. Obviously this was where that chop was coming from, and we began setting sail. The mainsail and staysail steadied us, but the chop was now on our starboard beam, and we were rolling uncomfortably.

The wind continued to rise as it grew dark, and I decided to take a double reef in the main. Velda and I wrestled with the sail, ordinarily a simple procedure, and we tied in the points.

The decks were cluttered with things I had forgotten to secure, or things I had secured, which had come adrift. And judging by the cry of anguish from Velda when she went below after the last reef points had been tied in, the below decks were in an equally sorry condition.

Velda struggled with the flying coffee cups, jars of seasonings, stray bits of clothing, tools, navigation gear and books all jumbled together, mostly on the cabin sole where pools of water leaking through the decks had accumulated. The boat was a shambles.

The wind continued to rise, and although the mainsail was double reefed, we were heeled over about ten degrees, an extraordinary degree of heel for *Prospector*. The seas were still building and as we approached North Cape, we found ourselves in a force six or seven sea condition. Occasionally, I could see the light at Cape Brett behind us when the swell lifting the boat coincided with the flash.

It was almost midnight, near the end of my watch, when I realized something was terribly amiss with the rig up forward. Now that I was focusing on it, over the weather noises I could hear a piece of loose gear crash and rattle somewhere in the fore part of the boat.

I yelled down the companionway to Velda, who was still valiantly trying to stow things below, to come on deck. We turned the boat over to the Autohelm, and crept forward to see what the trouble was.

When *Prospector* was rigged in the fall of 1940, commercial sail had all but disappeared, but men who knew how to rig deepwater sailing ships were still in the game. *Prospector's* rig is a faithful replica of the most successful commercial rigs.

Five feet from the top of her main mast, a pair of hounds were let into the mast on either side of the mast. They supported the trestle-tree, upon which the crosstree rested (the crosstree serves the same purpose as spreaders in a modern rig). This was cleverly locked together by the tenon cut in the heel of the topmast, which was stepped on this foundation.

The three-eighths inch chain jackstay we had installed in Costa Rica, about 35 feet long, hung from the hounds and was hauled taut parallel to and about eight inches in front of the mast by a large turnbuckle shackled to a ring bolt set in the deck. This jackstay provided lateral support for the yard, which was secured to the chain by a strong bracket.

At first, because of the spray coming over the starboard bow, and the wild motion of the boat, I didn't see the problem.

I worked my way forward on hands and knees. Velda was behind with the flashlight. Out of the corner of my eye, I saw movement and caught a glimpse of the end of the chain flick over my head, swing out over the rail, and back to the mast. *CRASH!*

The jackstay had come adrift! As I yelled a warning to Velda, I realized what that awful grinding noise overhead was. The bracket on the yard, normally supported by the jackstay, was sawing back and forth against the mast with every roll of the boat, chewing into the mast.

I found a piece of light line. After tying a noose in it, I worked my way toward the mast, being careful to keep out of range of the chain snapping and flicking over my head, swinging out and back, smashing against the mast. Finally, I was in position at the base of the mast, noose ready, waiting for the chain. It came flying in from the dark, crashing to a stop against the mast.

With a single motion, I slid the eye of the noose as far up the chain as I could reach, pulled it tight, and took a quick turn around a nearby belaying pin. The boat rolled, and I waited to see if the line would hold. It did. I took another piece of light line, threaded the end through a link, and made it fast to another belaying pin.

Half the turnbuckle had disappeared. Taking a longer piece of light line, I rigged a Spanish windlass. After hauling the chain taut with my improvised tackle, we faced a decision whether to keep going across the Tasman Sea or turn back to Opua for repairs.

There wasn't much need for discussion. We knew we would have been foolish to continue with a significant part of our rig held together by a jury-rigged Spanish windlass. I was worried about the attitude the officials might take toward the animals, but I thought we could make out a reasonable case of *force majeure*, the ancient law of the sea which obliges all civilized countries to open their ports to ships in trouble. I suspect the informal reception we received was standard.

We limped ("slunk" might be a more accurate description) back into Opua the following afternoon. The bush telegraph had been busy; our friends knew we were coming before we hove into view. Once ashore, I telephoned the authorities in Whangarei to announce our return. I was advised not to re-enter officially, but to make the necessary repairs as quickly as possible, and to stay close to the boat.

Everyone knew how ridiculous it had been for us to go to sea in such awful condition, but the average Kiwi is a mannerly person, and if any comments were made, they were well out of our hearing.

Wanderer V, owned by Susan and the late Eric Hiscock, the undisputed deans of long-distance cruising, was anchored up river from the boat yard. We had developed a wave and greeting relationship while we were at the yard. Then, to my surprise, before we left, Susan had come alongside with a parting gift of books. She appeared again, as an gracious gesture, as we were setting our anchor, saying "I knew it had to be you when I heard your little black dog barking."

This time, instead of party-party, we stuck to business, and quickly put things right again. The damage was spectacular, but mostly cosmetic. Of course below decks was a shambles, but Velda quickly straightened that out.

Four days later, a borrowed dinghy bumped against our topsides, and a young man came aboard.

"Hi," he said, "I'm Tom Sawyer (not his real name). I've had a lot of square-rigger experience, and I'm looking for passage to Australia."

He explained that he had recently come north from Antarctica, and the company paying his fare to the States didn't care whether his ticket originated from Auckland or Sydney. He wanted to go to Australia because a friend he wished to visit lived in Sydney.

When I came to know him better, I found it easy to understand why he was willing to sail a thousand miles out of his way to visit a friend. He couldn't have had very many friends.

I like aggressive young men with square-rigger experience, and after he told us some of his background, we were glad to take him along. That was the worse decision I made in four years of cruising. And I found it out very soon — but not soon enough.

Finally, repaired and rested, with everything that should be carefully stowed or lashed down, turnbuckles moused, and tanks topped up, we left New Zealand a second time. We motored out past Cape Brett, set the sails, and were on our way to Australia.

Chapter 9

Across the Terrible Tasman

$\mathcal{W}$hen we reached North Cape and turned west toward Australia, we were met by a steady southwesterly wind. During the first six days of the passage, our forward progress was nil. We had left the Bay of Islands on March eighth; incredibly, by the 14th, while we had logged 385 miles through the water, we had traveled only 85 miles over the ground.

We would get almost past the Three Kings — offshore islands north of Cape Reinga near North Cape — and abruptly, like a ball at the end of an rubber band, we would be hauled ingloriously back. Searching for clues, we studied the *Pilot Chart*, reread the *Sailing Directions*, and consulted *Ocean Passages of the World*. None explained the two-knot easterly current we were bucking.

The lack of published comment suggested that those currents were unusual. The only unusual weather phenomenon we knew about was a persistent and very deep high atmospheric pressure cell centered in the middle of the Tasman Sea, which had dominated the weather for the previous week.

When I came off watch, and was settling down in my bunk, reviewing the facts concerning our peculiar plight for the hundredth time, while waiting to fall asleep, I had a sudden intuitive flash of insight.

Sailors tended to associate high pressure with good weather and happy times, and regarded low pressure systems with fear and loathing. Ordinarily, that isn't a bad approach. Although high pressure systems often generate strong winds, they are usually steady breezes that provide good sailing.

High pressure systems have another, often overlooked, attribute.

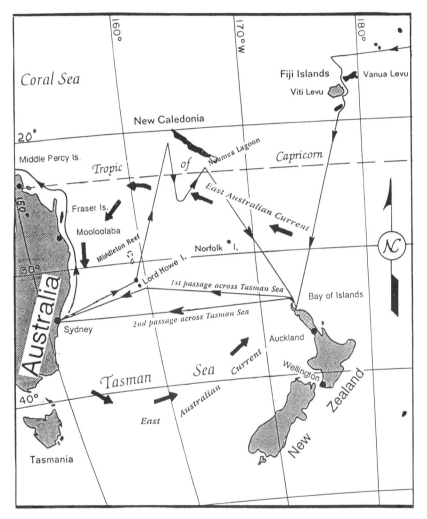

The Tasman and Coral Seas
depicting Prospector's voyages
(Chart 5)
(Note: See p. 264 for expanded chart and p. 287 for Noumea Lagoon)

Like the proverbial 20-ton elephant, a high pressure system sits wherever it damn well pleases, and when it sits, it is likely to squeeze whatever is beneath it.

Graphic demonstrations of the power of high atmospheric pressure occur many times every winter on ice-covered lakes in the Arctic because water is not easily compressed. I saw that effect every winter in Alaska, when the sheer *weight* of a high pressure cell would bend lake ice, often three feet thick and strong enough to support a tank battalion, forcing it beneath the surface of the water. Then the ice would break with a shattering BOOM that sounded like massed cannon, while untold thousands of gallons of water flowed over the ice through the resulting pressure cracks.

That same high pressure can also depress the ocean's surface by several feet. The displaced water, instead of squirting up through the ice as it will in an Arctic lake, flows laterally in the direction of the least resistance. Since the Tasman Sea is a semi-enclosed body of water with Australia blocking the flow of displaced water to the west; the cold, heavy waters of the Southern Ocean blocking it to the south; and the southeast trade winds piling up the Coral Sea preventing the displaced water from flowing north, the only route open was around the northern tip of New Zealand.

Thus, there was only one thing to do. Strap on the iron topsail and bull our way through that invisible bottleneck and into the Tasman Sea where the current would be less focused.

If only life were that simple. Tom was in a hurry, and he had suggested we start the engine the second day we were held back by the current, but I didn't think it was necessary. When he repeated his suggestion on the third day, I found myself flinching, and by the fourth day, when he began to insist on it, I felt the adrenalin begin to flow because by that time, I knew he was right. We had plenty of fuel, and to be perfectly honest about it, the only reason I didn't start the engine until the sixth day was because of pure stubbornness on my part. But then I swallowed my pride, and started the engine. We motored due west for two days before we picked up a breeze. By that time, we were well clear of the islands, and had settled into a shipboard routine.

It was not a routine I preferred, but it was predictable. Tom and I became embroiled in an almost constant quarrel. He was never satisfied with my performance or our daily runs.

Aided by 20/20 hindsight, I can see now that my relationship with Tom and other crew members who later joined us would have been improved and as a result, we would have had a happier ship, had I been more sensitive to any captain's subtle and unwritten responsibilities as a leader. It was my job, not Tom's, to take the initiative making sure our lines of communication were open. But I just didn't do it. As a father of six, I should have known, if anyone did, that impatience was characteristic of young people. Instead, I became the quintessential reactionary.

Tom was a superb sailor and his main interest was in a fast passage. Mine was to keep the overhead to a minimum. Those goals could have been complementary rather than mutually exclusive, if we had worked better together. But I had blinders on. All I knew was that ocean sailing can be inordinately expensive if you push things too hard. Spars break and sails tear. I saw in Tom a young man's judgment, and I questioned whether he knew the value of things, or had much experience paying for them. To me, he was representative of the kids who habitually borrow Dad's car and use his credit card to pay for the gas. The oceans are filled with young people like Tom; young, energetic, eager — and careless.

There was another complication. As a conscious objective, I tried to teach responsibility. To me, that meant the person on watch was in charge of the boat. I thought Tom took unfair advantage of that policy. When he came on watch, out came the reefs, or if the sail wasn't reefed, he would set the topsails, sails I never use at night.

Ultimately, of course, the skipper is always in charge. But my reasons for slowing the boat at night had a timorous and illogical ring to them, and I didn't want to be forced to defend them. Perhaps inevitably, one night while pushing the boat too hard, he ripped the foot off the mainsail. We sailed the last four days to Lord Howe Island in silence with a reef tied into the mainsail. I suppose this could be viewed as a penance for him, but all I saw was an expensive trip to the sailmaker when we arrived in Australia.

The Terrible Tassie was beginning to live up to her reputation. The weather began to deteriorate. Of course, even during the southern summer, at 36° south nasty weather was the norm. The log tells you what happened next.

March 17: Heavy squall at 4 a.m. Dropped jib on deck, put second reef in main. Sea up to 12–15 feet. Many breaking waves. Estimate wind SSW 45 knots at 8 a.m., with higher gusts.

March 22: *Last night at dusk, in a heavy following sea, steering cable broke. Struck all sails, rigged emergency tiller, heaved-to for the night. Wind SE 30–35 knots, seas high and breaking 20–25 feet.*

Prospector's steering system is a miniaturized version of a standard sailing ship's system, with wheel, drum, and tackles, all neatly tucked away in the wheel box and lazarette. She carries her rudder outboard of the transom, which creates a problem around docks and other boats, but which gives the rudder maximum leverage when forcing the keel sideways in close quarters.

The rudder head rises about ten inches above the taffrail to provide a point of attachment for an emergency wooden tiller that is kept lashed to the bulwarks nearby. It took only five minutes to rig the tiller, and less time than that to discover that the tiller was almost useless because the rudder was so heavy. We lashed the tiller for the night, and settled down to wait for dawn.

At daylight, Tom rummaged in the gear locker and found a pair of handy billys. In less than an hour, he had rigged them, one on each side of the boat, between the tiller and the bulwarks, leading their falls through blocks to the cockpit. He then opened the wheel-box, and taking four hard turns with each fall in opposite directions around the wheel drum, he tied their ends tightly together. The jury rig worked very well. Our steering system was again operational, so we set sail.

While we were jury rigging the steering system, we discovered (to me) a new method for estimating the drift **and** set of ocean currents. We had set the mainsail and the boat was beginning to move. Tom pointed to the Walker rotator line in our wake.

"Look at that," he said.

Instead of trailing obediently behind the boat, the line angled sharply away to the northeast, about 45 degrees from our course. The significance was instantly obvious. While we were lying dead in the water, the rotator at the end of its line hung straight down like a plumb bob because the boat and the rotator were both influenced by the same force and to the same degree.

However, as we began to move, the rotator and the boat came under different forces. The wind was pushing the boat *across* the current, which was still exerting a discernable pull on the rotator. As our speed increased, the angle caused by the northerly drift narrowed, and when we reached five knots, it disappeared.

I guessed, based on that simple observation, that we were in a northerly drift with a set of around a knot and a half. Had we been relying on dead reckoning, that would have been useful information. It seems possible that a way might be found to measure the variables and calculate the current's drift and set just like we can now calculate apparent wind.

We were close to Lord Howe Island. We weren't set on stopping there, but when we had left Opua the second time, Tim and Pauline Carr suggested that stopping there might be worth our while. The Carrs didn't often offer advice, but when they did it was worth listening to. They were owners of *Curlew*, a demon racing boat reincarnated from an 1895 Falmouth punt. The boat was only 28 feet long, but they have lived aboard and sailed her casually around the world and back and forth from one race to the next so often that proud owners of modern gel–coated rigs groan when they see her tanbark gaff–rigged sails approaching, because they know that more often than not, the Carrs would win.

I should think it would be embarrassing and irritating to own a Big Bucks Racing Machine, complete with coffee grinders, rod rigging and Dartmouth graduates, only to see the prize carted off by a worn out fishing boat that was designed by a carpenter and built during the Spanish-American War.

But Tim and Pauline had worked together so long that they function as a single entity with four arms and legs. Tim's secret weapon, apart from his superb seamanship, is a wardrobe of topsails that he uses with devastating effect on his opponents.

Speaking of skill, my navigational skills, such as they were, had begun to unravel by this time. It's one thing to make a decision about stopping at a particular place, and a different one to find it, especially with a person like Tom breathing over your shoulder. But I have only myself to blame, because this is where I learned another lesson I shouldn't have needed.

Every expert I have read warns time and again to check your sextant for index error *every* time you make an observation. But, because my sextant seemed always to have minus two minutes of error, and because of my immediate distractions, I had carelessly fallen out of the habit of checking it. There are always excuses — rough weather, the need for opportunistic sights, etc. But none of those are reasons. Just excuses.

With that preamble, you won't be surprised to learn that we missed the island. Lord Howe and Bonaire were the only landfalls I missed during our four-year cruise. I could plead that we passed it in the dark, which we did, but that alone could denote a serious navigational lapse, except when the island didn't appear when I expected it to, I had sensibly heaved-to.

The next morning at dawn, under clear skies, I took a series of star sights, and reduced them. *Aha,* I said to myself as I crossed their lines of position, *the island is ten miles to the southeast.* I didn't really expect to see it, but just to act out the charade, I went on deck — it was fully light by that time — and after glancing at the compass, faced southeast. There it was! But it wasn't ten miles away, or 15, or even 20 miles. Indeed, if it hadn't been so clear, I wouldn't have seen it. I later discovered the sextant was 17 minutes off. We were nearly 30 miles away from Lord Howe.

The wind was almost gone, and we motorsailed toward the island all day, arriving near the northern end at dusk, too late to attempt entering the lagoon. We heaved-to for the second night. Lord Howe has a reversing current that flows north on the flood and south on the ebb. We were carried five miles north at night, and when the tide reversed, almost the same distance south, so at daylight we were only a mile or so off the beach.

I called Lord Howe radio on the radio, and was rewarded by an immediate response. After identifying ourselves, I asked for advice about entering the lagoon. The operator told us to wait, that her husband would come out and show us the way in.

Within minutes, a little red runabout came boiling out of the pass, circled us, and the skipper waved and motioned us to follow. We did. He led us slowly through the pass into the clear, shallow water of the lagoon. The launch swung alongside.

"You can pick up that mooring," the young man said, pointing to a yellow buoy. "My name's Clive Wilson. I'm the harbor master."

When I asked about the piloting fee, he said, "Piloting is a courtesy here. Better check your mooring, though. Doctor and customs will be out directly."

With a wave of his hand, he gunned his engine and throwing

spray high on both sides, ran back across the lagoon to the dock on the shore side of the lagoon.

Tom put on fins and a mask, and went over the side to check the mooring. He found the buoy was shackled to a heavy piece of coral encrusted machinery, most likely part of a whaling ship sunk there in the last century.

While we waited for the officials, we took turns studying the shoreline through the binoculars. From the chart, we knew that the island lay on a north–south axis, and was about seven miles long by two miles wide. The southern third of the island was given over to twin mountains, Mt. Gower and Mt. Lidgbird, each rising nearly 3,000 feet. Dick McIlvride had warned that vicious down–drafts occur near the base of those mountains, and to give that end of the island a wide berth.

The lagoon was a long, shoal bay that enclosed much of the western perimeter of the island, beginning at the base of Mt. Lidg-bird, and extending north in a shallow crescent for about four miles, ending at a knoll near us. The coral barrier reef that enclosed the lagoon ran in a nearly straight line from the base of Mt. Lidgbird north to the knoll, passing less than 100 feet behind our mooring.

The twin peaks dominated the southern skyline. Turning to the left, we could see, with the glasses, what looked like an extensive lawn near the town dock, and behind that, a growth of palms and stately Norfolk pines. Apart from the lawn, the dock and a few power boats near it, and two other sailboats moored, like ourselves, in the outer part of the lagoon, there wasn't much evidence of human activity.

While we were studying the scenery, a second launch detached itself from the dock, and came toward us. These were the clearing officers. Both the doctor and the customs officer were in the same launch, but the customs officer remained in the boat until the doctor invited him aboard.

In the few countries that still require medical inspection aboard clearing vessels, the doctor is always the first official on board. Only after a letter of pratique has been issued may the customs officer come aboard. That is a relic of an earlier age, when small pox vaccinations were not universal, and communicable diseases had time aboard slow-moving sailing ships to incubate between ports.

In the dozens of ports we visited, we found that medical

inspections were required only in Fiji and Australia. But relic or not, even in this remote outpost, the officials took the rule seriously.

I was as ready for a cold beer as Velda was for a pack of cigarettes when the officials had completed their examination. We gleaned much useful information from them concerning stores, bars, the post office and other local attractions.

The customs officer warned us against swimming at night. "That's when the sharks come into the lagoon," he said. When an Australian warns you about sharks, it's well to pay attention. He also told us about the Bowler's Club, open to the public, and the only place on the island where you could buy a mixed drink.

Politically, Lord Howe is part of New South Wales — Australia's most populous state — and it is also a National Reserve. The population, we were told, was pegged at 290 people.

As I stepped off the dock and turned to face the woods, I was struck by an overwhelming sense of beauty. In some fashion, the ancient, gnarled, Norfolk pines, and the fringing coconut palms, backed by the expanse of carefully groomed lawn that ran from the beach to the road, melded together under the bright tropical sun in a symphony of green and shadow, of old and new, traditional and modern, which for me, set the tone of the place.

After tying the dinghy, we hiked up to the graveled road that ran parallel to the beach, and turned left, walking into a shadowy tunnel, the ancient pines closing overhead. Velda was enchanted by those huge trees. We surmised they must be indigenous partly because of their age, and because Norfolk Island lies only 500 miles upwind.

We soon came to a small store buried in the deep shadow. We found what we were looking for: cigarettes, and a cold beer. The storekeeper directed us to the Bowler's Club.

The walk took us back along the beach past the dock where we had left the dinghy, and past an intersection. The intersecting road ran off to the left, and at a glance, we saw signs indicating the post office, two more stores, and several unmarked buildings.

We continued along the beach road, passing several modest bungalows, a fourth store, and eventually we came to a sign reading BOWLER'S CLUB – VISITORS WELCOME.

We opened the gate, and followed the walk to a small building marked Clubhouse. It was early in the afternoon, but the clubhouse bar was busy. We ordered drinks and carried them to a table overlooking the bowling greens.

A game was in progress. The ladies wore modest white dresses; the gentlemen were in white trousers, long sleeved shirts, ties and straw hats. The spectators in the gallery applauded each well rolled bowl. I found it extraordinarily pleasant relaxing in the bar, watching – for the first time – the ancient game of bowls. I forgot, for the moment, the broken steering cable, the torn sail, our depleted funds, and even the misfortune of being inextricably linked to Tom for another three weeks.

Two days later, while we were enjoying breakfast, someone knocked on the hull. I climbed the companionway, and peered over the side. A dinghy with a young man and a boy was alongside. "Hello," the young man said in an unmistakable American accent. "My name is David George, and this is my son, Paul."

We shook hands, and I invited them aboard. David, originally from California, was a petroleum engineer. He had married a lovely and talented Australian lass named Joanne, and was now living in Australia. They had left Freemantle, on Australia's southwest coast, and had sailed their 38 foot steel ketch *Kailua* north along the somewhat barren west coast to Darwin, then east through Torres Straits, and south inside the Barrier Reef to Brisbane. Having nearly circumnavigated the Australian Continent, mostly up wind and against the prevailing tides and currents, they then sailed offshore from Brisbane to Lord Howe, arriving several days ahead of us.

We spent hours visiting with *Kailua's* people during the ten days we remained at Lord Howe. Early on, David was kind enough to help us out of a temporary financial crisis.

I had tried to change money in Paihia shortly before we left New Zealand. I had obtained the few Australian dollars the local bank had in its till. That was the money we used to pay for the groceries and our drinks at the Bowler's Club immediately upon our arrival.

A store near the post office and the post office itself served as agencies for two different Australian banks. Neither of them, however, was willing to exchange our remaining New Zealand currency for Australian, but since *Kailua* was bound for New Zealand, David was glad to exchange $50 Australian for an equivalent amount of New Zealand currency. We had a secret hoard of four American $20 bills, but that stash and the $50 Australian we had gotten from David was the extent of our bankroll.

While still in New Zealand, I had asked Buzzy to wire $2,000 to us in care of Westpac Bank in Sydney. I was confident the money would be waiting for us when we arrived in Australia.

Consequently, you can imagine my joy when I subsequently discovered a counter in the rear of Marie Thompson's store over which hung a WESTPAC AGENCY sign. I thought it probable the lady behind the counter could arrange a transfer of funds. I took my passport to the window and introduced myself. Mrs. Thompson obligingly called the bank in Sydney. Then she turned to me.

"It isn't there," she said.

An important consideration, when making telephone calls half way around the world, is to avoid dragging people out of bed. It never improves the quality of the communication when you wake people at 3 a.m., especially when you are asking for money.

I didn't have to worry about that here. Since we were six hours west of Seattle, Buzzy was eating lunch about the time we got up, and at noon, our time, Buz was sitting down to dinner.

However, when you place a call across the International Date line, it is helpful to know whether it is tomorrow or yesterday on the other end. It was yesterday in Seattle. Buzzy answered the phone and as usual accepted the charges.

"Well, this is a surprise," he said. "Are you there already?"

I explained our situation, and he promised to telex the money in the morning when the bank opened. And he did. The next day – in less than 24 hours – the Sydney bank called Marie Thompson, and authorized our advance. Once again, we were in the chips. And not a minute too soon. Tom's appetite, always healthy, had begun to resemble that of a bear preparing for hibernation. We had discovered a little grocery store that would accept a Master Charge card, but we may have overdone it; the lady who ran the store was beginning to look regretful when she saw us coming.

In the days that followed, we came to know the George family well. David was a perceptive observer, and he called our attention to the peculiar situation prevailing on the island.

Lord Howe had religion.

While the population was almost evenly divided between Seventh Day Adventists, and non–Adventists. The non–Adventists were strategically outnumbered because most of them, like the doctor, customs officer, weather forecasters and forest rangers, were government people. There was also a small but hardy minority who were neither government nor Adventists, like the fellow who ran the store where we bought cigarettes and beer.

Adventists are highly focused people who see themselves as a persecuted minority, primarily because of their rigid adherence to the Saturday Sabbath. While we were at Lord Howe, an incident occurred which brought that trait into sharp focus.

Largely on principle, the Adventists were enraged when the wife of a government employee had been selected as the new telephone operator, even though they knew it would by necessary to operate the telephone seven days a week – a condition no Adventist could possibly accept.

Adventists seem to dominate the tourist industry. Yet they effectively insulate their young from outside influences. Most guests arrive by air. They are met at the airport by taxicabs owned by Adventists, and are driven to Adventist-owned hotels. But the visitor is not likely to have any contact with young Adventists. The young people waiting tables, making beds and driving cabs are secular college students imported from the mainland for that purpose.

The only thing the Adventists couldn't control was the random arrival of visiting yachts. Family yachts like ours and the George's were not the problem. The problem lay in the lusty young men who crewed in the annual Brisbane-Lord Howe Ocean Race. They were the apples in that particular Garden of Eden.

I wasn't surprised to find the Adventists promoting an agenda calculated to discourage yachts from calling. We were charged a $20 fee for the mooring, which I thought reasonable. But there was serious talk of a $100 fee which would not be reasonable.

I've said a lot about Adventists, but I don't want to give a false impression. Our contacts with them invariably were pleasant and productive. Clive Wilson, the chap who piloted us through the reef and saw us to a secure mooring was an Adventist. So was Marie Thompson at the Westpac Agency who went well out of her way to help us.

Prodded by David George, I went to the met office at the airport, and arranged for a long-range forecast. It arrived (personal for *Prospector*) from Sydney the next day. The three-day outlook was good, and as it turned out, accurate. We had repaired the steering system properly, and Tom had patched our tired, mildewed old canvas mainsail in his usual Bristol fashion.

I cannot recall longing more fervently for a landfall then on the passage from Lord Howe to Sydney. Tom had learned how to goad me, and he did. By then, we had reached the point where he could accurately accuse me of doing or not doing something such as adjusting a sail, merely because he had suggested it.

Approaching an unfamiliar coast can be dicey. The New South Wales coast is flat and nondescript. There are no mountains or high landmarks. The morning we arrived, daylight overtook us while we were still miles at sea. The coast was an indistinct line, blurry through the haze. The breeze became fitful, and slowly died. I started the engine and began running on a heading of 265 degrees. Shortly before noon, we saw what appeared to be a flotilla of merchant ships. As we drew nearer, they proved to be ships laying at anchor waiting their turn to be called in to the busy terminals in Port Jackson. When I realized they were anchored, I knew the entrance to Port Jackson was near, though we still couldn't see it.

While I was examining those ships through the binoculars, I heard the roar of escaping air behind me. Although I had never heard that sound before, except perhaps in the movies, I knew instinctively that it was a submarine venting her ballast tanks.

Consequently, it was exciting but I was not surprised to see a conning tower emerge from beneath the waves not more than 200 yards away. The ship surfaced fully, water streaming off her main deck, and people appeared on her bridge.

I knew we couldn't keep up with her, but on the theory that we were both going in the same direction, I took a careful bearing on her heading as she steamed toward the coast.

Seeking Sydney Heads was like searching for a wild bee hive. You didn't look for the entrance; you looked for the bees. The tiny hole the insects use would be invisible without a steady flow of activity. Sydney Heads was a narrow gap in a low cliff. You'd pass it by, except for the amount of traffic buzzing around its entrance. Once inside, however, you find yourself in Port Jackson, one of the world's great natural harbors.

I called Sydney Radio, and was advised to anchor in Watson Bay and wait for the medical examiner and customs.

In many ways, entering a new harbor on a summer week end is like driving into a strange city at night in a heavy rainstorm. You are distracted by competing worries. Trying to find your way while avoiding the many hazards surrounding you is always tough. We found ourselves in the middle of flotillas of small sailboats racing madly around us, while we, in turn, were obliged to dodge the heavier, less nimble traffic, all the while anxiously scanning the shoreline for Watson Bay. We saw a thinly populated bathing beach on our right and a crowded beach on the left. Later, we learned they were Obelisk Bay and Lady Jane beaches respectively. We were too far away to appreciate it, but the former was the local nude beach, and the latter was where the gays went to meet and mingle.

Immediately adjacent to Lady Jane was Watson Bay. We were supposed to anchor near the pilot boats tied to a dock in the southeastern corner of the bay, but the guy who told us to do that had probably never tried it. The water was 60 feet deep. We ran slowly back toward the entrance, dodging other boats, watching the depth finder, until we found a suitable spot in 30 feet of water, where we dropped the anchor.

We saw a Ferris wheel on the beach turn slowly in the afternoon sun directly behind us. The faint strains of a steam calliope came across the water. Behind the amusement park, we could see two and three story buildings. I assumed those were apartments. The entire area, from our restricted vantage point, seemed to have a holiday air.

To the south, we saw dozens of high rise apartment houses, and to the right, the tops of skyscrapers, including the modernistic *Centre Point* building, rose over a wooded hill in the immediate foreground on the opposite side of the channel.

We waited an hour before a launch appropriately named the *Pasteur*, bearing on each side a large sign that said QUARANTINE came alongside. The boat nudged against us just long enough for the doctor to step across. By this time, I was calling attention to the opened gate so our official visitors would not find it necessary to step on the lifelines when they came aboard.

The doctor was a friendly young man. I invited him below to the saloon. He sat at the table and opened his brief case. Handing each of us a medical history form, he asked us to complete them.

While we answered the printed questions, he looked at Cap and Lara. "Are the animals healthy?" he asked.

234

Velda assured him they were, and we handed our completed forms to him. He questioned each of us, noting our responses. Then he took a document from his briefcase, filled it out and signed it with a flourish. "Here is your letter of pratique," he said.

"Don't forget to take the Q flag down," he added, as he stepped back aboard the launch.

As I was readjusting the flags on the starboard spreader, another launch arrived, this one bearing a varnished sign announcing **HM** CUSTOMS SERVICE. Two young officers came aboard, and began to look around.

It was immediately apparent that neither had experience on small boats, because both wore leather soled shoes. One smiled nervously at me, and confessed that ours was the first yacht he had attended. He didn't know what he was supposed to do.

Remembering the cool, professional way the customs officer at Lord Howe had gone about his business, I began to prompt the young men. While they were not well versed in yacht clearance, they had been well briefed on the fiscal aspects of their examination. I knew we had plenty of cash on deposit, thanks to Marie Thompson and AT&T. But it wasn't on the boat; it was waiting for us in the bank. I don't know if they believed me, but I was told to present myself with the cash at Clarence House on the following Monday.

The two officers held a short conference while looking at the animals. The bolder of the two said, "You know about the rules for animals?"

"You mean about staying mid-stream, not taking them ashore, that sort of thing?" I asked.

"There is more to it than that," the young man said. "You will have to anchor in the animal quarantine anchorage," he consulted his manual, "in Balls Head Bay," he added. "And you must post a bond. You can take care that in Clarence House Monday."

While he was talking, I had unfolded the Port Jackson chart, and spread it on the saloon table. "Can you show me where Balls Head Bay is?"

They studied the chart. I'm sure neither of them had seen one before. Realizing they were baffled, I pointed to major landmarks depicted on the chart. "This is the bridge," I prompted.

They conferred again. "It's above the bridge; you'll know the place when you see it," one of them said. "There are several boats there already. Some of them are Yanks, like you."

That was the end of the examination. Their launch was summoned, and they left. We pored over the chart. Sydney is a world class city, with a population of over three million people. But Sydney's busy docks and waterfront occupied only a fraction of Port Jackson's shoreline. Like the Bay of Islands, Port Jackson had deep water bays, prominent headlands, and unexpected peninsulas. Unlike the Bay, however, it also had many bedroom communities scattered around the shore.

In a more heavily populated area, those suburban communities would have been linked together and to the metropolitan center by an interlocking web of freeways and bridges, contributing to the universal traffic problems of all over-crowded cities, such as parking, smog, and endlessly frustrating traffic jams, and making water transportation difficult. Sydney had those problems in a modest way, but because many commuters rode to work on ferries and trains, the city was spared the worst of it.

Sydney's spectacular arch bridge linking the city with North Sydney was the only major bridge in the Port Jackson complex. Dozens of ferries scurried on their routes to and from the ferry terminal in the shadow of the bridge.

The world famous opera house, Sydney's international trademark, was almost immediately next door to the ferry terminal under the bridge. We began our chart search at the north end of the bridge. The first was Lavender Bay. We couldn't find the name of the second bay, but the third was Balls Head Bay.

In minutes, we had the engine running and the anchor secured. We went back into the channel, and turned south, hugging the bank, trying to stay out of the traffic as best we could. After about ten minutes, we came to a sharp bend in the channel. We turned the bend and *WOW!* The bridge was directly in front of us, and under it, to the left, was the Opera House.

The city, with its indistinguishable jumble of skyscrapers, and modernistic spires, lay on the left. Near us, in the foreshore, was what appeared to be a small Navy yard. Closer still was tiny Fort Denison Island in the middle of the channel almost completely covered by a massive stone structure. That was the punishment barracks used during convict days.

The bridge connecting
Sydney and North Sydney

The bridge traffic generates wind and noise in about equal proportions. But that was only annoying. The constriction of the narrow passage under the bridge creates a venturi effect increasing the flow of air and water currents. I felt the boat shifting uneasily in the turbulence. I was startled, looking back over my shoulder, to see a large ship bearing down on us.

I was uncertain about the controlling water depth, but I knew that in these restricted waters, a large vessel, even if she was overtaking, had the right of way.

The ship blew two short blasts on her whistle, signifying her intent of passing on our port side. I made the proper response with our Freon horn, and pulled closer to the bank on our right. The ship slipped effortlessly past. We heard the murmur of her engines over the hiss of water tumbling away from her bow.

The Sydney waterfront across the channel fell away to the left, and was lost in a montage of funnels, docks, warehouses, cranes and bustling tugs. Our ship, in the meanwhile, had abruptly turned to the right in front of us, and disappeared into a bay.

After leaving the bridge, we had gone past two bays; one with an amusement park, the other with several marinas. We came to the third bay where the ship had gone, and found her just inside the bay, tying to a coal dock.

Looking deeper into the bay, we saw a ragged assortment of yachts tucked away in a bight. I knew this was the place.

As we came closer, I saw several boats flying American flags. Two I noticed particularly, were *Le Papillon* and *Bali Ha'i*. We knew both boats had cats aboard.

Velda had brought Tom and D.L., owners of *Le Papillon*, to meet me in the hospital in Tahiti. We met John and Wendy Ettish, owners of the 37 foot Gulfstar *Bali Ha'i* at a wedding reception at Dick McIlvride's house in New Zealand.

Tom saw us coming, and climbed quickly down into his dinghy, and rowed out to meet us. He is one of those fortunate people with wonderfully organized minds. With him, it is always first things first. If we anchored here, we were likely to experience this. If we anchored there, something else might happen.

The famous Opera House (Note our stanchion in foreground)

"You see those steps over there?" he asked, pointing toward the shore. "You climb to the street, turn right, walk three blocks, and you'll come to Waverton. Besides the train station, you'll find a laundry, a deli, a small grocery store and a post office.

"What else do you need? Water? You can get water at the old power plant, over there. It will be a bit rusty, but let the faucet run for a minute or two."

That's Tom Lemm. A great guy, and all business.

John and Wendy came over that evening and brought us up to date. Fortunately, they only heard about our crew. They never had a chance to meet him.

Tom, our crew, had gone below while we were under the bridge exchanging whistle signals with the collier. He was packing. As soon as the anchor was set, we put the dinghy in the water, and I rowed him and his gear ashore.

My last sight of him was watching him struggle up those 128 stone steps, like climbing a pyramid, under the weight of his duffle. What a welcome sight that was! I don't think I stopped smiling for the rest of the day. However, I might not have been quite so happy had I known that before many more months passed we would be involved in a near fatal collision at sea.

Chicago of the
South Pacific

Balls Head Bay lies in a bowl, surrounded to the north and east by steep hills, but open to the southeast where Sydney's skyline was visible two miles away across Port Jackson.

The bay wasn't large; only half a mile deep and possibly a quarter mile wide. The portion set aside as a quarantine anchorage was a shallow indentation on the western side of the bay next to an attractive little city park.

Crumbling buildings backed against a wooded hill marked an abandoned power plant on a decrepit dock in the northeastern corner of the bay opposite the yacht anchorage. To the right of the power plant, on the other side of a stone dinghy landing, was a small Royal Navy facility. The dinghy landing was at the bottom of the steps where I last saw Tom Sawyer.

The anchorage was protected except in southeasterly winds, when the two-mile fetch from the city docks on Sydney's waterfront could generate significant waves.

We had arrived in Balls Head Bay on a Saturday afternoon. Following Tom Lemm's directions, we made a short sortie up to Waverton to get our bearings and needed supplies — fresh eggs, bread, beer and a newspaper.

Sunday was spent resting, reading the papers, and catching up on the news. It seemed strange that no matter how many days or weeks we had spent at sea, when we did catch up, only the names seemed to have changed. Everything else remained the same, except in small increments and insignificant detail.

Although the anchorage supposedly was reserved for foreign

yachts carrying pets, four live–aboard Aussie yachts shared it. These were *Madelline Ann, Aotea II, Vera,* and *Morning Star. Kiah* was permanently tied to the old power plant dock. Foreign yachts were in the majority, however, and at different times, American, German, English, New Zealand, and French flags were displayed.

Balls Head Bay anchorage

As a quarantine anchorage, Balls Head Bay had a lot to recommend it. Still, you wouldn't expect the Aussies to billet unpopular yachts carrying an unwanted cargo in a really prime location. They hadn't. During the War, this bay was a breaker's yard. Surplus, worn-out, and mortally wounded vessels were towed into the bay and dismantled. Ship breaking is a very untidy business. The bottom was littered with chunks of jagged rusting metal, causing serious anchoring problems.

Twice, during the five months we lived there, our anchor rodes were cut by debris on the bottom. No harm came of it because luckily, both times it happened during daylight hours. Still, knowing what was on the bottom, I wondered on stormy nights whether we would be adrift before morning.

The Royal Navy facility across the bay was a dive school. Several times a month a dive launch following streams of bubbles would come into our anchorage and circle the yachts. I suppose the trainees were practicing fixing mines on our bottoms.

When the trainee's arrival coincided with inexplicably shortened anchor rodes, we would ask the leading petty officer in the launch if the divers would untangle our anchor lines. They wouldn't always do it, but sometimes they did, and saved us the cost of hiring a diver.

Before we left Lord Howe, Marie Thompson had coached us concerning the Sydney subway system and how to find the bank's branch office where our money was on deposit.

We left the boat Monday morning and climbed the steps to Waverton. I bought our train tickets, and we walked down the ramp to the station platform where people were gathered.

Within minutes — the trains run at 20 minute intervals most of the day — we heard a train approaching from the north. It emerged from the tunnel like a huge mechanical caterpillar and ground noisily to a stop.

The doors clanged open and the passengers quickly boarded the nearest car. We found an empty seat, and studied a route map fastened to the wall of the coach. Waverton was the third stop north of the bridge. After crossing the bridge, the train would make three additional stops before it reached Town Station where the Westpac Bank office with our deposit was located.

The engineer's announcements were unintelligible, but the stations were well marked, and we had no difficulty finding our destination. The bank was in the Town Hall annex in the heart of Sydney's business district.

We surrendered our tickets to the guard at the gate and walked to the George Street exit. Instead of climbing the steps to the street level, we turned left and rode a short escalator to the front door of the bank. At the international transactions window, we identified ourselves, and received the balance of the money Buzzy had wired.

After deducting the $200 advance Marie Thompson had provided on Lord Howe, thanks to the exchange rate, we still carried away over $2,500 (Aus.) to show the officials. The bank teller, a friendly young woman, gave us detailed directions and again we were on the street with bulging pockets.

We had no difficulty finding Clarence House. It was three blocks north of Town Hall. The customs officer glanced at the wad of currency and made an entry in our file. I signed a $1,000 promissory note as a surety bond for our animals, and we were formally admitted into the Commonwealth of Australia.

Back in the anchorage, we met our new neighbors. Roger and Madelline Bodenham lived with an alleged dingo/dog and a brand new baby aboard *Madelline Ann*, a big fiberglass ketch Roger had built in Tasmania. Roger was an Englishman who taught fine art

241

at the University in Tasmania. Madelline, a former student, was an accomplished artist and also an art instructor. Roger introduced us to Birkenhead Pier across Port Jackson from Balls Head Bay.

Birkenhead Pier was an elaborate shopping center housed in a cluster of red brick buildings on a point of land immediately west of the city. Originally a munitions factory, it had been rebuilt since the War, and now housed a marina, a marine museum, two marine hardware stores, a large supermarket, a large butchers hall, an aggregation of green grocers, restaurants and an assortment of the small shops found in any shopping mall.

On a typical weekly shopping expedition, I would run the dinghy out of Balls Head Bay, and keeping a sharp eye for ferries and other traffic, I would run a half mile across open water in Port Jackson, Sydney's docks and the bridge now in plain view to my left, reaching the comparative safety of the south shore after a five-minute run.

Then I would turn slightly to the right and run past two small ship repair yards on the shore to my left, and the Goat Island Submarine Base on my right. That leg of the trip took another five minutes. Birkenhead was five minutes further, straight ahead. I could see the sailboat masts in the marina when I passed Goat Island. After tying the dinghy under the tide ramp near the fuel dock at Birkenhead, I always stopped first at the Franklin supermarket.

Franklin's is a big supermarket chain in New South Wales. The stores were comparable both in size and the variety of merchandise offered to any similar chain in America except you won't find a fresh meat counter or a fresh fruit and vegetable display in an Australian supermarket. Following the English tradition, those commodities are sold separately. Australian food prices would have brought tears to your eyes. They were higher than New Zealand's, but ridiculously low by any Stateside standard.

As a courtesy, you were allowed to retain your Franklin's shopping cart until you had completed all your shopping at the mall. I found that generous policy to be wonderfully convenient.

After leaving Franklin's, I would push my cart across the mall and down a short incline into the adjacent building that housed several small shops and the butcher's hall.

The hall was a room, isolated and glassed-in possibly for sanitary reasons, in the middle of the adjacent building. It was about 150 feet long by perhaps 100 feet wide. You entered it by pushing your cart through double swinging doors. Inside, customers found themselves in a wide aisle that looped around an island in the middle of the room. The continuous counters and display cabinets that lined both sides of the aisle were divided into individual butcher stalls, each with ten to 25 linear feet of counter and display space.

The room, including the aisle, was maintained in a spotlessly clean condition. Displays of roasts, steaks, chops, and other cuts of meat were fresh, wholesome and inviting.

There were about 30 stalls in this complex, most of which offered identical cuts of beef and lamb. Five stalls exhibited rabbit and poultry (which was very expensive), a wide variety of sausages and various cuts of pork. Since the goods in most of the stalls were identical, the hall was raucous with the sound of many voices, as butchers competed mostly by personality and cajolery. Every Saturday morning, the butchers sold the week's leftover meat at auction. It was a good chance to fill the freezer. I remember buying four small legs of lamb for two Australian dollars, which worked out to about 35¢ *each* in American money. Even the best cuts of beef rarely cost more than four dollars per kilo (or slightly less than two dollars per pound), and lamb chops were practically given away. American style bacon was unknown, so we bought deliciously seasoned bulk pork mince (sausage). That was an exceptional bargain, costing less than 50¢ a pound.

After buying the meat we needed, I would push my loaded cart out the swinging doors and through that building to the one behind it where the greengrocers conducted their businesses. There were 12 competing greengrocers. Like the meat exhibits, the fruits and vegetables were fresh, wholesome, and beautifully displayed.

The next stop was the liquor store. Spirits were even more heavily taxed in Australia than in New Zealand and therefore were very expensive. Beer was also expensive. A case of little 250 ml. bottles cost $16. A six-pack of Foster's beer was over six dollars. However, as in New Zealand, local wine appears to have escaped taxation. Consequently, not surprisingly, the national beverage appeared not to be beer, but "plonk." Plonk was cheap wine.

Usually, my last stop was at a Chinese carry-out near the dock where I would buy two egg rolls to eat while I was running the dinghy, loaded with my purchases, back to *Prospector*.

243

I would wheel the now heavily laden shopping cart down to the fuel dock. Then, after loading the groceries, and returning the cart, I would open a bottle of Tooey's beer, unwrap an eggroll and settle back for the 15-minute ride back to Balls Head Bay.

That trip was often exciting, because the dinghy was now deeper in the water, and therefore sluggish in its handling capability. I was often compelled to slow the boat and make emergency maneuvers to meet careless wakes thrown up by other, larger, boats.

Again passing Goat Island, I couldn't help but smile because it was clear to me that the Australian taxpayer, like his American cousin, was being taken on a military snipe hunt.

Like Americans, it seems the Australian taxpayers are forever condemned to pay for an assortment of expensive toys for the amusement and entertainment of their military elite. That submarine base was an exquisite example. During the six months we were there, I watched five submarines being taken out of the crate, so to speak, and prepared for active duty. But why? For what purpose?

Unless the Australian military psyche envisions an invasion from New Zealand (even as American military planners contemplated an invasion from Canada not so many years ago), I couldn't imagine why those subs were necessary. I realized many people thought that Australia would be compelled to defend herself one day against an Indonesian invasion. They may be right, although I doubt it; but even if they are, surely the Navy won't be counting on *submarines* to protect the Commonwealth against sampans in the shallow, treacherous, reef-strewn waters of the Arafura and Timor Seas. Personally, if I were planning a defensive war against Indonesia, I'd be spending my money on airplanes.

On the other hand, perhaps this was just the Navy's way of compensating for the loss of *HMS Melbourne*, the ill-fated and possibly jinxed aircraft carrier which was scrapped at about that time. Building a submarine force might have been the Australian equivalent of the American admiral's nostalgic impulse that led to the foolish reconstruction of an obsolete battleship Navy.

Frankly, I thought it was silly for a country with a population less than half that of California's to be squandering money on submarines. Military submarines, after all, are like loaded pistols. They have no friendly or peaceful uses. But where do you find rationality in defense programs? Look at our record.

America has always been generous with her youth. Each living generation of Americans, except the youngest, bear scars, mostly from other people's wars. To spare our former enemies the expense and inconvenience of protecting themselves, American taxpayers have maintained large garrisons in Europe and Asia without recompense for nearly half a century. That policy has sapped the economic vitality of the United States and therefore has weakened the global economy. It would be hard to top that performance.

Looking at those submarines reminded me of *Kiah*, another steel boat, and her owner–captain, John Bailey, who lived aboard. John was a gregarious bachelor, and a splendid host. It was he who showed us how to purge the old power plant's water lines of objectionable quantities of rust, and coax a cold shower out of the crumbling facilities.

By inclination, John was a *bon vivant*. By training, a marine engineer whose specialty was marine electricity. When I found that out, I quickly explained my problems with our starter.

John casually suggested we take the motor to a shop he knew. Early the next morning, I'm sure somewhat to his surprise, I was banging on his hull to let him know I had taken his suggestion seriously. In the bottom of the dinghy, wrapped in rags, was the infamous starter.

We had coffee – John was still asleep when I had arrived – then we drove in his car up the hill past Waverton, continuing until we reached an old fashioned suburb. The hotel, in the center of the small business district, dated from 1911.

"They call this district Crows Nest," John said, "because it's the highest ground around Sydney."

Turning down a side street, he parked the car and we went into an auto–electric shop. It was obvious that altruism wasn't his only motive when I saw the pretty young office manager. He explained the problem to her, and carried the starter out into the shop. I was told to come back the following day for a diagnosis and repair estimate.

It's a wonderful feeling to have experts focused on your problem. At last, thank God, something was going to get done. We returned to Balls Head Bay and had a self-congratulatory drink before I returned to *Prospector* with the good news.

The next day I hiked back to Crows Nest. It is marvelous how

245

the anticipation of good news will flatten even the steepest and most tedious of hills! But when I arrived, I got one of those good news — bad news jokes.

"The good news is that for some reason, although it was fitted to a diesel engine, your starter housing carries the marks identifying it for service in a four cylinder Hillman petrol engine, and that's the way it was wound." The shop foreman paused for effect. "What we have to do now," he went on, "is convert a Hillman starter back to one that will crank a Perkins diesel." He paused again, and pursed his lips thoughtfully. I scanned his face anxiously, looking for a sign that he had a ready solution.

"I've been calling around," he went on, "and nobody has the right armature." He permitted himself a small smile. "Too bad you didn't keep your old one. But I think we can fix that. It won't be exactly right, but it should do the job."

By that time, if he had proposed stuffing it with toasted marshmallows, I probably would have agreed. We left it that I would return a week later; by that time the starter either would be fixed, or we would know that repairs were impossible.

Mistaken assumptions lie at the root of many of life's problems. People think they have communicated by making the appropriate sounds but, as here, when one person said "starter" and thought Perkins, while the other said "starter" and thought Hillman, both thought they had exchanged useful information. But because neither told the other what they were *thinking*, only an *illusion* of communication had occurred.

When I returned a week later, the starter was ready. I paid the bill of $195 and hurried back to the boat, where I quickly reinstalled the starter, and turned the key. Nothing happened.

Well, that wasn't surprising. No doubt the batteries were low. John had a battery charger and shore power, so I dragged the 125 pound 8-D battery from the battery box, carefully lowered it into the dinghy and ran it over to *Kiah*. Handling a battery that heavy was not easy, but we managed it. Two days later, I reinstalled the battery, and turned the key. The "repaired" starter cranked the engine even more slowly than it had before I had taken it to Crows Nest. I was very discouraged.

I disconnected the starter again, and took it up the hill a second time. The foreman took it apart while I watched.

"Well, I'll be damned," he said softly. "It has been rewound for a Hillman again." Obviously, Les wasn't the only person who had communication problems.

He looked at me sadly. "I'm sorry about this, mate," he said, "let's have another go at it. Come back next week."

The following week, I trudged up the hill, collected the starter and returned to the boat. I installed it, turned the key, and – you guessed it – the same result.

The answer obviously did not reside in Crows Nest.

We were running out of time. Crossing the Indian Ocean is dangerous any time of the year, but the risks can be minimized by leaving Darwin no later than mid–August.

Darwin is almost 3,000 slow miles from Sydney. To get to Darwin in time, you want to leave Sydney in early May. By then, it was almost the middle of May.

The Lucas company, which is to the British Commonwealth what Delco is in America, had a factory repair center in Auburn, a Sydney suburb. The next day, with my wire cart and the starter, I took the train to Auburn.

The station master in Auburn pointed me in the right direction, and shortly before noon, I dragged the cart into the Lucas office. The shop foreman was courteous and helpful – up to a point. He fitted the starter to a test stand, applied power, and measured the torque the starter could deliver. It wasn't much. Definitely not enough to crank the Perkins.

"Well," I asked, "what's the matter with it?" The foreman didn't know. "Why don't we look?" I suggested.

"Oh, no," he said, shocked by the very idea. "I couldn't do that. It would be unethical for me to check another man's work."

I've been in and around organized labor most of my adult life, but that was a new refinement. "Look," I said, "I am roughly 12,000 miles from home. I'm going to be relying on that starter you are holding in your hand, to help get me there."

One thing led to another, and after an unnecessarily long debate concerning his obligation to me as a customer compared to any loyalty he might owe another tradesman, I overcame his delicate scruples, and he opened the starter. As I suspected, it was wound for a Hillman.

Now we went into the office. He sat at a computer terminal, and called up the inventory. "As I thought," he said cheerfully, "there isn't an armature in Australia to fit. This application is obsolete. Your bellhousing would have to be modified before a more modern starter could be fitted." He struck a few more keys and read the display.

"However," he added, "you may be in luck. This says the Perkins dealer down the road has a new starter like this in stock."

I made a third trip to the auto-electric shop in Crows Nest, dragging the cart and starter behind me. I told them what I had discovered. They apologized profusely and called Perkins, arranging for the new starter to be delivered, and giving me credit for what I had spent with them. Three days later, after handing over another $390 and my old starter, I took delivery of the new one, which I quickly installed. Then I turned the key.

Nothing happened.

I knew immediately that something else was terribly wrong. I had an awful feeling of foreboding as I fitted a wrench tightly to the flywheel nut. Then I slipped a pipe over the wrench handle for additional leverage. As gently as possible, I pressed on the pipe. The flywheel turned a fraction of an inch against enormous resistance.

Water began to trickle from the engine's air intake!

I didn't know whether to laugh or cry.

I climbed into the dinghy and went to the nearest pay phone, where I called Les Snowsill in New Zealand. Les had no idea what might have caused the engine to fill with water, but he told me how to fix it. Following his instructions, I removed the injectors.

There are some things such as brain surgery, the manufacture of sausage, and little salt water fountains spurting from your engine's injector ports, that non professionals should never see.

I rolled the engine over by hand to make sure all the water was out of the head, while squirting copious quantities of WD-40 into the combustion chambers. Satisfied that nearly all the water had been removed, I turned the starter switch, while continuing to pour WD-40 into the head.

While reinstalling the injectors, I ignorantly over-tightened the nuts holding them in place, and consequently broke two injector brackets. I thought it was absolutely essential, now that I had emptied most of the water from the engine, that any salt residue be flushed from the bearings before it could crystallize, or before the internal parts began to rust. It was imperative that the engine be started as soon as possible, certainly not waiting until next week. It was now past noon on a Friday and the Perkins dealer, in Auburn, was two hours away by train.

Stuffing the broken injectors in my pocket, I hurried up to Waverton, and caught the train. Two hours later, after walking briskly past a massage parlor, several Turkish groceries, and the Lucas building, I reached the Perkins dealership. I just made it.

I laid the two injectors on the counter in the parts department, and asked the clerk if he had replacement brackets.

"Sure thing, mate," he said cheerfully.

As he was writing up the bill, he asked, "Going to install them yourself, are you?"

"Sure," I said with a confidence I was far from feeling.

An older man who bore a remarkable resemblance to Carroll O'Conner was standing nearby listening to the conversation. "Better let me have a look," he said. "This is no job for a pair of pliers and a shifter."

I had noticed him standing in the doorway, and guessed he might be the shop foreman because he was wearing a shirt and tie. I nodded assent, and followed him into the shop. We went up a short staircase to a small room that opened on a balcony.

"This is the injector workshop," he said. "All the lads are gone by four o'clock of a Friday, you know." He unlocked the door, and we went inside.

He was right. Rebuilding injectors is no job for a pair of pliers and a Crescent wrench. Or for an amateur, for that matter. He subjected the injectors to a bench test, then quickly took them apart.

Holding one to the light, he squinted as he said to himself, "I thought so." Then, turning to me, he said, "This tip is broken. Both injectors have had salt water." He pointed to the tell-tale stains on the metal cylinders.

In less than ten minutes, he tested, disassembled, repaired and reassembled both injectors. When I inquired about the bill, he shrugged it off. "Just pay for the parts," he said. "Bring the others in next week, and I'll check them for you." He grinned. "I won't charge for the labor on them, either." Then he told me to get a torque wrench, and to tighten the nuts only to 12 foot/pounds. I stopped at a store in town and found a suitable wrench.

The next day, with injectors properly installed, but before I had a chance to start the engine, I heard a hail, and went up to the cockpit to see what was wanted. A little launch I didn't recognize, driven by an elderly man in greasy overalls, was lying in the water three feet away.

"Name's John Holmes," he said. "Tom Lemm (from *Le Papillon*) says you got engine trouble. Me and the Misses here," he paused and nodded toward a little woman wearing a brightly colored dress standing next to him, "we thought we'd stop by and see if we could give you a hand."

I remembered Tom mentioning a wizard mechanic he worked with, suggesting I get in touch with him. But we were counting our pennies again, and I was putting off as long as possible the inevitable call to Buzzy for more money. As you could imagine, the starter problem was standing our budget on its head, and I couldn't afford to hire mechanics, wizard or otherwise.

I quickly invited our benefactors aboard, and while Mrs. Holmes and Velda retired to the saloon, John inspected my work. He opened his tool kit, and began adjusting this and turning that, and eventually suggested that I change the oil again. Then they left, promising to return later. I went ashore and found the oil he recommended. When he came back, he had an oddly shaped piece of copper pipe.

"You need a syphon-break in that water line," he said. "This is the best I could do on such short notice." When we were ready to start the engine, I automatically reached for the gasoline soaked rag. He stopped me.

"Tom told me you were priming the engine with petrol," he said. "That's mainly why I'm here. Let me show you the proper way to start the engine."

He removed the air filter, and shot a blast of WD-40 into the air intake. Then he laid his callused palm across it. "I'm shuttin' off the air," he said. "I understand WD-40 has propane in it," he added. "Whatever it is, it makes a good starting fluid. Turn the key."

I did, and the starter whirred. The engine immediately revved up to 500 RPMs, twice as fast as the starter usually turned it. John jerked his hand away, and the engine instantly fired. "Nothing to it," he said, grinning, "when you know how."

He went on to explain that by placing his hand over the air intake, he was shutting off the flow of air into the engine. Without air, the pistons had nothing to compress; essentially the engine was rolling over in a vacuum. Thus, the only resistance the starter met was the internal friction of closely fitted engine parts bathed in oil slipping past each other.

Thus, the decompressed engine rapidly came up to speed. When he removed his hand, air was sucked into the chambers while the engine was spinning at the starter's maximum speed, and unless something else was wrong, it was certain to fire. Mr. Holmes was right. It was simple when you knew how!

Although engine and starter problems had preoccupied me for nearly three months, I had noticed other interesting things going on in the anchorage. For instance, one Sunday morning, I was startled to see an elderly motor yacht manned by Naval personnel, carrying depth char-

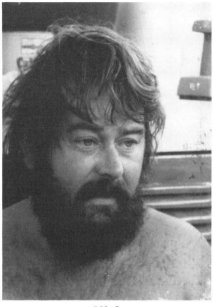

Nick

ges and armed with an antique machine gun mounted on the stern, steam past our mooring. Then I saw the cameraman.

They passed close to us. I gave them a wave. Much to the disgust of the cameraman, a slender Jack-tar standing by the machine gun waved back. Then the yacht disappeared around the corner.

A few days later, Velda sent invitations to everyone in the anchorage to join us for my birthday party. Jan and Nick Kositzin, owners of the motor yacht *Vera*, were among the first arrivals. We quickly learned they were participating in an amateur film reenactment of a little known incident of the second World War, the invasion of Port Jackson by two or three miniature Japanese submarines. Jan, of course, was the slender Australian sailor.

Nick was in a terrible auto accident as a very young man, and has serious physical and mental disabilities. He is partly paralyzed and dyslectic.

However, he's a winner. Subsequently, he became a window-dresser for a major Sydney department store. He has owned a series of motor yachts, each larger than the last, culminating in his beautiful old *Vera*, a 42 foot wooden yacht powered with twin English diesels.

Jan was a lovely young woman, willing to tackle about anything. Nick's disability prevented him from working on the engines. Because his work was seasonal, they couldn't afford to hire much work done. Therefore, although she had little mechanical ability, Jan cheerfully donned outsize coveralls and crawled down into *Vera's* bilges to attend to those big engines, as well as other chores which needed doing. She was quite a lady.

Craig and Louise Palmer from *Morning Star*, also accepted Velda's invitation. Louise was a young widow. Her son, 17 year-old Craig, was a SCUBA diver, and I soon learned to rely on him, rather than the Navy, to recover our anchors.

Everyone in the anchorage stopped by for a glass of plonk, or a Tooey's, or a sample of my Caribbean rum punch. It was one of those parties that seem almost spontaneous. Velda had cooked and served at least a gallon of her delicious onion soup.

Toward the end of our stay in Sydney, Velda and I were enjoying a brunch one Sunday morning, when we heard a woman calling, "Denny! Velda! Are you home?"

I went to the cockpit, and peering over the side, found a pretty girl standing on a small sailboat holding one of our stanchions. One look, and I called Velda. Our visitor was Julie Howe, the English girl we had met in the Marquesas. Julie was the sort of girl-woman who simultaneously provoked the best and the worst impulses in any aging male who saw her.

She had a delicately innocent air that aroused the protective impulse and a smile, as Jimmy Carter might have remarked, that provoked enormous lust in our hearts.

Julie had arrived in Taiohae Bay on a small South African sloop with a young man named Allen. I don't know what their problem was, but I know that although eventually they sailed off together, he left her twice, both times coming back on some silly pretext.

252

I also remembered that Jack and Ritva Curley on *Kulkuri* were practically ready to adopt her — she had that kind of appeal — and Ritva had even started making clothes for her.

Here she was!

I shook hands with Ross, her new boy friend, a well set up chap with dark hair and a bushy black beard. I liked him immediately. Julie indicated he was a shipwright and boat carpenter. If the little boat they had was a sample of his work, and apparently it was, then my first impression was correct. We were invited to dinner, and gladly accepted.

Albatross, Rosses' 19-foot sloop, was a thing of grace and beauty. It was obvious that many loving hours had been spent sanding and varnishing. Ross told me he had practically rebuilt her. He had done a wonderful piece of work. She floated so lightly, so gracefully, that I was sure she would respond to the slightest movement of air. An outboard motor hung on her quarter would have been an obscenity. Ross understood that and sensibly used a pair of oars as her auxiliary power.

At the lower end of George street, near the University and numerous Chinese restaurants, you'll find hanging over the sidewalk a small sign:

> ### Edwin Bowers & Sons Pty. Ltd.
> ### Nautical Instrument Makers

After climbing three flights of worn wooden stairs in an old fashioned office building, you'd soon discover that the gracious elderly gentleman waiting on you was the youngest and only surviving son of the firm's founder.

Although his shop was modern, bright and airy, in many ways, Mr. Bower was like a character from the 19th century, possibly from a novel by Dickens. He was a wonderful old gentleman. He re-silvered and realigned my sextant mirrors, repaired the ship's clock, and rebuilt the Walker log. With his directions, I also found a genuine old-fashioned ship's chandlery.

Those were the dark, crowded stores where you had your choice of white or red lead in pint or quart cans, where the rich smell of tarred hemp blended with the feel of wooden marlin spikes, and where Stockholm tar was sold out of a 50-gallon drum. Not a piece of plastic or stainless steel in sight.

When the clerk discovered I only wanted a gallon of tar, she rummaged around in the back room and found an empty soap container, which she rinsed, and filled with tar. When I paid for my purchases, I discovered the tar was free because her price list for tar began at five gallons, and she didn't think it was worth while to reprogram the computer to accept 11¢ for a piddling little gallon of the stuff. Like the injector repairs, this was another example of that wonderful Australian generosity.

I have somewhat earthy tastes, and I quickly discovered that Sydney had a robust red light district with a dozen porno shops, scores of streetwalkers, and several brothels in a five block radius around the Kings Cross train station.

While on the surface that may seem harmless, I'm sure there may be a darker side. An Australian journalist, Bob Bottomly, characterized Sydney as the "Chicago of the South Pacific," a comparison that flattered neither city. I don't know the present situation in Chicago, but Bottomly used the description to describe corruption that was pervasive in New South Wales.

Local newspapers stated that Sydney was the drug capital of the South Pacific. Later, we were to have some reason to believe that allegation might be true.

Any discussion of legality and illegality raises an interesting facet of the Australian character. There is no doubt in my mind that Australia's penal colony history influences public attitudes. I believe Aussies enjoy thinking of themselves as anarchistic rogues; as spiritual, if not physical, descendants of Ned Kelly, an infamous bush ranger from convict days. You could see that tendency whenever the average bloke on the street had an opportunity, through his trade union for instance, to give the government a stiff jab in the ribs.

Like the warders of an earlier era, you could always count on the government to retaliate. I thought governmental attitudes, policies, and actions were in many ways were unnecessarily harsh and restrictive. It seemed as if the government and the average citizen were engaged in a kind of ritualized confrontation, suitable to a relationship between guards and inmates or warders and convicts.

Sometimes, of course, when the convicts gained the upper hand, they could be harsher and more restrictive than the government. The Queensland boycott was an example. I have forgotten, if I ever knew, what provoked the argument in the first place. All I recall was what I regarded as unnecessary taunting and blatant provocation by Queenland's 73 year-old Conservative Premier to the Labour Party and to organized labor generally.

Organized labor controlled Australia's communication and transportation systems. The unions threw a figurative picket line around the State. All organized transport (rail, truck, air) was cut off. Even the mails were embargoed, and telephone service across State borders was suspended. To an American, it was an astonishing display, apparently countenanced by the Labour Government in Canberra. It seemed clear that the inconvenience and possible hardship that course of action caused the people of Queensland was of no consequence to either party.

A few months earlier, during the peak of the Christmas shopping season, the train drivers operating Sydney's subway system had gone on a ten-day wildcat strike in support of strikers engaged in a manning dispute on an obscure and remote train system in the coal fields.

Those were examples of convict-warder attitudes, and the inevitable resulting confrontation. But confrontation Australian style was not confined to institutional disputes.

Individuals were sometimes labeled "ockers" by their peers. That was not a complimentary term. It referred to people who behaved badly, were argumentative or unduly confrontational; people, in other words, you would rather avoid.

Because of the starter-related problems, it was late in the season before we were ready to leave Sydney. The conventional wisdom was that the opportunity for a safe passage across the Indian Ocean that year would have passed before we could reach Darwin. However, I thought we could make up lost time by sailing outside the Barrier Reef and north through the Coral Sea.

I was becoming concerned about our finances. I haven't said much about money, but Buzzy kept warning me the poorhouse was my certain fate if I didn't control our expenses better. Even discounting his sibling hyperbole, I was sure the modest stake we had invested when we began our travels must be running low.

We took *Prospector* to Birkenhead and bought an enormous quantity of groceries. As usual, our leave-taking was emotional. Our beloved friends boarded *Vera* and escorted us to the Heads. We passed *Endeavour*, a replica of explorer Captain James Cook's ship, inbound as we approached the Heads, and she paid us the huge courtesy of dipping her colors. That was the last really nice thing that happened to us for quite a while.

The day after leaving Sydney, while under power, we picked up a rope in the propeller which locked it and stalled the engine. That's no big deal if you have athletically inclined young people on board who aren't afraid of the water. But if you happen to be a senior citizen without much affinity for free diving, an immobilized propeller can be a serious problem.

Thinking I could cut the rope away in sheltered water, we tried to run back into the shelter of Watson Bay. Unfortunately, the wind was against us, and lacking the room to tack, we were unable to sail into Port Jackson.

Accordingly, we resumed our original course. On July 23rd, the wind began piping up at sundown, and by the end of my watch, I had two reefs in the main. We were sailing on a broad reach about 25 miles offshore from Newcastle, some 65 miles north from Sydney. It was almost midnight, near the end of my watch. The boat was heeled about eight degrees under the press of a force six wind and sea directly on our port beam, her steady rise and fall almost hypnotically comforting.

It was time to wake Velda for her watch. I switched on the Autohelm and went below. After putting the kettle on the stove, I gave her a call. As she sipped her hot coffee, I pointed to our approximate position on the chart. I was explaining my concerns about the currents when we were shocked by a sudden sideways jolt accompanied by a splintering *CRASH!!* in the forepart of the boat, as if a truck had rammed the bow!

Oh, my God! I thought we had hit a derelict container! I sprinted to the cockpit to see.

Less than a hundred yards ahead on our port bow a big fishing boat was rolling in the trough. I knew instantly somehow she was involved, but again I jumped to the wrong conclusion. I thought we must have hit her.

Almost without conscious thought, I cast off the Autohelm and mainsheet, and turned the boat into the wind. Wondering if any seams had opened, as soon as the mainsail began to flog, I ran below to see if we were taking water.

The bilges looked OK. Then I tried calling the fishing boat on the radio. No answer. I called Sydney Radio, perhaps the most efficient radio repeater system in the world. Using only our VHF radio, which normally had a range of 25 miles or so, we could reach Sydney Radio from anywhere along the several hundred miles of the New South Wales coast.

I reported who we were, carefully specifying that we were an American yacht, and told them we had been in a collision. I explained that we were not in immediate danger, or taking any water, but because of the quick way we had turned into the wind, I suspected that our headsails were gone. I also reported that because we also had a line in the wheel, we were immobilized. The operator asked to speak to the fishing boat.

I went back on deck. By this time, the fishing boat's deck lights were on, and I could see people moving about.

Cupping my hands around my mouth, I yelled across the water, "Hey! Is your skipper there?"

There was a long silence, and I was beginning to think they hadn't heard me, but then faintly I heard, "I'm the captain. What do you want?" *What did I want?* For a moment, I had trouble absorbing the implication of his response. *Were they pretending nothing had happened?*

"Sydney Radio wants to talk to you, Cap," I yelled.

"Why'd you bring them into this?" He shouted back angrily.

No doubt I should have listened in while he was talking to Sydney Radio, but it didn't occur to me. Instead, I took a flashlight and bracing myself against the erratically rolling and plunging deck, made my way forward.

The jib tack had broken, and the sail had blown back against the shrouds and was flogging wildly and noisily against the ratlines. Taking several sail ties, I climbed into the ratlines and gathering the sail in my arms, I lashed it securely to the foreshroud. Then, back on deck, I went further forward.

Fearful of what I would see, I directed the beam of the light to the bowsprit. Immediately, the crazily splintered stub of the bowsprit caught my eye. It had snapped across the stem head.

The broken piece, some 12 feet long, sagging down and off to the left, was held out of the water only by the pulpit, itself a mass of mangled junk, the weight of it carried by two brackets bolted to the stem and the lifelines.

I already knew the furling roller for the jib was gone, but I was shocked to see that the outer and inner headstays, and the starboard whisker stay also had carried away. In addition, about ten feet of the starboard bulwarks had disappeared.

It was a terrible thing to see, the more painful as I remembered the careful way Dick McIlvride had repaired the bowsprit months earlier in New Zealand.

The fishhook-like ends of the broken wires were flicking back and forth with each roll of the boat. I cautiously grabbed them one by one, and secured them to the mast. Then I crept as far out on the pulpit as I dared, and passed a line around the pulpit frame, securing it to the staysail halyard which I then hauled taut.

Sydney Radio evidently instructed the fishing captain to stand by and provide assistance if necessary. I told the skipper we needed a tow. He brought his boat alongside, and a member of the crew threw a one inch eight-plait nylon line to me. After threading it through the wreckage, I dropped its eye over the Sampson posts.

Judging by the way he was running his boat, the captain was very angry, because he rammed his throttles wide open. His powerful diesels caused his boat to lunge forward, and the towline came sharply against our bitts.

I barely had time to shout a warning to Velda and jump clear before the line snapped taut, stretched, and parted. A heavy nylon line carrying away under a breaking strain is very dangerous. It could inflict terrible injuries.

The skipper calmed down after that. He passed a second line and we tried it again. Perhaps he realized that his earlier recklessness bordered on the criminal, because this time he loaded the tow line sensibly, taking up the slack, getting *Prospector* under way, gradually increasing her speed to the point where she didn't want to go any faster. Her best speed under tow appeared to be about five knots.

Velda and I took turns trying to rest while we were towed back to Sydney. I was sick with shock and remorse. I could barely comprehend the terrible thing that had happened, and I was still dazed at daylight when we met the police tug, which towed us back into Balls Head Bay.

As soon as our anchor was down, the police came aboard to assess the damage and take a preliminary statement. When the officer asked me what had happened, I told him truthfully that I didn't know because I was below waking Velda when the collision occurred. He was sympathetic. He told me the name of the other vessel and her owner's name. He also told us that according to their preliminary statement, they had hit the tip of our bowsprit while overtaking and passing us. However, when they discovered I hadn't seen the collision, for some reason they changed their story, but I didn't find that out until the hearing, sometime later.

Collision damage.

A few days later, I was asked to come to the Water Police headquarters to amplify my initial statement. That's when I met the owner of the fishing vessel, a Mr. Carmello Musumeci. I knew I was in trouble when I saw the easy way he greeted the senior officer, Sergeant John King. Watching them exchange pleasantries, I was immediately reminded of the corruption allegations in the local papers.

Before the hearing, the police sent a launch so everyone could view the damage to both boats; *Prospector* in Balls Head Bay and *L.F.B. Vincenzann* in her berth at Pier Six. The first thing I noticed as we idled alongside the 100 ton trawler, was a fresh white paint scar on the leading edge of her port trawl door. The doors, weighing at least half a ton, were carried slung from a frame on her stern, with the leading edge splayed outward about 15 degrees from the side of the hull. I knew where that white paint came from — the tip of our bowsprit.

But my attention was mostly drawn to the boat's sharp high bow. I could barely repress a shudder. If that bow had sliced into our sides, we'd have gone down instantly in 100 fathoms of water. It's doubtful whether either of us could have survived.

The hearing was a farce. I still don't know why, but the fishermen now insisted we had collided while they were rushing back to Sydney to deliver their 1,000 pound catch to the market before daylight. The hearing officer, Captain Ken Edwards, concluded after hearing the testimony, that we were equally culpable. My culpability arose because I was off the deck when the collision occurred. Theirs was based on the undeniable fact that they ran into us.

Again we were on our own, but I was curious about the story the fishermen had told: that they were rushing back to Sydney with a 1,000 pound catch when the collision occurred.

I went first to the Fisheries office, and asked if I could see the fishing trawler's catch records for that particular day. Properly, the answer was no. Then, when I explained I was seeking back-ground information concerning a collision, I was referred to the Marine Safety Board. Boating accidents were more in their line.

So I went to the MSB office and asked the same questions. I gave the vessel's name, *Vincenzann*, to the young man behind the counter, and struck paydirt.

The young man behind the counter in the MSB office oblig-ingly opened his log and ran his finger down the list of entries for July 23rd. He laid the book on the counter, pointing to an entry. "See the entry on this line," he said. "This is where she checked out...let's see... ." He read the line, and pursed his lips thoughtfully. "She wasn't gone very long. See? Only 18 hours."

Oh, oh! That information added an entirely new dimension. Now, my curiosity was thoroughly aroused. Having spent nearly all of my adult life one way or the other in the fish business, I knew there was something very irregular about a 100 ton trawler running offshore for five or six hours, fishing for only two or three hours and then running full bore through the night in a heavy sea, to deliver a mere 1,000 pounds of fish to the market before daylight. That's what they said they were doing. That story may have fooled the cops and confused Captain Edwards, but to me it just didn't make sense. I don't know what they were up to, but I don't think honest fishing had much to do with it.

In the meanwhile, a local wooden boat club had put me in touch with a marine surveyor familiar with wooden boats. He came to inspect the wreckage, and recommended a solicitor with whom he had worked on other cases. I made an appointment, and Velda and I paid a call on the solicitor.

The lawyer was a warm and gracious man, who welcomed us to his office, and made us comfortable. We explained why we were there, and told him what had happened. He listened patiently, asking questions from time to time, and finally said, "If you were rich eccentric Americans, I would take your case, because I think you would win."

He went on to explain that the matter could be disposed of easily and cheaply if the other side would agree to try the case in a lower court of general jurisdiction.

"But they won't," he said. "Their insurance company won't let them. The insurance company will force you into the Admiralty Court, because this is an Admiralty case."

He paused, then went on. "The Supreme Court of Australia is the Admiralty Court. The docket is at least a year long. You'd have to wait a year before even coming to trial." I started to say something, but he held up his hand. "Wait," he said, "there is more. To plead a case in the Supreme Court, you will have to hire a Queens Counsel. The fee charged by most of them is now around $2,000 a day."

Again he paused, letting that unpleasant bit of news sink in. "One last thing," he continued, "like your courts in America, the Justices will award costs to the prevailing party, but no Justice is likely to award a fee for a Q.C. larger than his own salary. So you see," he concluded sadly, shaking his head, "even if you win you lose. That's why I said you'd have to be both rich and eccentric to want to try this case. Admiralty just isn't designed for small cases like yours."

He smiled. "I'm terribly sorry," he said. Then, when I asked about his fee, he said, "Just send a picture of your boat."

In retrospect, I'm inclined to think that it was a very fortunate thing that I called Sydney Radio when I did. The behavior of *Vincenzann's* crew may have been perfectly innocent, but I'm still not sure. I know our friends thought we had stumbled over a high speed smuggling operation. But we'll never know.

Neither the captain nor Musumeci made the slightest effort to help us put things right. Perfect ocker behavior. On the other hand, the Balls Head Bay gang quickly rallied around.

An English welder took the pulpit to his shop in Waverton. It was so badly mangled, however, that before he could perform restorative surgery, he needed a picture of it when it was intact. Luckily, we had one.

John Bailey knew a fellow who had recently built and was currently rigging a Cape Cod catboat. His friend thought the mast specified in the drawings was too heavy, and would make the boat tender. Consequently, he was building a lighter hollow spar and was willing to sell the original one at cost. I met the friend, and bought the mast on the spot. We lashed it to the roof of his car, and carried it down to the park behind Balls Head Bay, where I floated it out to the boat and lifted it aboard.

Another local resident had recently purchased new rigging, and I was encouraged to give his vendor a call. In a surprisingly short time the bulwarks had been repaired, the varnish was drying on the new bowsprit, and Roger (the welder) had hammered, cut and welded the pulpit fragments back into a pulpit. Also, the torn jib had been restitched.

By the last week in August, we had nearly repaired the damage. We had taken shameful advantage of our friends' generosity. Roger the welder, for example, charged us only $500 for his work. I'm sure the hours he put into that job were several times more valuable than the fee he collected. The carpenter who repaired the bulwarks worked by the job, and provided the materials. I did the rigging and organized the bowsprit.

We went to the (spring) boat show early in September with only one idea in mind — to buy a radar to reduce the possibility of another collision. AWA (Australia Wireless Amalgamated) Australia's leading marine electronics dealer, offered exactly the unit I thought I needed at a price I could afford to pay.

That was the Vigil radar made by the Mars candy bar people. A local writer had recommended it, explaining that the radar was a spin-off from Mars' experience with vending machines. He was unquestionably right; God knows we kept putting coins into it!

The installation slowed us a bit, but since we had abandoned hope of crossing the Indian Ocean that year, it didn't matter whether we left today, tomorrow, or next week.

Did you ever notice how much like a honeymoon it is when you are enjoying the euphoria of a new outboard motor, lawn mower, car – or radar? You resolutely ignore any suggestion of imperfection. If the car won't start, it's the fault of that idiot in the shop. The same thing with the radar. The fact that you and everyone else on board see a tanker that is invisible to your new radar somehow becomes the tanker's fault. That's the way our relationship with the radar began.

Nick and Jan went with us on a short shake-down cruise a few miles north of Sydney Heads. Half a dozen ships lay at anchor patiently waiting their turn to load or discharge cargo. As soon as we cleared the Heads, I turned on the radar.

Everything we could see the radar saw – except those ships. Even the most charitable assessment of the display ("I think that dot may be a ship... .") was unconvincing. We had a pleasant sail, but I was secretly worried about the radar.

Again the technician came out to *Prospector*. Additional adjustments were made. By this time, we were beginning to watch the calendar closely because our six-month visas were about to expire. I went downtown to the immigration office to inquire about a renewal, and while I think we would have gotten one, the person I talked to was such an unpleasant *warder*, and made me feel so unwelcome, that I just said to hell with it. We can leave when our six months is up – and we did.

Again we motored over to Birkenhead and anchored. Again we took the dinghy ashore, and made one last foray in the wide and hospitable aisles of Franklin's. We loaded up on greens, meat, beer, and catfood. Again, we had the benefit of a sendoff committee. This time, though, we did something differently. We cleared out formally. The customs officer came aboard, and checked the duty-free stores that had been delivered to us in Watson's Bay. He compared the animals with their photographs.

Finally, he said, "There is just one more thing. The $20 departure tax for the misses, here. You," he nodded in my direction, "are the captain, so you go free."

I paid the $20, and we were off to Noumea, on a passage that would make our collision seem almost carefree by comparison.

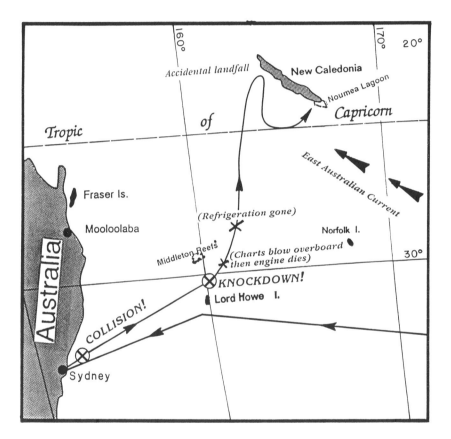

Western South Pacific
where collision, poop and knockdown, and
other inconveniences occurred
(Chart 6)

Chapter 11

The 51st State

$\mathcal{F}$our days out of Sydney, the morning of September 29th, the sky had a disturbing red hue. The old sailor's rhyme, "Red in the morning, sailors take warning," passed through my mind. Shortly after lunch the barometer began to fall.

We were approaching a submerged ridge anchored by Lord Howe Island at the southern end and two reefs, Middleton and Elizabeth, at the northern end. The reefs and Lord Howe were about 90 miles apart.

Our LAN on the 29th put us about 70 miles west of the ridge, on a latitude about midway between the two. The sun disappeared in late afternoon behind ugly black clouds coming out of the southwest. The wind was rising and I shortened the rig by striking the mainsail and rolling the jib.

I decided not to heave-to because I was afraid that if we did, the wind and possibly the currents might push us toward those reefs, now only 50 miles away. Also, because of the growing overcast, I was afraid we might have to rely on dead reckoning for the next day or two. Therefore, it seemed only prudent, since those reefs were very close and downwind, to keep moving west as long as possible.

I laid a course that slightly favored Lord Howe, and put the wind on our starboard quarter. By maintaining way and favoring Lord Howe, the angle between our course and the direction to those reefs widened with each passing hour, reducing the awful possibility of striking those reefs.

The darkness that night was absolute, unrelieved by starlight or even phosphorescence. During my watch, I was frightened and exhilarated by turns. I have difficulty estimating speeds in the dark, and I know I tend to overestimate, but I'll swear that under only the staysail, at times that night we were making eight or nine knots, almost planing in the stronger wind gusts. Perhaps it was reckless to press on, but I was still focused on those reefs in the dark somewhere north of us.

Velda relieved me at midnight. Yawning, I stumbled below, and began pulling my French fisherman's oilskin smock off over my head. Unexpectedly, the boat yawed viciously to the left and I lost my balance. Blinded by the garment around my head, I pitched forward, and before I could catch myself, I pitched forward and my muffled face smashed violently into the massive eight inch carlin, the timber that ties the cabin's coach roof and the deck together.

The skin over my cheekbone split, and the wound started to bleed. I put a cold compress on it, and took a Percodan before going to bed. I don't know whether the bone was broken, but I had a hell of a headache, and it was several weeks before I slept comfortably on my right side.

At daybreak, as I prepared to relieve Velda, although I had the mother of all headaches, I felt much better when I saw a flock of petrels in our wake searching for food. They were soaring over the tumbling waves and gliding down the troughs. If land was within a 20 or 30 mile radius, as the presence of the birds seemed to indicate, no matter in which direction it lay, it would be well behind us by dark.

As I took the wheel, I was struck by the peculiar way *Prospector* was sailing. Although we were still shortened down to the staysail, we almost seemed to be skipping from crest to crest, like a fast sailing dinghy; a motion hardly suited to a boat of our displacement.

The wind was still at near gale velocity, but curiously, instead of causing the sea to rise, the wind appeared to be compressing the waves, pushing them closer together. It's quite possible, I suppose, that the wave shape was related to our close proximity to the shallow summit of the north–south submarine ridge that connects Lord Howe Island with the northern reefs. Whatever it was, it made strange sailing.

We would seem to soar across a trough, which closed just as we reached it, only to fall into a watery hole on the other side of it with a spine jarring *crash*. It is no exaggeration that at times the bowsprit and the mizzen boom were simultaneously under water. Everything at that moment seemed so crazy, I remember wondering if a 43 foot boat could pitchpole in a 15 foot sea.

I simply wasn't thinking straight. Despite the Percodan I had taken, each sudden jolt sent strings of pain across my face, and coherent thought was difficult. I decided to take another pain pill. Velda relieved me while I went below to get it.

As I climbed the companionway ladder, returning to the cockpit, my horrified gaze fell on an overtaking rogue wave directly astern, already looming above the taffrail, the lazarette, and Velda, blocking the sky as it rolled toward us!

I was as mesmerized as a rabbit staring at a snake. Water began sliding down that ugly, monstrous, moving face. The spell was broken when, to my utter terror, I saw the crest begin to topple forward, propelled by countless tons of water behind it. In that instant I knew *Prospector* was doomed! *"LOOK OUT!"* I screamed.

Desperately, unthinkingly, I wedged myself as tightly as possible into the frame of the companionway and closed my eyes, as if my puny body were any match for the hundreds of tons of water beginning to fall on the boat. I was blinded and choked as a wall of salt water washed over me, but suddenly, as abruptly as it had arrived, the water disappeared, leaving me gasping for air and rubbing the stinging salt water from my eyes. A part of my mind wondered for an instant if I could be hallucinating.

As we later pieced it together, when that monstrous breaking wave crashed over us, the underlying ocean swell apparently lifted *Prospector* in a sudden corkscrew motion, hurling her on her port side, so the thundering wave — hundreds of tons of water — harmlessly landed on her side and was deflected by her stout planking. Instead of flooding below and instantly sinking her, the water flowed harmlessly back into the sea. There's no question the knockdown saved her.

Prospector righted herself almost instantly, and when we recovered our senses, we discovered that unattended, the staysail had filled and she was again under way!

Velda recovered sooner than I. At first, she thought the boat was sinking. As I regained my senses, I saw Velda frantically bailing the cockpit with a bucket. I grabbed a bailer; together we quickly emptied the cockpit. Then Velda took the wheel while I, still trying to clear my head, numbly went forward to assess the damage.

"LOOK OUT!!"

I don't think either of us realized, even then, that we had been knocked down. But the first thing that caught my eye was a dangling shroud. Incredibly, the port foreshroud turnbuckle had *pulled apart*. The barrel hung uselessly from its chainplate, while the upper tang, still bolted securely to the eye of the shroud, dangled in midair.

The only thing to do was heave-to and sort ourselves out. I flattened the staysail amidships, and Velda swung the bow into the weather, lashing the wheel one spoke past dead center.

We were like train wreck survivors. Our experiences were both intensely personal, and shared. We had each survived a catastrophic experience, but a bond between us had been forged out of a common disaster involving forces almost beyond comprehension.

Hearing my panicky scream, and understanding the tone if not the words, Velda had reacted instinctively by dropping the wheel and falling to her knees, throwing her arms around the binnacle.

The wave thundering into the cockpit temporarily stunned and submerged her; then, as the boat was flung on her side, Velda was hurled by the forces of water and gravity into the corner of the doghouse where she remained, stunned, sputtering and gasping. There is no question the doghouse saved her life. If ours had been the typical open cockpit fitted with a canvas dodger, without question, she would have been lost.

It's hard to imagine the forces involved that morning. Perhaps this will help: The energy in those huge waves has been calculated to exceed one ton per square foot of mass. The portion of the wave that inundated *Prospector* was the width of the boat, 15 feet, and possibly 25–30 feet high. In other words, since our rogue wave had a cross section of about 400 square feet, we were subjected to a force approaching *400 tons!* Imagine 400 tons of wet cement falling on you from a height of 25 or 30 feet.

It is no wonder we were stunned and, for a few moments, oblivious to our surroundings.

We shall never know, except by circumstantial evidence, but the energy in that wave probably thrust the boat forward while she was on her side. Quite possibly, the turnbuckle broke when the end of the yard entered the water and slammed back into the foreshroud. This must have put enormous strains on the entire rig, but especially on that turnbuckle. I think the only reason the yard survived was because it was braced by the squaresail's taut luff wire.

Also, I found that the chainplate that anchors the port running backstay broke; I've never understood why. Why the topmast survived is another mystery.

The clearest evidence of the size and shape of that rogue wave was not found until nearly dark. I must have stepped over it a dozen times while I was rigging a Spanish windlass to replace the broken turnbuckle, without realizing what I was seeing.

The VHF antenna, normally fastened to the top of the mizzen mast 25 feet above the deck, was laying on the deck. I picked it up. Looking more closely, I could see that three of the four two inch wood screws that had secured the metal bracket to the mast were still in the bracket and that fragments of wood still clung to their threads. They had been wrenched out of the mast by a terrible force. In my minds eye, again I saw that terrible wave rearing up, up, blocking out the sky.

The VHF antenna was on the side of the mast, while the radar was mounted facing forward. Curiously, the radar antenna — a much larger target — survived, although the aluminum bracket supporting it was cracked. Perhaps the mast served to split the falling wave, thus protecting the radar.

Down below, the boat was an awful mess. Everything, including pots, pans, food, clothes, our bunks, and even the cushions in the dinette, the instruments in the navigation center, and the books in our tiny library, was wet with salt water. Most things were displaced. Three of four coffee cups were found on top of the cupboards. The fourth was never found.

Our living quarters could not be restored merely picking things up. Clothing and bedding — any fabric — that receives a saltwater bath will stiffen but remain clammy until the salt is rinsed out. Hard things get sticky, and things made of iron, including stainless steel knives and forks, are sure to rust.

The wind continued to subside all evening, but we were content to rest and continue sorting things out, quietly rejoicing in the sweet knowledge that we were still alive.

The next morning, I saw the most beautiful sunrise I can remember. The skies were clear, the winds were almost calm and fair. I set the squaresail immediately after working my morning star observations. Then I opened the chart drawer.

That's when I discovered the drawer was watertight. My new

British Admiralty charts were soaking up the last of the water in the drawer, and were turning to pulp. I knew instantly what had happened. The companionway ladder is on the starboard side of the engine box, between the engine and the after water tank. The chart drawer is on top of the tank, under the chart table. The boat had rolled down on her port side when we were knocked down. Gravity had pulled the drawer open. It can't come all the way out because it comes up against the bilge pump. But it opened far enough to receive a good dollop of water. Then, as the boat recovered and rolled to starboard, the drawer slid shut.

There is only one cure for wet charts. Separate and dry them as quickly as possible. I lifted the sodden mass out of the drawer and laid the charts carefully on the cockpit sole. After peeling them apart, I hung each on the lifelines, securing it with clothespins. The charts looked like colored diapers as they fluttered gently in the occasional breeze. Unfortunately, I forgot, if I ever knew, that paper soaked in saltwater will stiffen with salt as it dries.

It was nearly noon when I finished. The last one was a beautifully detailed chart of New Caledonia showing the approaches to the Noumea lagoon, with inserts depicting the ten-mile channel through the reefs in the lagoon to Noumea. I pinned it next to its fellows, and after taking a careful look around, went below for lunch. The wheel was lashed, the seas were still rough, but calming. A fitful breeze would lift the charts and fill the sail, than die.

After lunch, I returned to the deck with my sextant, ready for my noon sight. After making myself comfortable on the doghouse roof, I squinted through the eyepiece, checking the index error.

Suddenly, with an awful feeling of dismay, I realized that those white specks in our wake were not, as I had first supposed, flecks of foam. They were charts. I scarcely needed a confirming glance at the lifelines to make sure. As they had dried they had stiffened, and even a whisper of air that lifted the stiffened paper was enough to pop the clothespins loose.

I rushed below, noon sight forgotten, stowed the sextant, called Velda and started the engine. While she turned the wheel, steering *Prospector* on a reciprocal course back toward the charts, I stood on the bowsprit pulpit trying to think of a way of retrieving them from the water without destroying them. What should we do? Spear them with a boat hook? Would one of us have to jump into the water and swim for them?

The engine suddenly revved up. Velda yelled, "I've lost power!"

Good God, I thought, *now what?*

I assumed at first the clutch had not been fully engaged, and had somehow slipped out of gear, but after a quick check, I knew that wasn't the problem. I crawled under the cockpit sole, and made sure the clutch lever was moving fully into position. It was.

Next I checked the fluid level in the transmission case. It was full right up to the mark. Maybe there is a bubble in the hydraulic system, I thought. I had Velda shift the gear lever forward, neutral, reverse. The lever moved easily and smoothly, but the propeller shaft remained inert.

I was out of ideas. Whatever was wrong with the transmission was beyond my limited ability to repair. While I was trying to absorb this new calamity, I reminded myself that my first priority still was those charts. Now how the hell was I going reach, let alone retrieve them? The only chart I considered really indispensable was the one depicting New Caledonia. The others could be replaced in Noumea. And I was sure, beyond any question or doubt the way my luck had been running, that the chart furthest away would be the one I needed most.

There wasn't enough wind to continue coming about, let alone beat back to the first of them. I briefly considered the possibility of launching the dinghy. But the outboard motor was unreliable, and I knew I would have to row. Our dinghy did not row well even in the best of circumstances, and mid-ocean at any time, even under the most benign weather conditions, by definition was not the best of circumstances.

Even so, I found myself speculating how long the weather would remain as it was — but luckily, common sense intervened and told me I was foolish even to think about it. If the wind came up while I was rowing off into the sunset, we'd be in much worse trouble than we already were. I'd never be able to catch up with *Prospector*, and Velda would have a terrible time trying to handle her alone.

Finally, I had to consider the awful possibility of becoming separated from *Prospector* in the dark. That settled the matter. I'm capable of wildly rash decisions, but there were some things you just didn't do. Leaving *Prospector* in mid-ocean was at the top of the list.

Charts would have to be added to the grimly lengthening list of things that were lost, broken, or that simply didn't work any more.

My log entry was brief but poignant:

October 4: Wind dropped off just before daylight, swells rapidly abating — still rolly at noon — running off under squaresail, LAN 25°12'S, 148°04'E. Walker log ruined, freezer dead, engine stuffed, sextant error 16'.

Let me explain first about the freezer. It was afflicted with a mysterious ailment which was often "repaired" but never cured. The truth of it was, I think we needed an exorcist more than a mechanic because our problem seemed to border on the supernatural.

Ours was a Grunart Versimatic, among the best small–boat refrigeration systems available. Like most such systems, it was water–cooled. Cooling water entered the system from a through-hull deep below the turn of the bilge. After a run of about 18 inches, the water intake line was interrupted by a standard filter. Then it ran laterally another four feet to a water pump mounted on top of the very expensive AC-DC variable voltage motor that drove the compressor. The pump was the highest point on the intake side of the water line, but at all times was about two feet **below** the boat's water line.

Although the line was automatically pressurized because of its relationship to the outside water depth, air somehow invaded the line *even when we were tied to a dock.*

The disorder was progressive, and had reached the point on the passage to Noumea, where I had to disconnect the intake hose from the pump and bleed the line *every day* before running the cooling unit. Every day I watched air bubbles escape, chased usually by a healthy slug of salt water that trickled down the side of the motor.

Although you might have expected the motor to fail because of that daily shot of salt water, when the system ultimately rolled over and died, ironically, it was the compressor that failed. In fairness to the compressor manufacturer, however, I should point out this was our *second* motor.

The next week passed slowly and uneventfully. And why not. Everything that could break, fall off, or malfunction had already done so. Even the new radar had gone to lunch. By this time, I wasn't foolish enough to have much confidence in its reliability, but during my night watches I liked to turn it on every hour or so just to watch the sweep go around; at least it kept me company and provided a comforting illusion of certainty. That wasn't asking for much, and I was annoyed when I was deprived of even that mild diversion. When the shorter ranges were selected, the whole picture would abruptly collapse to the size of an American quarter.

Very possibly that tendency toward a miniaturized display was a direct result of the rogue wave, but I could never decide whether its shyness toward shipping was worsened by the wave, or was simply the logical and unavoidable consequence of its lineage. Vigil radars are manufactured by the Mars candy bar people; therefore, my machine was the inevitably sad result of an unnatural union between a candy bar machine and a radio transmitter.

The radar was subsequently treated by experts in New Zealand, Australia, and years later, in Pennsylvania. I'm sorry to say the machine never was worth a damn and I finally gave it away just to get it off the boat. I realize it was an early model, but even so, I can tell you unequivocally that we'll never buy another Vigil radar.

By now, we had reached the southern version of the horse latitudes and the skies were constantly cloudy. We were near an invisible line separating the Tasman Sea from the Coral Sea.

Constantly gnawing in the back of my mind like the memory of an overdue tax return, was the certain knowledge that we were going to have to enter Noumea lagoon somewhat like Captain Cook did, under sail and without charts.

But there were differences. For one thing, he was getting paid for it. Besides, his ship belonged to someone else. And he had plenty of people on board, so he could send a small boat ahead to take soundings when he thought it was necessary.

By contrast, ours was a crew of two. We had no small boats to send out. *Prospector* belonged to us, and represented virtually our entire estate. Finally, not only were we *not* on someone's payroll, we were doing this for fun.

Yet we had something Cook didn't have. We had a copy of Alan Lucas' excellent cruising guide, *Cruising New Caledonia*. I think it's fair to say that book may have saved us. At the very least, it made life much more pleasant.

Lucas has done for the Western South Pacific what Earl Hinz has done for the Central and Eastern Pacific, and Don Street has done for the Caribbean. They have each written detailed and accurate cruising guides for their respective areas of expertise; books I consider essential for successful cruising in those areas. While it would be foolish and dangerous to substitute those guides for charts, in a pinch, because of the wealth of detailed information and well drawn sketches they contain, they will serve.

From a sketch in Lucas' book, I deduced that the recommended pass (Boulari Pass) into the lagoon was ten miles south of New Caledonia at 22°30′S.

Lacking an engine, I felt it was especially important to remain on a weatherly course, or upwind, from our landfall. There were several good reasons. One was to shorten this plague-ridden passage as much as possible. Another was to avoid any possible complications caused by the proximity of a large land mass to its surrounding marine environment; problems which included land/sea breezes and possible wind shadows. The little wind we had at the moment was from the sou'southeast.

I sailed as close to the weather as possible without pinching, but we still constantly inched above our rhumb line. Early in the morning of October fifth, our 11th day at sea, much to my disgust, the wind backed into the southeast where it remained: Fitful, temperamental, and seriously inconvenient because it began pushing us well north of our rhumb line.

With one eye on the telltales and the other on the binnacle, we steered a weather course in the narrow slot between pinching and falling off for nearly a week. We were rewarded with a miserly 50 to 75 miles a day, and despite our best efforts, the wind forced us further and further north. I was reluctant to come about, because I knew the wind would eventually veer into the south; besides, our heading on a port tack in that breeze would have been south-southwest, away from New Caledonia.

Although it's sometimes necessary, it is psychologically hard for me to sail away from a landfall. Especially in circumstances like this miserable passage, which, like our first awful trip up the Intracoastal Waterway, was beginning to resemble a nautical demolition derby.

A week went by without celestial observations. I grossly underestimated the cumulative effect of wind and current in my dead reckoning. Apparently, we were quartering into the invisible East Australian Current which flows in a northwesterly direction parallel to New Caledonia.

I discovered my error when we made an unexpected and quite unwelcome landfall on New Caledonia's northwestern coast. Velda had seen land almost from the beginning of her watch, but saw no reason to disturb my sleep. When I arrived for my turn in the barrel, through the glasses, we could see houses on the shore.

A landfall is usually a signal for rejoicing; but the happy ones are planned, and the navigator can at least pretend not to be surprised. I think most navigators will agree that the only thing worse than missing a landfall is making one you don't expect. I was not prepared for this one, and I found it deeply depressing. I felt as if a bitter joke had been played on me. Even the decision to come about had been taken away. We barely had enough way to come about on a port tack, and we drew slowly away from the island.

Any person who spends much time out of doors can tell you that the elements become personalized when they are persistently adverse, and here they were seriously and consistently against us, and I was almost becoming paranoid.

First the wind fell away and we were practically becalmed; left in that horrible intermediate situation where you get enough breeze to keep your sails up, but not enough to prevent them from slashing and banging. Nothing on this earth is as noisy and uncomfortable as a semi-becalmed sailboat. When the wind returned, it was from the wrong direction, blowing us south and away from New Caledonia. Instead of allowing ourselves to be blown back to Lord Howe Island, we decided to heave-to. It was just as well we did, because that little storm lasted three days.

Five days after our abortive glimpse of New Caledonia, the skies cleared and I got my first evening star sights in several days. Our position was 164°10'E, 21°40'S, or about 165 miles west-northwest of Boulari Pass into Noumea Lagoon.

At last things were looking up. We knew where we were for the first time in days, and with the change in weather, the wind had veered into the south. We let the sheets run, and soon were heeling to port, sailing on an easy broad reach, listening to the comforting gurgle of water running past the counter, and enjoying the lift and fall of the boat as she made her way over the swells.

The gloomy and nearly delusional pall that had clung to me since my first glimpse of New Caledonia nearly a week earlier fell astern, and my spirits lifted. Not even the prospect of sailing into a strange coral-strewn lagoon without an engine and charts dampened them.

The southerly breeze continued for the next 24 hours. My evening star sights on October tenth put us at 165°42′E, 22°10′S, or about 57 miles west-northwest of Boulari Pass. I was certain we had averaged five and a half to six knots through the water, possibly even more; yet according to my sights, we had only traveled 108 miles over the ground. I concluded that we were still bucking the East Australian Current.

Now, however, those problems were nearly behind us. Having a night run of fifty to sixty miles to your landfall, even against a contrary current of unknown velocity, was about right. You knew it would be light when you got there, but early enough so you'd have the whole day ahead of you to do what needed to be done. Except for one thing, especially important in our circumstances.

We would be sailing almost due east when we entered the pass. It is axiomatic in the tropics that you *never* want to enter an unfamiliar lagoon with the sun in your eyes. Even with Polaroid glasses, you can't see into the water when the sun is reflecting off its surface.

As the morning light strengthened, I saw an indistinct smudge on the horizon well north of our course. That was expected. I knew the lagoon extended south of the island, and according to a sketch in Lucas' book, the entrance into the lagoon was about eight miles below the southern tip of the island. Unless the currents had final tricks to play, I thought our course should take us directly to the pass. It did, but not before I climbed up to the yard and stood, legs braced, arm looped around the jackstay, anxiously scanning the horizon through our binoculars. Then I saw the slender minaret-like shape of Amedee lighthouse marking the pass. Since the pass opens to the northeast, Lucas recommends an approach of 050° true.

I had to ignore that refinement because the wind, from the south-southeast was on our starboard bow. We were sailing as close to it as possible, on a heading of about 095 degrees, a course that was carrying us straight to the northern edge of the pass.

I didn't think it wise to waste time maneuvering for a more favorable angle of approach because I didn't think we had the time. Our wind was only a land breeze. I knew it would be replaced around noon by a sea breeze which could have made it impossible to sail north through the lagoon.

Lacking an engine, I was becoming increasingly sensitive to the wind's nuances, and probably a better sailor for it. In our circumstances, I had to take the best possible advantage of the wind. At the moment, that meant maintaining our speed, while holding a course as close to the wind as possible, even though we were poorly positioned to enter a pass opening to the northeast.

Within an hour, the dirty brownish–green coral surrounding the lagoon was in full view, as was the lighthouse. I still couldn't see the pass, but I was encouraged by a smaller light fine on my port bow that I mistakenly thought was the lighthouse lead. I also saw a big schooner at anchor inside the lagoon where I thought we wanted to go. We were still making five knots, sailing into an ever narrowing funnel of coral. But I though as long as I kept the lighthouse lead on my port bow, we would be clear of danger.

As always in a tight spot, Velda was standing next to me. She was studying Lucas' book. In the same instant when I suddenly realized we were sailing straight toward a wall of stained coral that was not more than 100 feet dead ahead, Velda yelled, "That's not the lead, Denny!" She had turned the page and had seen the drawings of the navigation aids.

I was already spinning the wheel hard over to the right. We lost the wind; the mainsail began to flog. I hauled the sheet as fast as I could, meanwhile holding the wheel with my knee and watching the coral slide past, not more than ten feet from our port side. We slowly lost way as we awkwardly coasted toward the pass.

Finally – it seemed like an hour, but it couldn't have been more than a few minutes – the coral opened a bit to the left, allowing me to fall off and the jib to fill. Abruptly the coral disappeared. We were inside the lagoon.

I wanted very badly to sit down. I must have been holding my breath, because I found myself panting as if I had just run up a flight of stairs. I had thought for a moment that we would hit the coral. But again I had underestimated *Prospector*. I still think it was something of a miracle that she turned away from danger so quickly and adroitly , and while her ability to coast long distances is a tribute to her designer, the ability to glide that vital extra 50 yards as needed was pure *Prospector.*

It wasn't until we were sailing past Amedee light that I realized the lead I had been looking for was on the same platform, not more than 50 feet in front of Amedee light. That arrangement would be useful at night because you could line the two lights up and know when you were on the proper course. But it was no help in the daylight. It and the lighthouse are painted white; Tabou light, the one I had mistaken for the lead, is white with a dark band near the top.

Stranded and wrecked vessels are invariably sad. That lonely old schooner was no exception. She is a permanent resident on Tabou Reef. We passed close enough to see running rigging and blocks hanging from her spars, but not close enough to read her name or hailing port. A tragic thing to see. I was later told that she was Sterling Hayden's old pilot schooner, *Wanderer*, from San Francisco.

The passage through the lagoon to Noumea was anticlimactic. The wind was fair, so we furled the mainsail and set the squaresail. We followed Lucas' sketches as we sailed north, and we found the channel buoys exactly as he had drawn them.

The city of Noumea fronts on Baie de la Moselle, near the southwestern tip of New Caledonia. The approach to the city is obvious, once you reach Brun Island.

We chose to enter Old Harbor, rather than turn into a nearer bay sheltering the yacht club and navy yard, partly because we saw dozens of yacht masts clustered in the eastern portion of Old Harbor, obviously at anchor, and partly because I had never docked under sail, and my instincts told me that a French yacht club was not the place to learn.

By this time, it was barely past noon. The wind was blowing toward the city dock, and I didn't dare tie there up for fear I wouldn't be able to sail away. After rolling the squaresail, we coasted to within 200 feet of the wharf and let the anchor go.

Of course, we were flying our Q flag from the starboard spreaders just below the French courtesy flag. The Stars and Stripes were boldly displayed on our stern. We put the dinghy in the water. With our passports and ship's papers in hand, I rowed ashore. I was met at the dock by a friendly gendarme who inquired in excellent English why we hadn't tied up like everyone else?

I complimented him on his linguistic skill. Then I explained the problem with the engine, and offered to row him out to the boat. It may seem strange, but I have offered my services as an impromptu gondolier to customs officials the world over, and not once has anyone taken me up on it.

However, after I admitted we had arms on board, I was required to row back to *Prospector* and bring them ashore. Then I was told to come to the harbor master's office the next day to pay the harbor fees. These came to 3,500 CP francs, or around $25.

He filled out the necessary forms — God, how the French love forms — using his car fender as a desk, and with a flourish handed me my letter of pratique. "Welcome to New Caledonia," he said.

After cruising for a time in the South Pacific, the probability that you will see familiar faces in unfamiliar anchorages becomes a certainty. Old friends will be waving and calling. The more energetic ones will be coming alongside in their dinghies. It is a tight little fraternity, forged out of shared hardships and unique experiences, tempered by mutual respect, understanding, and even love.

After sailing across the harbor and settling into the small boat anchorage south of the ferry lanes, we found many friends. Wendy and John Ettish from *Bali Ha'i* were there; so were Doug and Mary Solomon on *Sundance Kid*, Gus Wollmar single handing *Diogenes*; our Lord Howe Island friends, the George family on *Kailua;* and Mike Davidson, our Aussie editor friend on *Ardright*, who was returning from Hawaii with a very pretty American deckhand.

New Caledonia was experiencing serious political unrest while we were there. The native Melanesians, locally called kanakas, were distressed by the rapidly growing European community. Now outnumbered by European settlers, they had no hope of winning a plebiscite. The French Government was seriously concerned because New Caledonia has one of the world's largest nickel mines. The French Army had its hands full. As fast as the soldiers tore them down, new posters appeared overnight in hundreds of conspicuous places around Noumea. The message was a simple one.

I can't say whether a substantial portion of the population really craved annexation to the United States, but I do know that many local people had a definite affinity for things American.

After spending nearly a year in the British Commonwealth where anti–American sentiment smolders just beneath the surface, it was as refreshing as a spring morning to find ourselves in a place where the people seemed genuine in their affection for America. A local family demonstrated how genuine those feelings were during a courtesy visit by a U.S. warship.

The *USS Cushing*, a relatively new and sophisticated missile destroyer paid a call in Noumea and held an open house a week after we arrived. We decided to take the tour.

We were the only Americans in our tour group, and our American accents were what our guide, a homesick young sonarman from Louisiana, needed to hear. He invited us to stay behind when the tour was completed. Then he told us this story:

The ship had come from Melbourne, Australia. Somehow, anti-American demonstrators in a small boat had eluded her guards, and had gotten to within spray paint range of her transom where, under the merciless eye of a television camera, they had painted several anti–American and anti–war slogans.

The first inkling the unfortunate captain had about this incident was when his admiral, having seen it on the evening news in Pearl Harbor, called, demanding to know what the hell was going on! Needless to say, the luckless Master at Arms was severely punished.

This incident, our young guide explained, had been very demoralizing. But when the ship was entering Noumea, a family of Melanesians standing at the edge of a bluff near the channel had suddenly unfurled a large, welcoming, American Flag.

The crew was standing in formation, and when the Officer of the Day saw the Flag, he ordered the ship's company, "About face!" Then as the sailors faced the small family on the bluff, he ordered them to salute. Instantly, the ship's morale was greatly restored. Darrell concluded his story by saying, "We all had wet eyes. God, it felt good."

Noumea was about the same size as Papeete, but it is much more European. Its architecture was somewhat reminiscent of Fort de France on Martinique. However, unlike the French West Indies where English is not usually spoken, the people in France's Pacific territories seem to regard English as a second language, and in the metropolitan areas, nearly everyone appears to speak it.

Noumea's waterfront was old fashioned, but clean and tidy. Two large markets, one a supermarket, were within easy walking distance of the dinghy dock. The largest occupied a city block, and was surrounded by small bars and cafes on three sides and a bus park on the fourth.

The town was built on an irregularly rising slope. Some streets running away from the waterfront were nearly level; others were quite steep. The cross streets, like frozen ocean swells, seemed to undulate, following the contours of the land.

We found three marine hardware stores in the same block, an inconvenient eight blocks from the dinghy dock. I arranged repairs to the Autohelm at one, and found charts and large galvanized turnbuckles for rigging repairs in another.

Originally, we had intended stopping only briefly in Noumea, then heading north to Vanuatu and on to the Solomons, where we planned to spend the hurricane season. But I found it hard to imagine a conversation in pidgin English with native tradesmen in Honiara on Guadalcanal concerning our various electrical and mechanical problems.

Moreover, after calling the AWA company in Sydney regarding the radar's peculiar behavior and learning that the guarantee on that exotic instrument would be honored only in New Zealand or Australia, we were convinced that instead of heading north, we'd better return to New Zealand. I was also sure that our best chance of getting the engine and refrigeration properly repaired also hinged on an early return to New Zealand. While New Zealand may not have the world's greatest starter repairmen, at least they speak something other than pidgin English.

Our old Evinrude gave up the ghost in Noumea, and we had to cast about for a replacement. We knew that in New Zealand, even though the duty was reimbursable, the price of a new motor would probably be greater than it was in New Caledonia, and we were equally certain our selection might be limited to English Seagulls.

I had learned to respect John Ettish's judgment. I knew he had recently bought a small Suzuki from a local dealer and seemed pleased with it, so we decided to follow his lead, even though I experienced serious sticker shock when I read the price tag, 68,000 francs. Wow! Even at the then current exchange rate of 142 francs to the dollar, that little engine cost almost $500. Still, it was that or buy new oars.

We had trouble obtaining visas because we had animals and had been in New Zealand within the previous 12 months. Eventually, they were granted, but not before we received a stern interrogation, especially concerning the livestock.

I was ferrying water and groceries out to *Prospector* the day before we planned to leave, when a young man sitting on the dock asked if we needed crew. He was an example of a familiar South Pacific phenomena. In an earlier life, he might have been a beachcomber, with a certain claim to status. Today, however, he was only a drifter, aimlessly going from place to place as free transportation provided. He lived in youth hostels when possible, and camped in his tent when there wasn't a hostel within reasonable distance.

He was a slender man, in his early 30s, with a strong German accent. He was somewhat vague when I asked about his previous boating experience, but steering isn't that difficult, and I remembered how wearing the watch schedule was when only two of us were on board. Besides, I wasn't expecting an easy passage. New Caledonia is northwest from New Zealand, and therefore downwind in the normal southeast trades, and I expected we would be sailing hard on the wind for most of the 900 mile passage. Also, I knew what to expect when we reentered the horse latitudes.

Moreover, because our mechanical and electrical gadgets such as the engine, refrigeration, Walker log and radar were still out to lunch, I knew the trip would be arduous. Unquestionably, an extra pair of hands would come in handy. We decided to take him on.

I had already cleared for sea with the harbor master and the immigration and customs officials, and had retrieved our firearms. Now, it was necessary for Willi to get his clearance.

As a West German, and a partner in the European Community, Willi had certain privileges not available to us. Informal arrival and departure procedures were among them. I also expect the officials were glad to see him leave. Transients like Willi contributed little to the tax base or the general prosperity of the community.

My initial impression was correct. Willi had almost no experience at sea. But since his civilian job as a fireman surely gave him an understanding of ladders, I assumed he would be right at home on the ratlines. In that assumption, I was dead wrong.

I now think that climbing ladders may have been the reason Willi gave up the life of a professional fire fighter, but that's the sort of information you won't get while you're standing on the dock conducting a pierhead interview.

The breeze was out of the south when we left Noumea, so we were obliged to tack back and forth all day between reefs and around coral heads in the lagoon, finally coming to anchor at dusk in the lee of Amedee light. The stranded schooner stood a forlorn watch over us as we slept.

I woke abruptly at 3 a.m., and lay in the dark wondering what had wakened me. Then I felt a subtle but distinct bump. It may be slight and even pass unnoticed by a landsman, but that's a signal that will invariably bring a sailor to his feet.

Thump! There it was again. I grabbed the flashlight and hurried up the companionway ladder to see what was causing the bumping. I looked over the side and caught my breath.

We were surrounded by coral heads, some barely under the water's surface gleaming whitely in the flashlight's beam. Clear water magnifies things, but I'm sure some coral heads were only inches beneath the surface. When we had anchored the previous evening, I had dropped the hook in 20 feet of water. Because of the gathering darkness, I hadn't noticed this reef. Evidently, a current or a breeze, or both, had pushed us up on it during the night. I wasn't sure about the stage of the tide, but I knew that the three hours remaining until daylight could make a profound difference.

We might float clear, or we could just as easily find ourselves hard aground by daylight. Also, while the wind was now flat calm, I knew a breeze would probably spring up at daylight. I also knew that maneuvering without an engine in those circumstances might require a greater degree of sailor's skill than I possessed.

As if to punctuate the urgency of a decision, the keel struck the coral again. By this time, Velda's sea-mind had wakened her, and she appeared in the cockpit. Willi, snugly tucked into the quarter berth, snored gently on.

Silently, I pointed the light's beam over the side.

We did the only sensible thing. I woke Willi, and as gently as possible, we shortened the anchor chain, pulling ourselves into deeper water. That seemed to work. After recovering about 50 feet of chain, the coral heads seemed deeper, and we bumped less often. I was concerned about dislodging the anchor. The last thing I wanted was to go adrift in the dark; I couldn't think of a more certain way to get into trouble.

At first light, a breeze began to stir the water's surface and we raised the mainsail. Then, while Willi and Velda operated the anchor windlass, I hauled the main sheet. We were underway as the anchor left the bottom.

While Velda and Willi wrestled the anchor over the lifelines, I cast off the jib furling line and gave the jib sheet a tug to start it unrolling. I almost ran into a coral head, but Velda had her eyes open, and she shouted a timely warning.

Sailing through the pass was almost too easy. The sun was behind us, and the opening in the reef was clear and obvious. With a final glance over my shoulder at the schooner on Tabou reef, and the 51st State, we set full sail.

If the trip from Sydney to Noumea was our worse passage, the sail from Noumea to New Zealand was the best. The only thing that marred the passage was Willi's complaining, and that didn't start until we were nearly halfway to New Zealand.

Our crew's personalities seemed to oscillate between Tom Sawyer's aggression and the sensitivity that Willi displayed. Frankly, I don't know which was worse. I don't mean to suggest that we wanted crass people, but a small sailboat inhabited by three people and two animals is not where a person of tender sensibilities is likely to be comfortable. And an uncomfortable person of tender sensibilities makes a damn poor shipmate. You can count on that.

One complaint that didn't surface until we were halfway to New Zealand involved our admittedly unsanitary practice of letting the animals lick the dishes after our meals. I realize that people are divided on that practice. Some would share Willi's revulsion, and might equate that practice with keeping goats in the living room. Others would agree with us.

Of course, after the problem surfaced, it was easily resolved. The key word, of course, is *surfaced*. None of us can read another's mind. Like my experience with Tom Sawyer, this trip could have been much more pleasant had I taken the initiative to establish better communications aboard. I now realize that no matter what my personal feelings were, as captain it was my responsibility to open and maintain lines of communication, and I'm sorry to say that I didn't do a very good job of it.

The winds, while not great or constant, kept us moving; and we were able, at one point, to strike the fore and aft rig and set the squaresail and raffee. We caught an albacore. It was good eating, but fish three times a day for more than a day or two was too much. Still, we didn't leave much to throw away, which could have had serious results. Luckily we got away with it.

Then, we were blissfully unaware that there even was such a thing as scombroid toxin (or histamine poisoning). I now know about it, although luckily, not by first-hand experience. The poisoning results in a serious, although not usually fatal, illness resulting from eating stale, unrefrigerated fish of the suborder Scombroidea. Unfortunately, that suborder includes most of the fish we catch at sea, e.g.: tunas, mackerels, wahoo and mahi-mahi (or dolphin fish).

Like ciguatera, this kind of food poisoning is particularly insidious because the fish tissues offer no hint of the danger within, and there is no effective means of testing for it. The fish may smell and look sweet and wholesome. This condition is caused by the abnormal breakdown of enzymes in the tissues of the dead fish due poor handling practices. Histamines are released into the tissue when the decomposition process is accelerated.

The best way to protect against histamine poisoning is to dress and chill the fish as quickly as possible after removing it from the water. If you lack refrigeration, keep the fish in the shade covered by wet cloths. If the fish is not refrigerated, I think it's best to get rid of it after the first 24 to 36 hours.

The Walker log had been overhauled (again) in Noumea, but it consistently under reported our daily runs. I found it was reporting about 78 percent of the distance we actually traveled. That was no big deal while the skies remained clear, but there is something foolish about making allowances for instruments because they are incapable of doing what they were designed to do.

We sighted New Zealand's North Cape at first light on the 17th of November. A pair of sperm whales — a cow and calf — crossed in front of us. By late afternoon, we were standing off the entrance to the Bay of Islands. Nine hundred twenty three miles in nine days, four hours. A dazzling performance for us, but we weren't there yet.

Willi then left something to remember him by. As he was striking and bagging the raffee, he lost the raffee halyard, which shot merrily up the mast, ran through the halyard block, and fell in a heap on the cabin top. That meant one of us was going to have to shinny up the topmast to rereeve the halyard. I was certain that someone would not be Willi, although before he left the boat in Opua, he offered in perfect sincerity to do it. I realized by that time, however, that possibly he had quit the fire department because he was afraid of heights. That was nothing to be ashamed of, but it was a serious handicap for a fire fighter or a sailor of tall ships.

We still had a few miles to go before we could drop our hook. And at that precise moment, the northwesterly breeze we had been enjoying backed solidly to the west, and we began the slow, tedious back and forth tacking, working our way into the outer bay, navigating carefully as it grew dark, still back and forth. God, how I wished we had an engine!

I would never have attempted this if I were a stranger to those waters, but I knew there was no obstruction in the pass into the inner bay. Finally, at midnight, we came around the corner in front of Russell, dropped the anchor in 15 feet of water and turned in. It had been a long day.

FORM 'A' ISSUED

Seen at the New Zealand
Consulate-General, Noumea

Good for a single journey to New Zealand

Within ..THREE.. months of date
hereof provided passport remains valid.

Period of authorised stay ....SIX....

...(6). MONTHS
                                    P.J. Wilkinson
(Sgd) ....Vice-Consul

Date 30.10.83 Nº 200/84.

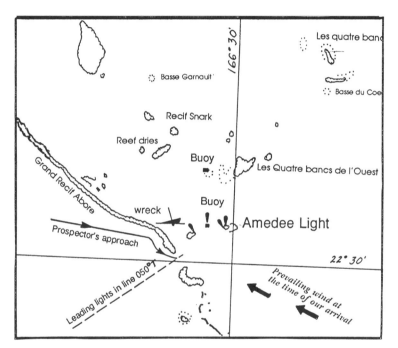

Entering Noumea Lagoon through Boulari Pass

(Chart 7)

Chapter 12

New Zealand Revisited

$\mathcal{H}$er Majesty's Customs launch was alongside first thing next morning. A clear complexioned, bright-eyed young Kiwi, neatly dressed in a sharply ironed uniform common to Her Majesties' tropical services, stood on the vessel's side deck, and politely told me that we had to go to Opua to clear in. I thanked him, and went below to finish breakfast.

The westerly wind that had plagued us the night before, was now very squally, and although the distance to Opua was only about five miles, it took most of the morning to get there.

The breeze was straight on the nose and we were forced to tack until we made the turn into the upper bay. Then, in sight of the Opua pier, we let the sheet run and enjoyed a brief reach. Les Snowsill had been watching for us, and came alongside in his yard launch, as I attempted to come about in the current. He towed us to a mooring buoy directly in front of his shed.

Our friend, customs officer Lou Sabin, was still making house calls. He and a new agriculture inspector named McNamara came to clear us in. McNamara's most noticeable characteristic, apart from an unnaturally red complexion, was his irascible disposition. The man was downright obnoxious. He was winding down what I'm sure was an undistinguished career to retirement. Believe me that no more righteous species of humanity exists than a low-level bureaucrat with a pension in view.

Even here, McNamara was in a class by himself. I'm sure that on his best days, asking for a liberal reading of the regulations would have been like asking him to renounce his faith. The trouble, as usual, was the unwanted presence of our two little furry friends. The only time McNamara smiled during his entire interrogation was when he offered to "put the animals down" as he phrased it.

John and Wendy from *Bali Ha'i*, Roger and Molly from *Sundowner*, Tom and D.L. from *Le Papillion* and Klaus and Babs from *Atair II* were already anchored in Opua when we arrived. Susan and Eric Hiscock were there permanently aboard *Wanderer V*.

Yard repairs began almost at once. After calling the Australian electronics dealer for instructions, I climbed on the bus to Whangarei with the radar display unit on my lap.

Various personnel changes had occurred at Deemings while we were away. Two former employees of Les's had set up a competing shop across the river. Les had replaced them with Leigh, a first rate diesel mechanic, and a 16-year old apprentice named Steve, a small lad, about Les's size, and almost as energetic. Les put Steve to work dismantling the rear end of our engine.

Our engine "room" was a tiny. very cramped cave beneath the cockpit sole. It measured only about 30 inches from the floors that supported the engine beds to the cockpit beams overhead. The engine occupied most of that space, except at the very rear where the transmission, the propeller shaft, the horn timber and the sides of the boat converged.

The transmission was a Borg-Warner, weighing some 140 pounds. Handling such heavy chunk of machinery in those tight quarters required more strength than most 16 year-old boys possess, and Les came out to help.

I could see two pairs of boots bracketing the engine, and hear muttered instructions, punctuated by serious exclamations, and the rumble of heavy machinery moving about.

"AHa!" — I took that as a sign of progress. "Got you now, you bloody so and so!" More progress. Eventually, Les squirmed his way back out of the hole behind the engine, and turning to me, opened his fists to display an odd assortment of oily springs and bits of torn metal. "This is yer drive plate," he said.

The drive plate, also known as a flexi-drive plate, is the device that absorbs the shock when you let the clutch out and an inert machine comes into sudden contact with whirling machinery. Or, reversing the process, when an marine engine stalls because a rope has inadvertently wrapped itself around the propeller.

That wonderful little plate, in other words, with its cleverly arranged springs, was an engineer's answer to a physicist's dilemma. The springs absorbed the shock, until they absorbed one shock too many, as evidently happened when we picked up that line right after leaving Port Jackson the first time. There was probably a fragment of the plate remaining, which allowed us, on our second try, to motor to Sydney Heads, but which crumbled when we had tried to recover those charts in mid-ocean.

A new drive plate was ordered and installed the next day.

"Start her up," Les ordered. I turned the key, and the engine sprang to life. Les only grunted when I pointedly remarked how nicely the starter worked. Then I engaged the clutch. For about five seconds, the propeller turned. Then it stopped and the engine revved up.

"Gor blimy," Les said. "It's broke again," he added.

When he removed the transmission a second time, we discovered that the five bolts holding the drive plate in place had sheared off. He took the flywheel ashore, mounted it in a lathe, and cut a rebate to receive the plate. Then he completed the repair by drilling and tapping *ten* bolt holes to secure it.

That's the heavier hammer approach, and frankly, I don't care much for it. I find it troubling when the doctor treats only the symptom and ignores the underlying cause. However, I was somewhat distracted as the Bay of Islands Tall Ship Race, sponsored by the Russell Boating Club, drew near.

Velda and I had become friendly with several local fishermen who knew about my commercial fishing experiences. One day, as two of them were lounging in the shade of our awning, one said, "Let's enter *Prospector* in the race."

You don't want to let ideas like that get loose. I looked him in the eye and said, "Neither she nor I have ever lost a race, and I intend to keep it that way."

They kept after me, and finally I said if they would put on air tanks and clean *Prospector's* bottom, and if Bill Sellers — an American resident of New Zealand who was a fine artist and a wizard sailor — would come along as sailmaster and tactician, I'd consider it. Bill, like Tim and Pauline Carr in *Curlew*, was a keen racer. But he couldn't enter his cutter *Nimbus* in the race because it was open only to vessels with more than one mast.

Sellers was willing to join us, but only if I would use his 600 ft. genoa. At first light the next morning, our would-be racing crew, none of whom had sailed before, were swimming around the boat, scrapers in hand, keeping their part of the bargain.

By evening, the bottom was clean. Sellers brought his huge genoa on board, and we decided to take her out for a sail. Sellers wanted to see whether his sail fit, and how the boat sailed. The crew was curious to see how a sailboat worked, and I was suffering a serious case of racer's remorse. And not without reason.

Racing imposes stresses on the vital systems of any boat. That's fine if racing is your boat's purpose. However, when your boat is your home and your only mode of transportation to faraway places, and you're totally reliant on a rapidly dwindling bank account for basic sustenance and repairs, you might want to think twice about racing. Those stresses can then become an extravagance. But things were happening too fast for me to brood on that unhappy fact for long. Shortly before the race, the handicap committee putt-putted around the fleet assigning handicaps.

The boat against which the handicaps were measured was *Cygnus*, a 65 foot Swan with coffee grinders and an 11 man professional racing crew. *Cygnus* was almost *America's Cup* caliber. By rights, she should have been required to sail the course twice so the rest of us would have had a decent chance.

Our initial handicap (with my fisherman crew) was a hilarious but flattering 0.60. But as soon as the Race Committee found that Bill Sellers had signed on, our handicap shot up to a wildly ludicrous 0.75. The legality of that was open to question, but the race was only for fun, so what the hell.

The race started well. Under Bill's direction, we crossed the starting line in exactly the right place, at precisely the right second, and for a brief moment of glory, we led the pack, including the mighty *Cygnus* – to the first marker. Our achievements after that were more modest, except that we were fouled (rammed) by another American boat whose skipper had difficulty distinguishing between her starboard and port tacks – we suffered a broken stanchion; but his pride was terribly battered because we had promptly hoisted one of Velda's scarlet T-shirts as a protest flag.

A big New Zealand training ship, the square-rigged bark *Spirit of Adventure* with a crew of 76 squealing teenage female cadets, had passed us nearly an hour before, but as the afternoon breezes died away, and we kept crowding on sail under Bill's urging, we began overtaking her.

The high point of the race occurred at the finish line. As we approached the line, we were on a dead run, all sails full and drawing, with the wind on our starboard quarter. Theoretically, we were supposed to make a last 180 degree turn on a starboard tack, coming about on a port tack, then crossing the line.

We caught up with *Spirit* in the final turn. She was well ahead of us, but instead of coming about by tacking her bow through the weather as a fore and aft rigged vessel would do, she had to wear about, as most square-rigged vessels would, tacking her stern through the weather, to come on a port tack for her approach to the finish line.

She didn't leave much room for us, but as she ponderously gathered way, I swung wide on the turn, maintaining a starboard tack, and approached her starboard bow. As the wind drew forward, and just before we began to pinch, I put the wheel hard over, exactly as I had in Boulari Passage entering the lagoon in Noumea, and sails flogging, we coasted across the line about 25 feet ahead of *Spirit's* bowsprit, missing the starboard buoy by less than five feet. *Spirit* crossed the line half a boat-length behind us. A big English schooner followed *Spirit* across the line.

Although our corrected time put us squarely in the middle of the pack, we didn't come away empty handed. The following Sunday, we had the enormous satisfaction of seeing on the cover of the weekly *Whangarei Advocate's Sporting News*, in living color, *Prospector* bowling along, bone in her teeth, pennants flying, looking almost like a serious racing boat. (*See Frontispiece.*) We may not have been the fastest boat in the race, but clearly, we were among the most picturesque.

The Opua Cruising Club, though the efforts of Harry and Marge Mitchell from *Whalesong* from Alaska, loaned the facilities to the visiting yachts for a Christmas party and people from about 35 boats attended. Our collision with the Australian trawler was still fresh in my mind and it seemed to me that this was a rare opportunity to inquire into the views and experiences of our fellow yachties. After all, where are you likely to find a saltier, more seasoned, bunch of small boat sailors than at a Christmas party in New Zealand?

I prepared a simple one-page questionnaire, and circulated it at the party. Two very experienced cruising couples, Dick and Pat McIlvride and Eric and Susan Hiscock, participated. I included their comments but not their mileage or years spent at sea in the aggregate totals. To do so would have distorted the results.

The 21 respondents (excepting the two mentioned above) had aggregated some 426,000 miles at sea in 94 years. The averages were 22,400 miles and nearly five years of cruising. I was surprised to learn that the *average* boat sails only 4,530 miles a year, spending 45 days at sea. Clearly, we were not typical; we logged more than twice the average time and distance at sea per year during our cruise. The average cruising boat was six years old, was 37.5 feet long, and carried a crew of 2.15.

Eighty-one percent of the respondents said they maintained 24 hour watches. Five boats (of the 21) reported collisions at sea, but the only collision involving another vessel was ours. Two were with whales, one with a container and one (reported by the Hiscocks) with a log or tree. That's not a very comforting number, when you think about it.

Over half the respondents considered collision to be the greatest hazard cruising yachts face. Uncharted reefs came in second, while fire, weather, and freak waves came last in descending order. I was astonished at how accurately our experiences reflected that poll.

I realize it could be misleading to extrapolate from this limited survey to the ocean cruising population at large, but assuming this was a fair sample, since it represented about five percent of the universe, you might conclude (a): that the probability is 1 in 4 that you'll have a collision with something by the time you've logged 22,000 miles; and (b): that you are twice as likely to have a collision with a whale as you are with a container, and equally likely to have a collision with a log as you are with another vessel.

Common sense suggests, however, that there are a hell of a lot more ships out there than logs, and while only Lloyds knows the number of containers that may be adrift at any given time, we believed the number was much greater than we would like to think.

Eric Hiscock flatly considered them the most serious hazard small boats face. Perhaps, because of our experience in Australia I'm biased, but I think shipping presents the greatest danger.

Dick McIlvride's greatest concern was a special kind of merchant shipping; ships operating under flags of convenience. As he pointed out, shipping companies use Liberian registry to avoid their national manning requirements, safety regulations, and other economic inconveniences.

Collisions between ships and yachts do not happen every day, but neither are they so rare that they happen only once in a lifetime (once in 94 years) as a literal reading of these data might suggest.

The only collisions you hear about are those between ships. Quite literally, you *never* hear of a collision between a tanker and a yacht. The reason seems both obvious and macabre. There are no witnesses. No one on the yacht survived and more than likely, people on the ship weren't aware that a collision had occurred.

At sea, it is our invariable practice to hail every ship we see on our VHF radio. Several times during our cruise, ships only three or four miles away responded to our hail with the disconcerting news that they couldn't see us visually on a bright sunny day, and in two cases, even on radar after we had given them our bearing.

That's not as strange as it seems. Most of us with experience in coastal waters know how difficult it is, even from a sailboat, to see a stationary skiff in the swells dead ahead. From a ship's bridge, even a tall sailboat is below the horizon, and is often hidden behind a swell, becoming an intermittent target. Think about it.

Also, according to Captain Jim Mort, writing in Australia's *Cruising Skipper* (Vol. 1 No. 5, 1984), ships rarely use radar at sea, and lookouts, when they are posted and paying attention, are looking for other ships, not nearly invisible yachts.

After you contact a ship on your VHF, the lookouts and the watch officer will know you're there. As a rule, watch officers were glad to break the monotony by chatting with us. But even this is not a foolproof arrangement. Consider Tom Lemm's experience the last time he crossed the Tasman Sea in his pinky schooner, *Le Papillion*.

About halfway across the Tasman, Tom saw a container ship on the horizon and gave her a hail. Her watch officer responded, and while they were chatting, a third party with a heavy Nordic accent broke into the conversation.

"Where is you fellers, anyway?"

Both Tom and the container ship reported their respective positions to the unseen ship. Tom automatically jotted down the container ship's position as he heard it; then he compared it with his own. The two positions were 18 miles apart! Tom suddenly realized that he had hadn't been talking to the ship he was watching, but to a ship he never saw and which never saw him, while the ship he mistakenly thought he was talking to sailed over the horizon oblivious that two other ships and a yacht were within a 25 mile radius. That can be scary.

While we were hauled out toward the end of our second visit to New Zealand, we had a wonderful surprise. I had just climbed down the ladder to get another bucket of paint when I happened to look up, and saw a familiar face peeking around the edge of the shop door. It was Sylvia!

I called up to Velda, then in two great strides was into the shop and had Sylvia in a bear hug. God, I was glad to see that girl! She was living at the time in Auckland, having returned from the delivery of *Aldebaran* to Hong Kong by way of the Philippines, Darwin and Sydney. A mutual friend in Auckland had told her we were at Deemings so she had prevailed on her current boy friend to drive her to the Bay of Islands for a visit.

We haven't seen her since, but one of these days, when we least expect it, one of us will look up, and see those happy blue eyes under the carelessly piled blonde hair peeking around another corner. The Sylvias of this world are more than shipmates; they become lifelong friends.

Time was running out. McNamara had written a nasty letter to us, again offering to put our animals down, so we were in the midst of a last minute orgy of preparations. The refrigeration system was operating again after restorative surgery. The Walker had been rebuilt, the Autohelm repaired, and the radar (temporarily) could distinguish between seagulls and tankers.

A few days before we left, a tall, skinny Australian kid hailed me from the beach. He had met Willi in a youth hostel in Auckland, who had told him we were preparing to sail to Australia. He had come to Opua hoping we might have a berth for him.

I must confess, I have seen more promising specimens than Alan Petersen. Tall, gangling, almost frail in appearance, he had none of that square-jawed, two-fisted determination Tom had displayed, and that I foolishly had found so appealing, under similar circumstances almost exactly a year earlier.

I almost rejected him out of hand but remembering our last experience with the Terrible Tassie, I told him that we would talk it over and let him know later that afternoon. We had heard about a Canadian woman at Opua who also was looking for a berth to Australia, and I wanted to interview her before making a final decision.

I ran the dinghy across to Opua and met Jane Weber, a short competent looking woman in early middle age, who seemed eager, but who didn't appear to know much about sailing. However, I liked her and reported my first impressions to Velda.

I talked to Alan again. This time, I discovered that this passage to Australia would complete his personal circumnavigation. I told him we were also considering Jane. Alan suggested that since we had two spare bunks, we might take both of them.

We hadn't thought of that possibility, but it made sense. We knew that *Le Papillion* routinely carried two or three crew, but she was bigger than *Prospector*. When I mentioned the possibility of two crew members to Jane, she jumped at it.

Alan returned to Auckland for his gear, but Jane moved aboard immediately. She was devoted to her Walkman, and in her baggage had an aluminum suitcase crammed full of camera equipment and cassette tapes. She moved into the pilot berth, stowing her precious tapes at the foot of the bunk. She was a great help to Velda generally getting the boat ready for sea.

Alan returned two days later and moved into the quarter berth. He and I tackled the deck work, and just two days ahead of McNamara, we were ready for sea. *Bali Ha'i* and *Le Papillion* were also ready, and we cleared together, betting a six-pack on our ensuing race to Sydney. A Soviet cruise ship, the *Aleksander Pushkin*, was leaving on the same tide, so the immigration and customs officials gave us a summary clearance.

We left the dock at Opua at 2:30 p.m., February 18, 1985. The wind was calm, the skies partly cloudy. The five-day outlook was for continuing high pressure in the Tasman Sea. History always repeats itself. Last year we had limped out of Opua with a sick starter, and now we were hobbling out again. This time, instead of using a gasoline-soaked rag to start the engine, we needed an extra case of automatic transmission fluid. Only we didn't yet know that. The moral of this story is: Never let the apprentice, no matter how energetic, bright, or nimble he may be, realign your engine.

Two days later, we turned the corner at North Cape, and like the previous year, we began bucking an invisible river as high pressure pushed water northeast out of the Tasman Sea. Only we this time, we strapped on the iron jib and went for it.

The fourth day out, we saw a small pod of whales. In sharp contrast to the previous year, on the 21st, we logged 135 miles, mostly under the squaresail and raffee. On the 22nd we logged another 123 miles and caught a nice mahi-mahi. I was beginning to worry about the consumption of transmission fluid, but the wind was fair, and I held engine time to a minimum.

I couldn't decide whether the Walker was under reporting, or registering a continuing contrary current until sharp-eyed Alan saw the rotator skip out of the top of a wave from time to time. A little extra weight on the chord fixed that.

We were forced to heave-to the next day. The weather suddenly turned bad with rain, squalls, green water on deck and slop coming over the combing into the cockpit. An especially big wave rolled into the cockpit and gave the Autohelm motor a bath, putting it permanently out of action.

Velda had a scary experience on her watch. She saw a long-liner steaming straight for us. She tried in vain to raise them on the VHF, and finally flipped on the deck light.

Ours is not an ordinary deck light. It is a 50-watt halogen automotive driving light, the kind people mount over the cab for off the road work. It is mounted on the mizzen mast, focused forward and slightly down. When it is turned on, and is glowing through the squaresail, we must seem to the onlooker be a visitor from outer space. Tom from *Le Papillion* swears we cast a loom above the horizon.

The ship continued steaming straight toward us. When she was almost within flare pistol range — Velda was holding the flare gun, loaded and cocked, someone must have looked up and seen the light. Perhaps they thought we were a patrol boat, or a ghost, or who knows? The ship suddenly swerved to miss us, made a 180 degree turn, and quickly disappeared over the horizon.

The refrigeration system broke down again, and we went on an orgy of meat consumption, trying to save as much as we could by eating it. I saw *Le Papillion* on the horizon that evening, and called

Tom on the radio, explaining that our refrigeration had failed again, and offered to pass over some meat if we could rendezvous in the morning. Unfortunately, at daybreak we were out of VHF range and the meat I wanted to give Tom went overboard to the sharks.

A few days later, we heard what we thought was a boat with the call letters *QE 947* calling *Le Papillion*. Tom had turned his set off, so we returned the call. *QE 947* was an Australian patrol plane. We identified ourselves, the plane gave us a "Roger" and I signed off, strangely comforted that for the moment, someone in authority knew where we were.

That night, we were treated to a spectacular phosphorescence show. We were all but becalmed, and were motoring through water livid with microscopic animals. Our bow wave was a sparkling necklace of beauty, and deep in the water twice I caught a glimpse of moving fins as something big kept pace with us. Spooky.

The next day, near the end of my morning watch, I saw what appeared to be a squall line directly in front of us, closing fast. I could see spikes of lightning, and judging by the roiling clouds, I knew we could expect sharp squally winds. Alan and I put on our oilskins, and tied a double reef into the mainsail.

Lightning began to crackle and sizzle around us, and the accompanying thunder, an almost continuous explosion, caused the deck to vibrate, and was actually painful. I sent everyone below, and after starting the engine, changed course to the northwest, hoping that would be the quickest way out of that mess. It didn't work that way. The weather seemed unaffected by the wind — we slogged through it for another two hours before we finally got clear.

Looking back, we could clearly see the dark angry clouds boiling up, and frequent lightning bolts darting from cloud to cloud. It reminded me of Grieg's *Storm on Bald Mountain* from the *Peer Gynt Suite*. I probably made that connection because the storm was so localized and appeared to be immobile.

At noon, after our midday observations, I realized the storm was directly over the Tauro Seamount. Later the same day, *Le Papillion* encountered the same storm at precisely the same location. Two days later, *Bali Ha'i* had an identical experience.

Two nights later, we saw Sydney's loom over the horizon before I laid down for the night, and when I came on watch at 4 a.m., I could distinguish the cadence of the Macquarie light against the bright city loom. Our landfall was perfectly timed.

At daybreak, while we were still several miles off the coast, I called Sydney Radio and asked permission to enter the port. I also asked them to notify customs and quarantine of our arrival.

We anchored in Watson Bay as directed, and settled down to wait. This crossing had taken 11 days, 19 hours. We had sailed 1,205 miles. We were getting better at it.

I didn't like the look of the weather. The glass was dropping fast, and the air was still, hot and muggy. I thought we might be in for a blow. When *Le Papillion* came in three hours later, Tom looked around, and decided to exercise his captain's prerogative by notifying Sydney Radio that he considered Watson Bay unsafe in the developing weather conditions, and would anchor in Obelisk Bay.

I would have followed him, except that we couldn't. We had been obliged to sail into Watson Bay because our transmission had run dry. Without transmission fluid, the engine was useless.

We were in a bad way. I didn't dare send Alan ashore for transmission fluid until we had been cleared, and the officials were in no hurry to clear us. Already, the wind was up to 20–25 knots, and little wavelets were beginning to crest with foam.

By noon, the wind had risen to 35–40 knots. Even if we were cleared instantly, the wind by now was too strong to consider sending Alan ashore. The wind continued to rise, and when the officials finally arrived, the wind was blowing half a gale. As sheltered as Watson Bay is, we were beginning to pitch and roll.

Clearing in was quick and painless, except the customs launch hit us hard enough to break a stanchion. The customs officers were beginning to look a little peaked. They left as soon as they could, the lady officer sensibly stuffing her shoes into her briefcase before climbing over the lifeline. The young man slipped on the rail and for a moment, I thought we would have to fish him out of the bay.

As soon as we cleared, Alan asked to go ashore for transmission fluid. The wind had slacked temporarily, and it looked as if this was our best chance. We put the dinghy in the water, and I gingerly handed down our new Suzuki.

Alan was gone a long time, and I had just about given up on him until the weather improved, when Jane called down the hatch, "Alan's coming!"

I hurried up on deck, and watched him expertly dodging the larger waves, working his way up wind to *Prospector*. Alan was a fine person, a wonderful shipmate, and a good sailor. He was one of the best crew members we had. Just watching his approach back to the boat gave me a good feeling.

It took only a few minutes to pour the fluid into the transmission. After bringing the Suzuki on board and doubling the lines to the dinghy, I started the engine.

Velda and Alan stood by the anchor windlass, and when I engaged the clutch and advanced the throttle, they pressed the windlass switch, and began retrieving the anchor chain. As soon as the chain was straight up, I shoved the throttle wide open.

The engine roared and clouds of smoke belched from the exhaust. We seemed motionless while the windlass brought the clanking chain aboard. Gradually we began to inch forward. Alan came back to stand next to me.

"Might be easier under the bluff," he shouted, pointing across the choppy channel. I agreed, but I wasn't sure we could get there. Besides, the hydrofoil ferries were still operating between downtown Sydney and the outlying suburbs. Crossing the channel under these conditions was like crossing a busy arterial highway on our hands and knees.

I steered outside a channel marker, and turned to the left so the wind was on our beam. *Prospector* began to gain speed, and I mentally debated setting the staysail. I probably should have done so. After we had gone a quarter of a mile, we came to the dogleg turn to the right, which takes you past the famous opera house and under the bridge.

Prospector reeled under the weight of the wind blowing under the bridge and the two mile fetch which caused us to lose way, and relentlessly pushed us to the left.

Shark Island was dead ahead. I turned slightly to the right to counter the thrust of those waves. Meanwhile, Alan crawled under the cockpit, and poured more fluid into the transmission, which was exactly what we needed.

It seemed like hours — but it was only minutes before we were past the opening, going peacefully into Rose Bay where we anchored in the calm shadow of apartment buildings.

Our crew, like all seafaring crews throughout history, couldn't wait to get ashore. After supper, Jane and Alan climbed down into the dinghy, and rowed to a landing at the head of the bay.

Although Alan came from Queensland, he knew his way around Sydney. He especially knew his way around King's Cross, which was within easy walking distance up the hill from the dinghy landing. That's where Alan got his revenge for Jane's incessant teasing and mock efforts at seduction during the trip from New Zealand.

As I said earlier, if it's defined as sin and you have the money to pay for it, you'll probably find in the King's Cross neighborhood. Just the place for a sailor home from the sea. Alan was chatting up a pair of Kings Cross birds, when Jane popped up, and insisting on being introduced to Alan's new friends.

"Girls," Alan said solemnly, "I'd like you to meet my mother."

During the night, the storm blew itself out, and by daylight, the wind was almost calm. We raised the anchor, and sedately motored back to the channel, past Fort Denison, past the Opera House, under the bridge, and on into Balls Head Bay.

Le Papillion was already anchored in her usual way, deploying six anchors like a spider web. As always, she was on the outer tier of yachts, infringing slightly on an area the Navy regarded as its own. The Navy viewed Tom's presence out of the bight as a trespass. On one occasion, a small Navy tug came dangerously close to *Le Papillion* and "accidentally" snagged one of her anchor lines. Seemingly unaware, the tug dragged her half way across the bay before anyone realized what was happening.

But the second time around for us was a homecoming. Jan and Nick from *Vera*, Louise and Craig from *Morning Star*, and John Bailey from *Kiah*, turned out to give us a rousing welcome as we came to anchor.

We also had new neighbors. *Blue Waters*, a Tahiti ketch belonging to a young woman named Elinor Davey, was anchored nearby, as was *White Horse of Kent*, an old boat belonging to a boat carpenter, and a Polish sloop named *Terra Incognita*.

I never understood how the Polish boat was organized. We were told it belonged to a cruising club in Gdynia. Yet, her crew of four young men seemed permanently employed in Sydney. Pawel, one of them, was seriously romancing Elinor, and they were talking marriage.

The next major passage for those making a circumnavigation, was the 6,000 mile Indian Ocean crossing. Unlike the Atlantic or Pacific passages, there is no time of the year when it is entirely safe to cross the Indian Ocean. Statistically, however, the least dangerous time is a narrow ten-week window from August first to the middle of October.

We began counting backwards. Since Darwin was the jumping off place for the Indian Ocean, and was on the northwestern corner of Australia, almost 3,000 miles away, the obvious question was how long it would take to reach Darwin. Bear in mind that over a third of that distance involved day sailing in the Barrier Reef, where 50 miles was a good day's work.

Taking everything into account, including stops along the way and possibly two or three side trips, we thought it would probably take three months to reach Darwin.

The first of May, then, was the best time to leave Sydney. We had arrived on March second, so we had about two months to cure the misalignment problem and provision the boat.

Elinor Davy, from *Blue Waters,* was interested in crewing with us as far as Mooloolaba, about 600 miles up the coast. She needed the sea time for her license. She also wanted to do some serious thinking about her relationship with Pawel. She had been single a long time, and she was not a person to take marriage lightly. We were glad to welcome her aboard.

It seemed as if I were going nonstop between the wonderful market in Birkenhead and the boat. I also spent much time wiggling the engine around, trying to get a perfect match between the coupling on the propeller shaft and its mate on the transmission. The ability to align engines mounted on wooden beds with long lag bolts is an art, passed from father to son. Unfortunately, my father was a trainer of polo ponies.

Two months whizzed by, and was barely enough time to get ready, but on May fourth, we exchanged final embraces with our friends, and by noon, we had the anchor up and were underway.

As before, we were escorted to the North Sydney bridge by *Vera* and several smaller boats. Velda called my attention to something at the coal dock. While I was distracted, Elinor quickly ran a large boxing kangaroo flag up the starboard flag hoist, then anxiously watched for my reaction. I think half the Bay must have been in on it; when the green bunting shot up to the spreader, our escort gave a hearty cheer. Not a bad send-off.

This time, we knew the drill, and we called in Watson Bay to clear for Darwin. I paid Velda's $20 departure tax — Elinor paid her own — and we cleared Sydney Heads. But we needn't have been in such a hurry. By noon of the first full day at sea, we were only 25 miles from Port Jackson. Twenty-four hours after that, we were merely 55 miles away. It was becoming embarrassing. By evening, however, we had a double reef in the main.

The East Australian Current can be a nuisance at times. Unlike the Gulf Stream, or the Agulhas Current off South Africa, the East Australian Current is unpredictable. Sometimes it runs like hell; three or four knots is uncommon, but not unheard of. Sometimes it barely trickles down the coast, and on rare occasions it can reverse.

We had encountered it in one of its more robust moods. The current running against a fresh southeast breeze kicked up a substantial sea and bounced us around, but those little storms don't last long, and by morning we were almost becalmed again.

It seems incredible, but that 600 mile trip to Mooloolaba took ten days. *Bali Ha'i* left Sydney two days after we did, and pulled into the breakwater off Mooloolaba minutes behind us. We were both set to anchor, when a police boat came out and directed us to the municipal moorings, where, for seven dollars a night we were moored between two yellow buoys in the river. The man who collected the money said we could expect to pay the same, or higher, fees further north. But he was wrong. We weren't again charged for anchoring or mooring in Australia.

People without animals were allowed to tie up at the local yacht club. We had a dog and a cat. People without a menagerie had electricity, showers, laundry facilities, and free nightly movies in the club house for one dollar a night more than we were paying. Sometimes I wondered about those animals.

Several friends had arrived before we did. The Bodenham family from *Madelline Ann;* Doug, Mary, and Cathy Solomon from *Sundance Kid*; and other folks we hadn't seen since Tahiti were there.

Mooloolaba was a staging area for the lower and central part of the Barrier Reef. I found the town pleasant, a typical Australian resort town, crowded with young people on the dole and their elders with many children looking for inexpensive lodgings.

At seven dollars a night, we wasted little time replenishing the larder. We had no reason to linger after we had bought the groceries we needed, but we had an important decision to make.

Fraser Island (shown on some charts as "Sandy Island") was about 100 miles north of Mooloolaba. It had a macabre history. It was named for the unlucky captain of an English ship, the *Sterling Castle*, which was wrecked on the island late in the last century. The crew was murdered by Aborigines who reportedly ate the captain. His widow, Mrs. Fraser, was spared, and was enslaved. She was subsequently rescued, and after her return to England, she lived out her days as a side show exhibit.

The island lies on a north–south axis, and like an iceberg, extends underwater far beyond what you see on the surface. The upland part is 27 miles long. Breaksea Spit, the portion of the island beneath the water, continues in a northerly direction for an additional 30 miles.

Most yacht skippers wisely chose the inside passage. Done right, that short trip (I'm told) was easy. You entered the strait at low water, and carried the flood until you were about half way through, when the tide would reverse, and you'd ride the ebb to the northern side. As a bonus, not only were you traveling in sheltered water, but you had an opportunity to visit Bundaburg, home of Australia's famous rum.

With those obvious advantages, why would anyone choose the outside route? If you didn't trust your engine, the deep water route was the only alternative. But I should have been more trusting. Going outside the island was a mistake.

After leaving Elinor in Mooloolaba, we sailed northeast for nearly 30 hours, and reached the southern tip of Fraser Island at dusk. The weather was overcast, but we had spoken with a freighter at noon, and had gotten a position, but that was eight hours earlier, and the East Australian Current was still raising hell with my dead reckoning.

It turned out to be an inky black night. There wasn't a glimmer even of phosphorescence to relieve the dark. The wind was blowing a steady 30 knots out of the south southeast, and we had a single reef in the mainsail. Velda and I had reverted to our six on, six off watch schedule. It was my watch, about 2 a.m. when I saw, or thought I saw, a row of six white lights running in a north–south direction, as if they were marking the eastern edge of Breaksea Spit.

I hated to wake Velda, but since the chart didn't show any lights, I needed someone to corroborate or refute what I thought I was seeing. After she came on deck, Velda saw them, too. Then they vanished. She took the wheel while I carried the binoculars to my perch on the doghouse and settled down to search for them. They never reappeared, and were almost forgotten when I heard Velda's distressed cry, "Denny! Something's wrong with the compass!"

Christ! There couldn't be anything worse than learning that the compass has gone haywire while we were off a dark and hostile sandbar in an onshore 30 knot wind on an overcast night.

I jumped down and hurriedly joined Velda in the cockpit in time to watch the compass card move slowly, turning with evident purpose, as it made a 360 degree rotation. It didn't slow down when the card was 180 degrees away from the magnetic pole, nor did it speed up as the card approached its proper orientation. The complete revolution took between fifteen and twenty seconds.

We must have presented a primeval picture, the two of us hooded in oilskins, like medieval monks, anxiously huddled in the middle of the night over a cabalistic shrine, a card under a plastic dome bathed in a reddish glow, waiting for the Oracle to reveal its Divine purpose.

After resting for three of four minutes, the card began another stately revolution, as deliberate, and as purposeful as the first.

What an awful thing to see! I found it hard to credit my sanity, except that Velda had seen it, too.

Although we carry a spare compass, for all I knew that one was screwed up, too. In our tiny physical universe, the wind was our only constant. I kept it behind my right ear, and sent Velda back to bed. I steered by the wind until daylight when I checked the compass against the sun's azimuth, and found, to my enormous relief, that it seemed restored to health.

I have no idea what caused the compass to behave in such bizarre fashion. I can only guess that we must have sailed into a powerful magnetic field, perhaps over a rich iron ore deposit. That, in itself, would not be surprising because Australia is heavily mineralized. But if that were the case, I find it odd that a magnetic anomaly of that magnitude could exist and not be reported in the *Sailing Directions*.

It seems possible, although I know nothing of the circumstances of her wreck, that the unfortunate *Sterling Castle's* compass might have been similarly influenced, causing her loss.

But I couldn't see how a magnetic anomaly could account for those mysterious lights. I don't know how to explain them. Perhaps the least complicated explanation was the one offered by Ebenezer Scrooge viewing the Ghost of Christmas Past — a bit of overripe cheese, perhaps. As for Velda's corroboration, the power of suggestion is a powerful force.

Until that peculiar performance, I had been very pleased with our compass, a Richie. It was the only compass I have owned that had no deviation. This was as much a tribute to Captain Winters who swung it in Annapolis as it was to the manufacturer. Its continued accuracy was even more remarkable when you consider that it was a northern compass which by that time had been in the Southern Hemisphere for several years.

However, it was months before I was comfortable with it again. I checked it against the sun every day for a long time. I still check it at least every second or third day.

Three days later, we saw two dark smudges on the horizon. These were Lady Elliot and Lady Musgrove islands.

Most 18th century explorers relied heavily on private patrons to finance their voyages. Captain Cook was no exception. The Pacific rim is dotted with the names of his patrons, the richer and more famous ones appearing several times, and on larger and more prominent landmarks.

The Ladies Elliot and Musgrove were patrons, but apparently not heavy hitters. Cook probably didn't realize it, but the "islands" he named for them are really coral atolls which mark the southern limit of Australia's Great Barrier Reef.

From the Ladies to the Percy Island group is a slow overnight sail — the last overnight sail we were to experience until we reached the Indian Ocean. We saw the cluster of the Percy Island group at daybreak, and found our way through them to Middle Percy Island. This island was well known in yachting circles. It had its attractions. Besides a lonely and horny emu that was likely to make love to your inflatable dinghy if you left it overnight on the beach, the place had an innocence that many people found enchanting.

We arrived shortly before noon. The anchorage, in a shallow cove, was on the western side of the island.

We sailed in under the squaresail, having struck the raffee when we entered the narrow channel between North Percy and Middle Percy Islands. We hauled the yard as far as it would go on a port tack as we came around the corner. Though the sail started to luff, it still gave us steerageway, and we came to anchor without starting the engine. The ability to maneuver under sail was becoming increasingly important.

As we entered the little harbor, I saw a handful of boats already at anchor near a cluster of buildings on the beach. I tried to get as close to them as seemed prudent because I thought they would be in quiet water. Lucas warns in another cruising guide, *The Coral Coast*, that despite the proximity of Pine Isle and its antique kerosene-powered lighthouse directly opposite the anchorage, swells penetrate the anchorage, which was often uncomfortable.

As we were anchoring, one boat caught my eye. After I rolled the squaresail and Velda rounded up into the wind so I could drop the anchor, I kept reviewing that boat's familiar lines in my mind's eye, but I couldn't remember where we had seen her last.

Just then a dinghy load of people came alongside. One fellow looked up and said, "You won't remember me, but we are from *Innocent Bystander*. The last time I saw *Prospector* was in the Atlantic, and you thought we were a gold plater."

At first I was puzzled, then as I followed his pointing finger, I recognized her satnav antenna and I had a sudden recollection of that terrible storm in the Atlantic, and the boat I had called for a position check. I also remembered saying something at the time about having a gold plater — a rich man's toy — in our midst over the VHF radio to a nearby boat, *Che*.

The fellow in the dinghy promised to stop by later, and I was free again to stare at that boat with those tantalizingly familiar lines. Where had we seen that boat before?

I pointed her out to Velda. She took a quick look, and turned back to me. "She looks just like *Prospector* to me," she said.

Chapter 13

Crocodiles and Sea Serpents

$\mathcal{R}$ichard and Kathy, owners of *Innocent Bystander*, came past our anchorage late in the afternoon, and invited us for cocktails in the early evening. We gladly accepted.

I vividly remember Richard's grin when he asked whether we preferred ice made by solar energy or wind power. He had both. His refrigeration system was an adapted Adler-Barbour. The original Adler–Barbours were air-cooled, but he had converted his unit to water cooling before the manufacturers did. Richard and Kathy were like that; constantly finding ways to make things a little more efficient, a little handier, a little better.

A day after our arrival, Roger and Molly Firey in *Sundowner* came into the bay and anchored near us. We had met Roger and Molly two years earlier in Tahiti, and again in New Zealand.

Although I thought a 32 foot Westsail was small for two adults and a cat, they seemed to get along very well with a hyperactive Siamese named Angus. Roger was a retired Naval officer, and I was always glad to see him, partly because of his experience and sound advice, but mostly because he and Molly were generous people who seemed never to run out of beer.

The cluster of buildings on the beach were the telephone shed, a large open-ended A-frame protecting half a dozen picnic tables, and a small pump house. An open cabinet in the A-frame held homemade preserves and jars of honey. A small sign indicated that the "store" operated on the honor system. A price list completed the notice.

The telephone shed, a small building with a large sign over the door saying TELEPHONE was the most interesting thing on the beach unless you counted the emu tracks in the sand.

The original settlers, according to Lucas' *Cruising the Coral Coast,* operated a sheep station on the island from about the time of the first World War until the early 1960s. The shed housed a telephone in those days, and visitors announced their arrival by calling the main house a mile away.

The building no longer serves as a telephone booth, but has become an impromptu marine museum containing memorabilia from hundreds of cruising yachts. A typical example was an oar suspended from the rafters with the yacht's name carved in the loom and the names of the crew on the blade.

The building was jammed full of carvings, bits of fancy work, painted life jackets, ring buoys, ship's stationary, and even oars, all displaying a vessel's name, date, and hailing port. Some things were tacked to the walls, others to posts supporting the roof, without plan or purpose other than the desire to leave a visible record of passage.

But Middle Percy's main attraction was the hermit. In truth, Mr. Martin was as much

The telephone building

a hermit as I am. People land there expecting Robinson Caruso. What they find instead, is an erudite middle–aged English gentleman eking out a living selling horseradish sauce, wine, preserves, goat hides and being picturesque.

Roger, Molly, Velda and I decided to visit the hermit. We hiked up the hill, following a well marked trail to the homestead. It was a long walk, especially for this sailor, but worth it. The hermit's headquarters were impressive. His large house was built on stilts. Because all the roofs in the compound were connected in an elaborate rain catchment–cistern storage system, I suspect the island may be arid. We saw rows of cisterns, like fat pillars, under the house. A large cistern, almost like an outdoor silo, dominated the yard.

We were greeted by the raucous screech of peacocks, but we

didn't see a hermit. We hesitated to open the gate without being invited, but we could see a well organized flower garden behind the house. Across the road, we saw an elaborate fenced truck garden. Guinea hens wandered around, unconcerned, staying in the shade of the citrus trees.

Andrew Martin's house

We were on the point of leaving when we heard people approaching. I suppose I was expecting someone dressed in animal skins. What I didn't expect was a deeply tanned man in his mid–50s wearing brief bikini trunks, carrying a rifle slung over his shoulder. I expected even less to see an entourage of five young people, three women and two men, following in his wake.

He stopped abruptly when he saw us by his gate. Staring at me, he demanded, "Who are you? How did you get here?" Satisfied by our startled explanations, he offered to shake hands and invited us into his home.

His winery was on the ground in the cool, shaded area under the house between the great water tanks. Judging by his set–up, he sold much wine. It was a sweet fruity wine that would distill easily into brandy. We stayed for lunch. I noticed how he made himself useful in the kitchen; mostly in an executive capacity. "Get this, do that," while the young women put things together.

Velda's earlier comment about the boat that resembled *Prospector* was much more perceptive than we knew. After lunch, one of the young men quietly said to me, "I saw you sailing into the anchorage yesterday. Where did you get the plans for your boat?"

I must have looked puzzled, because he added, "I read about *Prospector* in *Good Boats*, and I had an architect draw a set of plans from the lines given in the book. I built a new *Prospector* three quarters scale."

Perhaps a psychologist could explain why, when I told him our boat was the original *Prospector*, he seemed almost disappointed. Or why neither of us visited the other's boat, and why I kept neither the owner's nor the boat's name. I don't even recall that we had

311

much to say to each other after that initial exchange of confidences. Although we did not go aboard, judging from outward appearances, he had built a fine boat.

It happened that this was my birthday, and that evening, Velda prepared a birthday feast, as she usually does. We invited Roger and Molly to join us. During dinner, we discussed the alternative routes by which we could tackle the Barrier Reef system. Roger was planning to leave before daylight the next morning, and we decided spontaneously to tag along.

The first anchorage north of Middle Percy was an exception. Scawfell Island was 70 miles north. Seventy miles was a long daylight sail, and if we were to arrive before dark, we had to get a very early start. Roger agreed to give me a call on the radio when it was time to get up. We left the radio on all night, and promptly at 2:45 a.m., we heard his 3 a.m. call. Roger is like that. I heard his anchor windlass hauling his chain aboard, while I made our coffee. Then I started the engine, and we hauled our anchor while I sipped hot coffee, keeping an eye on Roger's stern light. Not bothering to turn on our own lights, we followed him until daylight, when a southeast breeze sprang up, and I set sail.

With both the squaresail and the raffee drawing, it wasn't long before we overhauled *Sundowner*, and hours later, when she caught up to us, we were already snugly anchored in the bay on the north side of Scawfell Island.

Our mechanical problems were becoming more serious every day. The new starter, unbelievably, was beginning to smoke badly when I switched on the ignition. Also, the automatic transmission fluid seemed to leak away almost as fast as I could replace it.

We were approaching the Whitsunday Island group. Roger and Molly wanted to explore Australia's premier cruising grounds, but all I could think of was finding a mechanic who could put us right. We sailed into Pioneer Bay and anchored off Airlie Beach, where we rowed ashore with a fist full of Australian 20¢ pieces. This was sometimes called the Gold Coast. A smaller edition of Mooloolaba, it was a resort town full of kids living on the dole, drinking plonk and improving their sun tans. I found a pay phone and a phone book and began calling nearby boat yards.

When the people at the other end discovered we had animals aboard and therefore had to remain midstream, it was "sorry, mate, hope you make it." Discouraged, we went back to the boat, where we studied the charts. It was 50 miles from Airlie to Cape Upstart. From the Cape to Magnetic Island was another 60 miles.

The third night, if all went well, we would anchor in the Palm Island group, the fourth night at Dunk Island, and by the fifth night, with luck, we could be in Cairns. Five days, five engine starts. Surely we had five more starts in that starter.

Why we bypassed Townsville, one of the largest cities on this coast, I can't say. Townsville certainly would have had the mechanics and anything else we might have needed. But for some odd reason I was focused on Cairns to the exclusion of everything else.

We left Airlie Beach the next morning, and by noon we were near Bowen, home of a boat yard I had phoned. I was tempted to go in, and let someone else work around *our* problems for a change, but why look for trouble? We tucked into Grey's Bay for the night, sailing on and off the anchor. There were many double-rigged shrimp boats that looked exactly like their American cousins.

Australia's eastern coastline is drab. All you see from the water is a series of dun colored sand dunes, small hills, scrub vegetation, and infrequent mining scars. Occasionally, on your right, you'll see small islands, and now and then, coral breaking the surface, The fairway that far south is wide, but no place for a stranger after dark.

We sailed out of the anchorage behind Cape Upstart while the shrimpers were still working. We stayed well clear of a long sand spit that nearly closes Bowling Green Bay, and sailed around Cape Cleveland, guarding Townsville from the south. Our goal was Horseshoe Bay on the north side of Magnetic Island.

We arrived abeam of Magnetic Island shortly before dusk, but before we quite got around the corner, we were overtaken, and blinded, by an intense electrical squall. Darkness came with the storm, punctuated by flashes of lightning, and sheets of drenching rain. Our visibility plunged to zero. Fortunately, I had already struck our sails, and we had the engine going. Running slow, I groped my way into the bay. An alert shrimper saw us, and rushed over to head us off. *"They's a shark net in there!"* he yelled, waving his arm vaguely toward the south."Follow me!" he ordered.

Gratefully, I swung the bow toward his boat, and followed him around the edge of a net I still didn't see. By this time, the rain had slacked off, and the lightning was gone.

It was pitch dark, but I could see anchor lights near the shore. The trawler slowed, allowing us to catch up.

"There's yer mites," the captain said, waving toward the lights. "Yer OK now." He stepped into his wheelhouse while we shouted our thanks. The trawler disappeared in the darkness.

We ran toward the lights, watching the depth finder, and when it read 15 feet, I closed the throttle, and we coasted to a stop. Velda went forward. I heard the anchor hit the water, and the rattle of chain running over the wildcat. I stopped the engine.

The following morning, as bright and crisp an autumn day as you are likely to find, we sailed off the anchor — I was becoming quite good at it — sailed around the shark net, which was easy to see in broad daylight, and out into the Sound.

We passed close to a big rock that broke the surface four miles north of Horseshoe Bay. A large runabout painted a bright orange, bearing the letters *RAAF* on her side, came running up. I knew what the man standing on her bow was going to say. We also have orange runabouts in Chesapeake Bay. But their crews were more civil than this fellow.

"Yer in the middle of a bombing range!" he bellowed. "Get out of here — and don't come back!"

We were already making our best speed, but remembering how formal things had become when the international aspects of our collision became known, I ran our flag up the mizzen topping lift and immediately felt better.

Suddenly we heard the shattering roar of a major explosion behind us, and looking back, we saw a column of water and smoke not over a quarter of a mile away rising in the air. The Aussies played war games with live ammunition. If that explosion was from an aerial bomb, the plane that dropped it was so high it was out of sight.

The Palm Islands were our next stop. This cluster, except Orpheus and Pelorus, was an Aborigine Reserve, and casual visits were prohibited. The best anchorage seemed to be in Hazard Bay on the northwestern corner of Orpheus. In his book, *Cruising the Coral Coast,* Lucas warned about a resort on the beach, saying "(It) is now (1984) owned by Carlo Cobianchi and Alessio Cioni who have developed it into a small, very exclusive resort. Boating folk are not permitted ashore."

We arrived in early afternoon and anchored in 15 feet of water in front of a small dock and a row of beach cottages. We could see a reef directly in front of the dock. We had barely anchored before an aluminum skiff with three young people with an offering of a six-pack of beer came roaring through the opening in the reef and out to *Prospector*.

Until I got a close look at the people and saw the beer, I thought possibly Lucas' warning was more serious than I had realized. Our visitors introduced themselves as staff members at the resort, and handed over the beer. We invited them aboard, and each of us opened a cold one.

"We thought that might hit the spot," one of them said. They described the resort, confirming what Lucas had written. Then, much to my surprise, they invited us ashore for supper. "We have a barbi," the girl said. "One thing about this place; we eat well."

We gladly accepted. Barbecued anything sounded good, and I have an unquenchable curiosity about forbidden places.

Our guests left soon afterward, and shortly before dark the boat returned with a new driver. This young man's name was Cameron Douglas, a polite, well spoken young fellow who almost immediately, while we were alone, asked for a berth.

I told him we'd think about it. In the meanwhile, our hostess was right. The staff was well fed. As promised, we enjoyed a delicious barbecue with fish, steak, salad, plenty to drink, and good conversation around an outdoor grill in the early night air.

Because of our collision, perhaps I was overly sensitive to Australians with Italian surnames, but the *Sydney Herald* had recently published a serial exposé about organized crime in Australia, and the Mafia appeared to control a major part of it.

The older staff members wouldn't talk about the lodge or its guests, but the younger staff members told us about the apparent shortage of paying guests, the reluctance of some guests to be seen by the staff, and the general aura of secrecy surrounding the place. I couldn't help but think of that old saw, "if it looks like a duck, talks like a duck and acts like a duck... ."

Yet, to be fair about it, I have to say that while it's possible the Hazard Bay resort was a Mafia hideout, the only criminal thing we actually saw was the price of rum. We paid $50 for a $15 bottle.

There are many things on this coast that are hazardous to your health besides gangsters and bombing ranges. While I was getting information from the old fisherman who served as Port Captain about anchorages ahead, he confided his formula for a long and successful career on the water. "I has me an deal with the sharks," he said. "I stays out of the water, and they stays out of the pubs." I have taken his advice, and I have yet to see a shark in a pub. People joke about sharks, but they are a deadly serious proposition.

While we were in Sydney, according to the *Sydney Herald*, a young woman standing in just over three feet of water on a crowded bathing beach was attacked, killed and *eaten* by a shark before hundreds of stunned onlookers, including her husband and three children. The animal's first strike cut her body in half. It consumed half of it on its second strike, and swam off with the remainder.

Theory has it that sharks near the equator have so much food that they seldom bother with people. That may be so, but the people who put shark nets in front of bathing beaches probably have good reason. I still don't know whether the nets are there to protect the people, or whether they are put there to catch sharks attracted by splashing in the water. If it's the latter, it's an interesting concept, using bathers as shark bait. Knowing the Aussie mind, however, I suspect it's both.

Cameron took us back to *Prospector* and repeated his desire to join us and sail with us at least as far as Darwin. He lacked sailing experience, but he seemed pleasant and was certainly well mannered. When I asked him about giving notice, he said the manager rarely bothered with it, and that "kids are coming and going all the time; hardly anyone stays longer than two months."

We told Cameron that if he could meet us in Cairns in a week, we would take him as far as Darwin; we would then decide whether to continue the arrangement.

These waters practically crawled with sea snakes, some of which were so venomous that death following a bite was invariable and almost instantaneous. Several times each day we sailed past one coiled in the water, the sun reflecting from its wet yellow and brown splotchy back. True, they were slow and sluggish, and they couldn't open their mouths very wide, but when I saw one, I could barely suppress a shudder. Those snakes got big. We saw some eight or ten feet long and as big around as my lower leg.

316

On the other hand, when you saw that many snakes, you knew there weren't many crocodiles around, which was a blessing. While crocodiles were more abundant in the Northwest Territory than they were in Queensland, even in Queensland visitors were warned that crocs were highly predaceous to man.

The sea wasp or box jellyfish was another potentially fatal pest. Fortunately, they were seasonal; they occurred only in summer during the typhoon season, and sensible cruising skippers were long gone by then. And, if you had to go ashore, although cannibals no longer threatened shipwrecked sailors, it paid to keep your eyes peeled for poisonous spiders.

I'm a real coward when it comes to things like this. The very thought of going ashore, going swimming or exploring mangrove swamps made my skin crawl. All I wanted to do was get to Cairns. Long before daylight the next morning, we had the anchor up and the sails set, hoping to reach Dunk Island before dark. By daybreak, we were abreast of Hinchenbrook Island.

Many Australians will be surprised to learn that Alaska has a Mount Hinchenbrook, Cape Hinchenbrook, *and* Hinchenbrook Island. When it was time to write checks for Captain Cook, Lord Hinchenbrook must have been a very heavy hitter, indeed.

The combined northerly setting current and the relentless southeast tradewinds carried us over 70 miles, but just before we reached Dunk island, the wind faded, and I started the engine.

Oh, oh! More trouble! Instead of the expected few passive wisps of smoke when I turned the key in the starter switch, I heard an ominous crackling sound and saw the red insulation on a ground wire connecting the starter to the engine begin to smoke, bubble, and melt. That is definitely a bad sign.

Nevertheless, the starter cranked the engine, but I was doubtful whether it would do so again. As we ran around a point into the anchorage in Brammo Bay on the north side of Dunk Island, I thought we'd have to let the engine idle all night because, from reading Lucas' guide, I was sure we would need the engine when it was time to enter Cairns, 110 miles to the north.

Dunk Island was a major resort, with rental boats, sunbathers, and people splashing happily behind the shark nets. We didn't feel like going ashore. All we wanted was a quiet night's rest.

Long before daylight the next morning, we had the anchor up

and sails set, motorsailing north. With daylight, a fair breeze filled the sails, and to save fuel, still not daring to shut the engine down, I shifted the clutch to neutral, and allowed the engine to continue idling while the propeller free-wheeled.

After we had been underway some three hours, I smelled smoke apparently coming from the engine compartment. I thought at first it was merely a slipping fan belt. When you've had the engine problems we've had, you become hardened to things like smoke issuing from the engine compartment, but this smoke didn't seem to be coming from the engine.

Flashlight in hand, I crawled under the cockpit next to the hot engine, and immediately saw a mixture of smoke and steam coming from the stern bearing. The packing in the stern bearing was smoldering; it was on fire!

Hoping I wasn't damaging the propeller shaft, I slacked the bolts holding the packing gland, and let water seep into the packing. There was loud hissing and much steam came from the bearing when the cool water ran over the hot propeller shaft.

I stuffed new packing into the gland. Then, assuming that friction from the spinning propeller shaft had caused the fire, I put a pipe wrench on the propeller shaft to stop it from turning; I didn't want to set the packing on fire again.

Long before we expected it, we saw the piling fence that led into Cairns extending well out from shore. The approach to Cairns was a channel 70 meters wide, 9,782 meters long, and seven meters deep. Think about it; a shallow ditch 20 feet deep, 220 feet wide and slightly over six miles long. That's a hell of a ditch.

The channel was sort of marked by twin rows of piling. They were only marginally helpful because they had been driven some 180 feet (more or less) from the nearest edge of the ditch. All I saw was twin rows of piling about 600 feet apart, knowing that some- where between them was the channel.

The engine, by now, had been running over 24 hours, but we still had plenty of fuel. I crawled into the engine compartment, topped up the transmission with automatic transmission fluid, opened the packing gland so a steady flow of water was running through it, and removed the wrench from the propeller shaft.

After striking the sails, I engaged the clutch, and with one eye on the pilings and the other on the depth finder, hoping we wouldn't run aground or set the packing on fire again, I began feeling my way up that long ditch to Cairns. It took two nervous hours, but by 4:30 that afternoon, we had the anchor down in the northern anchorage just ahead of the pile berths off the city dock.

I had realized, as we sailed north, that we had really been cooking. But not until the anchor was set, and I let my full weight down did I realize that we had actually set some sort of record for ourselves. Conditions had been ideal. The wind, a constant 25–30 knots, was on our starboard quarter and although our stern was lifting to the following sea, there was no swell. The raffee hauled us along like a powerful steam engine. Again, I wondered how valid that theoretical hull speed limitation was. We had left the anchorage at Dunk Island at 5:00 a.m., and we had reached the outer Cairns piling by 2:30 p.m., a lapse of 9.5 hours. The distance between the two points was 110 nautical miles. Any 5th grader could tell you that we *averaged* 11.58 knots. I can't tell you how much of that was wind current, but I seriously doubt whether the current exceeded two knots. That leaves us with a speed of almost ten knots in a boat with a theoretical limit of just under eight knots. Unbelievable!

Weary, but basking in a sense of accomplishment, I joined Velda for a cocktail. As we sat there reviewing the day's events, I suddenly realized that like Newton, I had been hit over the head with a revealed physical law. To that point, I had stubbornly insisted, expert opinion to the contrary, that locking the propeller was detrimental to a sailboat's speed. It seemed logical to me that a free-wheeling propeller would dissipate its energy by friction in the transmission and stern bearing; while dragging a locked propeller was like dragging an opened parachute.

I had only locked the propeller to avoid damage or a possible fire, but as Velda and I reviewed the factors contributing to our extraordinary day's sail, we concluded, after allowing for the wind, the probable currents, and the fair seas, that the additional speed could only be accounted for by the pipe wrench I had put on the propeller shaft.

To me, that was as good as an apple off my head. We never allowed the propeller to freewheel again, and I believe we probably gained at least a knot (one nautical mile per hour) in our relative speeds under sail thereafter.

The next day when we went ashore to make sure we were

anchored in the proper place, Cameron was on the dock waiting. He and Velda went shopping while I made my way to the Harbor Master's office, and cleared in.

Next, I went to the Cairns Yacht Club. When I told the club secretary that we did not have a yacht club affiliation in the States, she said, "I'll have to charge you ten dollars a week for a temporary membership. This entitles you to the facilities; showers, laundromat, bar and dining room."

Cairns was a major sugar port and served as the administrative center for northeastern Queensland. It was a lovely little town around 40,000 population, and full of friendly and helpful people. Everywhere we went, we met people who *cared* whether the engine was repaired, whether Cap's shots were up to date, and whether I could find the right kind of water jugs. Strangers consistently went out of their way to make things easier and to help us.

For example, within minutes of becoming a temporary member of the yacht club, I was advised to see a Mr. Harrison, owner of a nearby auto-electric shop, regarding our starter problems. The next morning, I carried the starter in our cart to his shop.

"Looks fairly new," he said when I handed it to him.

I told him the gruesome story, how and why I had bought this one in Sydney, and described its present symptoms. He was taking the starter apart while I talked, and before I finished, holding the armature under his light, he interrupted me.

"Just as I thought," he said, shaking his head. He pointed to a discolored area on the armature. "Lucas starters have a bad reputation for this kind of earthing," he added.

"You see," Mr. Harrison continued, "When they build these things, they put the insulation into the slots first. Then they put the windings in. That's where the trouble comes from."

"The thing is," he went on, "when those windings comes out of the machine that cuts them, they have tiny burrs on them. Them Lucas fellas can't be bothered to run a file over the burrs, so the burrs tear the insulation, and that's what has happened here. You have a dead spot on your starter. Sometimes you can fix these by moving the winding a few millimeters. If it works, it could save you a good bit of money."

With that, he began tapping the copper windings, then put the armature on the test bench and after fastening the alligator clips, pressed the button.

ZAP!

"No," he said sadly, "we'll have to find another armature."

I didn't know what to say. I was thinking, of course, of those folks in Sydney with their computers who told me there was no suitable armature closer than England. It seemed ludicrous that the proprietor of a little auto-electric shop located two blocks beyond the local brewery on the outskirts of an obscure little resort town in central Queensland now thought he could find one merely by making a phone call. But that's exactly what he did. He called a "spares" shop in Freemantle and found what I needed at a price I could afford to pay. We were to have it by air express the next day.

Then he turned his attention to our alternator, which was now barely charging our batteries. This was the same Ford alternator we had bought in American Samoa. All alternators apparently come equipped with three diodes, or little electrical check valves. These are conveniently mounted on a metal plate. In the United States, when a diode fails, a mechanic will unfasten the plate, and throw it away. Never mind that two perfectly good diodes have gone into the trash with the bad one, because that's "cost effective."

In Australia, they did things differently. Mr. Harrison carefully snipped out the damaged diodes and soldered new ones in their place. The operation took about 30 minutes, and cost five dollars for parts and ten dollars in labor. That was impressive, but the real Mr. Harrison wasn't revealed until the armature arrived. I walked into the shop as he was unwrapping it.

"I can't believe that bloody airline," he sputtered. "They charged you $20 for picking the bloody package up, another $20 for delivering it from the airport, and they had the bloody gall to charge you an additional ten dollar handling fee. Fifty dollars plus the express freight rate!" He called the airline to protest. Finally he turned to me. "I'm sorry as hell about this, mate," he said. "But there isn't a thing I can do. Let's see if it works."

He put the starter back together, put it on the test bench, and pressed the button. It whirred like a champ.

He turned to me and said, "There you are. The parts and air-freight, he made a long face, come to $141.50." He paused. "You got screwed so badly on that airfreight, that as an Australian, I'm bloody ashamed, and I'm not going to charge you for my labor."

Thus ended, after 18 months of constant worry, a year's delay and a cost of well over $1,000, the awful saga of my starter motor. It had started in New Zealand, when Les blithely "whipped it off" the engine in January, 1984, and ended in that little auto-electric shop in Cairns in mid-1985.

I hate to say this, but it seems that English manufacturers have much to learn about electrical gear, or maybe about sailors like me and boats like *Prospector*. I accept some of the responsibility, but for God's sake, look at the record! Two Lucas starters and one alternator *kaput*, two Autohelms (one motor, one "brain") down the drain. A Vigil radar that never worked properly, even when it was new, and a battery powered Kevin–Hughes chronometer which failed before we got to St. Thomas. Perhaps I expect too much. Or possibly *Prospector's* environment was too harsh. But our wake is littered with dilapidated, electronic gear and costly repair bills.

We had other problems. When I had removed the starter, I discovered a cracked engine mount. While removing it, I found that the mount on the opposite corner was also broken.

With the engine teetering on two mounts, it's no wonder the flax in the packing gland was smoldering. I tossed the mounts in the dinghy and went ashore to find a welder. The bartender at the yacht club was the best source for a referral. Within five minutes after talking to him, I had two names, and a sympathetic member who volunteered to drive me there. That same gentleman also took me to several marine hardware stores in search of dark water jugs. We eventually found some black ones.

I don't understand why American manufacturers insist on making water jugs out of translucent plastic. Water stored in such jugs quickly grows a veritable bouquet of algae because of the sunlight that such materials admit. Water jugs should be made of opaque material, but only Australians seem to understand that.

When you cruise long distances, you never know who you're going to run into. I walked into the yacht club bar one afternoon and although I saw only her back, I immediately recognized the woman talking to the bartender, although I hadn't seen her for several months. However, this was not a person I soon forgot. I quietly walked up behind her, and tapped her shoulder.

"Par ... ." was as far as I got.

She whirled around. *"DENNY!"* Julie cried, throwing her arms around my neck. We began babbling, both trying to talk at the same time. We carried our drinks to a table overlooking the little waterfront, and began comparing notes. She and Ross had sailed their tiny *Albatross* to Papua New Guinea where they had cruised for several months, mostly up the notorious Fly River.

They had recently returned to Australia, sailing in through Trinity Passage in the Barrier Reef to Cairns. *Albatross* sails like a dinghy, and they easily sailed up the ditch to Cairns.

We left the club after promising to have dinner together on *Prospector* at the first opportunity. I wanted to hear more about the Fly River, and whether they had heard any new rumors about young Rockefeller's mysterious disappearance some 30 years earlier. Besides, I always looked forward to seeing Julie again.

The quarantine officer, Mr. D.J. Daniel, a witty and literate gentleman who had written a witty and highly enjoyable guidebook for northern Queensland, *A Factual Guide to Cape York Peninsula*, had promised Velda that he would bring the local veterinarian out to the boat to administer a long overdue parvovirus shot to Cap.

I had an important errand ashore the morning the vet was to come out to the boat, but I hurried back as soon as I could. The quarantine launch was hanging from our stern when I got there.

Down below, the vet, a big, ponderous man, syringe in hand, was trying to push Cap into a corner. Cap was thoroughly aroused, his eyes were rolled back, his ruff was sticking out like an agitated porcupine, his legs were stiff, his lips were curled back in a menacing snarl, and a constant warning rumble came from his tense throat. The vet, already dripping blood from one bite, ignored our entreaties to give it up. I suspect his ego was in the way. It was obvious that schipperkes were new to him. The vet made a sudden feint toward Cap and instantly began bleeding from a second wound.

It was ludicrous that a 20-pound dog, no matter how aggressive, could stand off four adult humans. Cap was trembling with fear and anxiety, and he backed up against me. I reached down and grabbed him by the neck, then held him out at arms length off the floor.

The vet was in mild shock, so Mr. Daniel jabbed the needle under the dog's hide and pressed the plunger. After he withdrew it, I dropped Cap, and the offended little dog promptly ran into the forepeak to hide.

Julie and Ross came to dinner the following night. Velda gave us a first rate meal, and afterward we sat in the saloon trading stories and sharing reminiscences. Velda and Ross were sitting on the settee. Velda made a joking remark to him, and he retaliated by punching her lightly on the arm. Suddenly, 20 pounds of outraged Schipperke came flying out of the forward cabin, and the offending hand was bleeding. It couldn't have been prevented. We bandaged Ross, and shortly afterward they left.

By this time we had been in Cairns nearly three weeks. Our anchorage near the entrance to the channel provided a wonderful view of the traffic in and out of Cairns, and one by one, old friends, some dating back to Tahiti, came up that long ditch, and seeing us, came over to say hello. *Sundowner* came in. So did *Courier* with a very pregnant Sarah Smith and her husband, Parker; *Atair II* with Babs and Klaus, showed up as did *Innocent Bystander* with Richard and Kathy. Klaus anchored *Atair II* nearby, and not surprisingly, in the middle of the night, our boats started banging against each other. Klaus insisted we were the offending party, while I *knew* it was *Atair II* that had dragged.

Our electrical system was fully operational. I was reveling in the luxury of it. And the engine again was standing on four feet. I attempted, once again, to realign the engine.

And not a minute too soon.

Roger and Molly had consulted the vet about their cat, Angus, and the vet had said something to them regarding Cap that to us sounded ominous and threatening. We were afraid he would find out about Ross's wound, which might have given him an excuse to destroy our "vicious" dog. It was time to leave town.

Cameron and I bought and hauled supplies, fuel and water, and laid in another supply of automatic transmission fluid. We knew this next leg would be the long haul. If all went well, our next port would be Darwin, about 1,500 miles away. However, we also knew there were several possible intermediate stops if we got into trouble.

We left Cairns early the next morning. The two-hour trip down the pile-lined ditch was much easier than our arrival had been. We knew what to expect, and we had the luxury of choosing the stage of the tide. We left Cairns at the beginning of the flood so if, by chance, we had run aground, it would merely have been a matter of waiting for the flooding tide to lift us off.

Roger and Molly in *Sundowner* left at the same time, and were behind us when we left the ditch. We both anchored for the night behind the Low Isles.

The next morning we sailed around Cape Tribulation, so named by Cook after he worked his ship, *Endeavour*, off the reef by jettisoning a heavy anchor and several cannon (which are now housed in the museum in Cooktown). By sundown we were anchored in Hope Isle.

Sundowner left the next morning for a side trip to Cooktown. Roger had a professional interest in the museum that we did not share. Still, if I had read Mr. Daniel's Guide to the Cape York Peninsula more carefully, I would have known that Cooktown once rivaled Sacramento and Skagway, Alaska, as the gateway to a "river of gold," and we might have followed *Sundowner*.

According to Mr. Daniel, following the 1873 Palmer River strike, over 100 tons of gold were taken out. Cooktown mushroomed overnight into a city of 35,000, with 63 hotels, an equal number of brothels, shanties, opium halls and "temples of fun and wild living. Horses were shod with gold and Australia's first striptease shows were performed to the rustle of silks and satins and the pop of champagne corks." My kind of place!

Unknowingly, we passed up that rich historical lode; instead, we sailed on to Cape Bedford, where we anchored for the night. The channel between the mainland and the reefs was narrowing rapidly. Because of the considerable ship traffic, it was necessary to be well out of the channel before dark.

The ships were of little concern to the dozens of shrimp trawlers we saw. Each anchorage we entered sheltered several shrimp boats as we arrived. They went to work shortly afterward, and as we left the anchorage, usually at daybreak, the tired fishermen were just returning from a night's work. Although we shared many anchorages, except for that fisherman at Magnetic Island, they hardly even acknowledged our presence. And who knows, maybe the fellow who came out in the rain to help us avoid that net owned it.

North of Cairns the scenery was particularly tedious and monotonous, but it spiced the day not to be sure of our next anchorage until we saw it. In other words, the passage inside the Barrier Reef had little to recommend it — until you considered the alternative.

When I had planned to sail north through the Coral Sea in order to save time the previous year, I had failed to appreciate that what I was proposing to do was not simply another oceanic passage. Now I knew that if we had succeeded in making a landfall on Murray Island, assuming we got that far through waters primly described on Admiralty charts as "not examined," we would still have had to find our way from there to the Great Northeast Channel through increasingly dense thickets of uncharted reefs. If we had managed to accomplish all that, one last obstacle remained: Unless my navigation was spot on, we might have had to detour almost to Papua New Guinea, or at least as far as Dalrymple Island (which is supposed to have a light) to find the crucial Northeast Channel leading us back to Torres Straits. I doubt whether that circuitous route would have saved much time. The passage inside the reef may be tedious, but it is relatively safe. Even so, any diversion was welcomed. It even got to where I looked forward to seeing the next sea snake.

Successful cruising on a remote coast like this inevitably is at least partly a matter of luck. When you discuss luck with a sailor, it seems necessary to ask: Did you bring any suitcases aboard? Opened any umbrellas? Discussed horses, by some unfortunate chance? Or did you leave port on a Friday? These were factors any sensible sailor would consider in avoiding misfortune.

Whatever it was, poor Velda was apparently guilty of a serious trespass. When she woke the morning before we reached Lizard Island, the left side of her face was swollen. Not as if it was bruised or she had a sore tooth, but grotesquely, so that her features were distorted beyond recognition. Seen full on the left side in a strong light, her face looked like something fashioned from silly putty. Oddly, she was not in pain or discomfort other than the inconvenience of an eye swollen nearly shut, a mouth that was pulled out of position, and a lip so puffy that talking was difficult. Frankly, It was hard to look at her and keep a straight face.

Understandably, Velda refused to go ashore after we anchored. Cameron and I put the dinghy over the side and went ashore. We soon discovered that a cookout was being planned. I prepared our fellows for Velda's appearance, assuming I could succeed in persuading her to attend. Back on the boat, I pointed out that these friends of ours were almost like family; and besides, it would do her good to get off the boat for a few hours. She agreed, and we took some food from the freezer and went ashore.

After the incredulous stares and ill-concealed smiles, people quickly got used to her appearance, and we received tons of advice. One person suggested that she might have been bitten by a spider. Everyone agreed that the best thing would be to leave it alone, that it ought to straighten itself out in a few days. I was afraid that if the swelling was an allergic reaction, her next exposure to it might close her throat or interrupt another vital process. So we stayed at Lizard Island, which had a small airstrip and daily flights to Cairns, in case we needed to send her to the hospital. The swelling subsided, but not before *Atair II* dragged into us (for the fourth or fifth time) in the middle of the night.

Although we have since come to believe that her upper teeth were somehow involved, I thought at the time I might have stumbled on a different solution in Lizard Island's peculiar history.

According to Lucas, nearly a century after Cook named the island for the abundant monitor lizards he found, a Mrs. Mary Watson, her baby, and a Chinese servant, cast themselves adrift from the island in a cast iron tub in 1882, hoping to escape an angry band of Aborigines. Almost a second century would pass before the reason for the attack on the unfortunate Mrs. Watson, who did not survive, became known. According to Lucas, film-makers in 1973 found sacred Aboriginal ceremonial grounds on the island where the presence of women was absolutely forbidden.

Of course, I was being facetious. But while we might kid around that the medicine was weakening, since it cost one woman her life, but it just made Velda look funny, remember what happened to Sylvia after she sat on the head of a "live" Tiki guarding the Taipi Vai Marae in the Marquesas.

We stayed at Lizard Island for a week after the swelling subsided and we were reasonably sure it wouldn't return. Two days after leaving Lizard, we sailed around Cape Melville, which looked at first like every other headland, until we got close enough to see that it resembled nothing quite so much as an unimaginably huge, half-opened, bag of shiny but irregularly shaped marbles spilling into the water at the foot of the cliff.

As we drew closer, we saw that instead of a bag, we were looking at a collapsed cliff face, and instead of marbles, we saw a disorderly pile of huge polished black granite boulders, each as big as a house. It was a striking thing to see.

This was not a relic of an Ice Age, as I at first supposed. During possibly the worst cyclone of the 19th century, on March 5, 1899, that cliff face had collapsed on a fleet of pearl luggers taking shelter in its lee. Nearly 200 fishermen died when those boulders crushed them. Some 100 Aborigines, attempting to save the few survivors, lost their lives in the cyclone's tidal surge.

We reached Margaret Bay three days later. Barely inside the bay is an islet that was named Sunday Island by Captain Bligh (subsequent to the mutiny on the *Bounty*) who paused there briefly on the Sabbath to give his crew a needed rest.

As we sailed around Sunday Island, approaching the beach, we saw *Sundowner* and several European boats anchored close to the shore. There was a lot of activity on the beach, and through the glasses, I could see people carrying what appeared to be arm loads of brush to their dinghies.

"What the hell's going on?" I shouted across to Roger.

"They've found black coral on the beach," Roger replied.

"Black coral doesn't grow near beaches," I answered.

"Well, that's what they think they have," Roger said, adding, "come on over for a drink!"

Cameron wanted to go to the beach and make his fortune, so after dropping us off, he rowed to the shore, while the four of us sat in *Sundowner's* cockpit enjoying a beer, watching the coral miners at work, and exchanging what little we knew or thought we knew about black coral.

Cameron returned with what looked like a pile of brush, and urged me to return with him to the beach. "There is plenty for everyone," he said.

I looked at his treasure. "Cameron," I said, "that's wood of some sort, possibly mangrove." The material was black, and, although it was hard and tough, you could bend smaller pieces into a circle, and cut them with a knife. I'm sure it was wood, although we later heard fourth hand that the material was coral, and that the finders had gotten a good price for it in Darwin.

Two days later, on the Fourth of July, a large airplane appeared suddenly from behind a hill, and buzzed low over our masts. We saw the word COASTWATCH painted on the side of the fuselage. Knowing that Coastwatch planes routinely photograph boats they see, I felt a smug little glow of pride because we were flying our flag from the mizzen topping lift in celebration of the day. At least they would know we were Yanks.

I called the plane on the VHF and got an immediate response. They were looking for another yacht that we hadn't seen. After I told them who we were, the pilot acknowledged with a quick wiggle of his wings, and flew on to the next boat.

Again, we shared an anchorage with *Sundowner*. As usual, Roger was up and away before full daylight. Molly often claimed that when she was slow to rise, Roger would play *Stars and Stripes Forever* at full volume on the ship's stereo system.

Eventually, when *Sundowner* was nearly out of sight, we started the engine, hauled the anchor, and began the interminable cycle over again. We set the squaresail and raffee, but there wasn't much wind, and we had to keep the engine running to make sure we reached the next anchorage by dark.

Roger was a good two hours ahead of us, but it was quickly apparent we were going a lot faster than he. In less than an hour we overtook him. He was nonchalantly ghosting along in the light airs. Say what you will about Roger, insouciance is not his style. I knew instantly that something was terribly wrong.

"Hey, come on, Roger; get the lead out," I called.

He shrugged. "I can't," he said. "Injector pump's broken."

I shifted the clutch to neutral, and we coasted while I absorbed this awful bit of information. It was impossible for someone in Roger's position to fix an injector pump. That's a job requiring specialized training, tools and nearly sterile surroundings.

Repairing one at sea would be like attempting brain surgery with a knife and fork. In other words, Roger was in a hell of a fix. Worse by far than our similar predicament off Noumea, because the waters around the northern tip of Australia swirl with currents and tides as the Pacific and Indian Oceans meet. The problem is compounded because, since we were so close to the equator, we were out of the tradewind belt.

For a sailboat, light winds and strong currents are the worst possible combination. Moreover, he had no way of generating electricity without an engine. Presumably his batteries were fully charged, but they would likely not have more than a 200 amp/hour reserve, depending on their size, age and condition. In other words, as a practical matter, Roger had no radio, no navigation lights, not even an anchor light.

He yelled at us, "You guys go on; we'll be all right."

Roger is an outstanding seaman. There was no question about his ability to take care of himself. We both knew his wouldn't be the first boat, or the last, to pass through Torres Strait under sail. But what the hell. We've both reached the age where neither of us needs extra excitement. We weren't in any hurry. So we decided to stick around. As I told him later, "We just wanted to see how you'd get yourself out of that fix!"

We shut the engine down and ghosted with *Sundowner*.

"Let me know when you want a tow," I yelled over to him. Roger looked at the sky and his watch. "If the wind doesn't pick up," he said, "we may need help getting around Albany Rock before the tide changes. Let's give her another hour."

I waved an acknowledgement and sat back to review what I knew about Torres Strait. You started with the basics. Water always runs down hill. But it was not uncommon for a two hour flood to be followed by a ten hour ebb, interrupted by brief periods of reversing current. Moreover, the tidal flows sometimes reached six or seven knots; the record was 11 knots. This chaotic situation was caused by many factors, partly because the Pacific Ocean was higher, but more because there was no relation between the tides. The Pacific tides were moderate; while the Indian Ocean tides were ten feet greater. As Lucas pointed out, a neap low and a spring high could occur simultaneously only 30 miles apart!

But, with the blessing of modern computers, the Australian Department of Shipping and Transport has been able to prepare reliable tide and current tables for various checkpoints as you approach Prince of Wales Channel. We each had a copy.

By now, the hour had expired, and since the breeze remained fitful, we started the engine and passed a line to *Sundowner*. The tide was just beginning to turn as we brought her around Albany Rock, one of the checkpoints, and turned into Pioneer Bay. At that moment, the wind started to blow, and Roger, dropping the towline, sailed past us. When we reached the anchorage, he was already snugged down for the night. Velda and I rowed over to *Sundowner* after we anchored, to discuss what we should expect tomorrow.

I had worked out a transit plan involving the shallow, less traveled Endeavor Strait, but Roger didn't think much of the idea. He was worried about the shoals at the western end of the Strait, and had a preference for the Prince of Wales Channel, used by commercial shipping. Roger was a consummate navigator. He once did it for a living, and I was glad to follow his lead. As usual, he was right. The Prince of Wales Channel was the best route.

The key to a successful passage was timing. You timed your arrival at each checkpoint, neither ahead nor behind schedule, to gain the greatest advantage of a fair current through the Straits.

We decided if there was no wind, we would tow *Sundowner* through. We were slow under power, but there was plenty of time to reach the various checkpoints on schedule.

The next morning the sky was bright, cloudless, and calm. We had expected calm weather and had decided to wait until 9 a.m. before leaving the anchorage. We had 35 miles to go before reaching the Straits, but the tide even here would pull us along.

We watched Roger work the ratchet on his deck windlass, bringing his anchor up. We motored over, passed the towline, and slowly took up the strain.

By 11 a.m., we were slightly north of Cape York, and I was thrilled to see the northern-most tip of the Australian Continent, about 20 miles away looming high against the western sky.

To the right of the Cape, could see an indistinct low-lying land mass. That was the Torres Island group, including Thursday Island. TI, as it is known locally, is the Administrative Headquarters for Northern Queensland.

I doubt whether anyone seeing those islands for the first time, and knowing something of their history, could be immune to the power of their colorful and violent past. In the 19th century, attracted by pearls and shell, bêche-de-mer, sandlewood, and trochus, the Straits swarmed with pirates, rogues, and even cannibals and headhunters.

By 2 p.m., we were just entering the Prince of Wales Channel. The wind had freshened earlier, and *Sundowner* having cast off the towline about noon, was now slightly ahead of us. We watched her sail past the first navigation buoy we had seen in nearly 2,000 miles. We sailed past the opening into Endeavour Strait, and suddenly we were on a watery combination toboggan slide and ski jump!

331

Ordinarily, a 20 mile passage should require about four hours, but this one seemed to last only 15 minutes. It really took about two hours to pass through Torres Strait.

The channel was only about 200 yards wide at the narrowest place. On the left, we saw low cliffs and rocky headlands; and between the nearest islands, we caught a glimpse of Thursday Island. As we approached that opening, a launch scurried out into the channel, and circled first *Sundowner,* then *Prospector*, obviously reading our names and hailing port as we went past. The Coast-watchers keep a close eye on transient yachts.

On the right, the long, low, dirty browns and greens of coral reefs awash were only a few feet away.

Hammond Rock flashed past. This may be the most heavily instrumented rock in the world. It is located midway through the narrowest part of the channel, and is the source of current measurements upon which much of the tidal data is based.

The radio suddenly came to life. "Hello, *Prospector*, this is *Sundowner*."

"Go ahead, *Sundowner*," I said.

"I think we'll tuck in behind Booby Island for the night," Roger said.

I acknowledged, and indicated that we would continue toward Darwin.

Velda and I looked at each other. It seemed almost unbelievable, considering what we had been through, but we had successfully passed another of the great milestones in ocean voyaging. We had gone through Torres Straits and were now in the Indian Ocean.

Chapter 14

The Northwest Territory

$\mathcal{L}$eaving the Pacific and sailing into the Indian Ocean was a rite of passage. Things would never again be quite the same. The western side of the Straits *felt* different, and presented a set of problems I hadn't anticipated. In a way, it was like getting married. You eagerly looked forward to the event, entirely oblivious of the consequences that immediately follow.

I was tense and uneasy, partly because of the constant short waves striking our starboard beam as if trying to push us into the Gulf, and the certain knowledge that shipwreck on this remote coast could be one of life's more unpleasant experiences. In addition, having looked forward so long and with such anxiety to the Torres Strait passage, I may have been experiencing something like postpartum depression.

For example, after reading the chart, I "knew" the mouth of the Gulf of Carpentaria — the huge geographic U-shaped dimple on the northern Australian coast west of Cape York — was 300 miles across, but I hadn't realized it would be quite unlike other bodies of water we had seen.

As usual, Roger had used his head when he decided to spend the night at Booby Island. We should have done the same. We had a green crew. Night sailing was new to Cameron, as was a boat the size of *Prospector;* and he had never stood an unsupervised watch. Also, because of the stressful, cumulative effect of continuous day sails in the reefs, and because passing through the Straits had been such an emotional experience, we were just plain worn out.

Also, we were in a very congested and constricted waterway, sailing in company with dozens of ships, all of us worried about

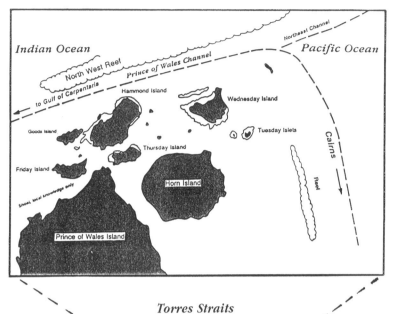

Torres Straits
Notice how Captain Bligh named the islands for the days of the week as he
sailed east in his longboat following the mutiny on HMS Bounty

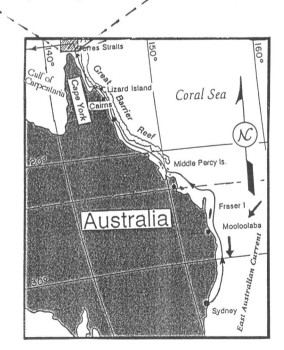

Australia's East Coast
(charts 8 & 9)

334

invisible and uncharted reefs on both sides of the channel.

Most ship captains in these waters will maintain a radar watch of sorts, but they are concerned about reefs and other ships, things which are hazardous to them. They sure as hell aren't examining every indistinct, intermittent, blip. The difference between a yacht and clutter may not be immediately obvious to the untrained eye. An electronic hiccup could be an errant wave — or a yacht. As usual, small boats were strictly on their own. I successfully indoctrinated Cameron concerning shipping, and was gratified to note on his first watch that he steered as carefully as we did, hugging the northern edge of the traffic lane. The first morning in the Arafura Sea, Cameron pointed to a dot dead ahead on the horizon.

"What's that?" he asked.

Peering through the binoculars, I saw what appeared to be a small boat. We kept watching it, and when we realized it wasn't closing very fast, I went below to take another look at the chart. According to my dead reckoning and the chart, we were looking at the Carpentaria lightship that guards a shoal in the middle of the shipping lane, immediately south of the rhumb line I had drawn on the chart.

We came abreast of the lightship by noon. Cameron had never sailed beyond the sight of land, and was impressed with my navigational skills. So was I. A spot-on landfall based on a doubtful series of star sights hours earlier, followed by sailing an additional 20 miles on a broad reach with God only knows what currents pushing us here and there, left a great deal to chance. But Cameron didn't know that, and I didn't tell him.

That tiny unmanned lightship was only a boat shaped buoy. I doubt if she was more than 20 feet long, but she was built in the classic whaleback style common to lightships the world over.

Originally a bright red color, she was covered with guano from the scores of seabirds roosting on her. Most of the paint and part of the word CARPENTARIA painted on her side was obscured.

Apart from her disheveled appearance, her size and her feathered crew, she was every inch a lightship, with a sturdy tripod mast supporting a horn and carrying a revolving reflector light at the peak. Nevertheless, that tiny ship seemed lonely with only seabirds for company.

A manned lightship would not have carried the large clapper

hung in the middle of the tripod that clanged dolefully every time she rolled; the sound would have driven a human crew mad.

At daylight, a week after passing through Torres, we sailed around the Cobourg Peninsula and tucked into the channel between Arnhem Land and Melville Island.

The island is about 70 miles long, and lies in front of Darwin. While it was possible to reach Darwin by sailing around Melville Island, that route was much further, and a portion of it would have been up wind. On the other hand, the inside route meant day sailing. However, with the winds light and fluky, it didn't make much difference. We had averaged only about 50 miles a day since leaving the Straits.

We spent the first night anchored behind Cape Hamm. We had seen dozens of ships, and just before we dropped the hook, saw the lights of a sailboat far behind us, but we anchored without thinking much about it.

The next morning, the wind was calm, and we motored from behind the Cape. Turning the corner, we saw the sailboat we had seen the night before. It was *Sundowner* with Roger and Molly.

I slowed the engine to an idle, and we went alongside while Cameron readied the towline, so he could toss it to Roger if he wanted a tow. Roger didn't have many alternatives. Sensibly, he accepted the tow. However, by mid-afternoon, a sea breeze began to blow so he cast off the towline and we both set sail.

The channel was well marked, but in places was only a few hundred feet wide. On the left side, the shoreline alternated between rolling hills with gravel beaches, and mangrove swamps probably filled with scores of hungry crocodiles. Melville Island, on the right, had less mangrove and more bluffs. There was a strong tidal flow through the channel.

On the second night, because the area was so sheltered, we simply found a convenient spot and dropped the hook. Roger anchored close by. At daylight, a slight breeze was blowing, and Roger was already gone.

Motorsailing, by mid-morning we overhauled him shortly before we entered the big flats 20 miles from Darwin. The wind had died. We tendered the towline. This time, however, Roger's pride got in the way of his common sense.

"No," he said, "I think we can make it under sail."

By early afternoon, we were within eyeball range of the city. We had a choice. We could join the dozens of other boats in a shallow bay straight ahead, or we could go into the commercial dock area and anchor in a creek on the opposite side of town.

We chose the bay. I don't care for industrial areas, but I wondered, as we felt our way into the anchorage, whether we had made the right decision. After motoring around the tip of a long sandbar, the depth finder showed a water depth of between 12 and 20 feet, miles from the nearest boats and the beach.

I knew the tidal range in Darwin was about 15 feet, but I didn't know what the stage of the tide was. Thus, when we dropped the anchor we were still a country mile from shore. We could have gotten closer, but I like swinging room, and I would rather dinghy an extra 100 yards to be reasonably sure that nothing was going to go bump in the night.

The officials had seen us coming, and as soon as we had the anchor down, they were alongside. The customs officer was a pleasant young man who quickly and efficiently checked us in. I was told to go to immigration in town the next day.

We launched the dinghy and went ashore. The Darwin Sailing Club was housed in a new brick building. A wide, shaded flag-stone terrace with outdoor furniture, overlooked the anchored yachts. Social activities were conducted on the terrace.

The beach, mostly clean white sand, began at the short, abrupt cutbank three feet high, showing exposed roots of the fringing palm trees and sea grapes, and ran (when the tide was out) for 100 yards to the water's edge. At high tide, the water almost reached the cutbank.

We had plenty of water where we were anchored, but at the beach, you had to adjust your socializing to the rhythm of the tides, or make other arrangements.

The wind was usually offshore. On the way to the beach, when I judged we were 100 feet off, I would drop the dinghy anchor over the side and allow the anchor line to run freely until the bow grated on the sand. Then, holding one end of a light 200 foot tag-line (the other end being tied to the crown of the anchor), I would give the boat a mighty shove, and tie my end of the tag line to a convenient sea grape branch. Our dinghy would be patiently bobbing on the waves while most of the other boats were high and dry above the tide.

When the time came to retrieve the dinghy, I simply untied the tag-line and pulled the anchor ashore.

This club, like the clubs in Mooloolaba and Cairns, was friendly and hospitable. A ten dollar fee covered our temporary membership, and provided access to the amenities.

The next day, Velda and I, following directions, went out to the highway and caught the town bus. Darwin isn't a very large place, and we had no trouble finding the immigration office in the lower level of a municipal building.

The officers were pleasantly interested in us because of Cap's ferocious reputation, which had preceded us. The officers pressed me for the bloody details of the combat between Cap and the veterinarian in Cairns.

Darwin reminded me of Anchorage, Alaska. Both cities had experienced and survived cataclysmic disasters. Anchorage was nearly destroyed by the Alaskan earthquake in 1964. Darwin took a direct hit from a cyclone that virtually demolished the city in 1975.

That's why the downtown buildings looked new. They *were* new. But cities are more than streets and buildings, bricks and mortar. Like people, cities have character. It is the spirit of the place that binds it together. That trait is particularly noticeable in isolated places like Anchorage, some 2,000 miles from the nearest support base, and Darwin, also at the end of a long, thin supply line.

Standing on the street corner in Darwin, you could watch the big trailer-towing Greyhound buses roll slowly down the street like pioneer wagon trains entering Fort Dodge, so covered with red mud and dirt that the familiar logo was all but obscured. You knew immediately that Darwin was on the frontier.

Two days after we arrived, we watched *Sundowner* sail past our anchorage and into the ship channel leading to town where mechanics and new injector pumps could be found.

Almost as soon as we arrived, we were made aware that the annual race from Darwin to Ambon (in Indonesia) was in the final stages of preparation.

Then, regular Indonesian cruising permits were impossible to get. However, the Indonesian Government was granting special

30-day cruising permits to everyone entering the race. Several friends entered the race primarily, I think, for the permit.

Kennemar, Innocent Bystander, and a New Zealand boat named *Charger* (we had met at Scawfell Island in the Barrier Reef), were among them. They urged us to join them, correctly pointing out that we might never again have an opportunity to visit Indonesia. I don't know if they intended to complete the race, but armed with the 30-day permit, they could call in Bali, Java, and Sumatra on their way to Singapore. To any cruising sailor, the mere mention of those magic names would start the adrenalin surging through the veins.

The Ambon Race became our symbolic fork in the road. The boats in the race would go through the northern Indian Ocean to Sri Lanka, the Maldives, and Aden, then north up the 1,000 mile "blow-torch" of the Red Sea to the Suez Canal, and into the Mediterranean Sea. Our paths would not again cross. Therefore, our mutual farewells had a special poignancy. Who could tell what lay ahead for any of us?

We could have gone to Singapore. We had made inquiries about boarding the animals there, and taking the train up the Malay Peninsula to Bangkok, returning by air.

The rub was that returning from Singapore to the Indian Ocean, we would either have had to backtrack to the Sunda Straits on the east end of Sumatra, or take our chances in the Straits of Malacca.

Although I will always regret not having entered the race, we resisted temptation partly because I knew we couldn't get ready in time, partly because I was afraid of the pirates, and partly because I didn't trust my engine in case we had to run for it.

There was another reason for my reluctance. I had already told Cameron that I thought it would be best if he found another boat, so we were short-handed again.

Our decks were a continuing source of trouble, Philip and his brothers in Fiji notwithstanding. Anything that might alleviate the problem was worth investigating. One day, while I was sitting on the terrace, cold Foster's in hand, I couldn't help but overhear a conversation between two local club members at the same table regarding a new material called Sikaflex.

I introduced myself and explained my problem. The younger of the two had recently been appointed territorial sales manager for the stuff. He described the material as a new seam compound, and told me what results I could reasonably expect, considering the age and condition of our decks.

I bought two cases of the stuff at the local marine store and spent the next two weeks on my hands and knees recaulking the decks. It worked pretty well; nothing is forever, but the effort I made at Darwin saw us across the Indian Ocean, around the Cape of Good Hope, and across the Atlantic.

We were thinking seriously about the next leg of our trip, and compared navigational strategies with Roger and Molly from *Sundowner*, and Tom and D.L. from *Le Papillion*. We had left Tom and D.L. in Sydney, but they had overtaken us when we reached the Whitsundays, and like Roger and Molly, had elected to do some sight seeing, while Velda and I pressed on because of our sick engine.

Even if the Sailing Club had a dock, which it didn't, we couldn't have used it. D.L. had a cat named Foolish, and they, too, were forbidden to go alongside a fuel dock. Luckily, we had three sturdy plastic 15-gallon jugs for fuel, and several five-gallon water jugs.

One of Tom's crew members was blessed with local relatives who loaned him a station wagon. We quickly discovered that the three 15-gallon jugs fit nicely in the cargo compartment. Our fuel and water problems were solved.

The beer problem was more complicated. Among the three boats, only Roger and I had any reason to investigate the potential of duty-free stores. Tom and D.L. met their beer needs for a long passage by buying two six-packs. But not Roger and me.

We hoped the Sailing Club could arrange it for us. They had done so for the Ambon racers. Trucks laden with beer, wine and spirits had appeared on the eve of the Ambon race and the racers had scrambled around, making sure their orders had been properly filled. The club declined, but, as was so predictable in Australia, a local club member quickly stepped into the breach.

He was one Ambon racer we won't soon forget. It seems incredible, but the day before *his* race started, disregarding the press of his own last minute needs, he drove us from customs brokers to liquor wholesalers, and back to the customs brokers, enabling us to buy tax-free liquor and beer. That spontaneous generosity is a basic characteristic that one soon learns is typically Australian. It's the way they were, and I hope they never change.

As our departure date approached, we loaded provisions, filled the tanks, located unrefrigerated eggs, bought Indian Ocean charts, and had both Autohelms repaired — *again*. D.L. found the eggs and fresh vegetables. The eggs were good value, but the veggies, having been held in cold storage, soon rotted in the open air. Velda visited a cut–rate grocery with the colorful name "Jack the Slasher," and we took on a new crew.

Cameron had found a berth on a Swan ketch, and left on the Ambon Race with his new shipmates. I wished him well. I think, looking back, that my problem with Cameron can be compared to the pessimist who, looking at a doughnut, sees only the hole. Cameron wasn't the problem.

The problem was a combination of the scary and hostile northeast coast of Queensland, the uncharted Arafura Sea, the sea snakes, crocodiles, and sharks. Cameron merely became the solution. I now better understand the social utility inherent in human sacrifice. In other words, this was another nutty case of blaming the tanker for the radar's failure.

Everyone, it seemed, had a crocodile story. The one I liked best, because it was about a creature which apparently shared my attitude toward outboard motors, had to do with a beast named Sweetheart. Sweetheart was a big crocodile, nearly 20 feet long, with an insatiable appetite for outboard motors.

According to legend, he would bite them right off the transom. Like most stories of its kind, this one is vague in detail; it doesn't tell us, for instance, what happened to the outboard's owners, or whether Sweetheart preferred running motors. If I were a crocodile, I would think a running motor would be more challenging. But you can never tell about crocodiles.

Sweetheart could be seen at the Darwin Museum because he was no longer full of outboard motor parts; he was full of sawdust. Someone had tired of his antics, and shot him.

Before our new crew found us, Jane Weber, the teeny-bopping Canadian grandmother who had sailed with us across the Tasman Sea, popped up. She had heard we were at the Sailing Club and had come by to say hello on her way to Europe, via Vietnam and the Trans-Siberian Railway from Vladivostok to Moscow. I don't recall how she planned to travel from Hanoi to Vladivostok, but it was probably by water buffalo.

The new crew candidates were definitely underwhelming. But

the idyllic setting – the lovely patio outside the clubhouse bathed in the bright winter sunshine, the clean, even flagstones underfoot, and everything crisp and new – was a setting created for optimism. You had to be optimistic when you looked at that pair.

Debby was a 19-year old Aussie girl whose mother lived near Sydney. Ian, her English boyfriend, was 23. His main ambition in life was to obtain permanent Australian residency status. I wouldn't have considered a couple, except that Alan and Jane had demonstrated that two crew members could be effective. I was just too dumb to recognize the subtle distinction between two crew members and a *pair* of crew members.

Neither had previous sailing experience, but they had backpacked over northern Australia, and I thought that if they were self-sufficient and tough enough to survive that, surely they would find boat life a pleasant and possibly luxurious change. Even so, we debated a long time whether to take them. And when we decided to do so, it was with serious misgivings.

The African passage involved two intermediate stops. The first was Cocos-Keeling, a lagoon almost exactly 2,000 miles due west from Darwin. The second stop would be in Mauritius 2,500 miles further on. The final leg of the trip was only 1,600 miles, but required us to swing around the southern tip of Madagascar on the way to South Africa.

We left Darwin at first daylight on August eighth, motoring all day to get clear of the Melville Island flats and away from the massive tides. Just before daylight the next morning, a light northeast breeze began to blow, and we set the squaresail and raffee. That was Ian's first sail-handling experience. He was as green as they come and knew nothing of knots, sails or rigging.

Debby was somewhat better. I think she was made of harder stuff, and given a fair chance, she might have become a useful crew member. Except for one flaw.

She was afraid of the dark, and refused to stand night watches. I'm not so old that I failed to realize that putting the two lovebirds in the cockpit at night was the same as not having any watch at all.

It didn't make much difference the first week, if you discounted my peculiar phobia about being run down by tankers in the middle of the night, because we were almost completely becalmed. We had assumed the first leg to Cocos-Keeling would take 20 days. It took

23 days, but at first, you might have thought we would never get there. I'm sure the kids felt that way.

Then things began falling apart. First both Autohelms failed. Earlier, I had cut the umbilical wires connecting the brain with the motor, and fit the cut ends with "waterproof" connectors, so instead of two machines, each comprising a brain and a motor, I now had four interchangeable parts. Instead of two combinations, I now had four. Both brains failed. One mindlessly insisted on turning to port at the least provocation, while the other became a vegetable. I had paid $100 to have them repaired, and they lasted about 100 miles. It's expensive steering when your Autohelm begins to cost you a dollar a mile. Once again, we were hand steering. I continued to use the motors as wheel brakes until they fell apart several thousand miles later.

A day later, the refrigeration broke down. The log doesn't provide details, this was such a common event, but immediately, we began canning and eating as much meat as possible. Although we gorged ourselves, and Velda partially cooked a half dozen roasts in an effort to save them, we eventually threw at least 100 pounds of meat overboard.

The Continental Shelf off northwestern Australia extends about 200 miles into the Indian Ocean before it reaches the Timor Channel. This huge expanse of shoals was dotted with atolls, and the edge of the shelf was marked by a well defined series of coral reefs and lagoons. We spent nearly a week on the shelf, ghosting along, making 25 to 39 miles a day. It was a million dollar experience, like living in the richest, most diverse ocean aquarium you could imagine. The water was very shallow — seldom more than 40 to 50 feet deep — and incredibly clear. The absence of wind riffles on the surface made it seem as if we were peering into the depths through a glass hull. A large school of zebra fish seemed attached to the rudder. Day after day, they followed it. Clouds of tiny pelagic animals drifted under our keel. According to the log:

August 11: 12°21'S, 128°37'E. Large shark swimming around the boat 20–30 feet deep. Tried to judge length by multiples of remora length, guess 15 to 18 feet. Very clear in the evening light. At dusk, six rays swimming fast, jumped clear of the water.

August 12: 12°14'S, 127°51'E. Our shark has company —

several sharks around the boat today — beef attracts them. Restless night, boat rolling badly. Lost hat overboard, but nobody wanted to swim for it. Velda canned pork tenderloin and salted butter. Bilge pump leaking again.

August 13: *(No position) Still becalmed. Dumped more meat. Sharks still hanging around.*

August 18: *13°08′S, 122°33′E, clear night, east winds force two. Saw **Atair II** on horizon, talked to Klaus via VHF. He said two boats ahead of us. Reading the Pilot, discovered we are very close to the banks. Chart isn't very reliable.*

August 20: *13°06′S, 119°58′E, saw bulk carrier, took successive bearings, discovered we were on collision course; talked to captain, checked my position against his satnav, found we were less than half a mile out for both longitude and latitude. Not bad.*

On the 27th of August, while Velda and Debby were sunbathing on the side deck, they were startled by a swarm of squid that flew on deck, landing on them. They gathered 30, enough for dinner.

The weather began to deteriorate that evening and all next day. By the evening of August 28th, we were in a force six breeze, sailing under the staysail.

No sights on the 28th, 29th or 30th of August.

Ian and Debby grew progressively more withdrawn. Debby seemingly was torn between a genuine interest in the boat and a need to nurture her boyfriend. Ultimately, Ian put us on notice that they would be leaving *Prospector* in Cocos-Keeling. I didn't like it, but naturally, I had to respect their wishes, but I warned them that their decision would be irreversible.

I was very explicit about it, because I wanted them to think it through before we reached Cocos-Keeling. I told them that if, after leaving the boat, they discovered that life ashore was not as pleasant as they had anticipated, they would have to live with it, because they would not be welcomed back aboard. I could not allow the boat to be a second-best choice. It would be better to sail short-handed, than with a sulky crew.

I got good morning star sights on September first, putting us 25 miles east of Cocos-Keeling. At noon, Ian, standing on the yard, spotted the lagoon. By late-afternoon, we were standing off the pass on the northern side of the lagoon. It was already getting dark because a serious squall was overtaking us.

Moments before the blinding rain began, I caught a quick glimpse of boats anchored inside the lagoon, and grabbing the microphone, I called, "Hello, hello, hello. Any boat in Direction Island, this is *Prospector* just entering the pass. It will be dark in a few minutes. Could someone please give us directions and possibly a light?"

"Hullo, *Prospector*," came a welcome response in a deep, unmistakably New Zealand accent. "This is *HOTTYD*. We can see you. Follow your present course, and you'll soon come to an iron marker with a ball on top. Stay on the same heading, and you'll see another marker. Steer close to it and take it on your port side. Turn 90 degrees to port, and I'll be waiting for you at the third marker with a torch."

The squall was full upon us, and the rain flooded down, as it does in the tropics, blinding us and reflecting back the beam of our searchlight. However, Ian quickly spotted the first marker. We came to the second stake. I saw a winking light off to the left.

"*Prospector*, this is *HOTTYD* mobile. I am flashing my torch at you. I can see your navigation lights. You are in the channel."

We turned toward the light, running dead slow until we nearly reached it, when I shifted the clutch to neutral. Something bumped against our topsides.

"Hullo," came out of the dark night.

"Come aboard," I called. Eager hands took the dinghy painter, and two sodden figures, one huge, the other tiny, hanging on to the mizzen shrouds, climbed over the lifelines.

The larger person thrust out his hand. "Name's Derek Blair," he said. Jerking his thumb toward his small companion, he added, "and this is my daughter Thiana."

Standing beside me in the cockpit, Derek piloted us into the anchorage, and showed us where to anchor. "Steady on," he said. "You can see our anchor light just to the right, there." Derek pointed slightly to our right. "I think this would be a good place for you," he said. I moved the control lever to neutral. Velda and Ian were already on the bow.

The swells had subsided by this time, and we coasted slowly

ahead. The depth finder indicated 22 feet. "Let her go!" I yelled. Almost immediately, I heard the splash of the anchor hitting the water, and the rumble of chain rolling over the windlass gypsy.

"Hold it," I yelled. I set the anchor and shut the engine down. Debby had heated water for coffee, and we crowded below in the saloon where I got my first look at our benefactors.

Derek was a bear of a man, appearing even more massive in his oilskins. Rain water was still dripping from his full beard as he sat down and gratefully accepted a steaming cup of coffee.

Thiana, also heavily bundled in foul weather gear, was a pretty girl, then aged 12 (going on 20), with a lovely smile to match her disposition.

I watched Derek sip his scalding hot coffee, wondering what sort of man would voluntarily leave the snug comfort of his cabin and venture out into a chilling cloudburst to help strangers. After I got to know Derek better, I realized this was a typical reaction. We needed help; Derek could offer it; nothing more need be said.

Studying his weather–beaten features, his large nose looming over his full and somewhat ragged beard, his large sunken eyes under heavy brows, and the good humored smile lines in his face, he looked like the sort of man I'd like to know better.

Thiana reminded me of my children. I wasn't surprised that she had volunteered to accompany her dad; my daughters would have done the same. I was surprised to learn that she was only 12. She was already maturing into a very attractive young woman.

Derek finished his coffee and pulling the hood of his oilskins over his head, bade us a good night, and left, Thiana following in his wake, a minnow pursuing a whale.

There is always a sag when the anchor is down and set. No night watches, no reason to study the sunset or sunrise for danger signals; just a silent feeling of relief, and a warm, happy feeling of accomplishment, somewhat soured here by our pending labor problems.

The next morning, before the sun was up, I climbed the ratlines to the yard and had a look around through the binoculars. It was like looking at a three–dimensional model of the chart.

Direction Island, where we were anchored in company with nine other yachts, was a motu or waterless coral island, at the extreme northeast corner of the lagoon. From my vantage point, I saw a series of smaller motus outlining the eastern edge of the lagoon, and several miles away, a large continental island identified on the chart as Home Island. Diagonally across the oval lagoon to the southwest was the other prominent island in this group, which the chart named West Island. The headquarters, the air field, and the quarantine station were on West Island.

The atoll once belonged to the Ross–Cluney family who maintained a seigneury under the benevolent authority of the Straits Settlement (Singapore) until they sold all but Home Island to Australia in 1955, and came under Australian rule.

Home Island is still a medieval fiefdom. We were told that the United Nations had even investigated allegations of slavery there. I couldn't imagine the basis for those allegations. Their labor policy was evidently similar to ours; workers were always free to leave; but if they did, they were not welcomed back. The place was cloistered and yachts were not welcome.

The authorities on West Island knew soon enough that a new boat had entered the lagoon, and shortly after breakfast, a quarantine launch came alongside. The doctor came aboard, sat in the saloon and began filling out papers. He asked the usual questions, signed our pratique, and said, "You may take your quarantine flag down."

Debby came in. "Can I ask a few questions?" she asked.

The doctor smiled at her. "Of course," he said.

I wasn't sure until now what the kids had decided to do.

Debby smiled back at the doctor. "Suppose we wanted to leave the boat here. Could we camp on the beach?"

Before the doctor could answer, I said, "Remember what I said, Debby. I meant it!"

The doctor must have sensed what was in the wind. Nevertheless, he said, "Of course you can."

Debby spoke to me first. "I know you mean it, Denny," she said. Then turning to the doctor, she asked about telephone service to the mainland, airplane schedules, and whether they could buy food in the local store. The doctor answered her questions, gathered his papers, and left. Harry jumped aboard.

In the tiny universe of Cocos–Keeling, Harry was an institution. Officially, he represented HM Customs on this speck of Australian territory. But Harry was more than a government bureaucrat. Harry was a friend. Short, stocky and balding in middle age, Harry reminded me of a retired Navy chief petty officer, with his friendly grin and genuine concern for the yachts and their crews.

His was a difficult job, acting as a go-between for the yachts and the indifferent (warder type) Australian officials on a desert island in the middle of the Indian Ocean. Harry quickly ran through the formalities, and explained the local ground rules. We were required to remain anchored at Direction Island. Home Island was strictly off limits, and we were not to cruise around the lagoon.

When we returned to the deck, we found the crew lined up at the rail, baggage in hand, ready to go ashore. It was a solemn moment. The silence was broken by Ian who, looking at Harry, asked if they could have a ride to West Island.

Ian and I shook hands. "Remember what I said," I cautioned. He shrugged nervously, and said, "We do." With that they climbed over the rail and left.

It is never possible to walk completely in another person's moccasins because no two people think, feel, or experience things exactly the same. However unflattering it may be, I now believe one or both of those kids was so terrified of me, or the boat, or the Indian Ocean, or all the above, that any alternative, even a desert island, was preferable. I don't know exactly what I felt as I watched them settle down in the launch. In a way, I was relieved. They were pleasant company, but neither had much interest or aptitude for sailing. Moreover, I'm too old to start raising a new family and those kids were terribly green.

The other consideration was that at least they had left the boat in an Australian port rather than waiting until we were in Mauritius. The days of Conor O'Brien, whose book, *Across Three Oceans*, was published in 1927, when you could casually pick up a crew here and leave them there, are gone forever. Anywhere yachts touch these days, the authorities carefully count noses to make sure you take the same number of crew you brought.

I knew the party wasn't over; that we could expect pressure from the authorities and, to paraphrase our Aussie friends, I wasn't wrong. In the meantime, however, the reaction of the other yachties was interesting. On the one hand, there was unease; as if we might be a Jonah, worsening the tenuous relationship the yachties then had with the authorities.

On the other hand, possibly because of our anticipated intimacy with the authorities, we became an informal yachtie ombudsman. People felt at ease sharing their concerns and problems with us. That's why we heard about the problems on Ashmore Reef, a lagoon near the edge of the Timor Channel, on Australia's Continental Shelf.

We had passed within 25 miles of it, and I had thought about stopping. Now I wish we had. This reef had an aquifer and fresh water wells. I'm sure Ashmore is not unique; but I don't know of another fresh water well in mid-ocean.

The wells were guarded by signs in English, Indonesian, and Tamil warning that the wells were infected with cholera. Those signs had been installed by the Royal Australian Navy. My informants also said they had seen a Navy shore party pour something into the wells.

After reading the signs and seeing the sailors dump something into the water, some yachties whose opinion of Australian officials wasn't very high to begin with, found it was easy to conclude that the Navy was poisoning the wells. Later, after we reported the incident in our annual newsletter, which was published in a national magazine, we learned that the Navy admitted putting salt into the wells as a public health measure to prevent people from becoming ill with cholera from drinking that water. The official explanation was that rats carrying cholera bacillus had fallen into the wells and drown. It's a nice theory. There *is* a thriving population of rats on the atoll, probably (and ironically), because generations of seafarers have landed on that atoll seeking sweet water, and undoubtedly they inadvertently brought the rats with them. However, biologists doubt whether rats would be drawn to the wells since they usually find sufficient water in their food.

It also has been suggested that since the reef is an important nesting ground for Indian Ocean sea turtles, degrading the water might discourage poachers from preying on sea birds and turtles.

That's another pretty theory, certain to generate applause from the environmental community, but I suspect the truth is that Australia's governmental *warder* instinct is in overdrive. It may be cynicism on my part, but I think the government is much more concerned about Indonesian attempts to colonize Ashmore Reef than it is about protecting endangered sea life. Rendering the water unpalatable would not have the same impact on transient poachers who undoubtedly would be carrying their own water, as it would on foreign (i.e. Indonesian) colonization efforts. However, I think it is so fundamentally wrong for humanitarian reasons to poison water under any circumstances, that for a government to do so merely to advance political objectives, borders on the atrocious.

We also had water problems. There was a freshly painted sign posted on a rain water catchment cistern that read, YACHTS NOT ALLOWED TO TAKE WATER. I found it both aggravating and disturbing. Luckily, we were able to do something about it.

The opening salvo in our incipient debate with the authorities regarding Ian and Debby's future was fired the next day. We had gone ashore to stretch our legs and visit with the other outcasts, when someone yelled, "Hey, Denny! Harry's here, and wants a word with you."

Harry came into the clearing where we were sitting. He walked up to me. "Can I talk with you privately?" he asked.

"Sure," I said. Together, we walked into the brush away from the others. "What's up?" I asked, knowing full well.

Harry was embarrassed. "I have to ask you if you will take the kids back," he said.

"Harry," I said, "you heard me tell them if they left the boat I wouldn't have them back."

"I know," he said solemnly, "and I don't blame you. I would probably do the same. But," he added, "it seems things ain't working out exactly the way they figured."

"Life is like that," I said philosophically.

"The girl called her mother in Sydney," Harry said, "and asked her to wire airfare for her and the boyfriend."

Harry's broad face creased in a grin. "For some reason, Mama isn't bloody keen on paying the boy's fare."

"Well, Harry," I said, "that's the way the cookie crumbles."

"I know," Harry said. "the Administrator thought that might be the way you'd see it. He told me to ask if you would come over to West Island to discuss this problem?"

"That seems fair," I said. Although he didn't say so, I'll bet he caught hell when he showed up with those two waifs in tow.

I had no quarrel with Harry, and I didn't want to make his life more difficult than it already was. We agreed on a time tomorrow and shook hands. I liked him.

After Harry returned to his launch, I told Derek we were making a command appearance on West Island the next day. Derek immediately inquired if our big 15-gallon diesel jugs were empty. If they were, he wanted to borrow them so he could replenish his diesel supply. Assuming, of course, that Harry was agreeable to providing the ferry service. Considering the circumstances, I was sure he would. I was glad to have a chance to do Derek a favor. The next morning, when Harry brought the launch alongside, Velda and I, Derek and his wife, Suki, and three 15-gallon fuel jugs were lined up at the rail. Harry was glad to take the lot across the lagoon.

West Island was strictly a government installation. As one of our peers remarked when our impending conference became known, "Cocos-Keeling is the only place on earth where it takes 400 civil servants to administer 200 natives."

Our first stop was at the store. It offered two categories of supplies – perishables and staples – to two classes of customers; local folks and the rest of mankind.

Perishables, which arrived twice weekly on regularly scheduled charter flights from Perth, were displayed along one wall. A small sign hanging over them said:

150% SURCHARGE TO VISITING YACHTS.

Cocos-Keeling was the only place in the world where we paid five dollars for a dozen eggs. I would have expected a different atmosphere on a frontier where the population could be counted in three digits and the mail came twice a week. But I guess what we found was what you might expect from warders.

After our brief shopping spree, we went to the local bar, a club for off-duty bureaucrats, and had a beer. That's where Harry found us to report that "the Administrator could see us now."

I thought we were invited guests. But now we were being granted an interview. Already irritated by my experience at the store, I took a deep breath and willed myself to be calm.

We followed Harry to the Administration Building, another military-looking, metal building, where we were told to wait out on the sidewalk. The walk was paved and lined with a chain on short posts, guarding a struggling but neatly trimmed lawn. The only identifying marks on the buildings were numbers painted over the doors. Exactly like a military post. Even to the street signs, completely unnecessary, but formally required. The nearest intersection was the corner of Cluney Boulevard and Ross Street. What an absurdity!

We could have been back in Panama. The waiting room was the sidewalk. There were no amenities such as shade or chairs. I don't know if the discourtesy was intentional or if it was simply another example of institutional (warder) indifference. We were kept standing on that walk in the sun for over 20 minutes.

It's one of the peculiarities of my disability that standing in place for more than a few minutes causes excruciating back pain. Of course, they didn't know that, but Velda does, and as she went inside to demand a chair, a clerk came out.

"The Administrator will see you now."

By this time, I was mad as hell and ready to go back to the boat. However, common sense prevailed; I knew it was doubtful whether Harry would take us back before we met with his boss.

Also, while the Administrator didn't have anything I wanted, there were a few things I wanted to say, and this seemed as good a chance as I was likely to have.

In retrospect, it was funny. Velda and I sat on one side of the table, armed with our agenda, while the Administrator and his staff sat opposite with their's. There was no commonality.

The Administrator, a personable man in early middle age, wanted to discuss Ian's airfare to Perth since Mama was such a poor sport about it. I wanted to talk about that snotty sign on the water tank at Direction Island, and the yachting communities' general need for water; the outrageous and probably illegal surcharge at the store; the poisoning of wells at Ashmore, to inquire whether other wells had been similarly treated, and finally, I wanted to make a few philosophical observations about Australia's cynical dole system that produced immature and irresponsible young people like Debby and Ian.

We didn't have much time to devote to Ian's airplane ticket, but that discussion didn't require much time. As you may recall, *passengers* leaving an Australian port must pay a departure tax. By bureaucratic fiat, all hands on a yacht, except the skipper, are passengers.

"Tell me," I said, "under Australian law, if I were operating a copra schooner, and those kids came on board in Darwin and decided to get off in Cocos, would I be obliged to provide on-going passage to whatever place they fancied?"

"No," he said.

"Well," I continued, "by definition of your customs service, those kids were passengers on board *Prospector*. Both have an absolute right of entry into Australia by reason of citizenship and residency. All I did was provide transport from one exotic Australian port to another. I didn't put them off the boat. Why should I pay?"

Velda was growing tired, and cut straight to the bone. "Are you going to deny us a clearance certificate?"

The Administrator looked mildly embarrassed. "We would never do that," he said. "Frankly, we don't have the means to compel you to do anything."

I wasn't through. I wanted to talk about the surcharge. "Suppose we were black people," I said. "In that case would it be legal to impose the surcharge?"

The Administrator smiled. "No."

"But it is legal to discriminate against us because of the kind of housing we have? Or because we are foreigners? Or because we are transients?" I asked.

I was getting close. The Administrator looked uncomfortable. "You see," he began, "we are under Singapore law here. . . ."

Next on my agenda was the issue of poisoned wells. When I mentioned them, he was puzzled. "I know nothing about it," he said. I believed him. The Navy wouldn't boast about it.

Nevertheless, I believe that sort of information ought to be provided on both aeronautical and marine charts, but it isn't. My Australian chart, corrected to May, 1985, contained no hint that anything was amiss on Ashmore Reef.

On the subject of water, I brought up the problem at Direction Island. Apparently, a private boating club had put up the sign. He told me to ignore it, and promised to find a way of routinely providing water to those needing it.

During the launch ride back to Direction Island, I tried to sort out our experiences to understand better the bursts of impulsive generosity we had enjoyed on an intensely personal level with the harshness of the institutional actions we had seen.

I had mixed feelings as our Australian visit was coming to a close. We had spent nearly 12 months in the Commonwealth, and carried away wonderful memories.

How do you reconcile people like Harry, or Mr. Harrison in Cairns, or the solicitor in Manly, or the Perkins shop foreman in Auburn, or Mr. Holmes in Balls Head Bay with an ugly sign that says **150% SURCHARGE TO VISITING YACHTS**?

What thread connects official, deliberate, degradation of water wells with the genuine help given us by the quarantine officer in Cairns who arranged Cap's parvo vaccination?

What do you think of a government that cynically maintains itself in power by corrupting a generation of young people, offering any kid out of school and over the age of 16 a dole for not working?

I liked Australia, but I had a problem with Australian Governmental institutions. I just don't like warders. None of us Ned Kelly types does.

Three days after our excursion to West Island, I heard Derek's hail from *HOTTYD*, "There's *Atair II*," he bellowed. I looked toward the pass we had entered a week earlier. There she was.

In a few moments, I saw Babs run forward and almost immediately, the gaff swung down and the mainsail lost its shape and wrinkled its way down the mast. The jib was the next sail to fall. Then the staysail collapsed in a heap on the foredeck.

Babs went back to the cockpit, replacing Klaus who ran forward, and as the boat entered the anchorage, he threw the anchor overboard.

We spent a pleasant three weeks at Cocos–Keeling. The sign forbidding our use of water disappeared, and Harry let it be known that we were welcome to take what water we needed.   Mostly, we just hung around, visiting back and forth, speculating about the weather – especially hurricanes – and planning the next leg of the Indian Ocean crossing.

Most of us, the less adventurous, planned to sail diagonally across the Indian Ocean from our present eight degrees south to Mauritius, at about 28 degrees south. We were leery of the Indian Ocean, partly because there isn't nearly as much information available about it as there is about the Atlantic or Pacific.

Klaus and Babs wanted to visit the Seychelles, so their route would take them north of Mauritius. They planned to head south through the Mozambique Channel (otherwise known as Hurricane Alley for very good reasons), meeting us in South Africa.

The only thing that prolonged our stay in Cocos was the lousy weather. Storm after storm, and for ten days the southeast wind never dropped below 35 knots. We just sat tight and studied the calendar and the barometer. Finally, on September tenth, everything looked just right, and we called West Island for a clearance.

The next morning, Harry came by to stamp our passports and wish us good sailing, and "No hard feelings, Mate?" We shook hands, and I started the engine while Velda went forward to begin hauling the anchor. Heading out into the Indian Ocean to an island 2,500 miles away was truly sailing into the unknown.

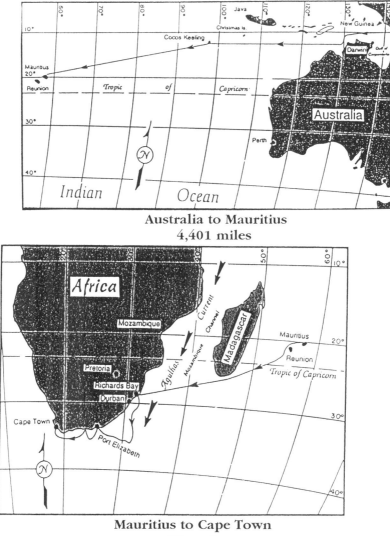

Australia to Mauritius
4,401 miles

Mauritius to Cape Town
2,662 miles

Crossing the Indian Ocean (Charts 10 & 11)

Chapter 15

An Asian Tower of Babel

$\mathcal{T}$he Indian Ocean is quite different from the Atlantic or Pacific because weather, like politics, is primarily the result of unequal pressures and much hot air. Unlike either the Atlantic or Pacific with their neatly defined equatorial Intertropical Convergence Zones (ITC), the peculiar geography of the Indian Ocean, bordered on the north by the Himalayas and the great Asian land mass, means that Indian Ocean weather is caused by terrestrial weather phenomena such as the Siberian high during the winter, and a deep low pressure system backing up against the Himalayas during the summer.

Also, it isn't as heavily traveled as the other oceans. Therefore, the weather isn't as well monitored. Where the Atlantic weather people make a terrible fuss about any tropical depression that leaves the Cape Verde Islands from mid–June to mid–October, the formation of similar depressions in the Indian Ocean is likely to go unnoticed.

I mention this because many people set great store by weather forecasts. I don't. I think we're better off to stay alert and rely on the single–station forecasting techniques described in the appendix. In the long run, I believe that in a dynamic environment like the Indian Ocean, we're better served by our barograph, the look of the sky, the feel of things like the wind and sea swell, and a few briny homilies such as "The time to shorten sail *is when you first think of it*." than by an distant forecaster working with incomplete data.

Concerned as we were by potential weather problems, we sometimes lost sight of the political problems we might face. Frankly, I was worried about the reception we might receive when we arrived in South Africa.

We had called at the South African Consulate in Sydney to apply for visas. That was an odd experience. When we arrived, we found the door tightly locked from the inside. Repeated knocking resulted in someone inside calling through the door inquiring who we were and what we wanted. Only after we satisfied the person inside that we were harmless was the door opened and we were admitted. What a hell of a way to run a public office!

Our efforts were futile. When the consular officer learned that we were traveling by private yacht, he told us that visas were no longer issued to people like us; that we'd have to write a letter to Pretoria asking permission to visit South Africa. Really strange.

No response from South Africa was received by the time we left Australia, so we didn't know what to expect. We were afraid, that the South Africans might retaliate against American yachts for the bad publicity and economic boycott South Africa was experiencing at the hands of our government.

Before leaving Darwin, we had ordered several charts from the Darwin chart agent. Included on the list was an Atlantic gnomonic chart, which is a flat rendition of a large part of the earth's curved surface. Those charts are used as planning tools. You can plot a great circle course merely by drawing a straight line between your points of departure and arrival, then transferring your course coordinates to a regular small scale navigation chart.

I was dismayed to discover, shortly before we arrived in Cocos-Keeling, that the chart agent had carelessly substituted a *Pacific* gnomonic chart. Looking further, I also discovered that instead of supplying the required sequentially numbered series of charts across the Indian Ocean, each covering a time zone (or 15 degrees of longitude), the agent had included two copies of the chart on which Cocos-Keeling appeared, and deleted the one immediately following.

It may seem foolish to spend good money for charts that depict nothing but water, although they contain information concerning magnetic variation, known currents, and so forth, but it is *really* stupid to buy and store charts without bothering to make sure you received what you ordered.

I had remedied that problem while we were still anchored at Direction Island by borrowing the missing chart from Derek, and plotting the necessary data on the extra chart that I had. But I couldn't do much about the missing gnomonic chart except hope the South Africans would be more hospitable than I expected.

The Autohelm was history. Again, we were locked into that killing routine, when we navigated and cooked, ate and slept only when we didn't have a watch to stand and a boat to steer.

However, the sailing from Cocos-Keeling to Mauritius was outstanding. We *averaged* 134 miles a day, far and away the fastest passage we made anywhere. We were pushed by monsoonal winds, and the trip, a distance of 2,412 miles, required only 18 days.

I realize this may seem tame to anyone accustomed to 60 mph on the nearest freeway, but for us, more accustomed to a stately four knots or 90 miles a day, this was life in the fast lane.

September 13: Winds rising all day. Struck the squaresail, set staysail, ran until dark, hove-to for the night.

September 14: Ran off all night under double-reefed mainsail and staysail. Seas very rough, force seven. We are getting tired. Velda doing most of the navigation, getting an occasional sight through the overcast.

September 15: Struck main as wind continues to rise. Estimate gusts 40 to 45 knots. Necessary to steer around swells. Decided to heave-to at dark. Staysail broke loose again. Velda fixed a great dinner.

September 18: Wonderful blue skies, wind still brisk but down to force five. Shook out reefs. LAN confirmed by two sunlines indicates we are fifty miles further southwest than we thought. At noon, seven days from Cocos, we are nearly a third of the way, at 15°11'S, 84°58'E.

During the ten day period from September 17th through the 27th, we ran *1,582* miles. On September 25th, we broke our all-time speed record for a 24 hour run. We ran an incredible *178* miles, averaging 7.5 knots.

That was a dazzling performance, reminiscent of the sprint we had made from Dunk Island to Cairns in the Barrier Reef, and confirmed my earlier discovery that we ran significantly faster when our propeller was locked. I still thought that result was akin to perpetual motion, but it worked; and that's all that counted.

Our landfall, on September 29th, was at dawn twilight when we saw the light on Flat Island about ten miles away. As the light strengthened, we saw looming behind it in shadowy profile, the huge bulk of Mauritius. The higher elevations of the island first caught the rising sun's light, and as we watched, the glow crept lower and lower on the island, turning shades of shadow to gray, and gray to green.

The chart showed many islets and reefs in a shoal area between Flat Island and Mauritius, and warned of reversing currents up to four knots in those shoals.

I steered a course well clear of those hazards. Sailing around Flat Island, we headed in a southeasterly direction, passing Gunner's Quoin, and other, smaller islands.

By 2 p.m., we were standing off Port Louis. I called the Harbor Master on the VHF, asking permission to enter the port and for clearance instructions.

We received detailed instructions, and after starting the engine, we struck the sails and began running toward the thickest, busiest, clump of shipping we could see.

Five ships were tied end to end along the harbor jetty to our left as we entered Port Louis. I smiled as I read the name *Nedlloyd Korea* on a container ship, remembering that it was she that had nearly come adrift in Papeete during hurricane *Veena*.

A row of huge steel mooring buoys marked the opposite edge of the channel. A few lighters were tied to docks behind those buoys in shallow water, but there was no visible activity.

The custom house, an orange roofed affair that resembled an Oriental Howard Johnson's, was situated on a short dock straight ahead, seemingly an extension of the street behind it. A row of rafted tugs were tied to each other and bow–out across the face of the dock. One tug, tied to its neighbor, extended beyond the dock. We saw sailboat masts behind her.

Evidently we were expected to motor around the last tug and come alongside the dock. As we drew nearer, I saw a uniformed official waving to us.

With the engine running at a slow idle, I swung as close to the nearest tug as I dared, and in response to the official's increasingly imperious gestures, I pointed to our yard and extended my hands helplessly.

I could have cock–billed the yard (tilted it so it would be nearly parallel to the mast) but he didn't know that, and I saw no reason to maneuver myself into that tiny space for his convenience. Instead, I put my cupped hands around my mouth and yelled, "How about tying up to the tug?"

The customs officer yelled back, "OK!", so we quickly nosed up to the outboard tug. Velda handed over the headline. I passed a stern line. We were in Mauritius. It was immediately apparent that English was not the language of the streets, although two crewmen on the tug had a smattering of it, and graciously toasted our arrival by passing down two bottles of beer and a greasy package of delicious smoked fish.

One enterprising young fellow asked why we were not flying a courtesy flag, explaining that it was a violation of the law not to do so. Then he displayed the flags he had for sale. The crewmen confirmed that it would be a mistake not to buy and display a flag. A simple transaction involving ten dollars, and we had a courtesy flag flying from the starboard flag hoist.

I was beginning to relax and enjoy myself when the customs officer arrived and explained that because the tugs had to leave, we were free to enter the port. The formalities could be taken care of later. Everyone seemed to know where we were to go, except us. One fellow wearing a heavy Turkish looking mustache, volunteered his services as a pilot. I gladly accepted.

Motoring past the tugs, we entered a narrow canal leading deeper into the port. It wasn't very long, certainly less than half a mile, but we motored past rust-streaked Japanese and Taiwanese longliners, fishing sampans, small freighters, and an odd looking Japanese reefer ship designed to service the longline fleet. Those vessels were tied end to end along the stained and weathered cement bulkheads on both sides of the waterway.

Dredging was in progress. We waited while the dredge completed a pass, then we were allowed to swing around it, and our pilot pointed to a decrepit wooden tug tied to the bulkhead.

"You tie there," he said.

We slid alongside and magically, Derek Blair, who we had left in Cocos-Keeling, stepped around the tug's wheelhouse to take our lines. We had come to the end of the canal and were in a cul-de-sac, or small turning basin, about 300 yards in diameter. The old tug, not much longer than *Prospector*, was tied to the west wall.

The north wall, directly in front of us, ran 300 yards to the right where it joined the east wall. The north wall accommodated two local fishing boats and three yachts. *HOTTYD* and five other yachts were tied to the east wall, directly across the basin from our berth.

Although there was no indication of the difference, Derek quickly explained that the portion of the dock where we were tied belonged to the Albion Dock Co. The opposite side where *HOTTYD* lay belonged to the city. He urged us to move to his side of the cul-de-sac because as tenants of the dock company, we would be charged a dollar a day. As a guest of the city, Derek paid nothing.

I can understand why Derek sometimes looks at me in a peculiar way. I reminded him that in the cosmic order of things, $30 a month was not a make or break proposition. Moreover, since we were 300 yards further than *HOTTYD* from the gate, potential thieves would have to walk past *HOTTYD* to reach us. I assumed the dock watchman would keep an eye on *Prospector* when we were ashore.

Finally and most importantly, after three weeks at sea on a running watch schedule, I'm just played out. When we get a line ashore, barring fire, pestilence or plague, I want to leave it there.

So we stayed put. Within minutes, the police launch was alongside with the customs officials. The formalities took about 30 minutes. Suki Blair, Derek's wife, was standing by with a CARE package of fresh bread and vegetables. By that time, it was late in the afternoon. We decided to wait until morning for our first look at the city.

We sat quietly in *HOTTYD's* large cockpit, drinking Derek's beer, exchanging memories of the trip just past, watching the play of light on the water as dusk turned into dark, listening to the alien sounds and smelling the strange odors of a new exciting and exotic port.

Long before daylight, we were awakened by the amplified voice of a muezzin calling the faithful to prayer. He was joined by a second and then a third, their voices blending in an exotic oriental harmony.

Port Louis was an Asian city. The ruling majority was Hindu. I doubt whether anyone knows, but I would guess the Creoles were the next largest group. I think of the Creoles as the indigenous population, because they reflected the historic ethnic, cultural and racial melding that distinguishes the populations of many island communities such as Tahiti and Hawaii. Part African, part Malay, part European, and with a dash of Chinese, Tamil and Arab thrown in, the Creoles have developed a unique culture during the past 400 years.

Indian Moslems were the third most populous group. When India's Partition occurred in 1947, many Moslems migrated to Mauritius, then a British Colony, instead of moving to what is now Pakistan or Bangladesh.

The island's political and social organization was similar to Fiji's. Hindus practiced the professions, wore the uniforms and ran things. Moslems drove cabs and operated small businesses. The Indian Christians found occupations such as hotel clerks and porters, which put them in close contact with Westerners. Port Louis also had a large Chinese population, mostly from Hunan Province. The Chinese operated restaurants, bars, small retail shops, and the casino.

The bottom rung of the economic ladder was occupied by Creoles and Tamils who earned a precarious living by carrying things on their heads. Coolie wages were 25 rupees/day ($1.75).

I found it inexplicable that although the British took Mauritius from the French in 1810 and ruled it for five generations as a Crown colony until Commonwealth status was achieved in 1968, and that the official language of the place was English, many people couldn't speak it at all, and hardly anyone spoke it voluntarily.

French, not English, was the language of trade, commerce, and the streets. This probably was a tribute to the stubborn tenacity of the French Jesuits into whose hands, by default, community educational responsibilities fell. Now, a Hindu optometrist told me, the French Government formally supports the movement to preserve the French language and culture on Mauritius.

Coming, as I do, from a society that is far below the linguistic poverty line, I found it astonishing that a $1.75/day coolie who could not write his name, was fluent not only in his native language, whether it was Tamil or the French patois of the streets, but equally fluent in French, reasonably fluent in the language of his co-worker, and his boss's language, which might be Urdu or Hindi, or the Hunan dialect, and as a fifth or sixth language, might even have a few words of English.

Since we had only a customs clearance, Velda and I spent most of the following morning searching for the immigration office. We left Cap in charge of the boat, and walked out to the road that ran past the Albion Shipyard gate.

Looking around, we found an aura of decay and neglect. The buildings were nearly all decrepit and covered with peeling whitewash. Signs were in a polyglot mixture of Chinese, French and English. A small single-story building supported a typically grandiose sign hanging over the sidewalk that announced the GREAT EASTERN BICYCLE CO. WHOLESALE AND RETAIL. The business apparently occupied a single room. Children peered out the window at us as we walked past.

We saw scores of loitering men, some standing on the sidewalk, some squatting or leaning against buildings, watching the traffic go by. These were coolies, some of them Tamils, mostly Creoles, waiting for work.

The road took us past the post office, a small stone building with the date 1872 carved over the lintel. The sun was high when, with the help of a street vendor and a clerk in the post office, we found Lyon Barracks, a former British Army post. After passing through the gate, and wandering along a graveled path through extensive lawns, we found a neatly lettered signpost in English that pointed toward the immigration office.

Shades of Costa Rica. This was another place where you stood outside and transacted your business through a window. We joined the end of a long line of people standing before the only open window under the immigration sign. Almost immediately, a formally dressed young man stepped from the doorway, walked up to us, and asked for our passports. He took them inside the office, and returned in a few minutes with the entry stamps neatly affixed.

"Enjoy your stay in Mauritius," he said.

On the recommendation of our Sydney bank, I had asked Buz to send our next remittance to the Hong Kong and Shanghai Bank in Mauritius. We had walked past it on our way to Lyon Barracks. Now we entered the bank's darkly varnished lobby.

The room was old fashioned, with heavy baroque carvings decorating the railings and the teller's cages. The atmosphere was gloomy and I wouldn't have been surprised to see clerks perched on stools, industriously scratching away with quill pens.

I approached the teller near the INTERNATIONAL TRANSACTIONS window, and identified myself, asking whether the funds had arrived. Taking my passport, she went to a card file and found a telex message.

Instead of returning to the teller's window, she took it to an officer seated at a desk near the windows. Something was up. Instead of coming to us and saying something like "Look here, old bean. We have a bit of a problem... ." the bank officers held a series of whispered meetings, looking toward us from time to time. Finally, a senior officer came to the railing.

I suspect the bank didn't have $1,000 in U.S. currency. It didn't matter to me,of course, but they probably couldn't imagine that I wanted local currency instead of dollars.

"I'm sorry, sir," he began, but anticipating what he was going to say next, I held up my hand.

"Please give me rupees instead of dollars," I said.

It's possible we might have gotten a better rate of exchange on the street, but if there was a black market in hard currencies, it was very discreet. I never noticed it, and I usually spot things like that.

"All of it?" he asked. His relief was almost palpable. When I nodded, I was rewarded with a bright smile. "Of course, of course," he said. "Please sign here, and here, and here."

Our $990 turned into slightly over 14,000 rupees, making an enormous pile of banknotes. I stuffed my pockets; Velda crammed notes into her purse, and when we were back on the sidewalk, once again I knew how it felt to be rich.

On the way back to the boat, we decided to stop and pay our respects at the Merchant Navy Club, a hospitable oasis and a friendly haven for the circumnavigator. The club was housed in a small mansion about five blocks from the Albion Dockyard gate. An iron grill separated the front yard and circular drive from the sidewalk. A wide porch was four steps up from the drive. Tall French doors opened from the porch into a large room with the bar to your left and the lounge on the right.

If you wished, you could walk through the lounge into a short hall that led to a covered gallery on the eastern edge of the back yard. An open air pavilion was on the left and small meeting rooms opened off the gallery to the right. At the end of the gallery, 100 feet from the house, was a gate opening on to the next road. The toilet facilities – including showers – (which were free) were found off the gallery next to the gate.

All that was required to become an honorary member was your

signature in the guest book. This wonderful place, operated by a charming English couple, had two serious flaws from the point of view of the typically impoverished yachtie.

Compared to local native bars, the drinks were expensive. And the waiters did everything but stand on your feet in quest of a tip. Both problems discouraged a large and faithful following among transient yachties.

Tico's Bar, two blocks nearer to the dock yard, on the other hand, had everything a yachtie might desire; a tolerant bartender, a reasonably clean bar and cheap beer. True, you learned to hold your breath when you went to the urinal, and I doubt that anyone ever took a shower there, but you can't have everything.

I don't know where the name "Tico" came from. Costa Ricans are sometimes called "Ticos", but in this case, most likely, years ago, someone named Tico owned the place.

When we were there, the place was owned by a young Hunan Chinese with a Vietnamese name, Van Ng, who operated it with the help of his widowed mother. She was a doll.

Her English was limited to "beer," and "whiskey-water." She cheerfully tended bar, and responded at length in spirited Chinese to any question or comment the patrons might offer.

I sometimes wondered what she said. I imagine it was obscene, partly because many Chinese have a ribald sense of humor, and several elderly Chinese men, regular customers, found her comments very funny, and partly because more than once, I saw Van (more popularly known as Tico, of course) roll his eyes and shake his head when she started her monologue.

One thing about yachties. We are a dependable lot. You don't have to worry that we'll want fancy cocktails or exotic call brands. Just give us a bottle of Phoenix beer (three rupees at Tico's *v.* five + tip at the Merchant Navy Club). Phoenix beer came in the same 500 ml. bottles we had learned to enjoy in Fiji.

The rum was also a local product. It was to real rum what moonshine is to bourbon. It was formally identified as cane spirits, and was sort of a pre-rum. It was clear like alcohol and would tear your head off if you weren't careful. The most popular brand was Green Island. You could buy it in any Chinese store, hardware or grocery, for 18 rupees ($1.29) per 750 ml. bottle.

Around the corner from Tico's was a doorway egg and poultry store operated by a family of Indian Christians who made sure their Western customers knew their religious preference. They apparently felt it was good business to advertise their affiliation. I've noticed that other Christians often do that.

When I describe the business location as a doorway, that's what it was. Their inventory was a pile of egg crates on the sidewalk. A crate of anxious looking chickens was piled on top.

Using the containers we had purchased in Costa Rica, we bought our eggs and an occasional chicken from them. If you wanted a chicken, all you did was point out the bird you wanted. They efficiently dressed the bird, and in less than five minutes, for about 50¢, you had a still warm Sunday dinner in hand.

Third world markets are efficient and fascinating. To a social anthropologist, I would think they might provide a measure of the relative sophistication of the community which supports them. For example, in Papeete, like New York, you must rise well before the chickens, but by 10 a.m., when the sun is high, the market closes. Also like New York, Papeete had numerous alternative supermarkets.

Mauritius had no supermarkets, and the iron gates of the market across the street from the post office swung open at sunrise. As you entered the market, you passed four small buildings, two on each side. Those were the butcher shops, and they eloquently reflected Mauritian religious and social diversity.

If you peeked into the one labeled BEEF, you would find Moslem butchers cheerfully reducing beef quarters into salable chunks of meat called "curry" beef. Hindus were in the building labeled PORK, cutting pork chops to order.

The ethnic or class lines were not as obvious in the other buildings, one devoted to eggs and poultry, the other to fish, sea slugs and turtle meat. But subtle or not, I'm sure they were there.

The vegetable market, next to the butcher shops, was a green, yellow, red and purple wonderland. For every vegetable I recognized, there were two I did not know. An aisle opened on a series of small stalls, each stocked with a dizzying array of spices. Shoppers were asked to sample them from saucers on the counter. Women, most of whom wore saris and nose rings, solemnly tested a pinch of this or sniffed suspiciously at that. Handcrafts, including straw and leather goods, took up an entire corner of the market. I had to duck beneath the displayed purses and baskets. And there was bread.

Any country where the French have had the slightest influence will forever after enjoy the baker's art. The French take their bread seriously; even in a place like Nuka Hiva in the Marquesas, lines formed at the bakery well before sunrise for breakfast croissänts.

Roger and Molly on *Sundowner* arrived in Port Louis ten days after we had. Almost immediately, they arranged with a local taxi driver for a tour of the island, and invited us to accompany them.

Craftsmen on Mauritius have earned a world-class reputation for ship models, and we visited a shop where expensive museum quality models were displayed for sale. We drove past three tea plantations; I was surprised to find that tea "trees" are really waist-high shrubs.

We spent a hurried hour or so wandering through one of the world's great arboretums and botanical gardens. I don't know the numbers, but I do know the arboretum collection was one of the most complete in the world. The grounds are beautifully kept, and the specimens are neatly and clearly labeled. It was not the sort of place you wanted to visit for only an hour or so. A few days or even a week was needed to do the place justice.

We also visited a small woolen mill, but I was more interested in talking with the driver than I was in trying on sweaters, so I waited with him while the others went inside. The driver was an Indian Moslem who had come to Mauritius with his parents in 1949. Having in mind India's bloody religious riots shortly after World War II, I asked how Indians of different faiths got along on Mauritius.

He knew what I was talking about; he was old enough to remember those riots. He told me they got along well, because everyone accepted the system. Since the Hindus were in the majority, they controlled the political apparatus. I sensed, however, that he wasn't altogether pleased about the Hindu domination because he reminded me that unlike the South Africans, the Hindus have been practicing a form of apartheid for centuries.

Possibly because of the prevailing caste system, each segment of Mauritian society seems to have maintained strong cultural integrity. All the Tamils speak Tamil, for example, just as the Hindus speak Hindi, the Chinese for the most part speak the Hunan dialect, and nearly all the Moslems speak Urdu.

Even though it's still the official language, it's possible that one day, the small amount of English now spoken on the street may disappear. People like Tico will remember it, because he valued his yachtie trade, and freely used his English to smooth the path for those of us with special needs.

It started when I casually mentioned to Tico my need for new walking shorts. He referred me to a nearby tailor. The tailor quoted 200 rupees for the job. Thirteen dollars is not too much to pay for tailored shorts, but Tico thought it outrageous. He and I together went back to the tailor, and it quickly developed that I had misunderstood. The price was 90 rupees.

It was wonderful having a Hunan Chinese run interference with the local merchants. It saved money and probably improved the quality of the goods we bought. As with the shorts, Tico always inquired after making a referral, "How much he charge?" If he was not satisfied with your answer, you would soon discover, after he had "conferred" with the merchant, that you had misunderstood the price. Tico looked after his customers.

In her way, Suki Blair was a lot like Tico. Besides her other accomplishments, Suki was a registered nurse. She discovered that some antibiotics in *Prospector's* medicine chest were four years old, and that we didn't know the age of other medicine. "That's it!" she said firmly, "the lot goes over the side!"

She explained that antibiotics lose their potency over time, and some can even become toxic. I hated to part with those pills, stale or not. We had invested several hundred dollars in them.

But Suki insisted, and even offered to help acquire replacement medicine in Port Louis. Reluctantly, but knowing she was right, I handed over the outdated pills. The next day, we went to a pharmacy where she was known.

Suki speaks enough French to get along, and made her needs known to the pharmacist. He directed us to a room in the back of the store, set off by a plywood partition.

Suki knocked on the door. Hearing a shouted invitation, she pushed the door open. A plump young Hindu woman in a doctor's coat, wearing a caste mark on her forehead and a stethoscope around her neck, sat behind a small desk.

Suki explained about our outdated medicines, and told the doctor that we needed to replenish the medicine chest. The doctor nodded understandingly and turning to me, she began taking my medical history. I wasn't sick, but she ignored my protests.

"Up on the table," she ordered.

She probed my abdomen, and began to sound my chest. Satisfied, she asked again, "What can I do for you?"

This time she paid closer attention as Suki outlined my needs. "Let me see," the doctor said, making a list. "You need something for sleep? Something for burn? Something for infection?"

A long discussion between Suki and the doctor followed, involving the medical needs of people aboard cruising yachts. I chimed in, making a special request for sulfa powder, and was rewarded by the doctor with a nod and an approving smile. We were accumulating an impressive stack of prescriptions.

I brought up another problem. Serious, chronic constipation can be almost as disabling at sea as a broken leg. It is a serious problem, brought on by any number of factors. Those factors include stress, inadequate rest, irregular meals, the boat's motion, and even, at times, the sheer inconvenience of going to the toilet, which, in a seaway, can become an athletic event.

The doctor nodded. "Of course, of course," she said, scribbling on her prescription pad. "This suppository is French, and it never fails to work." We also needed pain killers. More prescriptions were added to the pile.

We paused at the pharmacist's counter and handed the prescriptions to him on our way back to the street. The next morning, I poked my nose into the pharmacy.

"Oui, Monsieur," the pharmacist greeted me. He wasn't going to forget a 600 rupee sale. He lifted a carton to the counter. I saw little medicine boxes and gray plastic pill containers in it.

He picked up the containers, marking each with a grease pencil, as he spoke. "Thees wan good for burn," he said, holding a small box, laboriously printing "B–U–R–N." He continued to mark each container, and for antibiotics, their expiration dates.

I had acquired an odd assortment of labels. Some medicines, those with labels in English, came from India. The rest were European, mostly French and Swiss.

The disparity in prices was shocking. For about $45, which included the doctor's examination fee, I had nearly duplicated the medicine chest we had on board when we had left Virginia four years earlier, for which I had paid about $300.

370

Petty theft was a serious problem in Mauritius because we were tied to a dock, rather than anchored midstream, and therefore we were an easy target for thieves. Of course, that's why we carried a guard dog. Unfortunately, Cap was never territorially inclined toward the boat. His allegiance was narrowly focused on Velda. Consequently, we found it necessary to put him on a leash whenever we wanted him to remain in the cockpit; otherwise, at night, he would curl up next to Velda's bunk, and when we left the boat in the daytime, he would always try to follow.

One morning, I went out in the cockpit and instead of finding an enthusiastic little black dog, my eye fell on his leash leading overboard through a hole in the lifeline netting. *Oh, oh,* I said to myself. The leash was limp, and I was almost afraid to look over the side, fearing I would see a limp little carcass dangling in midair, Cap having strangled in his harness.

The harness was still attached to the leash, but it was empty. No Cap. *Oh, boy! Now what?* Obviously, Cap had gone into the water. I thought he had probably drown. The turning basin was solidly bulkheaded with a cement wall and I couldn't see any place where he could have climbed out of the water. I had no idea, of course, when he had gone overboard. Velda was as devoted to the dog as the dog was to her. I crept quietly back into the cabin so as not to waken Velda, hurriedly dressed, and quickly went back to the cockpit and stepped ashore.

Hoping against hope the little beast was still splashing around somewhere, but fully expecting to find a little black corpse floating in a corner of the basin, I quickly walked around the perimeter of the basin. No dog, dead or alive. When I returned to the boat, Velda was awake and dressed, sitting in the cockpit. Finding us both gone, she had assumed the dog was with me. As gently as possible, I broke the news. By that time I was assuming Cap's little carcass had sunk.

We decided to take one more melancholy walk around the basin's perimeter. Perhaps I had missed something. When we were standing next to HOTTYD, a little girl on another New Zealand boat tied nearby spoke to us.

"Are you looking for Cap?" she asked.

I indicated we were.

"I know where he is," she said archly. Then, seeing the look on my face, she quickly added, "he's down there." She pointed to a sewer outfall flush with the water level in the basin.

She was right. The outfall was a cement pipe about two feet in diameter, projecting from the bulkhead below the dock.

When we looked over the side, we saw an incredibly filthy, shivering little dog standing just inside the pipe look wistfully out at the water. I quickly dangled my legs over the edge of the dock, found the pipe with my feet, and lowered myself so I was standing on its lip, where Cap had been moments before.

It was a precarious foothold. Holding on with one hand, I bent over and reached into the pipe with the other. Although he growled defiantly as I touched him, and I thought he might bite, Cap let me get a firm grip on the nape of his neck. With a continuous sweeping motion, I brought him out of the sewer and back into polite society. He was a chastened dog. I don't imagine the rats in that sewer would have been very friendly.

By this time we had been in Mauritius for nearly a month. It was late October, and although we were at 28 degrees south, we were still well within range of Indian Ocean cyclones. It was time to move along. While Velda refilled our jars with meat from the respective Hindu-Moslem butcher shops, I worked out a deal with Tico for large quantities of beer.

We were still uneasy about the reception we might receive in South Africa. However, I had heard via the yachtie grapevine that the best place for transient yachts on the east coast of South Africa was in a new port north of Durban called Richards Bay. To make sure we would be welcome there, I found the overseas telephone office and called the yacht club.

The person with whom I spoke assured me there was ample room for us, that a haul-out could be arranged, and that the stores and banks were just across the street. It sounded delightful and unexpectedly friendly.

It is difficult to summarize my impressions of Port Louis. Looking at the place through one set of eyes, you would see a cluster of two and three-story buildings filled, on the ground floor, with dirty little shops operated by Chinese or Moslem shopkeepers, stocked with a wildly disparate array of merchandise; where Shanghai Alarm Clock Company products were displayed next to string-tied clusters of cans of tuna, or stacks of tinned Chinese mushrooms, next to a display of Green Island cane spirits, next to a barrel of salted codfish. Bundles of dried squid hung everywhere. Wood chisels were displayed next to sacks of rice and large empty glass jars.

The streets were narrow and dirty, and the sidewalks were crowded with vendors, loiterers, and coolies carrying sacks of rice. On one street, a dozen tiny shops offered pirated cassette tapes by well-known European and American artists. They cost less than empty cassettes might cost in New York.

That was the Mauritius Velda saw, and she didn't care much for it. But there were also the colorful Mosques, the happy, healthy children, Tico's genuine concern for his customers, the gentle people who went out of their way to help us, and several times each day, the muezzin's musical call to prayer. I liked it. It was a place I'd like to visit again.

Port Louis was much more than an Asian village with seedy shops and friendly people. It was also a modern commercial center. Consider our experience at the Bank of Mauritius.

We had gone through our 14,000 rupee bankroll, and we needed more cash. We went to the Bank of Mauritius. I handed over my Master Card, asking for an advance of 5,000 rupees. Within *ten minutes* the clerk had the necessary authorization from the clearing house somewhere in the States, and in another five minutes I was back on the street, 5,000 rupees richer.

On October ninth, we cleared the breakwater outbound from Port Louis, and I carelessly let the raffee halyard slip through my fingers and run through the block at the top of the topmast, exactly as Willi had done in New Zealand. If we had stopped in Reunion, a few miles southwest of Mauritius, as most of our friends did, I could have easily rereeved the halyard. It was a long climb to the top of the topmast; a mast band and a block fixed halfway up the topmast offer poor footing, but by standing on them, I would have been within six inches of the halyard block, and I could always contrive to shinny up that last six inches — *if* the boat was perfectly steady.

Unfortunately, however, Reunion was a French colony. We had received a threatening letter from the Tahiti hospital while in Australia, and we didn't know whether the Veteran's Administration had paid the bill. I was afraid to take the chance, because if the bill was still outstanding, French Customs might be on the lookout for us. Consequently, we avoided Reunion, and the raffee never came out of the sail bag on that passage.

Four days later, we discovered our stowaway. It was 4 a.m. Velda woke me for my watch, greeting me with a scalding cup of coffee and "Guess what?"

I'm not good with "guess what" games at any time. Especially at 4 a.m., when I'm trying to gulp my coffee.

On the other hand, Velda is not a frivolous person, and when she says "guess what," it's a good idea to find out.

"OK," I said, "I give up. What?"

"I think we have a rat on board," she said.

Anything is possible, but with a dog and an experienced mouser as big as Lara on board, it hardly seemed likely.

"I saw it," she insisted, "running along the deck just now."

We had seen plenty of rats in Mauritius. Sleek gray and brown Norway rats in the city and dock yard, and I imagine Cap saw more of them in that sewer pipe. Considering how we had tied up in Port Louis, if it weren't for our animals, I might almost have expected to have picked up a rat or two.

It was early in the morning, on my watch a day later, when I realized I wasn't alone. The moon was bright enough so I could see a chunky little animal, not more than four feet away, crouched over an egg container. By God, we *did* have a rat on board!

The little fellow, apparently sensing it had been discovered, scurried forward out of sight.

That was serious. A rat coming from a place like Mauritius could be carrying any kind of disease, including plague, typhus, cholera, and rabies. The most important thing was to prevent it from getting below decks where it would find food and many hiding places. It is very difficult to get rid of a rat once it has taken up residence.

Fortunately, sea-going sailboats are designed to keep the elements out. Except the companionway and the ventilation hatch over the galley (under the dinghy) our hatches were always closed tight when we were at sea. Now, we closed the galley hatch, and stuffed rags into the dorades.

I'm not foolish enough to think that rags would stop a thirsty rat, but getting through the rags could have caused enough stir so that the dog or cat might have wanted to see what was going on. This was a community effort.

Normally, the dog and cat behaved like passengers with

374

first-class tickets. They slept when they chose, begged unmercifully, and made general nuisances of themselves. But now that was changed. Now we had a job for them. Either one or both of the animals would live in the cockpit all the way to Africa. The companionway was the only opening we couldn't close.

By this time, we had personalized our unwelcome visitor, naming it Rodney, for no special reason except that "Rodney the Rat" had a nice alliterative ring to it. Neither of us saw Rodney again. If the animals did, they kept quiet about it. The cat was mildly interested in the awning stowed beneath the dinghy for a day or two after we saw Rodney, but her interest soon waned.

Although we had both seen Rodney, I might have thought we had only imagined him except that when I unrolled the awning, I found where Rodney had made a nest.

The cat was right. True to his little rat-like instincts, Rodney had taken up housekeeping in the awning. He had chewed a three-foot square area of the synthetic fabric into lace, and had left a generous supply of rat turds. But no Rodney and no forwarding address. We haven't a clue what happened to him. If one of the animals had killed him, I'm sure we would have heard the fuss; certainly we would have seen blood or fur.

I suspect one of the animals may have cornered him and forced him out on the bowsprit, where, in a weakened condition because of his diet of synthetic canvas, he slipped and went overboard. Whatever happened, luckily, he didn't last long.

This passage was less of a pleasure cruise than the previous leg had been. The log tells why:

November 6: Wind backing to NE and rising to force seven. Averaging six knots. Squaresail started to split – a seam high in the middle of the sail opened about a foot. Rolled the sail and set the staysail. Log-line became tangled with fishing line. The Autohelm motor, which we have been using as a wheel brake, fell apart. Seas up to 16-18 feet on the quarter. Breaking seas coming into cockpit. This morning at 3:30, rudder cable broke. Rigged the tiller and hove-to.

November 8: Spliced in a new rudder cable. Had a hell of a time passing rudder cables around the quadrant. Finally succeeded, and got under way at 3 p.m. Two hours later, squaresail split in half, rolled it and set staysail. Still using raffee.

To appreciate the significance of that last entry, remember the rudder quadrant was mounted outboard of the rudder, and was under water much of the time in a stern sea. The cables must be laid in the proper grooves, which required that I hang head down over the taffrail while Velda anxiously sat on my legs to keep me in the boat.

The squaresail Glen Housley had made six years earlier had served us well, but we were overdue for a replacement. I wasn't surprised when it ripped. I knew it was in bad shape, and had ordered a replacement while we were in Mauritius from Cheong Lee in Hong Kong.

Cheong Lee gave us wonderful service. During our trip, we ordered eight sails and an awning for delivery to diverse places such as Puntarenas, Tahiti, South Africa, Noumea and Australia. We were never disappointed.

November 9: Met and spoke to a ship at 1 p.m. Got a position check and a rundown on the latest weather. Wind up to force eight, still running off under the staysail. Took three cockpit–filling waves in rapid succession. Heaved–to at 11:30 a.m. Position 28°10'S, 44°50'E.

November 11: Underway at 5:30 a.m. Northeast wind dropping, seas abating, but southwest sky looks bad. Rigged storm trisail just in case. More problems: Staysail traveler worn out, must be fixed; steering suddenly went slack. Tensioning turnbuckle had backed off, cables came off quadrant again. Unpack lazarette, and do my balancing act over the taffrail again!

Our problems were caused by the uncharted unknown currents we were encountering south of Madagascar. The wind often ran against the current. When that happened, the results were spectacular, and damned uncomfortable.

November 13: Today the staysail halyard block broke. I had to climb the mast twice to fix it. Two days ago, the starboard jib sheet parted. Pressure extremely high, 1032 mb. Wind force 3, noon to noon, 118 miles.

At sea, the water is a dark blue color that reminds me of the blueing my mother used on the family wash and which, it was whispered, my grandmother's friends used on their sparkling white hair. At other times, the water was so dark it reminded me of Scripto ink. I found myself constantly, if mildly, surprised it didn't stain the topsides.

As always, the first indication of shoaling water was when the blue gave way to a dirty pale green. We had been in the dirty water for two hours before the indistinct thread of dark on the western horizon began to take shape.

The recommended approach to Richards Bay is to steer for the St. Lucia light, about 20 miles north of Richards Bay. The reason was because of the current; as you crossed the edge of the African continental shelf, you'd be squarely in the middle of the infamous Agulhas Current. That current, like the Gulf Stream or the Humboldt off the west coast of South America, is a major ocean stream. It is also the most dangerous current in the world.

When a southwesterly gale blows against the current, the Agulhas can develop 80 to 90 foot breaking waves. Many commercial ships and God alone knows how many small craft have been destroyed by such monstrous waves along this coast. If such a wave were to fall on *Prospector*, she would disappear in an instant. There would be no reprieve, no second chance. Knowing this, and because of our experience with that terrible wave near Noumea still fresh in my mind, I watched the barometer and the sky closely as we approached the coast.

My apprehension faded because the wind was fair and was actually smoothing the sea. I only hoped that was a good omen for the official attitude we would shortly encounter. The shore was visible by that time, I turned on the radio and called the harbor master, asking permission to enter the port and for directions.

Harbor Control responded to my call, "You may enter the port. Turn on the first green buoy to your right (none of our familiar "red, right, returning" in Africa; they follow the European buoyage system) and go straight ahead until you see the yellow (quarantine) buoy. You will be met there."

I couldn't find the yellow buoy, but our escort found us and led us to a large commercial wharf where we were told to tie up.

Like the dock in Fiji, this wharf had been rigged with huge tire fenders intended to protect a ship's topsides. The bottoms of the tires reached our lifelines, and a sea breeze was rising that was causing us to grate badly against the cement pilings.

Eventually the officials appeared. The immigration officer was disappointed to learn that we lacked visas — I told him that the South African Consul in Sydney had told us that no visas were issued to people traveling on yachts — and fortunately, I had the mimeographed instruction sheet to prove it. He seemed satisfied with my explanation, and as he began entering the visas in our passports, he looked up and said, "I can put these on a separate piece of paper if you like... ."

I recalled fearing we would not be welcome in South Africa. Yet here the clearing official was offering us the opportunity to conceal from subsequent passport examiners the fact that we had visited his country.

I was embarrassed, but I thanked him for his thoughtfulness, and indicated that it would not be necessary.

I told him, as he left, that I thought we would enjoy our visit to South Africa. He paused as he prepared to climb up to the dock, and smiled. "I'm certain of it," he said.

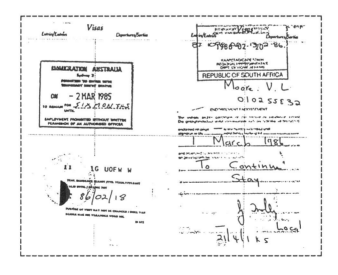

Chapter 16

South Africa

$\mathcal{F}$rom the moment I saw the indistinct coast through the haze, until we arrived at the yacht club, I was overwhelmed by the simple fact that we were in Africa. Whether my feelings were a reaction to years of conditioning by Edgar Rice Burroughs, Alan Paton, Winston Churchill, and Wilbur Smith — or a deeper, more elemental pull, I can't tell you. But it was one of awe and homecoming, as if I were entering a half-forgotten holy place of my childhood.

Shortly after the immigration officials left, a police launch came alongside. An officer called to us to follow them. Unfortunately, the wind by that time had shifted and freshened, and spring lines or no, we were pinned firmly to the dock. Remembering how fragile our taffrail was, I didn't want to try swinging the bow out by backing against a stern spring.

The problem was solved when the police impatiently passed a tow line and yanked us away from the dock. They led us through a confusing series of chambers to a circuitous canal in the northeast quarter of the bay. I kept glancing at the depth finder. We never had more than four feet of water under the keel, and I found myself bracing for what seemed an inevitable grounding.

The police boat swung back and forth across the channel, more or less following a row of PVC pipes sticking out of the water. The officer standing on the fantail kept waving his arm, urging us to increase our speed, but I knew the police boat did not draw nearly as much water as we, and I ignored him, maintaining our stately pace of about three knots. If we were to ground, I wanted it to be as gentle as possible.

We touched twice, but our weight and momentum carried us

over the high spot both times. Later, I learned there was no need for this; they were cutting corners, leading us out of the channel in their haste to complete the assignment and return to the station house, perhaps to an interrupted card game.

We passed a small island on the left, which we later learned harbored a resident troop of wild monkeys. Suddenly, the waterway opened before us. A neat row of yachts moored fore and aft appeared between the channel and the little island. Beyond them, less than a quarter of a mile around the next shallow bend, we saw the masts and buildings of the Zululand Yacht Club. Our escort stopped, waved us past, and with a roar of accelerating engines, wheeled around and rushed back the way we had come.

Approaching the sunken barge that formed the end of the yacht club dock, we saw people waving to us. Prominent among them was the dominant figure of Derek Blair from *HOTTYD*. This was the second time we had left him behind, only to find him waiting when we arrived. After tying up, we walked up the grassy slope past an open boat shed to a cluster of new brick buildings. The largest and newest of these was the yacht club. I introduced myself to the club secretary. She was expecting us. Our guest membership cost 20 rands/month. The mooring was an additional 30 rands/month. Then we discovered the magic economic realities for people with dollars visiting South Africa. While rands and dollars were once roughly equal in value, in 1985 you got two rands to the dollar.

In every respect except one, our situation at the yacht club was ideal. True, there was a large shopping mall near by, if your concept of "nearby" embraced a five-mile radius. The difficulty was that when I was told the stores and banks were "across the street," the phrase was purely rhetorical and was made by a person with a car. But the terms "across the street," "near by," and "easy walking distance" were not synonymous, at least not for me. There were no taxis, but fortunately, many yachties and all the permanent residents had cars. Those with cars were generous, providing free transportation and pick-up service.

Like the rest of the Richards Bay development, the mall was new. It was situated a country mile from the main road, and like many planned communities the world over, was miles from the nearest concentration of people. I doubt whether more than 500 people lived within a one-mile radius of it.

There were severe drawbacks to being an early arrival in a planned community. Buildings were spaced far apart, and there was no convenient or safe way to get from one store to the next because amenities such as sidewalks and street lights were planned to be added later.

The mall was laid out in classic fashion, with a large supermarket anchoring one wing, and the largest of three banks, the Standard Bank, holding down the opposite wing.

Besides the banks, two hardware stores, and a large liquor store, there were several smaller businesses, including a stationery shop, two jewelry stores, men's and women's clothing stores, and a chemist's shop.

The supermarket was a treasure. I'm a supermarket freak, possibly as a result of growing up during the Great Depression when basic nourishment was not always taken for granted by millions of Americans. It may require that sort of background to fully appreciate what a cornucopia a modern supermarket designed and stocked to European standards is, especially one with Dutch emphasis on cleanliness and dairy products. Prices were unbelievably low, even before considering the deep discount resulting from the favorable foreign exchange rate.

Much to my surprise, considering the religious underpinnings of the country, we found the same pricing policy in the liquor store that we found in the supermarket. Except for American Samoa and the U.S. Virgin Islands, this was the only English speaking place we visited where liquor was not taxed almost out of existence. Beer *retailed* for six dollars a case, vodka for two dollars a liter. Everything else, except American whiskey, was priced to scale. The same pricing schedule was followed in the yacht club bar.

The nucleus of any yacht club is the room set aside for casual conviviality and social interaction known as "the bar". And why not? Even in Fiji, where Moslem abstinence was a strong influence, the bar provided a meeting hall, social center, and a comfortable place to hang out.

The bar at the Zululand Yacht Club occupied nearly all the second story of the clubhouse. The bartender, a young Rhodesian named Eddy, had an almost encyclopedic memory and sense of modern southern African history. We spent hours discussing Wilbur Smith's descriptions of the early tribal wars, the Rhodesian conquest, and finally the independence movement culminating in the creation of Zimbabwe.

When you are in a country where the wage scale is reckoned by the day, and your boat has more than its share of brightwork, it seems only prudent to look around for local elbow grease. I made the appropriate inquiries in the bar, and a very active member named Bruce volunteered to help find three local laborers.

Under the law, when you wished to hire local help, you were supposed to go to the Native Labour Board, which would assign laborers and fix their wages. I don't know anyone who complied with that requirement. After all, a system suited to farm work was not necessarily appropriate for boats. Varnishing brightwork was not the same as spreading manure.

Occasionally, we were told, someone made a fuss about the illegal hires around the yacht club. When that happened, the authorities would come to the club and look around. I don't know what sanctions we might have faced had we been caught hiring local labor without the blessing of the Board, but I imagine they would have been much more severe on the hapless workers than on the yachties. On the other hand, we might have been ordered out of the country, which could have been very serious, indeed.

Bruce showed up one day with three young Zulus in tow. I was immediately reminded of Mauritius. Almost illiterate, these young men had powerful linguistic skills I greatly envied. They could barely spell their names, but each had a command of at least three wildly dissimilar languages. The ability to communicate accurately and effectively is undoubtedly an important key to survival for laborers in a multilingual society. That would be especially true where the economic scales were tilted so cruelly against those at the bottom of the ladder. As a native tongue, they spoke a Zulu dialect. I heard them speak fluent Afrikaans with our mutual friend, and they had sufficient English so we were able to communicate effectively.

Very likely, bright outgoing young men like those spoke other Zulu dialects, and the African *lingua franca*, or trade language. It's also possible they had a smattering of Portuguese, considering how close we were to Mozambique.

They carried brown paper folders which they shyly offered for my inspection. Those were the hated internal passports. I was embarrassed as I waved them aside.

382

Knowing the going rate for labor was eight rands per day, I offered them ten. We were expected to provide lunch as part of the bargain, and that consisted of a loaf of bread, a pot of jam, and tea or Coke. They consumed a full loaf of bread, half a pint of jam and two six-packs of Coke every day. They started slowly. None of them had worked on yachts before, but they were anxious to learn.

Christopher, who quickly assumed the foreman's role, was a strong featured young man, with a friendly good-natured grin. The oldest man, Sofney, was not as trusting as the younger men, but he was more spontaneous. Often, in mid-morning, he would begin singing. The others would laugh in delight, and quickly join in. Oliver, taller than the others and possibly the youngest, had an attitude problem. I'm not sure why, but I thought he might have outranked Christopher at home, and resented his leadership. Whatever it was, eventually I had to let him go. Their initial shyness wore off quickly, and soon we were enjoying each other's company.

I was surprised to find that they were afraid of heights, and even more surprised that they were not reluctant to admit it. I persuaded Christopher to sit in the bo'sun's chair while his mates hauled him aloft on the main mast, but I am certain nothing could have induced him to go up the topmast.

I don't know where they lived. I believe they traveled a good way to come to work. They arrived at daylight by bus every morning. I assume it was the same bus that carried them away in the late afternoon.

Although work on the boat was going well, things were not as amicable in the club. Strains were developing between us foreigners and some club members. This was the first year the government had encouraged significant numbers of foreign yachts to call in Richards Bay instead of going to Durban.

Consequently, the membership was divided on the sudden and, to them unexpected, invasion by foreign yachts. Some members, mostly those with the larger boats, empathized with the visitors, and tried to be as helpful as possible. But the board sailors were in the majority and mostly considered themselves seriously inconvenienced by our presence.

I don't mean that we faced overt hostility. On the contrary, except a temporary *contretemps* involving the New Year's Booze Cruise, none of the internal squabbling spilled over on us, but we heard about it from Eddy.

I think the complaining members may have lost sight of the government's *quid pro quo*. The entire Richards Bay complex, including the port, warehouses, rail terminals, and yacht club, was only about five years old. In exchange for keeping on eye on things and providing a temporary home for transient yachts (keeping track of them, and keeping them out of Durban, in other words), the government had granted a favorable lease on land belonging to the National Railway. The government also had built the slipway, and subsidized the construction of the new clubhouse. None of this, except the bar, meant much to the board sailors, many of whom found it easier and cheaper to keep their craft in their backyards.

Thanksgiving was approaching, and these problems were put aside for the moment. On the whole, South Africans seemed to like Americans. American movies, periodicals, and fashions were popular in South Africa, just as English movies, periodicals and fashions were important to New Zealanders.

Consequently, when some American ladies prevailed on the club authorities and the cook, a bouncy Canadian woman named Shirley, to allow them access to the kitchen so they could prepare a traditional Thanksgiving dinner, Shirley couldn't resist the idea, and the club Secretary gave his blessing.

In the meanwhile, several friends had arrived. *Atair II* had arrived in Richards Bay shortly before we did, coming down the Mozambique Channel. Klaus and Babs had a very difficult and stormy passage crossing the Indian Ocean.

John and Wendy Ettish on *Bali Ha'i* arrived after we did, and *Curlew* sailed into Richards Bay shortly after that. Tim and Pauline anchored a short way from our mooring. Before we left Richards Bay, Tim had replaced a guardrail on *Prospector*, and Pauline had assumed a major role in the clubhouse galley, helping prepare the Thanksgiving dinner.

I hope we began a tradition. We yachties contributed two dollars apiece, and an open invitation was extended to our South African hosts. Several attended as our guests. Dinner was served to about 100 people that afternoon. As the oldest American present, I gave a little talk explaining to our South African and European guests the origin and meaning of Thanksgiving in America.

A month later, the German contingent which was about as large as the American, again with Shirley's enthusiastic cooperation, sponsored the Christmas dinner. I well remember the candlelight tableau the Germans presented.

Our workers had not been left out. On Christmas Eve, when they arrived on the job, they were carrying gifts of fruit. After lunch, we had another round of Cokes and distributed our gifts to them. Velda had bought inexpensive digital watches for Softney and Oliver, and a Swiss Army knife for Christopher, who already owned a watch.

Velda had wrapped the gifts in traditional Christmas paper. To our surprise, they were reluctant to open their gifts in front of us. But we were selfish enough to want to see their reactions, and eventually after much urging, they peeked into their packages.

Sofney's reaction was the strongest. He made a tiny hole in a corner of his package. When he realized it contained a watch, his face lit up, and he clapped his hands in joy.

A week after Christmas, the yacht club was host to the annual Booze Cruise, otherwise known as the Durban–Richards Bay Ocean Race. It was a three day bash, complete with circus tent, rock and roll bands, and cultural diversions such as a massive tug of war and a wet T-shirt contest. This was a South African event.

At first, the visiting yachties were asked to stay away. But that seemed a bit churlish, and soon more charitable attitudes prevailed. Derek was a great asset to the home tug-of-war team, and Suki became a bellwether for the wet T-shirt contest, encouraging other local women by example, much to the scandalized horror of her two adolescent children, Thiana and Clough, to compete against those hussies from Durban.

I missed it because it coincided almost to the minute with the top of the highest tide of the month. Because of *Prospector's* draft, that was the only chance we had all month to haul her. Bruce, the chap who had helped us find laborers, operated the slipway.

I have seen *Prospector* taken out of the water in many ways, but this was new. The method was a cross between the traditional marine railway and an ordinary cement boat ramp.

A big, well anchored, single drum diesel-powered winch housed in a small shed on the bank provided the necessary pull. But instead of hauling a boat cradle rolling on railway tracks, the vehicle used here was a massively overgrown, eight-wheel boat trailer mounted on truck tires. The trailer was about 12 feet wide and 16 feet long, constructed of heavy steel "I" beams.

A heavy vertical frame of structural steel braced by stout hardwood timbers formed a railing rising about 12 feet above the trailer bed on its port side.

The procedure was simple. The trailer was rolled down the ramp into the water as far as it would go. Then the boat was floated over it and lashed to the frame rising above the water, which positioned the boat properly over the trailer.

While I was lashing *Prospector* to the frame, I heard the rumble of the idling diesel engine in the winch shed. When all was ready, Bruce opened the throttle and stepped on the clutch. Boat and trailer moved simultaneously toward the beach. Gently, the keel came into contact with the cross members of the trailer. Then Bruce stopped the winch and set the brake. Taking heavy wooden blocks, he swam under the boat and drove them between the keel and the trailer frame, distributing the load.

Now when he engaged the clutch, I could hear the diesel begin to growl with effort, and feel the trailer lurch forward as it took more and more of the load. Standing on the deck, I could also feel the boat begin to rise out of the water.

We stopped twice more while Bruce adjusted the blocking before the boat was removed completely from the water. Satisfied with our final position, Bruce set blocking between the boat's worm shoe and the ground, and drove big wedges into the blocking to take some weight off the trailer.

Prospector looked top-heavy perched up on that relatively narrow trailer. Mindful of the frequent sou'westerly gales on this coast, and remembering the fate of the boats up on the hard in Papeete during Hurricane *Veena*, I passed three long anchor lines from the crosstrees to windward where they were made fast to convenient trees.

Our Zulu laborers were excited to see what their boat looked like out of the water. She is an impressive sight, rather like a wooden iceberg. She has over 500 square feet of wetted surface. Her massive underwater configuration accounts for her stability, and explained her nimble recovery from the knockdown in the Western Pacific in 1984. But with that much drag, in light air we need the 1,200 feet of sail we carry in our full fore and aft rig.

We were out of the water for our customary ten days. Our

workers did a first rate job after they understood what was needed. But there was a problem. I could not get them to understand that the blue bottom paint was dangerous. I tried to explain it in English, and asked Bruce to explain it in Afrikaans. Tommy, the old Zulu night watchman, also tried to explain. None of it seemed to make an impression. They refused to wear the masks I had bought in Durban.

Finally I decided to have them wet sand the hull. At least that way they wouldn't be breathing the dust. They thought wet sanding was wonderful. I think they competed to see whose skin could become the most colorful, because I saw Christopher rub his torso against the wet hull. I sent them to the showers at least twice a day. They used a fresh bar of soap on the job every day.

The boat went back into the water on schedule, and ten days later, we said goodby to Christopher, the last of our workers. Knowing that Christopher had two sons, Velda had bought two toy dump trucks for them as a parting gift.

Christopher was moved when he understood the toys were for his children. We shook hands, and he walked slowly toward the gate, turned and waved. We waved back. He walked on a few more steps, turned and waved again. We waved back. We ex-changed waves five or six times before he turned the corner.

Two days earlier, I had learned a basic lesson about the relationships between blacks and whites in that tormented land. A young white South African lad named Sean had asked to join us for the passage around the Cape of Good Hope to Cape Town. He told us he was a 21 year old Navy veteran who needed a little additional sea time to complete the requirements for a coastal captain's license. He seemed a likely enough young man, and besides, he had a car. We took him on. The next thing I knew, Christopher was washing his car. *What the hell is this?* I asked myself.

"Christopher," I called, "why are you washing that car?"
"Boss tole me," Christopher said.

Sean was genuinely perplexed when I spoke to him about the incident. He could not understand why I thought it was inappropriate. In his world, white people drove cars and black people washed them. It was the natural order of things.

With the boat back in the water, and our annual refit completed, we thought about visiting the Kruger Game Park. It would have been an overnight trip, possibly longer, so we decided against it. We had animals to babysit.

Still, we made several overnight trips to Durban, and on one especially memorable occasion, we spent an evening at Stewart's Farm, 40 miles from Richards Bay.

That excursion was arranged by the yacht club. Two American friends, Al and Rita, circumnavigating in a small but shippy sloop named *Baroness,* had rented a car, and they invited us to accompany them to the farm. We had no idea what to expect. We knew only that the evening's entertainment cost 20 rands and included supper. But we were eager to see as much of the countryside as possible, so we accepted their kind invitation.

We left Richards Bay in the late afternoon and drove south on the main highway for about an hour. Rita was reading the directions, and told Al when to turn onto a secondary road. We followed that road for a mile, then took a left on a dirt track that abruptly ended in front of a waist-high growth of grass.

As soon as the car stopped, even before Al could turn off the ignition, we were ambushed by five young girls ranging in age from about 14 to 17, wearing only brief leather aprons and broad smiles. They jumped to their feet, waving their arms, shrieking "*Welcome, welcome*" in English and Zulu. The oldest girl – she might have been 16 or 17 – was truly beautiful, with classic features and a stunning figure.

We were helped from the car and led up the path 100 yards to the kraal, where we were invited to sit on a log near the cooking fire. Looking around, I saw several *rondavals*, as beehive huts are called in Afrikaans, of different sizes, and a larger oval hut on the opposite side of the fire. An old woman wearing a high flat-topped hat resembling a dark felt chef's hat, a vest and a leather skirt, was stirring the bubbling contents of a pot set in the embers of the fire. She paid no attention to us.

The sun was nearly gone when the girls escorted the last of the late-comers to the seating logs. Mr. Stewart, our host, asked for our attention. After thanking us for coming, he explained that we were sharing an authentic evening in a traditional Zulu kraal.

He then introduced Thomas, the chief, who wore his ceremonial costume, and carried his ox-hide shield and stabbing sword. His headdress had bits of lion mane worked into it. As Stewart explained, his costume was intended to intimidate the enemy.

"Young girls wear those aprons," he went on, "until they are married. Then they must cover their breasts and wear longer skirts." He explained the traditional significance of the clothing worn by the older women.

By this time it was very dark. The only illumination was from the cooking fire. A group of villagers filed out of a hut and sat around the fire. The singing and dancing began. The young girls danced in unison, then each performed a short solo. The boys — none of them older than ten — gave their interpretation of the elephant dance. One enthusiastic youngster stamped his bare foot so hard he was thrown off balance and fell in the dust.

We were invited into the large hut and given millet beer and offered native food. We were also given liberal quantities of wine that was far more intoxicating than the beer.

After we returned to the sitting logs, a witch doctor, possibly the most disheveled person I have ever seen; it was impossible to guess whether it was a man or woman, crept to the fire. It was too dark to see what the person was doing, but sulphur or gunpowder was thrown on the flames which flared up in strange brilliant colors.

Stewart maintained a running commentary, so low-keyed that the experience became almost real. After the performance, I was asked to say a few words on behalf of the assembled yachties to Thomas, the chief, expressing our appreciation for his kindness in receiving us and showing us their way of life. I'm sure our glimpse into a traditional Zulu kraal was contrived in the sense that much of what we saw mirrored the past rather than the present.

Mr. Stewart denied it, explaining that while Thomas's warrior's costume was historic, the remainder of the tableau was strictly contemporary. Perhaps he was right, but I wish we had seen Christopher's kraal.

The only males present were young boys and the chief, probably in his mid-50s. Nobody explained the peculiar absence of the men, and I felt it would not be polite to ask. The absence of males inadvertently may have authenticated the evening entertainment. My guess is that the men were away working as contract laborers. After the performance, we were invited into Mr. Stewart's store where we paid the fee and bought souvenirs.

By chance, we saw another facet of the South African puzzle almost immediately after our visit to Stewart's farm. A young South

African housewife, whose sideline was selling Italian–made gold chains, struck up a conversation with Velda at the yacht club bar. Shortly after meeting Sally, Velda learned that her husband, Angus, was on leave from an anti–terrorist unit of the South African Army, recovering from a leg wound.

Soon the four of us were having drinks in the bar, and the next day we and their two lovely little daughters had a picnic on Monkey Island, directly behind our mooring, where, to the delight of the little girls, we coaxed wild monkeys out of the brush with bits of banana.

By that time, Angus knew I had also been a patient in military hospitals. I suppose it was that similarity that drew them to us. Combat veterans, especially those with bullet and shrapnel scars, share an unspoken camaraderie that seems to transcend geography and time. I saw the trouble in Angus's eyes, and the way he held his mouth. It was obvious he had serious emotional problems.

Angus at the Christmas party

When he spoke about his experiences, I understood his pain and shared his feeling of hopelessness and frustration. His war was far from over, and it was plain he did not expect to reach old age. He hated the black terrorists so desperately that tragically, he was beginning to hate all black people. Whatever other costs may be reckoned against the tragic price of apartheid, the loss of Angus's generation is one South Africa cannot afford.

South Africa is a police state. We heard South Africans describe it that way. Although we were free to travel, yacht club visits were not optional. A person accustomed to utilizing yacht club facilities might not have noticed the difference, but for us, this was a new experience. Local boats were equally restricted in their movements, and were required to maintain a yacht club affiliation, so the government could keep an eye on them.

The key to understanding governmental policy, at least at our level, could be summed up in a single word: *control*. Immigration officers are called Passport *Control* officers. You will deal with the harbor *control* office instead of the harbor master's office.

I believe such exaggerated concern about yachts and the methods chosen for controlling them reflects both a lack of understanding of maritime affairs and a rural bias on the part of the Afrikaner National Party, which has dominated the country for the past forty years and is responsible for the insane apartheid laws.

The country was divided by a number of issues. Scars left by the Boer War, like those from our Civil War, have endured for generations. They divide the rural, God–fearing Dutch, or Afrikaners as they prefer to be called, from the more urban English "speakers" who live in coastal cities like Durban and Cape Town and on farms on the Indian Ocean.

The black members of the society are fragmented and divided along tribal, occupational and geographic lines, although the Zulu nation is by far the largest cohesive group in South Africa. The demented apartheid laws have artificially subdivided most South Africans into a potpourri of groupings based primarily and arbitrarily on skin color. Officially, they are White, Bantu, Colored, and Asian.

To aid our understanding of the country, several South Africans urged us to read *The Covenant* by James A. Michener, who repeats the story in his book about Joshua Slocum's encounter during his circumnavigation with Paul Kruger, then President of the Transvaal. Kruger supposedly accused Slocum of blasphemy and denounced him as a heretic for insisting that the world was round. If true, it's worth remembering that it occurred less than 100 years ago. Even today, the relationship between the government and the Dutch Reformed Church is very close. Religion, like control, overlies everything.

On our first trip to Durban, I watched for the kind of racial segregation and discrimination that appears to be endemic in America, but I saw something quite different. I hasten to add a caveat, however, because my observations were limited to only cursory glances at a very small part of the total population in cities with strong English traditions. I realize they were hardly typical of what one might expect to see in Sowato, or on the border where Angus's war was being fought.

In the United States, segregation and discrimination is illegal, but covertly permeates the society. Conversely, discrimination and segregation are legally obligatory in South Africa, but the most striking thing I saw was that paradoxically, casual interactions between whites and blacks in Durban, and to a lesser extent in Cape Town, were remarkable for their courtesy and genuine friendliness.

Despite the ravages of 40 years of apartheid, and Angus's travails notwithstanding, the Africans we saw in the city respected and liked each other without reference to skin color or social status. Thus, while housing, public education and public toilets were segregated, I saw no discrimination in public transportation, restaurants, stores, or theaters.

The Richards Bay–Durban bus dropped us off in the middle of the downtown business district. We met it for the return trip to Richards Bay at 4:30 p.m. sharp at the curb in front of Woolworth's in the heart of downtown Durban. Everything we needed – marine hardware stores, the yacht club, chart stores, and the American Consulate – was within easy walking distance from the bus stop.

At first, we had gone to Durban for paint and other supplies in preparation for the haulout. Bottom paint was very cheap. We were using Micron 33. It was a top-of-the line product that listed in the United States for $175 a gallon, and sold in U.S. discount stores such as *Boat U.S.* for $108. We paid 25 rands/liter, or about $50/gallon for it in Durban. Other hardware made in South Africa was equally inexpensive. But if we asked for gear of American or European origin however, the clerk would smile apologetically and say, "I'm sorry, but with the embargo... ." as if it was his fault. It was embarrassing.

It was on one of those earlier trips that we ran into Roger and Molly near the yacht club. They had elected to skip Richards Bay and go directly to Durban. So had several other friends. They showed us the dock where foreign yachts were accommodated.

It was a barge about 50x100 feet, with 30 small sailboats of different nationalities rafted alongside. It was a terrible mess, and couldn't be compared to the mooring we had in Richards Bay. Larger boats like *Le Papillion* anchored out on the flats, away from commercial traffic, but where they were exposed to the frequent gales that sweep up the coast from the Southern Ocean. *Sundowner*, at 32 feet, was small enough so she could remain at the dock.

Roger knew what a dollar was worth, and had the same interest in good food as Gary Parker. So when he and Molly urged us to join them for dinner, we were glad to accept. The restaurant they selected was a pleasant but ordinary appearing steak house. The menus had that slick plastic appearance characteristic of roadside family restaurants throughout the United States. Also like them, the entrées were reasonably priced. Velda ordered a filet mignon, while I settled for a T-bone steak.

Roger knew what to expect, of course, and was amused at my reaction when the food arrived. I was astounded. My steak was an *enormous* slab of meat. It smothered the plate and was at least two inches thick. It probably weighed more than two pounds. It was perfectly cooked to my taste; somewhat charred on the outside, a succulent, glistening pink on the inside.

I've read about Japanese beef where the animals are fed beer and given daily massages. The texture of this meat was probably similar. It was firm and resisted cutting with a butter knife or the edge of the fork, but it yielded easily to a table knife, and had the mouth-watering flavor found only in properly aged meat.

Unbelievably, I ate the whole thing. I also ate the potato, the mushrooms, the salad and everything else I was offered. It was a superb dinner, and it cost only 15 rands.

Another overnight trip was made to Durban so we could attend Chris Bonnet's lecture on rounding the Cape of Good Hope. The lecture makes clear why "Good Hope" expresses a wish concerning the Cape's *real* name: the Cape of Storms. Chris operated a book store, and has had enormous experience on that coast. He offered the lecture as a public service to anyone contemplating the trip. He knows every bolt-hole, rock, and current in those waters. He has also seen the tragic results of carelessness, bad preparation, and inexperience. His respect for the Agulhas Current bordered on the religious.

I made still another trip to Durban to clear a shipment from England. I had ordered a long list of marine hardware from Thomas Foulkes, Ltd. including chain, a new toilet, rigging, etc.

It shouldn't be a hassle to clear freight shipments consigned to *YACHT-IN-TRANSIT*, but invariably it was. Although those precise words on a bill of lading have specific meaning, understood by customs *agents* everywhere, they are not commonly seen by suspicious customs *officers*. Therefore, to clear a shipment, it was necessary to present myself and our ship's papers, with a customs agent who (for a fee) would vouch for me. The procedure varied, but the suspicions were constant. The South African procedure seemed especially convoluted, and required both my and the agent's presence in the red brick Customs House most of the morning when the container where my shipment was stowed was opened.

Agents (brokers) don't work cheaply, but they do the paper work, and there are usually tons of it. In this case, they also arranged for up-country shipping. It would have been impossible to carry a marine toilet, 100 meters of three-eighths inch chain, and a crate of lines and miscellaneous plunder on the bus to Richards Bay.

Clearing from a South African port was even more difficult than entering. Many yachts leaving Richards Bay or Durban cleared for Port Elizabeth, 400 miles south of Richards Bay. I didn't want to make any intermediate stops, and even if I had, the mind-numbing bureaucratic procedures required every time you enter or clear a South African port would have discouraged me.

To give you a flavor of it, obtaining our clearance in Richards Bay involved visits to four different offices scattered around the port, where the clearing officer stamped, signed, sealed or approved my stated intention. Unfortunately, the appropriate officer was not always available. He might be on a ship, out to lunch, or even on leave. If it hadn't been for a kind young woman who lived aboard a neighboring trimaran and owned a battered old Chevy, I might be still wandering around Richards Bay working my way through the bureaucratic thicket.

South Africa was the only country we visited that still used sealing wax on official documents. I watched the officer melt the wax on our clearance certificate, and press the seal into the warm wax with much the same feeling I had watching the witch doctor at Stewart's farm.

After the *external* documentation was completed, I had to get my *internal* clearances by doubling back to the yacht club for a statement that all fees had been paid, then to the Harbor Control office where the harbor dues were paid.

At last, with the sheaf of clearance documents in hand, I climbed the hill to the Signals Office at the radio station so that Signals would know we were legally cleared and would know when we planned to leave the port.

Following Chris Bonnet's advice, we left Richards Bay on a

favorable three-day forecast. We motored from the yacht club through the maze of PVC pipes until we came to the breakwater. Then, with a final approval from Signals, we left Richards Bay. It was 10:35 a.m., January 24, 1986.

Chris also recommended using a thermometer to find water with a temperature of at least 25°C, which would indicate we were in the middle of the Agulhas Current. An hour after we cleared the breakwater, by the time we reached water of that temperature, presumably the middle of the current, our speed had almost doubled. The Agulhas was flowing south at about four knots, and the first 24 hours, we made an astounding 191 miles over the ground.

The most important thing, on this coast, was to keep a close eye on the barometer, because this coast was particularly prone to fast-moving, tight and very intense low pressure systems that appeared almost without warning and generated instant gales. A falling barometer was your only warning, and I had carefully calibrated our glass with Signals when we left Richards Bay.

Chris had hammered on this point repeatedly. If the glass began falling, *sail inshore*; get out of the current as quickly as possible, because a 60-knot southwesterly gale blowing against a three or four knot current could produce the infamous Agulhas waves that, while not an everyday occurrence, were responsible for the loss of thousands of tons of merchant shipping on that coast.

Carefully following Chris's recommendations, we steered a course about 20 miles offshore, approximately in the middle of the current. That far off, we couldn't see much of the African coast because, like the coast of New South Wales, it is mostly low-lying and nondescript. That's one reason why this stretch is so dangerous. There are no capes to duck behind if the weather should turn sour.

It was a long way to Port Elizabeth from East London, and there is no place to hide in between. Therefore, as we approached East London, it was important to consider whether the glass was falling, and if it was, how fast. If the rate of fall was one millibar per hour or more, we were to shelter in East London and wait for another favorable forecast. On the other hand, if the pressure was at least 1012 millibars, and was steady or falling only at the rate of one millibar every *four* hours, it was safe to continue on to Port Elizabeth.

I foolishly assumed that Sean had told the truth about his

background; therefore, since he had nearly completed the requirements for his coastwise ticket and was a Navy veteran to boot, I
think it was not unreasonable to assume he would know simple
things, such as how to read a compass and steer the boat. It turned
out, however, that he had no more idea about steering by the
compass than a hog knows about Sunday.

During the morning hours of his first solo watch, while Velda
and I trustingly slept, Sean steered us east of the current and into
dark oceanic water, thirty miles from our projected course. Luckily
the weather was good. Otherwise, we could have been in trouble.

It was foggy the next morning. The wind slowly died away, and
by evening we were becalmed although we had managed to work
our way back into the green current. We started the engine at dusk,
and when it was completely dark, I saw far in the distance the Bird
Island light outside Port Elizabeth. I raised Port Elizabeth on the
radio, and up–dated our "float" plan, after identifying ourselves to
the port authorities. Then I was given a new weather bulletin.
Things still looked good.

But 24 hours later, during the night of the 27th, we saw
considerable lightning in the southwestern sky. The glass looked
good. It was steady at 1018, well above Chris's doomsday reading of
1012. We were close inshore, and saw the Cape Francis light as we
sailed past. At daylight, the wind abruptly veered from the southeast
to the southwest, and began strengthening. Also, the glass began to
fall. After tacking for several hours against the rising wind, I decided
it might be better to run back to Cape Francis and wait for more
favorable weather.

According to the chart, if you entered Francis Bay from the
southwest, you needed to give the light a 200 yard clearance to
safely clear a reef extending to the northeast.

Chris had warned that in this instance, the chart was wrong. The
reef extends not 200 yards from the light as shown on the chart, but
three times that far. If you followed the chart in the dark, you would
surely strike it!

I find it odd that a dangerous error of that magnitude would go
uncorrected on charts issued by a country with such a meticulous
and precise attitude about most things. Perhaps, like their yacht
policies, this was another result of the government's *landbouer*
orientation, which seems committed to the idea that the known

396

world ends at the high water mark. We gave the reef a wide berth, glad that it wasn't dark, and ran inside Francis Bay toward the shore. We were still half a mile from the beach when the depth finder showed 20 feet. It was getting dark by that time, and we weren't planning to go ashore, I decided to drop the anchor. Then I rigged the anchor light and we settled in for the night.

By morning, it was blowing half a gale out of the southwest. Though the fetch was causing us a moderate roll, I was content to sit tight. This bay was tricky, and I remembered an episode involving it reported by the late Eric Hiscock in his book, *Come Aboard*.

Like us, he and Susan in *Wanderer IV*, had sought shelter in Francis Bay, but they had gone further in, across a shallow bar and into a small stream where they became landlocked. It required several months and the use of heavy road building machinery before they could extricate themselves. From our anchorage, I could see the stream mouth as Eric had described it.

Shortly before noon, a small runabout carrying a woman and two men came alongside. "We thought you might like this," the woman said, holding out a plastic bag. I took it and passed it to Velda who opened it and peered inside.

"Thank you," Velda said. "This is very kind." To me she added, "look, a liter of milk, fruit, and a loaf of bread."

We invited our benefactors aboard and thanked them again.

"Well," the young woman said, "we saw you anchored out here. We realized it had probably been several days since you'd had any fresh milk, so we thought we'd bring some out. I'm sorry we couldn't get fresh eggs, but the store was out... ."

Another example of the spontaneous hospitality we enjoyed so much in South Africa. Our guests spent an hour with us telling us about this part of the country.

Early the next morning, the wind abruptly switched back to the northeast. We hauled the anchor with some difficulty, since it was wedged in a rocky bottom, and tore a fluke in the process.

Because the wind was fair, we set the squaresail, and were on our way. We had a good run all day and the following night, but the wind died at first light. We struck the squaresail and set the fore and aft rig. I had a powerful feeling that we were in for another south-wester, and I was right. Luckily we were close to Cape St. Blaize, guarding Mossel Bay (or Mosselbaai as it appears on the South African charts) when the wind reached 35 knots. We quickly ducked around the Cape and into the bay.

Instead of finding another rural settlement similar to Francis Bay, I was surprised to see a huge cement seawall that looked exactly like a medieval fortress inside this bay. From the water, we saw a portion of the town rising on a series of low hills behind the wall. The harbor looked crowded. Besides, I wanted to make this as informal as possible. The lower the profile, the better, since we weren't cleared for Mossel Bay, and I didn't know what kind of welcome we might encounter if the authorities found we were there. So instead of going in behind the seawall, we ran around it and anchored in front of the local yacht club.

Sean and I decided to go ashore. We were nearly out of eggs, and we could always use more grog. We put the dinghy in the water. When we drew near the shore, I realized why the seawall had been built. A strong back swell was running and we had a hell of a time landing without getting wet. As we were tying the boat to the dock, a man stepped around the corner of the club house.

Nodding toward *Prospector*, he asked, "You off her?"

We nodded. Then he said, "I suppose you'd like a shower." It was a statement, not a question. We nodded again.

"Well," he said, "club ain't open on week days; just week ends." Then he grinned slyly. "But I got a key." We followed him around the corner, and he opened the club house door into a dressing room. A propane water heater was mounted on the wall opposite the door. He turned a valve. I heard the pop of igniting fuel.

"Shower's in the next room," he said. Then, pointing to a cabinet, he added, "That's where we keep the towels." Then, as he was walking out, he said over his shoulder, "Lock up when you're through." We never saw him again. I never before had been offered the use of facilities as freely as that. It was just another example of the hospitality we encountered throughout South Africa.

Refreshed, we hiked up the hill into town. This was my first visit to a rural Afrikaner community. Most of the older buildings had two entrances, one for whites and one for blacks. On our return to the beach, we saw a large sign advising all blacks and coloreds that it was illegal for them to bathe on that beach. The sign looked new; it wasn't a relic of an earlier day.

We left Mossel Bay the next morning, though the radio was warning of gale force winds at Cape Agulhas 120 miles ahead. By now, we were well clear of the Agulhas Current which had spread out over several hundred square miles of shoals. My concern now was avoiding being trapped in a southerly gale. It seemed best to stand well offshore until we rounded Cape Agulhas, the southern-most tip of the African Continent. From there, it was only 60 miles to the Cape of Good Hope, which officially divides the Indian and Atlantic Oceans and is the cape for which Cape Town was named.

This 100-mile stretch of coast is one of a half dozen places in the world where massive quantities of cold, nutrient-rich water are lifted to the surface by great warm water currents. Those nutrients are exposed to the sun, resulting in enormous blooms of algae at the base of the marine food chain. These so-called "upwelling" areas are huge protein factories, generating the growth of a rich diversity of marine life.

The variety and quantity of seabirds was astonishing. We referred constantly to our copy of Harrison's *Seabirds*. I was particularly intrigued to note that here, gannets fly in formations, and seemed wilder than their cousins in New Zealand, where those spectacular birds hunt alone. We also saw scores of seals, which might account for the bird's wariness. I've never seen a seal catch a bird, but that doesn't mean it doesn't happen.

We stood so far offshore that we didn't even *see* Cape Agulhas. The weather was partly to blame; visibility was severely restricted in fog, and a fine drizzle fell much of the time. At night, it was impossible to see anything, and you could never be sure whether that was because nothing was there, or because the mist and fog was hiding it.

The only vessels we saw were South African fishing boats. Commercial shipping probably stayed further offshore, which suited me fine. As it grew light that morning, much to my surprise, we found we had passed Cape Agulhas, and were outside False Bay. We were moving much faster now than the engine's 1500 RPMs warranted. Almost before we realized it, we were crossing the mouth of Haut Bay, only 20 miles from the Cape Town. Minutes later — much too soon, I thought, — we came face-to-face with Green Point light-house at the entrance to Cape Town, whose great fog horn both welcomes and warns anxious mariners.

Later I realized we had gotten a powerful lift from the mighty Benguela Current, which sweeps from the Southern Ocean along the western flank of Southern Africa as a lesser stream might brush against a boulder in a stream.

The Green Point horn was silent the morning of our arrival; the weather was bright and clear, and strangely, the wind was calm. I called the authorities on our radio, asking permission to enter the port, and for berthing instructions.

We were directed to M Dock, there to pick up a stern mooring and to tie ourselves bow in to the quay. I acknowledged the instructions, and we began searching for M Dock.

Except for the silhouette of Table Mountain overshadowing the city, Cape Town looked like every seaport we had entered during the previous four years. Dirty, congested, and confusing.

We motored uncertainly into the turning basin. Many ships, including foreign stern trawlers, were tied along the main wharf in the shadow of a dozen huge, long-legged, gantry cranes. As we turned into the inner harbor, a police boat idled alongside.

Making a megaphone with my hands, I yelled across to the officer on the foredeck, "Can you direct me to M Dock?"

The policeman pointed to the far end of the main wharf. "It's there by the Navy Yard, where those sailboats are," he said.

I thanked him. I couldn't see a Navy Yard, but through the binoculars, I saw two sailboats tied in a dead end where the main wharf ended. Beyond them, I saw a thicket of masts.

When we drew near, I saw that M Dock was a short dock perpendicular to the main wharf, which provided a base for two long finger piers parallel to the main wharf. Seen from the air, the long main wharf, M Dock, and the nearest finger pier would have resembled a gigantic squared letter J, with M Dock at the bottom of the letter. We found a row of small conical buoys, about 50 feet apart and roughly 150 feet from the dock. These moorings, we later learned, had been installed the previous year to accommodate the boats in the Whitbread Around the World Race.

We found our assigned stern mooring. We stopped. I bent a line on the mooring and stationed Sean on the starboard quarter, explaining that he was to check our forward progress by snubbing that stern line on the king post when I gave the word.

We had plenty of time. Table Bay was flat calm. There wasn't a breath of air stirring. The nearest moving boat was the police launch, a quarter of a mile away and moving away from us. Certain that everything was under control, I returned to the cockpit and engaged the clutch. It was now, in the shadow of Table Mountain, that Sean distinguished himself. As I write this, I have trouble believing it really happened.

One of the boat's best structural features, the one that saved Velda's life in the Pacific, was the dog house. But the dog house was not designed with close maneuvering in mind. I'm of average height, but when the cabin top was blanketed by the dinghy and with the furled mainsail and gaff bulking high above that, my forward visibility was practically nil.

I found it best, in those circumstances, to stand on the wheel box and steer with my feet. That way, I could see both sides of the boat and, with limitations, what lay ahead. The problem was, I couldn't reach the throttle and clutch from that position. They were mounted low in the cockpit beneath the steering wheel.

Instead of watching Sean over my shoulder, I was watching the quay and the big boat on my port side. When I judged it was time to take the way off her, I jumped down and as I bent over to shift the clutch into reverse, I sang out, "Snub her down!"

But Sean didn't have any line to snub. The line I had bent on the mooring was too short. Rather than say anything, he had let the bitter end slide through his fingers and go overboard.

Twenty-four tons of boat in motion was not easily stopped. Desperately, I pushed the throttle wide open, causing our stern to swing gently into the big boat on our port side, but with no discernible effect whatever on our forward speed. We speared the cement quay with our sturdy 12 foot bowsprit. The shock of that impact carried back to our deck furniture, the twin madeira sampson posts absorbing most of it. One post snapped off flush with the deck; the other split in half.

I was so upset that I noticed, but paid little attention to the skipper of the big blue boat we had brushed against. His face was crimson with choleric rage, and he screamed at me at the top of his lungs. Poor Paddy. I understand he died in mid-ocean a few weeks later, much to the great consternation of his crew. Perhaps it was that wicked temper that did him in.

I had ideas along those lines for Sean when it was suitably dark, but once again, he was a jump ahead of me. Before I could kill him, I had to check in with the authorities. I hurried through those procedures as quickly as possible and returned to the boat only to find that Sean had departed. I never saw him again.

Sean was a poor shipmate from the beginning. While we were tip-toeing south near Port Elizabeth, I saw in him what I suspect may be a new and perhaps unforseen additional penalty to South Africa arising out of apartheid. Sean was a sturdy young man, and looked strong and physical, but he was unaccustomed to exertion. His approach to a heavy lift was dainty and awkward. While it's possible that this might just have been Sean, it might also have been the inevitable result of always having had someone with a darker skin nearby to do the heavy lifting and serious sweating.

He was a product of middle-class South African society. Personable and well mannered, he was the sort of young man people think of as a credit to his parents. But if Sean was typical of his generation and social status, then between his indolence and the corrosive hatred Angus had developed, I think South Africa's leaders have much more to worry about than merely how to untangle the barbed thicket of apartheid.

Although we didn't notice it at first, the policeman was at least partly correct. To an Afrikaner policeman, it might have looked like a yard, but to my eyes, the Navy "Yard" directly across the quay from our berth more closely resembled a small Coast Guard station. Surrounded by a chain-link fence, its most conspicious feature was a small two-story barracks housing possibly 25 men. There was also a repair shed and a small dock. Three PT-size patrol craft were tied to the dock. From our berth, you walked along the quay 100 yards or so toward town, then turned left and walked an additional 200 yards past the Navy Yard, to the Royal Cape Yacht Club in whose care *Prospector* had been consigned.

After clearing with the officials, I walked down to the yacht club. While I was in the club Secretary's office paying for our temporary membership, I heard Derek Blair's booming laugh in the hall. He had gotten ahead of us for the third time, and was waiting for me when I left the office.

"Heard you had a bit of trouble over on M Dock," he said, not bothering to conceal his grin as he extended his hand.

How fast bad news travels, I thought. I smiled back. "Well Derek," I said, "if you had been there to take my line like I expected you to, you could have pushed us off."

He told me that Roger and Molly, from *Sundowner,* were there, as were Doug and Mary from *Sundance Kid* — we had seen them last in Mooloolaba. Babs and Klaus on *Atair II* and *Curlew* were tied up in Hout Bay. Somehow, Derek had managed to wedge *HOTTYD* into a tiny slot at the yacht club.

Harbor Control assigned berths to ships on a logical order of priority. Cruise ships got top billing. They docked a mile away, near the city. Container ships were next. Freighters and coastwise container ships stood third on the ladder. Next came the stern trawlers; Spanish, Polish, and Korean. At the bottom of the list were the foreign yachts that could not fit into the yacht club facilities. That was us. Permanently berthed next to us at the nearest finger pier, beyond our irascible neighbor, *Paddy Pelham*, were two huge salvage tugs, (the world's largest, so I was told) and ships undergoing repairs at Global Marine Works, Cape Town's major marine repair shop.

We quickly became acclimatized to our new environment, which was quite different from Richards Bay. The Royal Cape Yacht Club was much larger and infinitely more traditional and formal than the Richards Bay yacht club had been.

We saw black and brown members in the dining room and at the bar. I don't believe the club practiced racial discrimination, but unlike the situation in Richards Bay, I can assure you the *Men's Bar* in the Royal Cape Yacht Club was strictly off limits to females, and they were deadly serious about it.

More than once, I saw a budding feminist get the heave-ho. The bartenders tried to be tactful, always pretending the female had entered those sacred premises out of ignorance. Mostly, the ladies left without a fight; but sometimes not.

About ten days after our arrival, I happened to be sitting in the bar when I overheard two members discussing an item in the Cape Times, and heard them mention *Innocent Bystander*.

Good Lord, I thought, there must be a mistake. Instantly, I remembered how proud Richard and Cathy had been at Middle Percy Island, when they asked if we preferred ice made from solar energy or wind power. We had parted in Darwin. They were returning to England via the Red Sea and the Suez Canal.

403

I interrupted the men, and asked if I might see the paper. On page 10 of the Cape Times (February 6, 1986), I found the following:

English Yacht Sunk

Innocent Bystander lost in South Yeman civil war!

Innocent Bystander's launching

Mr. Andrew Hardman, chief officer of the 13,360 ton Sri Lankan freighter *Pacific Universal* said that the morning of the 14th, *Innocent Bystander* took a shell from one of the South Yeman gunboats through the forward cabin.

Mr. Hardman said that Innocent Bystander had ran away from her attacker. Seeing a Jacob's ladder on his ship's side, they came along side. The gunboat followed. The people had been no sooner been helped on board than, in "an act of pure savagery and senselessness," one of the gunboats came slowly astern, and without warning fired a single shell into the yacht."The gunboat then put seven or eight more shells through the yacht, damaging it badly and setting it afire," he added. Consequently, the ship's crew was obliged to cut the burning yacht free. She posed a serious risk to the ship.

Clearly, the deadliest risks we faced were those posed by our fellow men. While they might be as benign as indifferent fishing trawlers, careless crew or unseeing tankers, they could also be deliberate and deadly as in this case. Either way, the result was often the same.

It was a long time before we

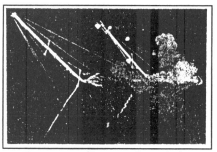

Innocent Bystander sinks

got over the horror of *Innocent Bystander's* savage end. We had known her in three oceans over a span of four years. She was a beautiful boat, maintained with loving care by Richard and Kathy. Unhappily, her name proved prescient.

I was surprised when I realized the harbor was an ecological disaster. No matter how strict or finicky the port authorities may be, garbage always finds its way into the waters of every commercial harbor in the world. Inevitably you'll see a grapefruit rind or part of a lettuce crate and other junk bobbing in the tide streak.

I would have thought the Afrikaners, with their Dutch sense of order and cleanliness, would have maintained water quality in Table Bay at least at that level. But Cape Town had the filthiest, most polluted harbor we saw in four years of cruising. Perhaps, like the Francis Bay chart, this was another example of an official *landbouer* attitude.

Because of prevailing southerly winds, most of the garbage in the harbor was trapped in our corner. I'm not talking just about orange peels and egg cartons, either. Several ships, especially the stern trawlers tied upwind from us, were in advanced stages of decomposition. To remain afloat, some operated their bilge pumps almost constantly, and every gallon of water pumped overboard was laced with fuel oil, and I don't mean diesel oil.

The factory ships and stern trawlers used a heavy oil called Bunker–C, similar in some respects to the tar that was once poured on country roads to keep the dust down. Thick, black as midnight, sticky, and virtually indestructible, it collected in our little corner of the harbor, and with other accumulated filth, bobbed ceaselessly against the cement bulkhead and our topsides. An honest egg carton or grapefruit peel was a welcome sight in the sea of tar that surrounded us.

I measured the oil in the water directly below the bowsprit. Unlike diesel oil, which is one molecule thick when it has room to spread out, this stuff had windrowed against the bulkhead to a thickness of *four inches* around our bow. Our topsides quickly became a hopeless mess of gray, shading to an inky black.

The Cape winds were another source of pollution. Although the little shunting trains that ground and clanged back and forth along the docks no longer burned coal, there was plenty of diesel soot, sand, and grime stirred up by the trains and constant vehicular traffic that was delivered to us by the prevailing winds.

Our decks became scruffy with sand and grit. The running rigging turned gray, and soiled our hands when we touched it. Our eyes stung, and we felt the grit between our teeth. Everything below became coated with a film of dust.

Except for the filth in the water, and the distance to town, ours was an ideal setting. Table Mountain in all its moods was on our immediate right. Table Mountain's famous tablecloth was a certain predictor of the frequent Cape gales. When the cloud began sliding over the edge of Table Mountain, I always stopped to watch one of nature's most spectacular shows.

The "tablecloth" was a thick, snow-white cloud, brilliant against the deep blue sky, smothering the top of Table Mountain like icing spread by an overly generous baker.

When it began to move, it moved ponderously as a unit, like chilled whipped cream pouring from a bowl, or a waterfall in slow motion. As it slid over the edge of the mountain, the cloud maintained its thickness and shape, and it followed the profile of the slope until it reached a point about halfway to the bottom where it disappeared as abruptly as if it had been poured into an invisible container. It was truly sensational.

Another attraction M dock held for me was the daily procession of a dozen or more brightly dressed whores going to the ships and fishing boats. They were a colorful lot. Mostly Eurasians or Malays, they dressed in bright colors, saved from looking gaudy by the girl's youth and perky demeanor. They chattered and skipped along like school girls on an outing which, in a way, I suppose they were. They always stopped to chat through the wire fence with the sailors in the Navy yard, and soon I developed a nodding acquaintance with the regular girls. It would have been hard to resist their spontaneous friendliness.

Before I knew prior approval from Harbor Control to operate the dinghy in the harbor was required, I carried our damaged anchor in the dinghy around the finger pier to Global Marine.

The shop foreman was puzzled by my appearance, and didn't know what to make of this Yank dragging his broken anchor into the shop. Still, he was a good sport about it. I pointed to the bent fluke, and the tear in the metal. He thought perhaps one of the lads might fix it on his lunch hour. When I inquired about the price, he said, "just bring him a bottle of whiskey."

The next day I went back, bottle in hand, and the anchor was ready, fluke restored and a reinforcing bar welded across the tear. Yet another example of South African generosity.

Apart from its proximity to the yacht club and the Global Marine repair yard, M Dock was a poor mooring. It not only collected the harbor garbage, it was a long walk to town.

Cape Town had a large Malay population. The Malays were brought to South Africa in the 18th century by the Dutch as slaves. Now, under the apartheid laws, they were obliged to live apart. We would later see the grossly unfair economic cost of that policy to its hapless victims. But first, I would see the indirect results of that cruel policy as it pertained to the children.

One of the most pernicious consequences of apartheid was the limited education available to children on the wrong side of the color line. Twice, I saw at first hand how profound those consequences were. The first time, I was sitting in the waiting room at the American Consulate, when a matronly Malay woman with a teen-age girl struck up a casual conversation. When I finished my business, and returned to the waiting room, I was mildly surprised to see them still there. But they left the waiting room behind me and followed me down the hall and into the elevator. Then, the woman shyly asked if I would have coffee with them in a coffee shop around the corner.

I'm undoubtedly one of the world's easiest pick-ups. I cannot resist an unexpected encounter. We sat in a booth while I listened to her story. The girl had been admitted to a boarding school in Lexington, Kentucky. However, an American had to vouch for her character so she could qualify for an educational visa. I was the only American they knew.

I spent an hour talking with them. The mother, like mothers the world over, answered for her daughter, interrupted her when she tried to answer my questions, and generally got in the way.

I didn't find much out about the girl's character, but it was obvious they were mother and daughter, and accordingly I signed my name on the form which the mother placed in front of me.

Just as I was excusing myself and standing up, the mother held up her hand. "There is one other thing," she said. "Where is Lexington, Kentucky?"

That simple question brought the ugly business of apartheid into stark, chilling focus. Here was a mother sending her young daughter to strangers in a place neither of them could find on a map, halfway around the world, possibly forever, because that was an Asian girl's only hope for a decent education.

The second incident was similar. I had visited a marine store, looking for a powerful detergent to cut the tar on our topsides, and the clerk had sent me to a shop that sold industrial cleaners.

Following directions, I found the shop and explained to the clerk that I needed a powerful detergent that could clean the oil and grime from my topsides. The clerk gestured helplessly at a rack of 50-gallon drums. I had not thought to bring a container.

The manager, a middle-aged Malay woman in Moslem robes and headdress, came out of her office to see what the problem was. After the clerk explained, she smiled and said something to her in Malay. While the clerk was gone, the manager explained, "This soap is very strong," she said. "I have sent for a small container. Then you shall try it. If you like it, you may bring a suitable container."

The clerk returned with an empty paper coffee cup and lid. She deftly filled it with a thick white paste that oozed from the spigot in a drum. She snapped the lid on and handed it to me with a flourish. I had my wallet in my hand, but the manager smilingly waved it away. "This is only a sample. See if you like."

The stuff was terrific! Of course, South Africa, like many smaller countries, never heard of the Environmental Protection Agency. I imagine they use chemicals and chemical compounds that long have been outlawed in the United States. It's not surprising their fly spray kills flies at 50 feet, and their soap cut the harbor filth so easily.

I took an empty Clorox bottle with me the next time, and for two rands bought a gallon of the most effective boat soap I've ever used. The only American cleanser I know that approached that soap was an Amway product called *Industrial Clean*.

By chance, I met the office manager on the street a week later. A young boy in a school uniform was with her.

We exchanged greetings and she introduced him to me as her son. Then, very matter-of-factly, she explained that she and her husband were saving to send the boy to school in England.

Suddenly, she interrupted herself. Her face flushed and she

blurted, "We have to get him out of this country. I will not allow him to remain!" I learned much in the next ten minutes about the really limited educational opportunities available to Asian boys.

Another aspect of South Africa was laid open to us two weeks later when a tall, slender, middle-aged South African hailed me one morning from the quay. I invited him aboard, and he introduced himself as Denzil Penny. We told him a bit about our travels, and he invited us to join him and his charming wife, Jane, for a drive through the countryside the following Sunday.

Denzil was a correspondent for *Cruising World.* He and Jane were members of the yacht club whose avocation was befriending visiting yachties. They took us to Stellenbosch, in the heart of the South African wine country. This quiet town was a University town and an important historic shrine.

On the way, driving past the Crossroads gate, Denzil stopped for a small procession of 30 black men and women, led by a man in a bright green suit and a woman beating a bass drum. Looking neither to the right nor left, they marched across the highway in front of us. The women wore long, fluttery head cloths.

We watched in silence. Then Denzil said softly, "Pure Africa. That's a Baptismal party."

He turned off the paved road on a dirt track. We looked around. There wasn't much to see. A few huts scattered here and there, a few children playing in the dirt. That was the Asian relocation site for the Malays from Cape Town. The Malay Quarter, like the French Quarter in New Orleans, historically occupied a valuable portion of the downtown area. Now, the Government was "relocating" the Malays to this new settlement miles out of town. I don't know what restitution, if any, the Government made. In a tragic way, it reminded me of the forced Japanese "relocation" in 1941–42 that moved thousands of Americans of Japanese heritage from their homes on the west coast to the desert in Nevada and Utah following the bombing of Pearl Harbor and the outbreak of the war with Japan.

We passed five men walking along the road, and Denzil greeted them in Afrikaans. They grinned as they responded.

"A remarkable thing about these people," Denzil said, "is when you pass them on the road and look back in your rear view mirror, you'll see them waving, even as your dust covers them."

Although it scarcely resembled it, Stellenbosch put me in mind of our Mount Vernon. Wide streets were shaded by overarching oaks, some of which actually have been designated national monuments. Many buildings were constructed of mud and wattle, but were so beautifully maintained that they seemed built of masonry. Most of them were roofed with skillfully tied thatch that looked like composition roofing. The buildings were uniformly white, and most bore historic society plaques. A small powder magazine prudently set in the midst of a large surrounding lawn bore over the arching doorway the word MAGAZINE. Above that appeared the date: 1777.

As we returned to M Dock late in the afternoon, Denzil noticed that *Queen Elizabeth II* was tied at the main wharf. He suggested we take a short detour and get a good look at possibly the last of the great passenger liners. As we drove along the wharf to the ship, we passed a sturdy little ship. Denzil, who knew by then that I had spent many years in Alaska, called attention to her. Her name, *St. Helena*, meant nothing to me. "When this little ship was in Canadian registry," Denzil said, "her original name was the *Prince Edward*."

I was stunned. Forty years vanished. It was early in May, 1946, in Vancouver, BC. I was on my way to Alaska, to make my fortune as a watchman on a salmon trap, but I was off to a bad start. It was raining, and the ancient straps holding my plaid portmanteau together had burst on the dock, and I struggled up the gangplank of the *Prince Edward* holding the bag closed with my arms, my cheeks pink with embarrassment.

Denzil was delighted when I shared that bit of nostalgia with him. After that, the *QE II* was little more than a large artifact.

There are two things tourists in Cape Town should do. One is visit the Cultural Museum on the Government grounds near the summer Parliament House, in the middle of a beautiful garden. The museum effectively explains how the people of South Africa have come to this painful and costly point in their history.

The other thing is take the cable car ride up Table Mountain. We had seen the cable car from the boat, but I hadn't thought of taking the ride until after Roger and Molly did. They came back and enthusiastically urged us to do it.

We had just returned from the Cultural Museum, and we thought they ought to see that. The next day while they went to the museum, we went up on Table Mountain.

The view was stunning. On a clear day, to the south you see as far as the Cape of Good Hope, and on a super clear day, you could even see Cape Agulhas. It was immediately apparent, as you studied the Cape mountain ranges, across the Cape flats to the south, why Cape Town had so many gales. The mountains formed a funnel that channeled winds from the Southern Ocean straight to Cape Town, which was sprawled before us.

We could distinguish M Dock and a speck that was *Prospector*. The view to the north was obstructed by mountain ranges.

Fat, brown, furry rodents about the size and configuration of rabbits but with short pointed ears and a very short tail, called drekkies, were playing in the rocks and sunning themselves.

We spent an hour on Table Mountain, studying the view, watching the animals, and breathing deeply of the African air. Knowing our visit was nearly over, those moments were poignant, and I made a conscience effort to impress each vista indelibly on my mind. Then, reluctantly, we took the car down.

We also faced the question of crew. We hadn't discussed it, but I felt, considering our experience in the Indian Ocean with Ian and Debby, and the recent one with Sean, that we might be better off going it alone. Except one thing. I had been denied a visa for Brazil because my passport was stale. Without visas, we couldn't break the trip in Brazil. Thus, we were facing an 1,800 mile passage to St. Helena, and a further 3,600 mile passage from St. Helena to the Windward Islands in the Caribbean.

If we couldn't stop in St. Helena, we faced a 5,400 mile passage across the equator and through the uncertainties of the Intertropical Convergence Zone (ITC). That was a serious thing to contemplate. You never know what to expect when you leave one weather system and enter another. Your passage can be so slow you worry about running out of things, or so wild you sail for days under only the staysail. And, of course, I was also thinking about that six on — six off watch schedule.

At that precise moment, a young man called to me from the dock, "Do you know anyone looking for crew?"

I can tell when Providence is nudging me in the ribs. "What's your name?" I asked.

"Rupert," he replied.

"Come aboard, Rupert," I said.

This kid was no Alan Petersen, but he was young, reasonably agile, seemed healthy, and was broke.

Today, for yacht skippers, destitute crew members can be a problem. Some countries won't let destitute crew off the boat. Others take the view, as the Administrator on Cocos-Keeling had, that broke or not, once you take them on board, you are forever after responsible for them. It can be difficult unloading crew in a foreign country. At the very least, you might find yourself unexpectedly buying an airplane ticket. However, if your crew members possess appropriate visas, being broke won't matter except in places like Polynesia.

Rupert told me he wanted to go to France to study fashion design. He thought that working his way to Martinique would be the first logical step. Overlooking the fact that most yachties, ourselves included, normally *charge* $100/week for board and room, I sent him to the French Consulate for a work-study visa. To my surprise, within a few hours he was back with one in his hands. My estimation of Rupert went up considerably.

He was a big help. We scurried around Cape Town collecting this, buying that, and arranging for our duty-free stores. One bargain that stands out in my memory were Velda's cigarettes. We bought a case of 5000 cigarettes (25 standard cartons) for 66.5 rands or U.S.$33.25, which worked out to $1.33/carton.

Finally, after hauling fuel in the dinghy and carrying water to the boat in buckets, on March first after four months in that oddly beautiful but tormented country, accompanied by the doleful moans of the Green Island fog horn, we left South Africa. My last impression was hulking Robbin Island in Table Bay, where political prisoners were held. If I were younger, I would be sorely tempted to try my hand in South Africa. I think the country has a tremendous future.

Chapter 17

The Home Stretch

$\mathcal{W}$e ran four hours under power before a light land breeze began sending cat's paws across the glassy water. When the breeze steadied, we set three lowers and the gaff topsail. We sailed at a steady three knots through the night.

I was surprised the next day to find we had made good 130 miles over the ground. Obviously, we were getting two knots, or 50 miles a day, from the Benguela Current.

Rupert was mildly seasick at first. I gave him a patch to wear behind his ear, which made him more comfortable. His basic problem, I think, was leaving home (at age 28) for the first time, and living with strangers in a strange and foreign environment.

Frankly, I take a cavalier attitude toward seasickness. I think there has been a lot of nonsense written about it. Of course, there are those who are prone to motion sickness, but luckily, not many people have that problem. For most of us, present company included, I think it is often a state of mind. A high percentage of first-time sailors *expect* to get seasick when they go to sea. But as soon as the novelty wears off, or the weather improves, or when they discover the boat isn't going to sink or capsize on the next wave, or the fear of the unknown wears off, the malady disappears.

I believe the best remedy for seasickness is to keep the patient busy. If you let them stay in the bunk feeling remorseful and sorry for themselves, you may never get them on their feet. Rupert probably thought he had signed on a hell-ship, the way I drove him from task to task. But he quickly recovered from his malaise, and for a time seemed to be enjoying his adventure.

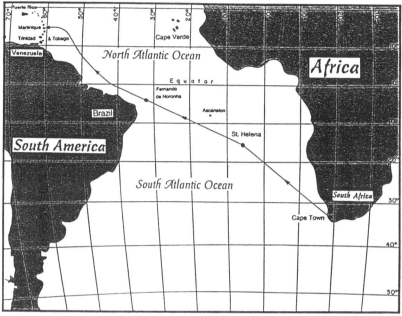

Cape Town to Martinique
5,535 miles (Chart 12)

By noon, March fourth, we were eight degrees or almost 500 miles north of Cape Town. Every day, my noon observations had consistently placed us 40 miles ahead of the Walker log's reading. Clearly, we were in the current. We began to see flying fish regularly, and night watchstanders were beginning to leave their sweaters below. Three days later, the log read:

March 8: Tradewinds! Broke through 25° south; good noon sight puts us at 24°48'S, 04°12'E, or about 975 miles from Cape Town. Had a small electrical fire in the engine room; saw a small but unmistakable green flash at sunset, and hooked (but lost) small dorado.

The insulation from a hot wire had chafed against an engine mount. The resulting short circuit caused the accumulated grease and matted animal hair clinging to the mount and lower block to burst into flames. The *only* good thing about animal hair is that it stinks like hell when it's on fire. I smelled that stench coming from the engine room, and within seconds, I had the flames smothered under a blanket of CO_2.

The next morning, after Rupert relieved me at the wheel, I took my customary little walk around the deck, making sure things were properly secured, and that there was no apparent chafing anywhere. A sailboat is an incredibly dynamic environment, and things will rub together, so you can't avoid a certain amount of wear. But by keeping your eyes open, you can minimize the damage.

I found myself studying the squaresail. Something was not quite right. Then, standing at the base of the mast and peering up toward the hounds, I found the trouble. The squaresail was pulling like a mule, but as the boat rolled, the yard appeared to be swinging freely in a two foot arc in front of the mast!

That wasn't right. Normally, the yard was prevented from swinging from side to side by a taut jackstay wire which held a bracket fastened to the yard. The wire ran from the hounds on the mast to a ring bolt set in the deck.

We had first rigged the jackstay, then a length of chain, in Costa Rica. As time went by, the bracket had chafed through the chain, and we had replaced it in Richards Bay with a length of heavy galvanized wire rope. Now, somehow that wire rope had magically stretched several inches over night. I had no idea what was wrong. But I knew there was no sense sending Rupert up to inspect it because he wouldn't have known what he was looking at, let alone what to look for. This was something I had to do.

As I've mentioned before, the hounds and crosstrees on *Prospector* are 35 feet above the deck. I don't know how many times during our cruise, I asked myself *What's a trifling 35 feet compared to the 100–150 foot climbs, and even higher, that sailors a lot older than I am routinely made in all kinds of weather on those old Cape Horn windjammers?* it was obvious that life, 100 years ago, was a very serious business, indeed!

I climbed the ratlines and quickly found the problem. A stainless steel guy wire bracing the yard had slipped from its notch on the bracket and had partially sawn through the jackstay as the boat rolled. Several strands of the softer wire had been cut, causing about three feet of the jackstay to unlay.

I quickly returned to the deck. We set the fore and aft rig, and then struck the squaresail and raffee while Velda stopped the boat from rolling by steering the boat across the wind.

Trying to guess the most effective way of repairing the damaged jackstay wire, but knowing I'd have to improvise as I went along, I cut a three-foot piece of chain, and stowed that with several bulldog clips, shackles of various sizes, seizing wire, and several tools in my canvas rigging bucket.

I went up the ratlines again, hauled the bucket up, tied it securely to the rigging, and set to work. Rupert joined me standing on the yard. Together, we spliced the chain to the jackstay, and locked the undamaged portion of the wire with a bulldog clip to prevent it from unwinding any further. Then we cast off the jury rigging that temporarily held things together, and returned to the deck. After striking the fore and aft rig, we reset the squaresail and raffee. I don't know about Rupert, but I felt as if I had put in a full day's work — and it was only 10 a.m.

As it grew light on March 14, we saw St. Helena looming high on our port bow. By 9:30 that morning, we had sailed into the very open and rolly roadstead anchorage outside St. Helena's only town, Jamestown, and had anchored near *Sundowner*.

This tiny island was best known as the last home of exiled Napoleon Bonaparte. The French still maintain as a national shrine the estate where he passed his final days, but his tomb is empty. The remains were taken to France long ago.

As we were putting the dinghy into the water, Roger and Molly came alongside in their Avon, while Derek and Thiana from *HOTTYD* approached from the opposite direction.

The happy and excited greetings following a successful landfall went right past me, as did the fact that we had traveled 1,755 miles in 13 days, for a respectable average of 135 miles per day, because I was suffering from that most dread helmsman's afflictions, boils on the buttocks. We also had financial problems. We had only $85 in cash on board, and I was distressed to learn that we already owed the government of St. Helena £16 (then $25) for dropping our anchor in their roadstead, and that when someone went ashore to pay the fee, the landing fee would be an additional £3 per person.

There is no airport. Everything — mail, groceries, fuel, passengers, livestock — arrives or departs by sea. The mail arrives monthly on the *St. Helena* but could be dispatched on visiting yachts sailing northwest to Ascension Island. Boats volunteering for this service were forgiven anchoring and landing fees.

Sarah and Parker Smith, whose baby had been born in the Empangini hospital in South Africa, volunteered to carry the mail to Ascension. Nothing remarkable about that, until you learn that the Smith's yacht was named *Courier*.

Rupert and I tried to get ashore, but at the last moment I backed out. It was calm, but I wasn't feeling well, and I found those five foot swells crashing against the landing and swirled up its concrete steps discouraging. We sat in the dinghy for a few minutes watching the swells restlessly surge against the cement structure, then abruptly fall away, baring the pocked and seaweed festooned structure. A sturdy gallows-like frame had been constructed over the steps. It supported dangling knotted ropes to facilitate arrivals and departures. Dinghies best timed their landing approach to coincide with the top of the swell. At the appropriate moment, the passenger grabbed a rope for support, and leapt in the landing's direction. Because of my affliction, however, I decided not to try it.

Velda and Rupert went ashore. The economy seemingly was grounded on two basic industries: Squeezing visitors and selling stamps. Velda described Jamestown as a row of cottages on the left side of the road and a row of net racks on the right. The cottages housed the bakery, the pub, and the police station where fees were paid and passports stamped.

Several local young men hung around the landing operating a sort of valet parking service. When a dinghy operator wanted to come ashore, he would stop the engine, grab a rope, and kick the dinghy away. A young man would then dive into the water and swim the boat out to a bright yellow polypropylene hawser anchored 100 feet off the landing. When you wanted to return to your boat, one of the lads would swim out to the hawser and bring your dinghy back to the landing for you. As we soon found out, this system was not without flaws.

We remained at St. Helena for five days. I kept tinkering with the jackstay and the jury rigging, while my boils slowly succumbed to massive doses of antibiotics. Rupert made many trips to the landing at Jamestown, but his last return to *Prospector* was spectacular. I had sent him ashore with six five-gallon water jugs. I thought we had plenty of water for the remainder of the trip across the Atlantic, but since it's just as easy to carry full water jugs as empty ones, and you can never tell... .

I knew as soon as I saw the returning dinghy wallowing in the swell that Rupert was in serious trouble. But not until he was nearly alongside did I realize that he was sitting in water nearly up to his waist. The boat would have sunk, but for the two large flotation tanks Les Snowsill had installed in New Zealand.

It almost seems axiomatic that sooner or later, your crew will get you. Although I had carefully told him to fill the jugs and swim them out to the boat, Rupert had decided it would be easier to fill the jugs *in situ*, so to speak. It's possible, of course, that he didn't believe me when I told him full fresh water jugs would float. Consequently, he had prevailed on some lads hanging around the landing to help him drag the dinghy ashore, which they happily did. Rupert then filled the jugs with about 200 pounds of water and asked his pals to help drag the boat back down the steps into the tide.

I can't imagine how he managed to row the boat, but fear is very inspirational, and that boy was scared, as he should have been. Our boat had a cathedral hull, and I imagine the three keels left indelible streaks of paint, gel coat, fiberglass and roving on the steps as the boys cheerfully dragged the boat across the rocks and coarse cement. After we lifted the boat out of the water, and stowed her, upside down, over the galley hatch, I found that the central keel was open for about 18 inches near the bow.

We left St. Helena the next morning for Martinique. The current carried us to within two miles of the Naranha Fernando Island group off Brazil, and we had a near mutiny.

Rupert had quite a different personality from the other young people we had carried as crew. In some ways, he reminded me of Willi, who had sailed with us in the Pacific the previous year. He kept things bottled up. All I saw as the days went by, was a progressively sulkier young man. Again, I'm reminded that had I been more sensitive to my subtle responsibilities as captain, this might never have happened, but in our nearly four years of cruising with an assorted cast of characters, we had been spared serious problems and I had never felt compelled to worry about communications.

Apart from the inevitable sunburns and minor cuts, and the psychologically distressed kids we left on Cocos–Keeling, ours had been, if not always a happy ship, at least one without serious physical or mental traumas. So I was quite unprepared when Rupert decided, in mid-ocean, to go on a hunger strike.

Perhaps it was the whiff of land he had gotten as we sailed through that little Brazilian archipelago. My first impulse was to say, *let him strike. So what?* But as all successful sailors quickly learn, you can never afford to ignore little problems. If you do, one thing invariably will lead to another, and the first thing you know, you can have a serious problem on your hands.

Eventually Rupert changed his mind, but his morale remained at a low ebb. Since he had a French visa, I offered to put him ashore in Cayenne, French Guiana. It's off the beaten track, and wisely, he declined my offer. Personally, I thought the place had a certain macabre appeal since it was the situs of the infamous Devil's Island.

On March 29, eleven days out of St. Helena, I was thrilled to see the Big Dipper on the northern horizon for the first time in over three years. It was hard to believe that we had been that long in the Southern Hemisphere. Crossing the equator in a sailing vessel can be serious business, and I think most ocean cruisers read, if they can't always follow, the advice offered in the British Admiralty's venerable *Ocean Passages for the World*.

To give you a flavor of those directions, let me quote directly from the 1973 edition:

> *9.41.01 TO CROSS THE EQUATOR follow the route to the English Channel as far as 5°E and then steer with a fair Trade Wind toward Isla Fernando de Noronha. On reaching 10°S, at about 30°W, stand more to the N, so as to cross the equator between 31° and 34°W, and as soon as the North-east Trade has been picked up, steer through it, and thence as follows:. . ..*

I tried to follow the advice in *Ocean Passages* because it represented the accumulated experience of sailing ship masters over many years. However, there is one important *caveat*. The directions were written for sailing *ships*, not yachts. Thus, while the "Roaring 40s" was a preferred route for Australian grain ships, it was hardly suitable for a small yacht run by senior citizens.

I believe that book deserves a place next to the two-volume set of Bowditch, *American Practical Navigator*, which is *the* basic navigational text. Those three books, a set of H.O. 249 tables, the current Nautical Almanac, and the Rules of the Road would comprise a basic ship's library.

The Intertropical Convergence Zone (ITC), is an area where Northern and Southern hemispheric weather conditions come into contact. This area is usually about six to ten degrees wide and occurs in the Atlantic and Pacific oceans near the equator. Seen on a satellite photo, the ITC, unlike the tidy equator drawn by geographers, undulates in gentle curves generally north of the equator according to the season, across the two oceans (and sometimes the Indian Ocean). Its shape is revealed by its constant cloud cover. As its name implies, it is a dead area between the northern and southern weather systems, and forms an impenetrable barrier to even the most ferocious hurricane.

In late March, we expected to find the center of the ITC about six degrees north of the equator. However, the rain normally associated with it began at 5°S (or 300 miles south of the equator). It was a miserable time. Our bunks were sodden, and Velda again began sleeping in her oilskins, while I reverted to my youth, pretending I was sleeping in a wet sail.

We caught a white marlin, and as Rupert was dressing it, he inflicted a nasty cut; one that could have used a stitch or two. I offered to sew him; we had pain killers and sterile sutures, but he didn't think that was a good idea.

You don't want to fool around with fish poison. We put him on antibiotics, and his finger steadily, if slowly, healed. But I had gotten to the point where I had no idea what Rupert was thinking. Already sullen, he became even more distressed. To be honest about it, I was beginning to fear that he might even become suicidal.

We were completely becalmed. However, unlike the great Cape Horners, we had an iron topsail, and we spent days listening to the muted rumble of our Perkins as we were driven slowly north through a continuous deluge on a glassy sea that was eerily calm.

Visibility was frequently less than a mile, and when it lifted, it seemed we were motoring on an unmarked highway, with distinct building-like squalls spaced more or less evenly on both sides. Occasionally, a squall would roll over us; when that happened, the volume of rain increased while visibility was reduced to a few yards.

As long as sailboats have auxiliary engines, the debate whether it is better to run the engine in search of wind will continue. Some people, like Mike Davidson in Australia, lack the patience to wait for wind. His boat, *Ardright*, was fitted with an outsize Mercedes diesel, and when *Ardright* slowed to five knots or less – speeds I consider very respectable – he started the engine. I have great patience, and if it were not for considerations such as food, water, or propane – or the temperament of the crew, I could wait a long time for wind.

Despite Rupert's dark looks and muttered imprecations, I refused to rush through this miserable streak of weather. All things being equal, 1,200 engine RPMs translates into about ten horsepower or three knots of speed. At that conservative rate, we consume about two quarts of diesel per hour. This clearly is our most fuel efficient speed. I didn't know when we would get through the ITC, or pick up the Guyana Current, which flows north from the Amazon following the South American coast into the Caribbean, and I definitely didn't want to run out of fuel in mid-ocean.

On April fourth, we spoke to an English container ship. I wasn't sure where we were, not having had any observations for several days. The captain gave our position as 02°00′S, 33°02′W. I was about 30 miles off in my dead reckoning.

He cheered us immensely by telling us that we were already nearly through the ITC, and when we reached the equator, the weather would change.

Again the log tells the story:

April 5: Drifted all night; totally becalmed. Velda's watch produced only three miles. Rained like hell yesterday afternoon. We are surrounded by great black squalls that reach from the water up into the stratosphere. Position: 01°12′S, 34°20′W.

April 6: Ran engine ten hours. Squalls, lots of rain, no wind. Still 12 miles from the equator. Every day I hope it will get better. Two sperm whales swam past the boat.

April 7: 80 miles in rain, rain, rain. I'm sure we got across the line, but no sights.

April 8: Becalmed last night – got underway at midnight in force four easterly wind. Heavy rain last night, must be a southeast intrusion. Making five knots under four lowers. Good LAN, position: 01°25′N, 37°39′W.

April 9: Drizzly morning, force five northeast wind today. Rupert's finger healing nicely. Looks like we are out of the soup at last!

We had just crossed the equator, and we had a polliwog on board who needed to be introduced to King Neptune.

Velda prepared a lovely holiday dinner and we had a mild celebration utilizing the last three bottles of beer Velda had hidden. But we weren't there yet.

April 11: Weather still fair, force four northeast trades. Fingers sore as hell. Gaff topsail downhaul parted last night, had a hell of a time getting the sail down, but it is now reset. We are in the Guyana Current, picked up 15 miles yesterday.

This shows you what a moment's carelessness can do. A sailor's hands are his most important tools. It is not an accidental whimsy that the ancient call summoning sailors to their duty is a call to "All hands!"

Two weeks earlier, we had experimented with various sail combinations. I was using our jib topsail. This was a large sail, 350 square feet with a 39 foot leech.

I had secured the tack to the bulwarks, and was holding the clew ring with two fingers from both hands when the sail slipped over the side and went into the water. We were moving at five knots.

My first sensation, after the whip-lash jolt that nearly wrenched my arms from my shoulders, was a dull ache in my hands that quickly spread up my wrists and arms as the clew flew overboard. Unfortunately, my fingers had been jammed tightly into the D ring, and when the sudden strain came, they were locked in place. I couldn't let go. Two fingers on each hand were swollen, tender to the touch, and painful when I used them, even gingerly making log entries. I'm sure there must be better places for the convalescence of hand injuries than in the middle of a trans-Atlantic passage.

Rupert and Velda did their best to help, but they had things to do, and eventually I learned to ignore the pain.

I had other problems. Both shortwave radio receivers died and our two chronometers, my $25 Casio digital watch and the $49 Seiko stop watch, disagreed with each other by one minute, two seconds. In navigational terms, that disagreement produced a built-in error of 15 miles. In mid-ocean, a 15 mile error isn't important, but when you are making a landfall, it can make the difference between gracefully docking and being shipwrecked.

Since I had been using the Casio regularly, I was sure that its normal gain of four seconds/month had not changed, so I stuck with it. A few days later, I checked our time with a passing freighter. This confirmed that my Casio was two seconds fast, while the Seiko, which I rarely used, was now a minute slow. The log continues:

Diamond Rock

April 12: About 1,020 miles to Martinique, eight or nine days. We are running short of diesel. Good sailing in a force four northeasterly breeze on a beam reach.

April 14: Set raffee, turned due west to pick up current on 100 fathom contour. Position: 06°27'N, 49°35'W.

April 15: Water color changed to dark green. . ..

April 18: Sun directly overhead at noon. . ..

April 19: Raised Barbados on port bow at daylight.

April 20: Sailed past Diamond Rock in the St. Lucia Channel at ten a.m., thereby closing the circuit!

WE HAVE SAILED AROUND THE WORLD

April 20: (con't) Dropped anchor in Bai du Fort de France at 1:20 p.m. From Cape Town, 45 days, 5,520 miles, from St. Helena, 32 days, 3,765 miles.

I found myself staggering slightly as I walked down the dock to the trailer that serves Martinique as an immigration office. It was the same trailer we had visited nearly four years earlier when we obtained our exit permits.

It was a few tense moment when I realized the huge black immigration officer would be examining Rupert's South African passport. I scarcely dared breathe as we stood in front of him, watching him carefully study Rupert's passport and visa, and his long and searching look at Rupert's face.

Satisfied, he nodded. Rupert was off the crew list! I wanted to cheer. Common sense prevailed, however, and I pushed Velda's and my passports across the counter instead.

I pointed to one of the earliest entries in them, a faded and water-stained six-sided exit stamp from Martinique dated *3 Juin 1982,* which signaled the beginning of our epic downwind voyage. "Would the officer be kind enough to put our entry stamps in the same squares?" I asked politely.

The officer looked puzzled for a moment. Then I saw a comprehending grin cross his face.

"This is indeed an honor, *Monsieur,*" he said, "congratulations!" He offered his hand. Then he carefully aligned his rubber stamp, and thump! The deed was done. It was official. There, for all the world to see, was our entry stamp dated 20/4/86, three years, ten months and seventeen days later. I thanked him.

The circuit was closed, but our trip was not over. We paused briefly in St. Barths, where we discovered my brother, Buzzy, had reported us overdue to the Coast Guard.

My first inkling that we were on the *Securite* list, a list broadcast by the Coast Guard at regular intervals of lost or overdue boats, was when a young chap rowed his dinghy alongside and asked if we had just come from South Africa. "Because," he went on, "if you did, there's a *Securite* message out for you. I just heard it on Saba Radio."

After thanking the alert messenger, I called Saba Radio on the VHF, and reported that we were safe and sound.

I later learned that the Coast Guard had made a serious effort to find us. Thinking we were overdue, Buzzy had contacted the Search and Rescue Unit in Seattle, which had relayed the information to SAR headquarters in New York, which in turn, had notified Miami, and ultimately San Juan, Puerto Rico.

The Coast Guard began the search by calling the harbor master in St. Helena. Finding we had cleared St. Helena on March 20, they had put out the *Securite* call. Before they could began a serious Caribbean search, Buzzy received a letter I had mailed in Martinique.

From St. Barths, we sailed to Great Bay on St. Martin, where we were briefly reunited with Rupert, who had found a group of expatriate South Africans living under the tolerant eye of the Dutch authorities, and was cleaning charter boats at Bobby's Marina.

More for sentimental reasons than any other, we also stopped in Marigot, where, to our surprise and delight, we found Hans and Elly Lutt, our Dutch friends from *Solitair* we had seen last in New Zealand. They were planning an early return to Holland.

Like most of us, they were finding that a midlife retirement, while eminently sensible, is not entirely practical in this materialistic world. In other words, like us, Hans and Ellie were running out of money. We didn't linger in Marigot, and reluctantly again said farewell to our friends.

We were becoming uneasy about the approaching hurricane season; if possible, you want to leave the Caribbean by mid–June. Consequently, we sailed directly to St. Thomas. From the water, Charlotte Amalie looked very much the same in 1986 as it had in 1981. There were changes, but Yacht Haven Marina still accepted garbage from yachts anchored in the harbor, but there were more yachts in Long Bay than there had been, and the Crew Bar had been replaced by a fast food place. I noticed one thing that was decidedly different: There was much less overt nudism than before, and you didn't see people swimming around their boats any more. Progress was beginning to exact its payment.

A sad thing happened while we were resting in the harbor. The beautiful replica of a Baltimore clipper, the *Pride of Baltimore*, was lost in a white squall with loss of life about 200 miles north of Puerto Rico. The mate, an Irish-American named Flanigan, whom we had met in Darwin, had taken command of the raft full of survivors. They drifted more than a week before they were picked up.

That tragedy was very much on our minds when, a few days later, we left St.Thomas for the States. If it could happen to a strong, well found ship like the *Pride*, it could certainly happen to us, and it almost did.

I planned to reenter the United States in Port Everglades near Fort Lauderdale. Since we had been out of the country nearly four years, I was sure this would be an excruciatingly painful and complicated procedure.

The passage from St. Thomas to Florida through the Bahamas was an easy, routine, downwind sail. However, Port Everglades was a circus. I'm sure, now as I look back on it, that we were a part of the problem. Neither *Prospector* nor I do well in a crowd. Her long keel and full underbody is a decided liability under circumstances requiring the nimble responses of a modern fin-keeler.

Her power plant is only marginal. Handy enough when you need an extra push to get through the doldrums, but not nearly muscular enough for the stop-and-go driving you'll find in a major seaport like Port Everglades.

Those are my alibis. The *real* problem was that her skipper had just spent four years enjoying wide-open spaces and sparsely populated harbors, and found the chaotic atmosphere of a crowded port more than he could comfortably handle.

It was chaotic. The movement of traffic was continual. Tugs scurried from job to job. Stately tankers were being eased in and out of their berths, and yachts were moving up and down the waterway. Running through the whole tapestry of marine activity like beads of quick silver rolling across a table, were dozens of "fizz" boats — overpowered runabouts — dodging, turning, darting in and around the other traffic, randomly and carelessly throwing sheets of water into the air.

I was unnerved by the unaccustomed tumult, but when I saw the Ft. Lauderdale bridge open ahead, I grimly ignored the activity around me, and headed for the opening. A little sooner, and we might have made it. As we steamed toward the opening, I heard the warning horn and saw the twin bridge spans, silhouetted against the sky like huge arms raised in supplication, begin their ponderous closing journey. I knew we wouldn't get through.

Even then, I realized the bridge-tender was merely acting out his Divinely ordained role as the yachtsmen's natural and mortal enemy. He could hardly be blamed for being what he is. But it was the final straw for me. I panicked.

We turned tail and ran, back through the breakwater to the friendly, familiar sea. I knew that Morehead City was also a port of entry, and I was sure we would find none of this insanity in a quiet fishing port.

Unfortunately, several friends, including Dr. Reid who had made my lower plate in Puerto Rico, and John Rixe, with whom we had maintained a steady correspondence, were expecting us in Fort Lauderdale, but we had no way of communicating with them. They were disappointed.

After leaving the breakwater, we sailed into the Gulf Stream while it was still light. In a situation like that, especially on a coast as busy as the Atlantic seaboard, if the current is fair, you'll want to stay as close to the middle of it as possible because there, you are unlikely to meet any on-coming traffic. No sensible skipper is going to buck the Gulf Stream just for the hell of it.

The flip side is that other captains will have the same idea. This is when you'll wish you had eyes in the back of your head. You must keep a close watch over your shoulder, and realize the only light an overhauling freighter will see is your stern light, which, on most sailboats, is mounted much too close to the water to more than marginally useful. Be sure it isn't obstructed. Also, you must always assume the lookout on the overtaking ship has gone below for a cup of coffee, or is standing with his back to the wind, lighting a cigarette. In other words, *always* assume that your stern light hasn't been seen. When we are overtaken at night, we usually flick on the big deck light. True, that light temporarily destroys our night vision, but it is sure to be noticed by anyone within ten miles.

We saw surprisingly little water traffic, but from the water, south Florida is a surrealistic light show. Wall to wall condominiums are punctuated by landing lights at airport after airport. Often the approach beacons extend out into the water. I wonder what it must cost to keep those lights burning all night.

Once we were abreast of the continental land mass off Georgia and South Carolina, we began running into frontal systems. The weather turned squally and nasty.

I was worried. Because of the continual cloud cover, we were forced to rely entirely on dead reckoning, which is not easily done when you are in a current of unknown velocity.

Our last known position was off the Georgia coast. Based on that and a series of assumptions, such as assuming the Gulf Stream's velocity was nearly constant and that the Walker log was accurately reporting our speed through the water, I plotted a dead reckoned course which proved to be surprisingly accurate.

But we didn't know that when a low-flying Coast Guard patrol plane dropped down on us from the clouds. We had evidently been spotted on their radar. I turned on the VHF and tried to call while the plane flew over, circled and came back. I needed a position check the worst way. This is a dangerous coast when you have to rely on dead reckoning, The plane was low enough so I could see faces peering from the windows, but the pilot wouldn't return my call. Instead, the plane turned and flew off into the clouds.

Perhaps the pilot thought we looked too scruffy to deserve a response (somehow, I think if we had been a 125′ Feadship, he would have answered). We also could have used a current weather forecast.

Visibility on the water that afternoon was less than a mile. These are the worst conditions imaginable for avoiding a collision, and I was alert and watchful. It's a good thing I was.

I was startled to see at first hazy and indefinite, but rapidly gaining substance, a wall of water rushing toward us from our port side. With only seconds to spare, I threw off the main sheet and ran forward to the fife rail around the mast, where I frantically cast off the peak halyard. The gaff was still falling when that wall of wind-driven water, traveling probably in excess of 100 miles per hour smashed into us like a speeding train.

The boat rolled deeply to starboard — Velda was pitched out of her bunk — but with the gaff down, the impact was only temporary, and the boat quickly recovered. Velda came on deck, bruised and angry, wondering what the hell I was doing, and determined that I stop it. This was the same kind of white squall that had killed *Pride of Baltimore*.

After the squall passed, the wind suddenly backed from the southwest to the southeast. I let the boom jibe across. It was getting dark, but with the wind shift, visibility improved and I saw a lighthouse in the far distance off our port bow. Using the stopwatch, I timed the sequence of flashes and compared them with the sequences shown on the chart. There was no question. We were looking at the Cape Lookout light.

Then I saw the first buoy. I couldn't find a buoy with a corresponding number on our chart, but our charts were five years out of date, and important changes had been made to navigational aids in the years since we had left. I assumed this was one of them.

Bearing on the light, we came to a second buoy, and a third. I couldn't find anything on my chart to match those numbers, but they were leading us to the light, so we followed happily along.

On a small vessel, fatigue can be as deadly as the most virulent plague. The victim rarely understands how fragile his remaining defenses, how blurred his vision, or how distorted his judgment may be. I'm certain it was fatigue that cost Ann Gash her boat on the Australian coast as she completed her single-handed circumnavigation, and I know it was fatigue that nearly cost us *Prospector.*

When we were a mile from the light, I turned on the depth finder and discovered we were in 15 feet of water!

I spun the wheel, cast off the mainsheet and ran forward to drop the anchor. It hit the water, and as soon as 30 feet of chain followed it over the bow, I tightened the brake on the winch to set the anchor. It dug in well. Then I released another 70 feet of chain, stopping when I heard Velda, watching the depth finder, scream, "*We have only ten feet*!" sending a cold cannon ball of fear into my stomach. I tightened the brake wheel a second time and set the chain stopper.

We swung around into the weather. Up to now, I had seen only the backs of the waves, but now we were facing rows of curling breakers smashing around us. We had anchored in the surf! Luckily, we were in a shallow pocket of somewhat deeper water.

It was nearly dark by this time, and the rising wind, now between 35 and 45 knots, was straight out of the southeast. We were in a desperate situation. It was too late to move; all we could do was hope that our precarious toehold would not give way.

The more I thought about it, the more frightened I became. We were wide open to the Atlantic in less than ten feet of water. I had no idea what the stage of the tide might be — but I knew that eight and ten foot tides were not unusual on this coast.

The incoming rollers battered old *Prospector* unmercifully, causing her to pitch and yaw with demented ferocity. When she came up hard against her ground tackle, every minute or so, I was reminded that we were laying to an anchor that had been repaired. I hoped those welds were holding!

We thought about setting another anchor, but the motion was so wild and erratic by this time that we were afraid to try manhandling the big CQR for fear one of us would be hurt. If that happened, we would be in very serious trouble. Neither of us slept that night. We sat in the dark, listening to our boat fight for her life.

When daylight finally came, the wind slacked off, and I went forward to see what had happened to our ground tackle. Although I had shared every crashing blow, every snap and jerk as *Prospector* rose and fell in the oncoming seas, I was unprepared for the havoc I found.

The anchor chain had broken the bow roller and had sawn through a piece of heavy-duty two inch galvanized pipe at the base of the pulpit. It had also *torn* the chain stopper out of the deck with such great force that a piece of the deck, a chunk of teak eight inches long by four inches wide, by one and a half inches thick literally had been wrenched out of the *middle* of a deck plank.

Looking out to sea, I marveled at our survival. As far as I could see, huge angry rollers, white with foam, were marching up the spit, only to crash and expire on the shoals around us. It was terrifying. Somehow, I had to get our boat out of that terrible surf. I knew she couldn't last another night like the last one.

I studied the breakers on both sides of us, and as I watched the waves, I began to see a possible escape route. A private buoy bobbed in calmer water about five hundred yards away, to our right. I don't know why it was there, but it gave me something to steer toward.

Before hauling the anchor, I had to check the engine. Routine checks are very important when survival depends on reliable power. I knew the fuel tanks were low, but when the sounding stick came up **dry**, I felt something akin to an electrical shock.

We had a quart or so of lamp kerosene in its container. There was fuel in the fuel lines, and in the Racor sight glass. I poured the kerosene into the fuel tank. We had enough fuel to run the engine at least 15 minutes — and possibly as long as half an hour.

We were so numb with fatigue and so conditioned by that time to living on the ragged edge of disaster, that I don't think either of us was frightened. Nor did it occur to us to use our radio to call for help. I knew there was a Coast Guard station less than ten miles away, but like so many of my peers, I tended to think of the Coast Guard as a punitive police force, rather than as an agency concerned about distressed yachts. The refusal of the aircraft pilot to answer our call the previous day was a typical example of Coast Guard behavior many of us have come to expect.

I started the engine. Then I ran to the bow and pressed the switch on the anchor windlass, while Velda engaged the clutch and drove the boat slowly forward into the surf.

The chain came up easily until it was straight up and down. Then the clutch on the gipsy began to slip because, since the bow roller had broken, the chain links were snagging on a piece of angle iron that was part of the pulpit frame.

I thought that by jamming a short piece of wood under the frame, I could provide a smooth surface for the chain to slide over. I found a short piece of two by four and got down on my hands and knees. As the bow fell into a trough, and the chain went momentarily slack, I slipped the wood under it. Only I miscalculated.

As the bow rose on the next swell, the chain snapped taut, slipped off the wood and before I could move, landed on the fleshy inside web of my right thumb, crushing it against the steel frame. The skin split, opening a wound nearly two inches long, which began bleeding profusely, making it very difficult to work.

I realized then that we couldn't save the anchor. At first, I thought of cutting the chain, but hi-test chain is made of hardened steel, which is difficult to saw through under ideal conditions. Sadly, I concluded we'd have to slip the chain. I indicated to Velda which direction to steer, released the brake on the winch, and let the chain run over the side. I had my knife ready, and when the bitter end emerged dragging its lanyard behind it, I cut the lanyard with a single stroke of the blade.

When we reached the yellow buoy, I went below and tightly wrapped a paper towel around my thumb — it was still bleeding badly — and secured the towel with a piece of duct tape.

Then I shut the engine down and set the main and jib. I knew where we had spent the night, and we could see the lighthouse, but where was Morehead City? Our charts were not sufficiently detailed. We saw two shrimp trawlers rafted together, and I sailed as close to them as I dared.

"Where's Morehead City?" I yelled.

The fisherman pointed to a water tower. "She be rait ther," he said. Those watermen are funny birds. They knew about our predicament — they couldn't have avoided it. But none of them would volunteer assistance. Not, you understand out of meanness or indifference, but out of courtesy. To offer assistance in those circumstances would have implied that they thought I had made a mistake, which, of course, I had.

On the other hand, nobody would be quicker or more eager to help if we had asked for it. But you have to ask.

When you enter Morehead City from the sea, you do a series of sharp turns, first to port to clear the big commercial dock, and then 200 yards further on, you turn to starboard for an additional 200 yards when you make another 90° turn to port. Then you sail the length of the town waterfront and anchor out of the way, in the lee of a small island.

We came booming up the channel with a fair wind, carried on a flooding tide, turned, turned some more, finally had her hard over, but the tide was carrying us remorselessly sideways into a Polish container ship innocently tied to the end of the dock.

In desperation, I cast off the main sheet and started the engine. I don't think we cleared the ship by more than a foot, but in gaining control over *Prospector*, I had pushed the throttle to the wall, and couldn't make that second turn. Instead, I felt the boat touch, and the bow rise as she ran hard aground on the little island that guards the waterfront.

This was our first real grounding in four years!

But the more you knock around this old world of ours, the less excited you are likely to be about inconsequential things like running aground on a flooding tide. Why sweat it? You know you'll float off in an hour or so, perfectly OK.

I swear I don't know where that water went. Where *I* came from, when the water comes up the creek, that's called a flooding tide. In Morehead City, when the water comes up the creek, that's a falling tide. Three hours after we ran aground, poor *Prospector* was lying on her side.

That's when I went to find the Customs Service and clear back into the United States. We put the dinghy into the water, and taking the ship's papers, our passports and a five-gallon diesel jug, I rowed ashore. First, I found the customs office.

A pleasant middle-aged man wearing a uniform, seated behind a desk, looked up as I entered, and asked me to sit down.

I put the passports and ship's papers in front of him, and explained that we were just returning to the United States after a four-year cruise around the world. He took a piece of paper from his desk and copied information from the passports and the ship's document. Then he asked several questions. Finally he gestured out the window.

"Is that your boat out there?" he asked.

He had a wonderful view of the poor old girl on her side.

"Yes, it is," I confessed.

"Well," he said somewhat querulously, "you don't expect me to inspect a boat lying on her side, do you?"

"I guess that would be unreasonable," I admitted.

He stood up. "Congratulations on your trip," he said. "Too bad it ended that way." He nodded toward the window.

"What else do you want me to do?" I asked, not at all sure where this was taking us.

"Nothing," he said. "You have just been readmitted. That's all there is to it."

It cost $50 to hire a small tug to help us off when the tide reached its highest point, but we were so close to the barn by this time that nothing could stop us. We stayed overnight in Morehead City, then began the tedious job of running the Intracoastal Waterway back to Norfolk.

By this time, we were on familiar ground. We reached the mouth of the Potomac on July first, anchoring in Cornfield Harbor. It was late, after 11 p.m., but the Coast Guard boarded us as soon as we dropped the anchor. Two young fellows came aboard, and listened in awe to my brief summary of our trip. Their inspection was cursory; they looked us over and left.

We arrived in Washington, D.C. on July third, and after paying the anchoring fees, dropped anchor in the Washington Channel outside the Gangplank Marina. The Marina graciously loaned us a key to the gate, and allowed us to use the showers and other facilities.

Velda's sons, Keith, Tim, Tom, Andy and Bill, sister Joy Marie and her family and brothers Keith and Larry with their families, arrived to greet us, as did our friends Jim and Kathy Hogan, who had faithfully corresponded with us throughout our trip. If there was one thing we could always count on at the next port, it was a letter addressed to us in Kathy's neat hand.

On the evening of the Fourth, as we sat absorbing the warmth and love of our friends and family, watching the fireworks, listening to the night sounds of Washington D. C., somebody had to ask,

"Would you do it again?"

The End

Appendix

Table of Contents

Appendix A

Epilogue

What has changed since 1986 and where are our friends today?

We understand the Australian Navy no longer salts the wells on Ashmore Reef. Moreover, the hated perishable foods surcharge of 150% imposed on (transient) yachties has been revoked, and the Cocos-Keeling administration has greatly improved living conditions on Direction Island by making water freely available, and providing some shore facilities such as showers. That's the good news.

On the other hand, New Zealand now charges $25 – $30 for the weekly quarantine inspections. The French no longer issue visas for the hurricane season, and anchoring fees are becoming the rule rather than the exception.

As for our friends, the last we heard, John Bailey (Balls Head Bay) had taken *Kiah* north to Queensland.

Eric Hiscock passed away shortly after we left New Zealand. Susan sold *Wanderer V* and has moved to England. Jim and Kathy Hogan still live aboard their ketch *Traveler* in Chesapeake Bay.

Julie Howe is married and lives in Tin Can Bay on the Queensland coast with her husband and two lovely children. John Kelly also has married, and lives with his wife and three boys in Silver Spring, MD. My brother has retired and lives on the shores of Puget Sound. My son is married, has two children, and lives in Alaska. Mike Orbach is on the faculty at East Carolina University. Jack Wise has retired from the government and has an active consulting practice.

We met some folks not long ago who had recently visited New Zealand. They told us that Lou Sabin is still clearing yachts in Opua. Les Snowsill has retired. Tim and Pauline Carr, according to Susan Hiscock, are spending the current summer on South Georgia Island, at about 55°S. Tim is working in the whaling museum.

John and Wendy Ettish from *Bali Ha'i* are living in Florida, as is Len Ackley from *Melusine III*. Ralph and Cheryl Baker still live aboard *Flying Lady,* and are tied up in the little town of Anacortes, north of Seattle on the shores of Puget Sound. Suki and Derek Blair, from *HOTTYD* (an acronym for **H**old **O**n **T**ight **T**o **Y**our **D**reams) are still aboard, living in the British Virgin Islands. The David George family in Australia sold *Kaihua,* and have a new, bigger boat, which they are readying for the day David retires.

Ritva and Benjamin Curley are living in Santa Barbara, but Jack is still cruising. *Kulkuri* was featured on a recent cover of *Cruising World* magazine. The last we heard, he was in the Indian Ocean.

Le Papillion is moored in Coral Bay, St. John in the US Virgin Islands. Tom and D.L. Lemm are managing the marine store there.

Rain Eagle was sold, and Bill Wridge now lives in the Seattle area.

Sandcastle has changed hands several times in the 10 years since that terrible night in Great Bay, and is still active in the charter business in the eastern Caribbean.

Our Dutch friends, Hans and Elly Lutt, have a baby boy and are temporarily living on a barge in the Netherlands while they prepare for another cruise. They have sold *Solitair.* Doug and Mary Solomon sold *Sundance Kid* and bought a bigger boat which they are presently chartering in the Caribbean.

Sundowner, with Roger and Molly Firey (and a new cat, Angus having gone to cat heaven) are two-thirds of the way through their **second** circumnavigation, and are somewhere in the Indian Ocean as this is being written.

Nick and Jan sold *Vera* shortly after we left Australia, and presently live ashore north of Sydney.

Windjob came to a violent end in Hurricane Hugo. She was caught in Christiansted, St. Croix. Her skipper, Dirk Winters, prudently took her away from the dock on the eve of the hurricane, but she came adrift during the storm and was blown ashore on the gigantic seas associated with the hurricane with such force that she was deposited on one of the downtown streets.

Eye witnesses who found the boat when they first ventured out as the storm was abating, saw an old man crawl out of the wreckage. Obviously dazed and apparently oblivious to the terrible devastation surrounding them, he asked whether the coffee shop was open yet.

They told him the hotel, coffee shop and all, had been destroyed in the storm, whereupon the old fellow shook his head, and said he'd wander up the street and find a cup of coffee somewhere. They never saw him again.

But now, three years later, as a storm victim, Dirk has a 30-year mortgage from the Small Business Administration, and has nearly completed a new home on St. Croix. I thought at first that was a pretty ambitious undertaking both for the government and for Dirk. But since he recently celebrated his 85th birthday wearing a T-shirt that read "Kiss Me You Fool!" I expect we'll still be corresponding when he reaches his centenary

Appendix B

Itinerary

Date	Places	Miles
	1981	
10/20 – 10/30	Wash. DC to Morehead City	350
11/07 – 11/22	Morehead City to St. Thomas	1,350
	1982	
02/18 – 02/25	St. Thomas to St. Barths & return	225
05/02 – 02/07	St. Thomas to St. Martin	100
05/13 – 05/27	St. Martin to Martinique	75
06/03 – 06/04	Martinique to Bequia	72
06/07 – 06/11	Bequia to Bonaire	405
06/13 – 06/20	Bonaire to Cristóbal (Panama)	733
06/25	Panama Transit	45
06/26 – 07/04	Balboa to Puntarenas, C.R.	490
12/03 – 12/04	Puntarenas to Ballena Bay	66
12/07 –	**1983**	
01/26	Ballena Bay to Hiva Oa, F.P.	4,127
01/27 – 01/29	Hiva Oa to Nuka Hiva	90
03/22 – 04/06	Nuka Hiva to Papeete	703
09/05 – 09/07	Papeete to Bora Bora	180
09/17 – 10/01	Bora Bora to Samoa	1,191
10/12 – 10/19	Samoa to Fiji	680
11/17 – 11/27	Fiji to New Zealand	1,260
	1984	
03/08 – 03/26	New Zealand to Lord Howe Is.	866
04/01 – 04/06	Lord Howe Is. to Sydney, Aus.	489
07/22 – 07/24	Sydney to *collision* and return	130
09/25 – 10/15	Sydney to Noumea.	1,230
11/07 – 11/16	Noumea to New Zealand	923
	1985	
02/18 – 03/02	New Zealand to Sydney	1,205
05/04 – 07/08	Sydney to Torres St. (Indian Ocean)	1,957

07/08 – 07/15	Torres St. to Darwin	650
08/08 – 09/01	Darwin to Cocos–Keeling	1,985
09/12 – 09/29	Cocos-Keeling to Mauritius	2,416
10/29 – 11/18	Mauritius to Richards Bay	1,687

1986

01/24 – 02/03	Richards Bay to Cape Town	975
03/01 – 03/14	Cape Town to St. Helena	1,755
03/20 – 04/20	St. Helena to Martinique	3,780
04/22 – 04/23	Martinique to St. Barths	65
04/25 – 04/25	St. Barths to St. Martin	10
05/15 – 05/17	St. Martin to St. Thomas	110
06/10 – 06/20	St. Thomas to Port Everglades	1,165
06/20 – 06/24	Port Everglades to Morehead City	650
06/26 – 07/02	Morehead City to Washington, DC.	350

Total miles 34,602

Appendix C
What did it cost?

Traveling around the world on a sailboat bears many similarities to a snail's progress through the garden. It's slow, but you always have a place to sleep.

I don't have exact numbers, but this is about what the trip cost:

BOAT EXPENSES

Original cost of boat	$ 37,500
Five years routine maintenance	6,000
Six sails and two awnings	4,200
Radar and other electronics	11,490
New equipment (stove, head, pulpit, dinghy, outboard motors)	6,000
Misc. carpenter work	2,000
Repairs from collision	3,500
Misc. supplies and fees	1,500
Vessel costs	$ 71,190
less residual value of boat	– 25,000
Thus, transportation and lodging cost	$ 46,190
or, on average, $ 9,238 per year.	

PERSONAL EXPENSES
(per year)

Food, booze, cigarettes, etc	$ 3,600
Clothing	250
Personal	1,200
Pro rata medical costs	300
subtotal	$ 5,350

Thus, our annual cost of operation was approximately $14,588. As you know by now, much of this money was spent foolishly; More complete information, better planning and more judicious buying would have reduced boat expenses by at least 25-30%.

On the other hand, we did **not** carry insurance. Marine

441

insurance is frightfully expensive — when it's available at all. Since we and the boat were in this together, if the boat went down, so did we. Insurance would have come in handy when we had our collision, but even that is problematical considering that we would have had a high deductible in any case.

To put this is a little different light, if we had it to do over, I'd lighten up on the electronics. Notice that fully a quarter of our expenses went into the bottomless pit labeled "Electronics." And we have damn little to show for it. Some disconnected dials in the cockpit bulkhead, and a mish-mash of wires running nowhere. The wind instruments were replaced by a windsock I made from a scrap of canvas and a metal clothes hanger. This was lashed to a jack staff made from a broom handle that was hauled to the top of the topmast, and which faithfully reported wind direction across three oceans.

Nor did we spend much for clothing. Most yachties quickly learn to shop thrift stores and are perfectly content wearing second-hand clothing.

I can understand why people stock up on spare parts for the engine and other machinery on board, but that's where you seriously need to look yourself in the eye and ask yourself if you are likely to overhaul your engine in mid-ocean. Or, more realistically, if you are even capable of it. Some people are. This is not meant for them. This is for people like you and me. I bought spare parts like the Pentagon does. Except that it was **my** money that was going down the toilet. Why did I carry a complete gasket set for my engine? Or even two spare injectors? Simple. Because the salesman told me I needed them, and I didn't know better. I watched $400 worth of spare Perkins parts slowly rust away.

The salesman will give you a "what if" list. Be skeptical. Be realistic about your own abilities and ask the awkward questions. Don't let him talk you into a bunch of stuff you don't need and will never use.

Appendix D

The Opua Questionnaire

The Questions:

1. I (we) have been cruising___years. Our vessel is___feet, was built in___. Our normal crew is___(number). To date, we have cruised ___miles (nearest thousand). At sea, we maintain watches (24 hours), (at night only), (other) please explain. We carry radar reflectors (yes/no) and believe they are useful.

2. Have you ever had a collision on the high seas? (yes/no).

3. Have you ever *almost* had a collision? (yes/no).

4. Do you see whales (frequently), (occasionally), (rarely)?

5. Do you consider whales (dangerous), (sometimes dangerous), (not dangerous)?

6. Have you been attacked by a whale? (yes/no).

7. Do you personally know someone who has been attacked by whales? (yes/no). If yes, do you know what species?_____. Where did it happen?_____.

8. Have you seen a derelict container at sea? (yes/no). More than one?____(number). Where?_____.

9. Do you personally know someone who has seen derelict containers at sea? (yes/no). Where?_____

10. Have you hit one at sea? (yes/no). Where?_____.

11. As an experienced yachtsman, is your greatest concern at sea (fire), (striking an uncharted reef), (collision), (other) please explain _____ .

And the Answers:

1. Average cruising time was 4.48 years. Average vessel was 37.5 feet long and nine years old. The average number of crew (like an average family) was 2.15 persons. The respondents (except for the Hiscocks and McIlvrides) aggregated 426,000 nautical miles for an average of 20,285. Eighty percent of the sample maintained 24 hour watches, and all but two respondents believed radar reflectors were worthwhile.

2. Five of the respondents reported collisions. Two were with whales, one with a container, one with a log and one was with another vessel at sea. (This latter was our collision with the Australian fishing trawler.)

3. In addition, eight respondents reported **almost** having a collision. **Seven of the eight events were with ships.**

4. About half the respondents saw whales occasionally. The others saw them rarely.

5. Four respondents did not believe whales were dangerous, even though everyone at the party knew that a boat enroute from Suva to New Zealand two months earlier had been attacked *and sunk* by one. The species identified as aggressive were pilot whales and sperm whales. These episodes occurred in the West Indies, near Mexico, near the Galapagos, near Hiva Oa, and between Costa Rica and the Marquesas. Two respondents who reported hitting sleeping whales did not consider them dangerous.

8. Four containers had been sighted.

10. One respondent hit a container near Kandavu Is. and saved his boat by sailing across the reef and beaching her as she was sinking.

11. Half the respondents ranked collision as the major concern. Uncharted reefs were second, and fire and weather came third. One singlehander expressed concern about going overboard. Another person mentioned freak waves.

Appendix E

A Ditty Bag of Sailor's Tricks

(1) Collision Avoidance

The answer to questions two and three (above) is alarming. Over half the sample had experience with sea collisions, but *Prospector* was the only vessel that physically came into contact with another vessel — and lived to tell about it.

I believe, as did the majority of our sample, that the greatest risk deep water yachts face is collision with a ship. There is a good chance that people on board the ship will be oblivious to a contact that would destroy a yacht. This may be a grim explanation why we hear so little about such collisions.

Most helmsmen will take sequential bearings on an approaching ship. If the bearing remains constant, they will know to take evasive action. But many do not know how to calculate the distance and speed of the approaching vessel. In this connection, there are two generalizations worth keeping in mind. The ship you're watching is a lot closer than she seems, and she's traveling faster than you think.

To estimate how close the ship is, you must guess how much of her topsides is still concealed below the horizon. Most laden ships carry a freeboard ranging from 20 feet for a small freighter or tanker to perhaps twice that for a large ship, and three or four times that for a cruise ship.

When you see only the ship's superstructure on the horizon (which often seems, oddly, to resemble an old-fashioned out-house), you can guess there is about 30 feet of ship hidden below the horizon.

The method for calculating her distance is (a) find the square root of her concealed height, (b) multiply that square root by 1.14, and (c) add your distance to the horizon.

Suppose all you see is the superstructure of the vessel. If it's not a cruise ship (which would be immediately apparent) You could safely guess that about 30 feet of her vertical hull height is hidden beyond the horizon. The square root of 30 is 5.48. Multiplying that result by 1.14 tells you the ship is about six and a quarter miles on the other side of your horizon. (note that the result is not much different, even if your guess is off by 10 feet either way: If you overestimate by 10 feet, the ship is still 5.1 miles on the other side of the "hill", and if you under-estimate the hidden height by 10 feet, your ship will only be a mile further away than your original estimate.

You must add to that result your calculated distance to the horizon. From the deck of a yacht, your height of eye above the water is probably around ten feet. Using the same formula (or Table 8 from *Bowditch*), you'll find your distance to the horizon is 3.16 miles. By adding the two distances, yours to the horizon and the horizon to the ship, you'll discover the ship is about ten miles away.

But, if you see a good portion of her hull, she will be much closer, perhaps only five or six miles, and if you see her bow wave, she is on *your* side of the horizon, less than three miles away.

It is not uncommon today for freighters to travel at 18 to 22 knots. If you are making 5 knots and meeting a ship head-on, your closing speed is 23 to 27 knots, or nearly a mile every two minutes. Which doesn't give you a lot of time to make up your mind.

We carry a radar reflector on the same theory that a lot of people go to church; it can't hurt and it might do some good. Nevertheless, I think that relying on your radar reflector is like snapping your fingers to keep the elephants away. I *always* assume that merchant ships have their radar sets turned off. Thus, neither a reflector nor a radar detector will be much use. Instead, we use our radio. If we can't raise the ship on channel 16, we try 13, the bridge to bridge channel.

Without a doubt, your best defense is to let the ship's watch officer know you're there. **Nine times out of ten he won't see you.**

No matter how careful we are, some risks can't be anticipated. For example, there's the enraged 50 ton sperm whale cow whose sleeping calf you might accidently ram in the middle of the night, or the container awash upon which you might impale yourself. Even here, however, there are steps you can take to reduce the risk.

If you have seen whales during the day, play your stereo at night. Sound carries well through the water. Whales will hear you coming, and they'll get out of the way. Keeping a rigged collision mat stowed on deck is a way of preparing to deal with a hull puncture that might be inflicted by a derelict container. I've never seen one offered for sale, but they are not hard to make. Ours is a 3 x 3 foot heavy canvas envelope enclosing a thick rubber bath mat. Lines are spliced into grommets in the upper corners, and short lengths of chain (to add weight), to which longer lines are spliced, are shackled to the lower grommets.

To deploy our collision mat, we would first pass the bottom lines under the bobstay, then slack the mat into the water (it would be pulled down by the weight of the chain), and fish it over the hole by manipulating the four corner lines, which then would be secured. At the first opportunity, in our wooden hull, I would go over the side with a lead patch, a hammer and a fist full of roofing tacks, and nail the patch over the mat, covering the hole.

(2) Necessary Ground Tackle

Books have been written about anchors and anchoring, and it is not my intention to usurp their function, but merely to offer an addendum based on our experience.

MOORINGS

We survived Hurricane Hugo in the Virgin Islands on a mooring I designed to a safe working load (SWL) of 9,000 pounds. The basic component was a 12 foot piece of RD–8 Caterpiller tractor track which was stood on edge and bent into a circle. After chaining the ends together, I shackled a 40 foot piece of ⅝" chain to the track's rail, bringing the other end of the chain to a 1" swivel, to which I secured a short piece of hardened ½" chain which was supported on the surface by a 1½ foot buoy. A 1" nylon pendant (which I doubled in heavy weather) secured *Prospector* to her mooring. The Crosby shackles I used were rated at 13,000 pounds.

The track weighed about 600 pounds, but I was more interested in its bulk, because when we set it, we were careful to place it on edge. The action of water currents quickly caused it to sink into the bottom, where it became an immobile object.

This was hardly a typical situation, not because the ground tackle was a permanent mooring, but because I selected its components with a maximum storm in mind, and I was not obliged to compromise. This, of course, is never the case with portable ground tackle.

ANCHORS

Perhaps the most useful approach would be to describe *Prospector's* ground tackle as it evolved. We started with a 50 lb. wrought iron plow anchor on a ⅜" proof coil chain. The chain broke in a storm on Chesapeake Bay. We lost the anchor and went on the beach. I replaced the original anchor with a 60 pound Danforth which I was subsequently forced to abandon near Morehead City.

Before we left Washington, D.C. in 1981, I had bought a 75 lb. C.Q.R. plow — the anchor which saved us in Great Bay. It was lost subsequently in Charlotte Amalie harbor when a second ⅜" proof coil chain broke. We replaced it with a 60 pound C.Q.R. and 300 feet of 3/8 inch *hi-test* chain.

We also carried a 75 pound fisherman (yachtsman) anchor, which proved to be too light. It was replaced with a 125 pound fisherman. We also acquired a 44 pound Bruce.

I bought the Bruce because it was available when a replacement for the Danforth was not. I'm not sure it's fair to compare it with a 60 pound fluke anchor, but it has dragged in circumstances where I'm sure the Danforth would not. Still, it is a rugged anchor, and in a rocky bottom, it is less prone to damage than the Danforth.

Obviously, it's best to use the style(s) suited to prevailing bottom conditions where you cruise. Much of the east coast has a soft bottom. There, a flat fluke anchor would be my first choice. Elsewhere, in rock or coral, a fluke anchor will snag, but may be damaged. Also, a light fluke anchor may not penetrate a hard clay bottom. This is where you'll want a plow, a Bruce, or even a heavy, old fashioned fisherman.

Anchoring in sea grass is a bad idea. A fluke anchor may not dig in, and when it comes out of the ground it's almost certain to tear a divot loose, causing irreparable damage to valuable fishery habitat.

To my mind, there's not much question about size. Within reason, use the heaviest anchor you can handle. If you have a choice, always go to the next larger size. Anchors are rated according to a theoretical holding power standard, and if you use the tables below, you should be able to chose the appropriate anchor.

RODES

Here, you must consider several factors.

For many people, chain is a logical choice because (a) it is almost chafe proof, (b) it increases anchor efficiency by holding the anchor stock down, (c) because of its relative density and weight it has a catenary which acts as a spring, absorbing the shock of waves lifting and dropping the vessel, (d) is easily stowed, and (e) is easy to work on deck with existing anchor windlasses. But chain is far from perfect.

Except for hi-test chain, it is relatively weak compared to nylon, is much more expensive, heavy, and prone to rust. Hi-test chain seems more prone to rust than proof coil. In a deep anchorage like Bora Bora, the weight of the chain is more of a factor than the weight of the anchor. Conversely, in heavy weather in a shallow anchorage, the catenary effect is lost and the chain is subjected to sudden, jolting, shock loads that may cause it to fail. There is also an important environmental consideration. Chain raises hell with coral. It's true that a fiber rode will chafe in coral, but there are few places where anchoring in coral is absolutely necessary.

Combination rodes — part chain, part rope — have much to recommend them, since they combine the best features of chain and rope, but they are difficult to handle, unless you haul your anchor hand over hand. If you use an anchor windlass, you haul the rope by taking three turns around the drum. But bringing the thimble and shackle over the roller, and switching from the drum to the wildcat can be difficult.

Polypropylene is not usually considered a suitable anchor rode, but the late Bob Griffith, with at least two circumnavigations under his belt, preferred a polypropylene-chain combination. His theory was that a short piece of heavy chain increased anchor efficiency, while the buoyant polyprop floated straight up, thereby avoiding chafe.

I've never tried it, but his theory makes sense, except in an anchorage where a floating anchor line would be sure to snag passing traffic. Polyprop is available in black as well as yellow. Black will be more sunlight resistant, but it will also be harder to see in the water.

Nylon has become the standard for anchor rodes. It is incredibly strong, but it has shortcomings. Because it's so soft, *laid* nylon has a distressing tendency to hockle or accidently unlay, especially if it is used on a mooring without a swivel. It is almost as prone to UV deterioration as polypropylene, and is so slippery that unless knots are well set, they can slip. Moreover, laid nylon is susceptible to chafe.

Plaited nylon is not commonly available in the United States, but an abundance of *braided* nylon lines are available. Braided lines meet most of the objections in the previous paragraph, and although they tend to be 40% more expensive, in the long run they are worth it.

In selecting a nylon anchor rode, often the *tensile or breaking* strength is used to describe a line of a particular size. The *safe working load* (SWL) for new nylon recommended by the manufacturers is only ten percent of the rope's tensile strength. My experience suggests that a SWL of 25–30% of its breaking strength might be more appropriate. But this is a matter of personal preference.

(3) Safe Anchoring Practices

Safe anchoring has three components. These are (a) the wind resistance of your vessel, (b) wind velocity and sea conditions, and (c) the match of ground tackle to both.

Calculating wind resistance

Larger vessels present greater resistance to the wind. Beyond that simplistic observation, however, most people have no idea how to calculate a vessel's windage. This is how I calculated *Prospector's*.

Anchored vessels in a seaway often yaw about 30 degrees from the weather. When they do, they present a target about halfway between their width and their broadside profile. The easiest way to calculate that target is by measuring each component of the vessel's broadside profile

449

and dividing by two. The vessel's total wind resistance is the sum of those calculations. Consider, for example, the first entry describing her hull. It is 43 feet long (divided by 2) and has an **average** freeboard height of 3½ feet, yielding 75.25 square feet.

PROSPECTOR'S WIND RESISTANCE

Structure	Dimensions	Square Feet
Hull	[43÷2] x 3.50	75.25
Cabin	[12÷2] x 1.50	9.00
Doghouse	[6÷2] x 4.00	12.00
Bowsprit	[12÷2] x 0.75	4.50
Main boom, gaff & sail	[22÷2] x 2.00	22.00
Pulpit	[48÷2] x 0.10	2.40
Yard & sail	[30÷2] x 0.75	18.00
Crosstree	[12÷2] x 0.20	1.20
Lifelines	[160÷2] x 0.03	2.40
Mainmast	40 x 0.75	30.00
Topmast	18 x .050	9.00
Mizzen mast	25 x 0.50	12.50
Lifeline stanchions	75 x 0.10	7.50
Standing rigging	500 x 0.03	15.00
Running rigging	400 x 0.06	24.00

(Table I)

By adding the right hand column, we see that *Prospector's* wind resistance **(WR)** is 244.75 square feet.

Calculating wind pressure

After finding your vessel's wind resistance (**WR**), it is easy to convert that **WR** into the weight exerted by wind velocity and sea conditions on your ground tackle.

At first, the formula seems a bit daunting:

$$D = C_d \; x \; \frac{P}{2} \; x \; V^2 S$$

Where: D = wind pressure
C_d = coefficient of vessel drag
P = air density
V^2 = wind velocity squared
S = your vessel's **WR**

For cylindrical shapes, C_d equals 1.00. Both Struemer and Skene (see bibliography) believe a fiberglass hull should have a C_d of 0.75 to 0.80.

However, I tend to be conservative in such matters. Since vessels yaw and plunge in a heavy seaway, it's hard to guess the pull exerted by the weight of the waves and the drag of the current. I think a clean fiberglass hull should have a C_d of 1.0, while an older wooden boat like *Prospector* with ratlines, a semi-dirty bottom, and irregular shapes on deck might have a C_d as high as 1.10, which is the value I used in the calculations which follow.

Air density varies with barometric pressure, but for this calculation can be held constant at 0.0034. The formula is now less forbidding:

which may be reduced:
D = [V^2x250] x 1.10 x [.0034÷2]
D = [V^2x250] x 1.10 x .0017 or,
D = [V^2x250] x .00187

The only variable in this formula is the wind velocity. Notice the difference in wind pressure between 10 and 20 knots at the top of the scale (140 pounds) and between 90 and 100 knots at the bottom of the scale (875 pounds).

I didn't carry the tables higher than 100 knots. However, we survived 150 knots during Hurricane Hugo in a bay on St. John, USVI, on a mooring designed with the aid of these tables.

We were riding to a mooring I had designed to a safe working load of 9,000 pounds. According to the formula, 150 knots of wind will generate over *five **tons*** of wind pressure on *Prospector*!

Bear in mind, however, that in any wind over 100 knots, survival is a crap shoot. If you're lucky and nothing goes wrong with your system, sure as hell someone will drag into you, which is what happened to us. Our mooring held *both* of us.

Wind velocity (knots)	Calculation [V²250] x 0.00187	Wind Pressure (pounds)
10	[100 x 250] x .00187	50
30	[900 x 250] x .00187	420
50	[2,500 x 250] x .00187	1,170
70	[4,900 x 250] x .00187	2,300
90	[8,100 x 250] x .00187	3,800
100	[10,000 x 250] x .00187	4,675

(Table II)

Let's put this all together. Let's suppose that according to *Table I* above, the wind resistance **(WR)** factor of your boat is 130 square feet. The strongest wind you're likely to experience is, say 60 knots. Look at *Table II*, and solve for D at 60 knots. Thus, D = 875 pounds.

That's about the way the charts in marine hardware stores will come out. But I wouldn't buy a *minimum* anchor. Danforth claims their 14 lb. fluke anchor will hold 920 pounds. But the next size will hold, they say, 1,300 pounds. That's a little more like it.

In choosing the appropriate rode, you find another peculiarity. Three/eighths nylon has a tensile strength of 3,340 pounds. Thirty percent of that is 1,100 pounds. But my hands no longer comfortably grip 3/8 inch nylon. Even 1/2 inch anchor line seems a bit dainty to my taste, yet it has a tensile strength of 5,750 pounds, and a safe working load of 1,728 pounds. On the other hand, 5/8 inch nylon gives me a comfortable grip, has a tensile strength of 9,350 pounds, (remember, it kept *Prospector* off the beach in Great Bay), and it will last a long time.

452

(3) Single Station Weather Forecasting

Predicting Wind Velocity

It is nice to have accurate, timely weather forecasts, but when you are well out of sight of land, often you'll have to rely on your skills as a weather forecaster. It is especially important to know the storm's center and direction relative to your own. No matter how skillful the distant forecaster might be, except in a very general and somewhat abstract way, that vital information can only be obtained by the local observer — by you, in other words.

The small boat skipper knows three things from the barometer. First, whether the atmospheric pressure has fallen or risen, second, how *fast* it's falling (or rising), and third, how *far* it has fallen (or risen).

While forecasters equipped with synoptic charts will forecast wind direction and speed partly by measuring the spread and direction of plotted isobars, you can do somewhat the same thing based simply on the spread between ambient barometric pressure and the pressure predicted on your weather-fax or at the time of the observation.

This formula was developed in a effort to provide the U.S. Navy with a simple method for predicting hurricane strength winds in the Western Pacific by Dr. Robert Fletcher who was then the Director of Scientific Services, Air Weather Service. The formula seems to work equally well in less strenuous storms. This is how you do it:

Look at your log (or a pilot chart for the current month), and determine the *ambient* barometric pressure for your location and season. For this exercise, assume an ambient pressure of 1010 mb. Subtract from that number the pressure at the time of your observation. Find the square root of the remainder and multiply that by 16.

Take as a practical example, our experience in Hurricane *Nano,* (see page 120, *et seq.*). The difference between 1010 mb. and 987 mb. was 23 millibars. The formula thus read: $\sqrt{23} = 4.8 \times 16 = 76.73$ knots.

Locating Storm's Center and Direction

Weather broadcasts can predict the general weather you might expect, but they can't tell you where the center of the storm is in relation to your position. Only you can do that. Here's how:

A 19th century Dutch scientist, Dr. Buys Ballot, demonstrated that you can find the center of a revolving storm by facing the wind and, (in the Northern Hemisphere), extending your right arm straight from your body. The storm's center will lie about 10 degrees behind your right hand, (or between 100 to 110 degrees to the right of the prevailing wind). Since weather patterns in the Northern and Southern Hemispheres mirror each other, in the Southern Hemisphere, you would extend your left arm.

By taking a series of those bearings over several hours, and plotting them on a regular plotting sheet, you will know where the center of the storm is, and as the plots accumulate, you will be able to deduce the storm's approximate heading and even make an intelligent guess about its speed.

Evasive Action

Knowing the direction and speed of the system's center, and having some idea what to expect in terms the storm's ferocity, you may be able to get into the navigable semicircle, or at least minimize your exposure if you find yourself in the dangerous semicircle.

The winds circulate in a counter clockwise direction around a cyclone in the Northern Hemisphere, and in a clockwise direction in the Southern Hemisphere.

After plotting your bearing from the center of the storm and determining the storm's approximate heading, you can determine your best strategy. In the Northern Hemisphere, you particularly want to avoid the starboard (or right-hand) side of a storm's track because this is the "dangerous" semicircle where the wind velocity is generally greatest, and may tend to sweep you into the storm's path.

The area to the left of the storm's track is called the "navigable" semi-circle because of the wind's reduced velocity and its tendency to push you away from the storm.

In the Southern Hemisphere, of course, directions are reversed. The area to the left of the storm's track is the dangerous semi-circle.

Appendix 7

(Note: Strictly speaking, this is not a bibliography because not all these works were mentioned in the text. However, these are books you will find on *Prospector's* bookshelf. These books were invaluable shipmates on our voyage and in the preparation of this book.)

Blewitt, Mary. *Celestial Navigation for Yachtsmen*. Tuckahoe, N.Y., John de Graff, 1967

Bowditch, Nathaniel. *American Practical Navigator,* (Two Vol.), Defense Mapping Agency, Gov. Printing Office, 1984

Corser, Frank and Rose, *Tahiti Traveler's Guide,* publisher unknown, (3d ed), 1981

Culler, R. D., *Boats, Oars, and Rowing*, Camden Me. International Marine Pub. Co., 1978

Eastman, Peter F. Dr. *Advanced First Aid at Sea*, Cambridge, MD, Cornell Maritime Press, 1977

Griffith, Bob with Nancy. *Blue Water*, Boston, Sail Books, Inc. 1979

Harrison, Peter. *Seabirds: An Identification Guide*, London, A.H & A.W. Reed, Ltd. 1983

Harding, Capt. Edwin T. and Kotsch, Capt. William J. USN, *Heavy Weather Guide*, Annapolis, Md., Naval Institute Press, 1965

Hedrick, F. M. *The Captain's Notebook*, Camden Me. International Marine, 1979

Hinz, Earl. *Landfalls in Paradise*, (Pub. Unknown)

Hiscock, Eric. *Come Aboard*, Oxford, England, Oxford University Press, 1978

Hiscock, Eric. *Cruising Under Sail*, 3rd Edition, Oxford, Oxford University Press, 1981

Howland, Waldo. *A life in Boats*, Mystic, Conn. Mystic Seaport Museum, 1984

Hydrographic Office Pub. 249, (3 Vol.) Defense Mapping Agency, Gov. Printing Office, 1985

Kinney, Francis S. *Skene's Elements of Yacht Design*, New York, Dodd, Mead & Co., 1973

Lucas, Alan. *Cruising New Caledonia and Vanuatu*, Netley, So. Australia, Griffin Press, 1981

Lucas, Alan. *Cruising the Coral Coast*, Melbourne, Aus. Castle Books, 1984

Norgrove, Ross. *The Cruising Life*, Camden, ME, Int. Marine Publishing Co., 1980

Norton, Lt. William, USCGR, *Eagle Seamanship*, New York, M. Evans and Co. 1969

O'Brien, Conor. *Across Three Oceans,* London, Granada Publishing Co. Ltd, 1927

Ocean Passages for the World, Third Ed. Hydrographic Dept., British Admiralty, 1973. (1st ed., 1923; 2nd ed, 1950)

Sailing Directions, Series, Defense Mapping Agency, Gov. Printing Office.

Street, Donald M., Jr. *Cruising Guide to the Eastern Carribean*, (4 Vol.), New York, W. W. Norton Co., 1980.

Street, Donald M., Jr. *The Ocean Sailing Yacht.* (2 Vols) New York, W. W. Norton Co., 1973

Street, Donald M., Jr. *Seawise,* New York, W. W. Norton Co., 1979

Stuermer, Gordon and Nina. *Deep Water Cruising*, New York, McKay, 1980

Stuermer, Gordon and Nina. *Starbound*, New York, McKay, 1978

Taylor, Roger C. *Good Boats*, Camden Maine, Int. Marine Pub. Co., 1977

Van Dorn, William G., *Oceanography and Seamanship*, New York, Dodd, Mead, Co., 1974

Note: A excellent source for English, Australian and New Zealand titles:

BOAT BOOKS
39 ALBANY STREET
CROWS NEST, 2065
AUSTRALIA

For South African books, publications, and detailed information about rounding the Cape of Good Hope, write to:

CAPTAIN CHRIS BONNET
APPLETISER OCEAN SAILING ACADEMY,
38 FENTON ROAD, DURBAN, 4001
REPUBLIC OF SOUTH AFRICA

Prospector's sail plan and
accommodations

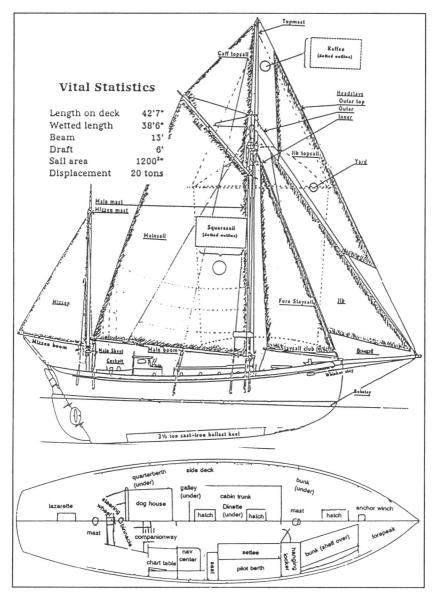

Vital Statistics

Length on deck	42'7"
Wetted length	38'6"
Beam	13'
Draft	6'
Sail area	1200²ⁿ
Displacement	20 tons

458

Glossary

ACCOMMODATION:	Spaces on board where the crew lives.
AHULL:	Riding out a gale broadside to the seas.
ALOFT:	Above the deck; in the rigging of a sailboat.
APPARENT WIND:	Combined ambient wind and wind generated by vessel's forward speed.
ATHWARTSHIPS:	At right angles to vessel's centerline.
AWASH:	Level with surface of the water.
BACKSTAY:	Rigging that supports a mast from behind.
BALLAST:	Weight placed low in a vessel for stability.
BALLAST KEEL:	Iron or lead mass bolted to bottom of keel.
BAROGRAPH:	Recording barometer.
BEAM ENDS:	When a vessel is on her side.
BEAM REACH:	Sailing with wind at right angles to direction.
BEARING:	Direction of object from observer.
BEAT:	Sailing to windward (or to weather).
BEAUFORT SCALE:	Universal system for describing weather at sea.
BELAY:	To fasten a rope (line) to a cleat or pin.
BELOW:	Living space below main deck.
BEND:	To tie lines (ropes) together, or to tie a line to an object.
BERMUDA TRIANGLE:	An area enclosed by a line drawn from Miami to Bermuda, from Bermuda to Antigua, and a closing line from Antigua to Miami. Mysterious disappearances supposedly have occurred in that area.
BERTH:	(a) A sleeping place on board; (b) employment aboard a vessel; (c) space allocated to a vessel

459

at a dock.

BILGE: (a) Inner compartment below a vessel's floors, often wet; (b) the curve in the hull where the bottom meets the sides.

BINNACLE: Compass housing in a cockpit or on deck.

BITTER END: Inboard end of line (rope) or chain.

BITTS: Strong vertical fitting on deck designed to receive mooring lines and anchor cables.

BLOCK: A pulley inside a shell made of wood or plastic.

BO'SUN'S CHAIR: Seat designed to carry worker aloft.

BOBSTAY: Heavy wire or chain stay extending from stem at waterline to end of bowsprit.

BOLLARD: Strong posts, usually iron, set on docks to receive mooring lines.

BONDED STORES: Duty-free liquor and tobacco for consumption at sea.

BOWLINE: A knot tied to form an eye which will neither jam nor slip. One of a half dozen basic knots every sailor must know.

BRIG: (a) Two-masted square rigged vessel; (b) jail.

BRIGANTINE: Two-masted vessel square rigged on foremast.

BROACH: Lose control in following sea, slewing violently to one side, in imminent danger of capsize.

BULWARKS: Solid extension of sides rising above main deck.

BUYS BALLOT LAW: See Appendix C.

CABLE–LAID: Proper name for twisted (laid) rope.

CAPE HORNER Colloquial for large cargo-carrying sailing ship.

CAPSTAN: Heavy machinery with vertical drum for hauling large lines (ropes).

CAREEN: Vessel deliberately beached and "hauled down" (rolled over on her side) so bottom can be repaired, cleaned and painted.

CARLIN: Heavy structural member joining cabin sides with decks.

CARRY WAY: Momentum remaining after engine is stopped or wind is lost.

CAULK: Fill plank and deck seams with plastic material and/or oakum or twisted cotton and pitch (tar).

CEILING:	Vertical lining inside hull.
CHAIN PLATE:	Strong metal fitting bolted to hull, to which fixed (standing) rigging is attached.
CHANDLERY:	(a) Gear necessary for fitting out a vessel; (b) a store where such gear is sold.
CLOVE HITCH:	A basic knot for securing gear on deck. Another of the required knots and hitches,
COMING ABOUT:	Changing course to a new tack.
COMPANIONWAY:	Main hatch through which vessel is entered.
COMPASS CARD:	Flat magnetised card with cardinal marks printed on upper surface, floating in compass bowl.
CONTINENTAL SHELF:	Submerged land near continental land mass extending seaward to a depth of 200 meters.
CROSSTREES:	A short horizontal piece of timber at top of main mast and beneath top mast. Crosstrees serve as spreaders, helping support topmast.
DEFENSE MAPPING AGENCY:	Agency of Department of Defense, U.S. Government, responsible for preparing world-wide nautical charts and other navigation materials outside the United States. The cover of this book is from a DMA chart.
DRIFT:	Velocity of a current. (See *set* below.)
FALL:	The hauling portion of a line (rope) suspended from a block.
FALL OFF:	Steer the boat away from the wind to gain speed.
FATHOM:	Length measurement of six feet primarily to measure water depth and length of line.
FETCH:	Distance traveled by wind over open water.
FIFERAIL:	Railing around mast carrying belaying pins.
FLOOD:	Part of tidal cycle when water is rising.
FLOTSAM:	Junk floating on the tide or at sea.
FORCE MAJEURE:	(Fr.) Superior or irresistible force; Act of God.
FORE:	Near or toward the bow.
FORE–AND–AFT:	Parallel to the vessel's centerline.
FORE–AND–AFT RIG:	Sails set parallel to the centerline. This class of sail includes all rigs except square rigs.

FOREDECK:	Part of the maindeck forward of the mainmast.
FOUNDER:	To fill with water and sink.
FURL:	To gather and secure (or roll) a sail.
GAFF:	Spar which carries the upper edge of a four-sided (gaff-rigged) fore-and-aft sail.
GALE:	Marine cyclone with winds 34 to 47 knots.
GALLOWS:	Permanent frame which supports main boom at rest.
TO "GHOST":	Means sailing without apparent wind.
GLASS:	Colloquial expression for barometer.
GLASSES:	Colloquial expression for binoculars.
GOLD PLATER:	Colloquial expression for ostentatious yacht.
GROUND:	Touching the bottom or running aground.
HALYARD:	Line or tackle used to hoist a sail, spar or flag.
HANDY BILLY:	Small block and tackle used for temporary purposes.
HEAVING-TO:	Stopping the boat at sea by backing the staysail (or jib) and lashing the wheel amidships or lightly to leeward.
"HELMS-A-LEE!":	Traditional cry by helmsman coming about on a new tack, warning that the boom will be swinging across as the bow passes through the wind.
HITCH:	Specialized knot that unties easily.
HOCKLE:	Where a laid line (rope) accidently unlays and with each strand developing reverse kinks.
HORSE LATITUDES:	Area between 25° and 30° north (or south), where the weather is unsettled, and winds are usually light and variable.
HOUNDS:	Wooden shoulders let into the mast near the top to support trestle trees upon which crosstrees rest.
HURRICANE:	Marine cyclone with winds over 64 knots.
JACKSTAY:	Fixed (standing) rigging that supports moving parts of a sailing rig.
JETSAM:	Gear or cargo deliberately discarded at sea.
JIBE:	When a vessel with fore-and-aft rig changes

	from one tack to another as the stern passes through the wind. (See *wear about*, below).
JIGGER:	Colloquial for mizzen sail.
JURY RIG:	Temporary repairs at sea.
KING POSTS:	Strong posts rising through the deck a vessel's quarters to receive towlines and stern lines.
KNOCKDOWN:	Serious accident when vessel is violently thrust on her beam ends by wind or wave.
KNOT:	(a) Unit of speed at sea equal to 1.15 (statute) miles per hour. (b) A fastening in a line (rope).
LAN:	Local Apparent Noon. A series of noon observations to establish observer's position.
LAND BREEZE:	Early morning breeze blowing offshore.
LATITUDE:	Geographic term. The angular distance north or south from the equator.
LAZARETTE:	Small storage compartment in the stern.
LEE:	Direction *toward* which the wind is blowing.
LEEWARD:	Downwind. A vessel falls off to leeward.
LINE:	All rope aboard (except the bell rope and foot rope on a square-rigger) becomes "line" when it is put into service.
LONGITUDE:	Geographic term. Meaning angular distance east or west of a given point expressed in degrees.
LOOM:	Glow from lights below horizon reflected from clouds or atmosphere.
LORAN:	Long range radio navigation system.
"MAYDAY":	International distress call when life is endangered (from the French *m'aidez* – "help me").
MEET:	Steering technique anticipating ship's heading.
MESSENGER:	Light line used to transport a heavier line.
MIDSHIPMEN'S HITCH:	Useful hitch for belaying (and releasing) a line under tension. One of the six essential knots.
MOUSING:	Wire fastened to shackle pins and across hooks to prevent accidental release.
NAUTICAL ALMANAC:	Annual joint publication of celestial data by U.S. and British authorities.
NAUTICAL MILE:	Officially 6,076.12 feet, but actually 6,077 feet.

SEMICIRCLE: The leeward side of a storm's track (the left side in the Northern Hemisphere, the right side in the Southern Hemisphere).

NOON: In navigation, means the precise moment the sun is directly above your position.

NULL: Radio navigation term meaning the point at which an incoming radio signal becomes least audible because the receiving antenna is pointed directly toward the transmitter.

ON THE WIND: Close-hauled; sailing to weather, sailing up-wind.

OVER THE GROUND: Actual distance traveled.

PAINTER: Line permanently attached to dinghy's bow.

"PAN–PAN": International distress call when safety is in question (French *panne* — "break down").

PARACHUTE FLARE: Hand-held distress rocket which ejects a red flare at 1,000 feet visible for 25 nautical miles. Flare burns at least 40 seconds at 40,000 to 100,000 candlepower.

PART: When rope, chain, or wire breaks.

PASSAGE: Journey by sea between two (or more) places.

PEAK: (a) After end of gaff lifted by peak halyard; (b) the forward-most compartment of a vessel.

PILOT: (a) Person licensed to guide vessels through restricted waters; (b) official British Admiralty publication describing features of a particular area or region.

PILOT BERTH: Curtained bunk usually built above settee in vessel's saloon.

PILOT CHART: Monthly or quarterly chart issued by the Defense Mapping Agency depicting average oceano-graphic and weather phenomena for a specific area (e.g. North Pacific Ocean).

PINCH: Sailing too close to the wind, thereby losing speed and control.

PINRAIL: Wooden rail fastened horizontally to shrouds to receive belaying pins.

PITCHPOLE: Disastrous accident when vessel cartwheels,

464

	stern over bow, usually in following sea.
POOPED:	Serious, possibly disastrous, accident when overtaking wave breaks on top of vessel. This sometimes causes a vessel to sink.
PORT:	(a) Left hand side of vessel, indicated at night by red light; (b) place where commerce occurs.
PORT OF ENTRY:	First port where foreign vessels may call to comply with customs and immigration laws.
PORT OF REFUGE:	In international law, a place where any vessel may shelter from *force majeure*, make repairs and take stores aboard.
PORT TACK:	Sailing with wind coming over port side.
PRATIQUE:	Certificate indicating vessel has been released from quarantine.
PREVENTER:	Line secured to boom to prevent it from jibing.
PULPIT:	Stainless steel frame surrounding bowsprit.
QUARTER:	Area of a vessel on either side from amidships aft to stern centerline.
QUARTER BERTH:	Bunk extending under side deck.
QUAY:	Stone or cement dock with solid vertical sides.
RADIO DIRECTION FINDER:	Radio receiver with directional antenna.
RATLINES:	Short lines or pieces of wood lashed like a ladder between shrouds to serve as steps for climbing aloft.
TO REEF:	Means to reduce sail area.
REEF POINTS:	Short lines sewn into both sides of a sail that are tied together when the sail is "reefed" or partly lowered, to prevent the unused portion of the sail from flogging in the wind.
RHUMB LINE:	Navigational term describing the shortest course between two points.
ROADSTEAD:	Anchorage in the open sea outside port.
ROARING FORTIES:	Roughly between 40° and 50° south where strong westerly winds prevail. Term derives from the sound the wind makes in the rigging.
RODE:	Anchor line or chain.
ROLLER JIB:	Jib secured to a rolling mechanism fixed to the

	end of the bowsprit. *Prospector's* squaresail is fastened to the yard with similar mechanisms.
ROLLING HITCH:	Handy hitch for temporarily relieving a strain on another line, lifting a spar and holding an anchor chain. Another of six required knots.
RUDDER QUADRANT:	Heavy metal bracket fixed to *Prospector's* rudder around which rudder cables, coming from opposite directions, are fastened.
RUNNING RIGGING:	Movable rigging such as halyards and sheets.
SAILING DIRECTIONS:	Official American (DMA) publication describing features of a particular area or region.
SALOON:	Main living compartment in a yacht.
SAMPSON POST:	Strong post or posts rising through the foredeck to receive mooring, towing, or anchor lines.
SARGASSO SEA:	Area in North Atlantic between 30° and 50° west which is blanketed by sargassum algae.
SATNAV:	Satellite navigation. Electronic navigation based on orbiting satellites. Newer system is based on stationary satellites.
SEA BREEZE:	Afternoon breeze blowing toward land.
SEAKEEPING:	Seaworthy characteristics of a vessel.
SEACOCK:	Valve for through-hull fittings.
SEAKINDLY:	Superior seakeeping abilities.
SEAMANSHIP:	Collectively, practices necessary for the safe handling of vessels.
SEAWORTHY:	This term embraces both the condition of the vessel *and* the degree of seamanship displayed by the crew.
"SÉCURITÉ":	Warning of navigational hazards, inquiry concerning vessel safety.
SET:	Direction a current is flowing.
SHEER:	Curve of the deck as seen from the side.
SHEET:	Lines that control sail trim.
SHROUD:	Fixed rigging that provides lateral support for the mast.
SLIPPERY HITCH:	Useful for securing lines and small articles on deck. A quick release hitch, this is one of the essential knots.

466

SMALL STUFF:	Light cordage and marlin.
SPANISH WINDLASS:	Method of tightening rigging by twisting parallel lines with a stick.
SQUARE KNOT:	Classic Boy Scout knot; of limited utility, but essential for tying reefs. A basic knot.
STANDING RIGGING:	Stationary rigging such as shrouds and stays.
STARBOARD:	Right hand side of vessel, indicated at night by a green light.
STARBOARD TACK:	Wind coming across starboard side of vessel. Sailing vessels on this tack have right of way.
STAY:	Fixed rigging that provides fore and aft support for a mast.
STEERAGE WAY:	A vessel slowly making way barely fast enough to be responsive to her helm.
STORM:	Marine cyclone with winds 48 to 63 knots.
TO STRIKE:	To lower, furl, or bag a sail.
STUFFING BOX:	Fitting attached to the stern through which the propeller shaft passes.
TACK:	Changing course by steering through the wind and taking wind on opposite side.
TACKLE:	Generic term, usually meaning a handy-billy or similar equipment involving block and tackle.
TAFFRAIL:	Railing, often ornamental, across the stern.
"TENDER" VESSEL:	Vessel that lacks stability and heels too easily.
THIMBLE:	Metal (or nylon) lining to protect spliced eyes in anchor rodes, etc.
TOPPING LIFT:	Specialized halyard used to support the boom while the sail be being reefed or furled.
TOPSIDES:	Part of the hull normally above water.
TRANSOM:	Portion of the hull across the stern.
TURNBUCKLE:	Threaded fitting inserted in standing rigging between shroud and chainplate to tension the rigging.
UNSEAWORTHY:	Unfit for sea because of vessel defect or inadequate crew.
VHF:	Very High Frequency, the FM limited range radios required to be carried on all ships, and which are carried by many yachts. Channel 16

is the standard calling frequency, and ships are required to stand by that channel at all times. Channel 13 is a bridge to bridge frequency, and if channel 16 doesn't work, try 13. *This is very important.* (See Appendix C.)

WATCH:
Period of time a crew member oversees the boat, her course and her safety.

WATERSPOUT:
Marine equivalent of a tornado.

WAY:
Directed movement through the water.

WEAR ABOUT:
Changing course by passing stern through wind. Standard maneuver for square rigged ships.

WEATHER:
(a) Opposite to leeward; (b) steering towards or nearer the wind; (c) successfully passing to windward of a headland; (d) to survive a storm; (e) climatic conditions.

WEAVER'S KNOT:
Last of the essential knots. Excellent for joining lines of unequal size, will never jam if tied properly.

WELL FOUND:
An able, well equipped, well manned vessel.

WET BOAT:
Vessel that habitually runs with lee rail awash.

WHITE HORSES:
Breaking waves with white foamy crests.

WINDJAMMER:
Colloquial term for large sailing vessels.

WINDLASS:
Mechanically driven horizonal drum used for lifting heavy loads such as anchors. (Compare with *capstan* above).

WIND SHADOW:
Area on lee side of high islands, under cliffs, and near high structures which block or distort wind flow.

Index

C

D

E

Vigil radar, 262-63, 273, 296

F

H

L

M

N

O

P

(Note: **bold** indicates former shipmates)

474

476

Hull configuration, 386

Rig, 220

Replica of, 311

Speed record, 359

Steering system, 225

PROVISIONING:

Birkenhead Pier, 242–43

Duty-free stores, 412

Groceries, yachting surcharge, 351, 353-54

Quantities, 2, 107–08

Unsuitability of refrigerated produce, 341

R

RACES:

Ambon (Aus.), 338-39, 340-41

Durban–Richards Bay (R.S.A.), 383-84

Tall Ship (N.Z.), 291

RIG AND RIGGING:

Bowsprit, 211

Handy-billys, 225

Jackstay, 107, 221, 415-16

Spanish windlass, 219, 270

Topmast, 118, 187

Yard, 67, 120, 415-16

S

SAILS:

Cheong Lee, 376

Fore and aft rig, 386

Gaff Topsail, 226

Genoa, 292

Housley, Glen, 376

Raffee, 2, 107, 316

Squaresail, 15

Staysail, 266

Storm trisail, 145

Topsails, 194

SALTWATER, ADVERSE EFFECT OF, 270

SCOTT'S RESTAURANT (Fiji), 181-83

Z

Credits and typographical note:

All artwork except cover, title page, and sketches appearing on pages 153 and 311 were the work of Betsy A. Lampé.

All charts, except the world map in the front pages, were drawn by Captain Jim Hogan.

Frontispiece and photo appearing on page 164 were reproduced by permission of the *Whangarei Northern Advocate* of New Zealand. *Power Images* of Ft. Lauderdale prepared the original (badly faded) newspaper page for publication.

Picture and quotations about *Innocent Bystander's* sinking on page 404 was reproduced by permission of *The Cape Times* of Cape Town, South Africa.

Photo of *Innocent Bystander* being launched was by Richard Cottier.

All other photos were by the author.

The book and book jacket were designed by Prospector Press. The typeface selected for the body of text was ITC Garamond Book (10.5 pts). Typesetting was done on an 800 DPI LaserMaster printer.

The book was printed by Walsworth Publishing Co. of Missouri.